MORE PRAISE FOR *THAILAND*

'An important book at a pivotal moment. Zawacki brings clear eyes and rigorous research to one of America's most complicated and historically important Asian relationships.'

Shawn W. Crispin, Southeast Asia Editor, *Asia Times*

'Zawacki's carefully documented and balanced analysis lifts the curtain on a gradual, often invisible, but seemingly inexorable geopolitical shift. It provides a thorough explanation of the circumstances that have led Thailand, once seen as an unequivocally staunch US ally, to lean increasingly toward a pragmatic and strategically assertive China.'

Michael Herzfeld, Harvard University

'Presents a powerful counter-argument to the conventional wisdom that China's economic rise alone explains Thailand's pivot from the US to China. In thoroughly researched detail, the book traces a sorry trail of US condescension and clumsy diplomacy.'

Daniel Fineman, author of *A Special Relationship: The United States and Military Government in Thailand*

'Now comes the rare American deeply informed of a "faraway country" of whose people "we know nothing", in a profoundly disturbing study of how the world-changing US–China dynamic unfolds in Thailand. Read and weep.'

Jeffrey Race, author of *War Comes to Long An: Revolutionary Conflict in a Vietnamese Province*

ABOUT THE AUTHOR

Benjamin Zawacki was a visiting fellow in the Human Rights Program at Harvard Law School in 2014–2015, and a term member on the Council on Foreign Relations through 2016. He was Amnesty International's Southeast Asia researcher for five years, and served as a policy advisor to President Jimmy Carter and two other "Elders" in Myanmar. A regular contributor to the media in Southeast Asia, he has lived in Thailand for fifteen years. He holds degrees from the George Washington University Law School and the College of the Holy Cross.

ASIAN ARGUMENTS

Asian Arguments is a series of short books about Asia today. Aimed at the growing number of students and general readers who want to know more about the region, these books will highlight community involvement from the ground up in issues of the day usually discussed by authors in terms of top-down government policy. The aim is to better understand how ordinary Asian citizens are confronting problems such as the environment, democracy and their societies' development, either with or without government support. The books are scholarly but engaged, substantive as well as topical and written by authors with direct experience of their subject matter.

Series editor: Paul French

Previous Titles:
North Korea by Paul French
Ghost Cities of China by Wade Shepard
Leftover Women: The Resurgence of Gender Inequality in China
    by Leta Hong Fincher
China's Urban Billion by Tom Miller
A Kingdom in Crisis: Thailand's Struggle for Democracy in the Twenty-First Century by
    Andrew MacGregor Marshall
China and the New Maoists by Kerry Brown and Simone van Nieuwenhuizen
Myanmar's Enemy Within: Buddhist Violence and the Making of a Muslim 'Other' by
    Francis Wade

Forthcoming:
On the New Silk Road: Journeying through China's Artery of Power by Wade Shepard
Last Days of the Mighty Mekong by Brian Eyler
Hong Kong: Markets, Street Hawkers and the Fight against Gentrification by Maurizio
    Marinelli

Thailand

Shifting Ground between the US and a Rising China

Benjamin Zawacki

ZED

Thailand: Shifting Ground between the US and a Rising China
was first published in 2017 by Zed Books Ltd, The Foundry,
17 Oval Way, London SE11 5RR, UK.

www.zedbooks.net

Typeset in Garamond Pro by seagulls.net
Index by John Barker
Cover design by Keith Dodds
Cover photo © Mark Henley/Panos

A catalogue record for this book is available from the British Library.

ISBN 978-1-78360-870-6 hb
ISBN 978-1-78360-869-0 pb
ISBN 978-1-78360-871-3 pdf
ISBN 978-1-78360-872-0 epub
ISBN 978-1-78360-873-7 mobi

Printed and bound in the United States of America

for Ella Nour and May Yasmine

Contents

Foreword and Acknowledgements

I am an American. Having lived and worked in Southeast Asia since late 2002, I am an "ex-pat" only in a colloquial sense. I retain not only my US passport and citizenship, but an inherent if self-conscious American perspective as well. Reminded by the late historian Howard Zinn that "you can't be neutral on a moving train", I forfeit any claim to neutrality in this book.

Two mitigating factors are at play. First, I am as much an ex-patriot as expatriate: someone who cares deeply about his country, but whose experience abroad has made him wary of nationalism. In just my years away, US foreign policy has not only fallen short of the "values" and "ideals" that supposedly inform and inspire it, but has given rise to another more negative set of standards. As costly as American policy in Thailand has been in just the 21st century—since Thaksin Shinawatra took power in Bangkok and global terrorism struck Washington—it does not compare to that in other regions. Deliberate and purposeful under Bush, halting and confused under Obama, US foreign policy has yielded few wins and a great many losses—not least in the defense and advancement of human rights. This book traces one such policy failure whose causes and consequences resonate well beyond its particular theatre.

Second, I place little stock in the adage among ex-pats that "If someone says he understands Thailand, he is misinformed." I do not claim to understand all of Thailand or to understand its more accessible aspects all of the time. It *is* a complex country. Yet to forfeit any claim to understanding on the basis of nationality is intellectually negligent and culturally orientalist. When for six months prior to a coup in 2014 millions of Thais called for replacing electoral democracy with selected leadership, one was to properly understand them as anti-democratic.

In 2002–2004 I represented Chinese asylum-seekers and assisted in their escape to Cambodia (after getting them into a Linkin Park concert). In 2006–2007 I wore UN blue in camps from which Thai authorities pushed refugees back to war and persecution in Myanmar. And as an Amnesty International researcher I interviewed torture victims in the deep south in 2008, documented Bangkok's violent confrontations in 2010, and sparred with Prime Minister Abhisit over Thailand's *lese majeste* law. Twice in eight years I watched tanks roll into the capital and take over the kingdom.

There are more people associated with this book than I am able to thank. Thanks to friend and mentor Sam Zarifi, David Mathieson, and relentless journalist Shawn Crispin for their early support. Aticha Chaivichian was a brief but competent research assistant, while Greg Lowe provided valuable publication advice. I am grateful to Harvard University, whose law school's Human Rights Program hosted me as a Visiting Fellow in 2014–2015, and whose new Thai Studies Program provided context and relevance. Tyrell Haberkorn at Radcliffe provided welcome advice and encouragement. It is notable that until 1940 all American foreign policy advisors to Siam/Thailand were drawn from the law school, and that Thailand's King Bhumibol was born nearby in 1927. Alongside Thailand's two longest-serving foreign ministers, the king died during the course of this book in October 2016. And my deepest gratitude to Jeff and Chu Race, whose hospitality and friendship provided warmth amidst a superlatively cold Boston winter.

It was my great privilege to interview over ninety engaged individuals, thirty-two of whom, all from their nation's foreign service or military, asked to remain anonymous. Several spoke entirely off the record, others exercised an occasional "line item veto" on particular points. Nearly all spoke with candor and conviction and occasionally emotion. In August 2015, after several failed requests, deposed Thai Prime Minister Thaksin Shinawatra granted a rare and extensive interview in London. I was given an exact time and location, where his security detail stood by the door (and bought me an expensive coffee). A man whose policies defy the easy characterizations often applied to them, Thaksin was forthcoming and generally forthright. Many others were notably hospitable: Kraisak Choonhavan answered questions for literally four hours in his Soi Ari garden; Denny Lane offered not only his recollections and rolodex, but the guest room of his cozy Washington home. Some would do Southeast Asia hands a great service and even greater pleasure by sharing their stories more fully.

Thank you: Abhisit Vejjajiva, William Aldis, Ammar Siamwalla, Anand Panyarachun, Chris Baker, Bhokin Polakul, Stephen Bosworth, Ralph "Skip" Boyce, John Brandon, Chalermsuk Yugala, Chaturon Chaisang, Chuan

Leekpai, Chulacheeb Chinwanno, John Cole, Anthony Davis, Robert Fitts, Nirmal Ghosh, Gotham Arya, Denis Gray, Karl Jackson, Jakraprob Penkair, Kantathi Suphamongkhon, Karuna Buakamsri, Kasit Piromya, George Kent, William Klausner, Jim Klein, Kobsak Chutikul, Korn Chatikavanij, David Lyman, Kim McQuay, Noppadon Pattama, Nick Nostitz, Panitan Wattan-ayagorn, Pansak Vinyaratn, Peter Bunnag, Pisan Manawapat, Jim Pollard, Pravit Rojanaphruk, Lionel Rosenblatt, Sarasin Viraphol, David Steinberg, Jim Stent, Sulak Sivaraksa, Sunai Pasuk, Surakiart Sathirathai, Suranand Vejjajiva, Surapong Tovichakchaikul, Teddy Spha Palasthira, Tej Bunnag, Thanet Apho-rnsuvan, Victor Tomseth, Michael Vatikiotis, William Warren, Paul Wedel, Weng Tojirakarn, Matthew Wheeler, William Whorton, and Derek Williams.

Heartfelt thanks to friends near and far who offered nothing but encour-agement: Will and Amanda Adamczyk, Keith Baldi, Matt Bugher, Tina Chen, John Cheverie, Gary DeAngelis, Justin DeVito, Skip and Susan DeVito, Tim and Kim Mooney-Doyle, Brittis Edman, Marshall Flowers, Todd Gustin, Jim Hayes (S.J.), Leah Kim, Medhapan Sundaradeja, Jeff Paterno, Nigel Pickles, Matt and Amy Smith, Ralph Steinhardt, Jenny Thambayah, and Veerawit Tian-chainan, among others. Thank you to Noom and Yo of Bangkok's Passport Books. Special gratitude to Donna Guest, without whose unflinching guidance and trust this book would not have been possible.

Finally I wish to thank my family in the United States—brothers Andrew and Ryan and parents John and Cathryn—who in numerous ways enabled this project and have never questioned my choice to live as an American in Thailand.

Benjamin Zawacki
Bangkok, April 2017

Continental drift: The gradual movement of the continents across the earth's surface through geological time.

Preface

Date: Early 1976

Location: Udon Thani, northeastern Thailand

Facility: United States Seventh Radio Field Research Station, known as "Ramasun" or the "elephant corral". The station is second in size and sophistication only to another in Germany.

Purpose: Ramasun anchors the US Integrated Communication System in Southeast Asia, designed to intercept communications and monitor military movements and operations. It is capable of intercepting platoon-level signals as far away as Vietnam and China's Yunnan province.

Legal status: Ramasun is the subject of the only written agreements between Thailand and the United States concerning an extensive network of bases and facilities in the country. Signed secretly between militaries in 1964 and 1965, they confer on the US unrestricted use of the land and facilities for an indefinite period. The station and its several thousand "technical" personnel have been known to Thailand's prime minister and Foreign Ministry for less than a year.

Public status: Ramasun is the only US facility never to have had a nominal Thai commander, and Thai officials are seldom allowed inside. The station is made known to the Thai public in late January.

Dispute: Talks between the two countries regarding the withdrawal of US forces from Thailand are ongoing. In February, Thailand conditions retention of Ramasun on US acceptance by 20

March of Seven Principles. The US objects to five of the Principles, in particular that "American facilities and personnel shall be subject to Thai jurisdiction".[1] Thailand contends that the US seeks continued diplomatic privileges and immunities for its personnel and control of Ramasun.

Resolution: The US is silent until 12 March, with its embassy in Bangkok left uninstructed. Thais speculate on a lack of interest in Washington or expectation that the Thai military might force a change in policy. An acceptable compromise appears close, but the US insists it will be effective for only three months. An agreement is not signed before the deadline, and the complete US military withdrawal from Thailand commences on 20 March. Ramasun closes on 20 June.

Result: The US forfeits the "brain behind the Vietnam War"[2] and its primary facility for intercepting communications and collecting intelligence on the People's Republic of China.

Introduction:
Points of Departure

On the early evening of 22 May 2014, I received a call from Al-Jazeera, asking if I could get to their Bangkok studio immediately for an interview. Two days before, Thailand's army had invoked martial law. When they asked if I could make it home before curfew, I knew that there was more to the story: Thailand's second coup in eight years was underway.

Martial law was codified in Thailand during World War I, and transfers nearly all rights from citizens and other authorities to the military. In contrast, international human rights law, late to the table after World War II, has never taken root in Thailand beneath a positive rhetorical surface. Signatures in Geneva and New York are of little concern and consequence to Bangkok's men in uniform, who have ruled Thailand for all but about fifteen years since. In the modern era, whether Thailand has experienced the rule of law or rule *by* law has in large measure turned on the passivity, persuasion, and pressure of foreign powers.

Other nations began responding immediately to Thailand's latest troubles that May evening. Two stood out, as indeed they have in Thailand for seventy years: the United States of America and the People's Republic of China. Yet their responses could hardly have been more different. Mere hours after the coup occurred, the US secretary of state issued a statement that he was "disappointed by the decision of the Thai military to suspend the constitution and take control of the government". He added that, "there is no justification for this military coup".[1] Two days later, his government suspended $3.5 million in military assistance, one-third of all aid allocated to the country. It suspended all non-essential official visits. And it urged Americans to reconsider traveling there. Significantly, the secretary also called for the release of political leaders, the reopening of media outlets, a return to democracy, and respect for human rights.

China did not issue a statement, but at a routine press conference the next day a Foreign Ministry spokesperson commented that, "We hope that all sides can exercise restraint, step up dialogue and consultation and restore order to

1

their country as soon as possible."[2] Three days later another spokesperson added that "the Chinese Embassy in Thailand is performing duties as usual and operating normally. We hope that no matter how the situation changes, friendly exchanges and mutually beneficial cooperation between China and Thailand can keep going".[3]

The timing and nature of the responses suggested or outright betrayed two points. First, they were utterly indicative of the countries' respective policies on Thailand, which have been solidly in place for decades. While quietly encouraging and embracing several of Thailand's nineteen coups over the years, the US has never publicly offered support and has almost always issued public criticism. China, in contrast, has never publicly condemned or condoned a Thai coup, instead maintaining a neutral hands-off approach. Although keenly interested and invested in Thailand's political game, China's policy has consistently been not to judge its "internal affairs".

Second, and counterintuitively, reactions to the coup spoke to the efficacy of the two countries' policies on Thailand—to their respective levels of influence. Since at least the turn of the century, influence has been declining for a geographically distant, politically distracted, and strategically drifting America. For a close and confident China, influence has been ample and growing rapidly. The content ("disappointed") and timing of the US statement betrayed both surprise and sudden concern that recent policy had failed and future policy was in jeopardy. Chinese intelligence was almost certainly better informed and Chinese interests protected regardless ("no matter how the situation changes"). Far more than their public concerns for "human rights" and "order" is at play.

THAKSIN

Coinciding with and partially consequent to the election of Thailand's Thaksin Shinawatra in 2001, American engagement decreased in degree and constructiveness. As illustrated by ill-advised anti-terror agreements and fruitless free trade negotiations, the US–Thai relationship waned and weakened. A 2006 coup was thus not unwelcome in Washington as a clean, swift, and redemptive reversion to a military it had supported for sixty years. China, in contrast, saw its political, diplomatic, economic, and military links with Thailand all grow in number and strength under Thaksin. Not only did Thailand proactively reach out to Beijing, but for the first time in a half-century, China was both able and eager to reciprocate.

Moreover, focus of the junta that took over remained on China, while its confused economic decisions had a greater effect on American trade and investment than on the more flexible Chinese. Much of the Thai military's 60 percent budget increase was spent on weapons and materiel from China. As per US law, military assistance to Thailand decreased after the coup, but in contrast to the law's design to punish and deter, so did US influence. In exercising discretion as to what programs to cut, Washington predictably and purposely harmed relations. But it failed to do so in a manner effecting appreciable change in Thai governance. A microcosm of US policy on Thailand since the turn of the century, the response was indecisive, miscalculated, and self-defeating, with neither the democratic principle nor a shrewder (and China-like) pragmatism prevailing. More significantly, Thailand's generals did not want or need American approval as much as they did in the past.

Elections in 2008 brought two more Thaksin nominees to power, amidst protests, crackdowns, and the use of the courts as a political battleground. While the instability suited neither the US nor China, the former disadvantaged itself further by replacing a superlative ambassador with one lacking the requisite experience. By the time a party with strong historical links to the US regained power in late 2008—with critical assistance from the Thai military—such links proved to be only that: historical. Poorly maintained for a decade and challenged by new Thai connections to an ambitious China, US ties to Thailand's old elite were in terminal decline.

Following a disruptive preview in 2009, in 2010 Thailand experienced its worst political violence in eighteen years. The military intervened as unlawfully on behalf of a government it supported as it would four years later against another it opposed. Statements by the US were again lame, equivocal, and either ignored or claimed as support by one side or another. China's silence spoke concentration and assurance. When a 2011 election then saw Thaksin's sister Yingluck take office, the US supported Thais' right to vote but was newly concerned by the results. Indeed, Yingluck inherited a network of contacts and relationships with the Chinese that dwarfed their American analog in both quantity and quality.

By the time President Obama made Thailand his first foreign visit only eleven days after being reelected in November 2012, the gesture was far too little, far too late. Despite describing Thailand as "America's oldest friend in Asia", his language admitted a friendship neglected: "restoring American engagement", "reaffirm the importance of upholding democracy", "revitalize our alliance".[4] And as if to underscore the point, two days later and just four days after his successor was selected in Beijing, outgoing Chinese Premier Wen Jiabao arrived in Thailand with an itinerary closely resembling Obama's. But he stayed two days to Obama's one, spoke pragmatically of interests, strategy, and progress, and referred to Thailand not as friend but as family "since ancient times".[5]

CAUSES AND EFFECTS

At the start of the 2000s, and again by the time the Thaksin era was summarily closed in 2014, Thailand's views of its Western ally and Asian neighbor were consistent with theirs regarding Thailand. Although Thaksin himself was initially responsible for the shift, the fact that it did not stop in either 2006 or 2014 shows that it is not linked to an individual, family, party, faction, or color-coded political persuasion in Thailand. The move into China's sphere of geopolitical influence (and away from that of the US) has become an institutional, cultural, *national* consensus. It not only transcends Thailand's domestic "Yellow v. Red" divide, but is a rare contract between them.

Moreover, the shift is manifest not only in Thailand's foreign affairs but in its domestic policies and practices—with roots even more firmly planted in the Thaksin administration. The "China Model" of an authoritarian government overseeing a liberal economy has been steadily replacing any semblance of democracy in Thailand since the turn of the century. That Thailand's Foreign Ministry did not issue an independent statement after the 2014 coup indicated its role as a glorified translation and messaging service for decisions made by Thailand's strongmen, Thaksin and the generals.

Differences between Thailand's 20th and early 21st century bastions of power are limited to pedigree and province. The former is a conservative and reactionary "Yellow" alliance of monarchy, military, and moneyed elite, based in Bangkok and provinces further south. Against it is pitted a "Red" amalgam of Thaksin supporters, nouveau riche, and repeatedly disenfranchised populations in Thailand's north and northeast. While both vie for claims on Thailand's democracy and "true voice", neither is remotely democratic or fluent in more than fallacy. Their political parties are unwilling to act as a responsible opposition; their rank-and-file are willing to use violence against their opposite numbers; and their leaders seek power only for themselves rather than any fair conception of the electorate.

Attendant to this rhetorical arms race on "democracy" in Thailand has been a rise in "human rights" assertions. Yet growing Chinese-style authoritarianism has only exposed a heavily politicized and highly selective rights agenda through (and including) the second coup of 2014. Thaksin's tenure was characterized by egregious abuses in his "War on Drugs" and southern counterinsurgency, and against the media. His subsequent nominees and the governments led or backed by men in uniform, all distinguished themselves by the persecution of refugees, stark violations of freedom of expression, and staggering impunity throughout. That Thailand joined (and soon led) the UN Human Rights Council in May 2010—literally as its soldiers were using lethal force unlawfully against demonstrators—was as shameless of the country as it was shameful of the Council (both the US and China voted for Thailand).

Rewinding the clock, Thailand as a theatre for the interface of domestic politics with international relations is informed and driven by historical and cultural factors. A hundred years ago, "Siam" only avoided colonization per se by preemptively surrendering rights and territory to Western powers, while adopting a quasi-irredentist approach to lands and peoples not firmly within Bangkok's control. This external concession and internal consolidation has characterized Thai leadership and people ever since, resulting in a nation devoid of ideology. Thailand experienced a bout of republicanism in the early 1930s, a shallow-rooted communist insurgency lasting twenty years through the mid-1980s, and brief displays of democratic fervor in the 1970s and early 1990s. Otherwise, the only ideological sentiment has been an undefined and increasingly manipulated "royalism".

Thai royalism manifested itself in a pro-American foreign policy at the end of World War II and at the start of King Bhumibol's reign a year later. The proximity of the two events was not coincidental; born in the US and deeply opposed to communism, the king helped cultivate, maintain, and encourage Thailand's relations with the world's most powerful nation. For twenty-five years these were based on anti-communist policies that were also overtly or de facto anti-China. Even as Thailand began to see both as less threatening, however, the latter's persistent espousal of communism and steady rise as a global power kept Thailand on-side until the turn of the century. Likewise was Thailand's regard for democracy and human rights consistent with US policy throughout. Advancing authoritarianism in Thailand through the 1970s before deciding that their interests would be better served by a more open system, the Americans successfully encouraged liberal reforms in the 1980s and 1990s.

Thai relations with the Chinese go back not decades but centuries, characterized by patronage and tribute, communication, and trade. Until 1949, Thailand's 20th century links to China were far more cultural and economic than political, the result of intensive Chinese immigration and their express exclusion from non-economic endeavors. Relations over the next quarter-century were adversarial on account of communism, with the Chinese in Thailand alternately tolerated and targeted for discrimination and persecution. In the late 1970s Sino-Thai relations began to thaw, followed by ethnic Chinese advances. By the 2000s, the former were set to grow and flourish, the latter to lead in nearly every sector in Thailand. Both the international and domestic dynamics had done a complete about-face from a half-century before.

Neither Thailand's military–monarchy elite nor the US had reason to resist this phenomenon until it posed a direct challenge to both in the person of Thaksin Shinawatra. But by then the game was late and the 2006 coup a last resort. It failed on all counts. It failed to uproot Thaksin, causing instead an eight-year extension of his influence and power. It failed to correct the benign neglect of the US toward Thailand, leading instead to a more rapid and consequential deterioration of ties. It failed to arrest deepening Thai–Chinese relations, accelerating instead China's geostrategic gains in Southeast Asia at US expense. And it failed to reverse the growing attraction across Thailand's political divide of the "China Model", resulting instead in a hastening decline in democracy and human rights.

Thailand's subsequent coup in 2014 was simply the starkest illustration and most dramatic product of its predecessor eight years earlier; nothing succeeds like failure.

MEASURES AND MEANINGS

This book illustrates three distinct but related reasons that the evolving political landscape in Thailand in the early 21st century warrants attention. First, a US politician once famously quipped that "all politics is local"; national and international issues have meaning, effect, and importance in smaller and constituent communities. Conversely, globalization asserts that local or national matters—ideas, products, systems, cultures—can outgrow their geographic origins and achieve application or acceptance on a global scale. That these two norms sometimes directly interact is not new. The politician's remark came in 1982, when fears of global communism and capitalism led their respective champions in

Moscow and Washington to interfere with the leaders and affairs of small and distant places. Those places, in turn, affected the politics and policies of the superpowers, as best illustrated in Southeast Asia by the US war in Indochina and the "domino theory" that informed it.

This book takes as axiomatic that the world is again more bipolar than multipolar in the distribution and projection of political power, and that such will only increase over the course of the 21st century. Whether the ability of the US to effectively wield its power abroad is in gradual, qualified decline or has merely leveled off—peak v. plateau—is debatable. But it will remain for the foreseeable future one of two dominant features on the global landscape. The People's Republic of China is the other, and will continue to separate itself from the other "BRICS" (Brazil, Russia, India, South Africa) and from the European Union and Japan. It will sooner rival the US than resemble any other "rising" (read: regional) power, but will differ from it in one major respect: only the Americans will continue to maintain democracy and human rights as at least nominal pillars of their foreign policy.

Although the US and China publicly accept the other as global "partner", they are of course competitors; bipolarity may be the current and near-term reality but it is not the goal of either nation. Which of the two will advance at the expense of the other will be determined "locally"—one country, border, UN vote, airbase, sub-region, waterway at a time. Overt territorial enlargement is likely more a characteristic of centuries past than the present one, but "spheres of influence" à *la* the Cold War remain the order of the day. As Chinese forces occupy disputed islands and construct new ones, the South China Sea is a partial exception to this rule. The reach and effect of international human rights law, however, is a perfect example. Thailand, as a nation in which the Americans and Chinese compete for geopolitical influence, is another.

Second, if all politics is local then it is also entirely *relative*. Bipolarity character-izes the power of two countries relative to that of all others. But it is also a measure of the two nations' power relative to each other. It is a zero-sum scenario whereby, in Thailand, the US has surrendered as much as China has gained, resulting in a balance of power that no longer favors the former and is beginning to favor the latter. For the Americans, Thailand has gone from a long-time and loyal ally—ideal for a global power—to one of ambiguous or conditional reliability. For China, Thailand has come to essentially hold the same status, only representing an advance rather than a loss, and is continuing to turn in its direction.

On the other hand, a country seeking allies in global powers is usually better served by strategic ambiguity. For Thailand it is *not* a zero-sum situation; two conditional allies in *both* the US and China are better than just one of almost any other nature. This includes a strong but exclusive alliance driven mostly by necessity, as it had with the US during half the 20th century. And in a nation where neither has deep roots, democracy and human rights can thrive or wither under either scenario, depending on the priorities of its ally/allies.

Third and finally, the changing political landscape in Thailand in the early 21st century warrants attention, put simply, because it is occurring in Southeast Asia. Although other regions will certainly play a role in the US–China balance of global power over the next several decades, none is likely to surpass Asia in importance. This is both a cause and an effect of Obama's "pivot" to the region, itself a response to China's rise. Thailand is not among the largest or most powerful countries in Asia by any measure. Yet Japan, India, the Koreas, even Indonesia are not only allied to greater or lesser degrees with the US or China, but it would take an unforeseeable combination of efforts and events for that to change in even the medium term. One glaring exception is Pakistan, which has endeavored to simultaneously cooperate with US military campaigns in South Asia and counter US–India relations by befriending China as well. Most of the Asian nations that will determine the US-to-China power ratio are small and currently of limited political clout—with the latter characteristic set to change, based initially on little more than a map.

GEOPOLITICS AND ITS DISCONTENTS

Between the mid-1980s and early 2000s, what separated Thailand from the nations above was that, due to global events and priorities, it was geopolitically unimportant. Conversely, for the dozen or so years since, Thailand has joined those countries because its geopolitical importance has increased substantially—not unlike it did in the wake of World War II. The key difference between the postwar period and today is that where the US assigned the most importance to Thailand then, China is doing so now.

Countries are never only the solid-colored nation-states on "political" maps. They are also the earth-toned areas that run through, around, between, and among them on their "physical" counterparts. For Thailand, this means the Chao Phraya, Mekong, and Salween Rivers. It means the Gulf of Thailand, Andaman Sea, and hour-glass-thin Isthmus of Kra that separates them, as well as their maritime extensions in the Straits of Malacca, South China Sea, and Bay of Bengal. It means part of twenty sets of hills or mountain ranges. And it means what lies beneath, within, and above these physical bodies, as well as, potentially, what lies next to them or where they might lead. Countries are *geo*political entities, contested and aligned with for geopolitical reasons.

The Straits of Malacca is an enormous maritime short-cut and ideal location for a naval blockade in the event of international conflict. Why? Because it is the waterway through which one-third of global trade and two-thirds of the world's oil and liquefied natural gas passes. Every day, three times more oil transits through the Straits than through the Suez Canal, and fifteen times more than the Panama Canal. China is the world's largest net importer of oil and one of the largest markets on the planet. That the US navy has essentially controlled the Straits for decades thus serves US geopolitical interests.

Since the early 2000s, China has responded to this US maritime dominance. It is developing a blue-water navy and projecting sea and air power in the South China Sea. In Laos it is building and financing dams to shore up energy supplies in China's southern Yunnan Province. In Myanmar it is expanding oil and gas pipelines from the Andaman Sea and Bay of Bengal—replete with ports, roads, and other secured infrastructure. China controls 20 percent of Cambodia's coastline. Energy and littoral access are the desired results.

China has also utilized territorial Thailand in ways that the US has not since the early 1970s, imposing new realities to which the US—when acting at all—is reacting. Where the US has publicly opposed the largest of China's dams in Laos and belatedly changed its isolationist policy in Myanmar since 2011, China has been investing in road and railway links across Thailand for two years longer. The sum of Obama's "pivot to Asia", announced the same year, has been the still incomplete deployment of 2,500 marines to Australia and the movement of a few ships to Singapore. China has meanwhile constructed over 3,000 acres of artificial islands in the South China Sea, and threatened to enforce a no-fly zone above them. The irony is that, although a response to growing Chinese power, Obama allowed his policy to fade through the end of his term while China has gone from strength to strength.

Economics has always been an element of geopolitics. In explanation of why his government did not bail out Thailand in the wake of its devastating financial crisis in 1997—the way it had Mexico several years prior—a US official remarked that, "Thailand is not on our border".[6] Despite being then only a regional economic power and doubtless *because* Thailand lay in its near abroad, China offered the country a billion dollars.

However, since a US–China trade deal and the latter's membership in the World Trade Organization (WTO) in 2001, the ability-*cum*-necessity of nations to pursue their economic interests separately from (other) geopolitical policies has risen. Most countries accept that global economic integration benefits their adversaries as much as themselves and their allies, but also accept its necessity for their own benefits to be realized. Thus, in contrast to the over-arching geopolitical contest between and among nations, the economic element is generally *not* zero-sum and so can be removed from the equation by either choice or necessity. Nations choose either when their economic interests are truly minimal (e.g. US trade embargo on Cuba after 1992), or when a nadir in relations causes them to subordinate those interests (e.g. US/EU sanctions against Russia in 2014). The growing rule, however, as most dramatically illustrated by the global financial crisis in 2008, is that nations are forced to protect their economic interests regardless of other geopolitical priorities. The US was no more on China's border in 2008 than Thailand was on the US's in 1997, but China was (and remains) the US bond market's primary creditor. In the 21st century, wars over trade will remain extremely rare and "trade wars" technical sideshows.

China's inexorable rise in recent years has naturally increased its economic importance to the United States. And yet, despite China's proximity and deepening economic links with Thailand, US economic policy toward Thailand has not been similarly strengthened. China signed a free trade agreement with Thailand in 2002, and between the 2006 coup and late 2014, it went from the Thais' third largest trading partner to their largest. The US and Thailand have no free trade agreement, and during the same period the US dropped from second to third on its list of trading partners. In 2014, direct investment from China into Thailand was expected to double over the next five years, while the US ranked sixth in that sector, accounting for a mere 2 percent. Whether viewed as a contingent element of geopolitics or a separate undertaking, US economic relations with Thailand are far from robust.

DEMOCRACY AND HUMAN RIGHTS IN GEOPOLITICS

When asked by reporters about Tibet, Taiwan, and human rights on a trip to China in February 2009, Secretary of State Hillary Clinton replied that, "our pressing on those issues can't interfere with the global economic crisis".[7] If the crisis exemplified a new economic imperative, then democracy and human rights were other geopolitical elements it might preempt or outweigh. Clinton's calculation (compounded by her public admission) spelled a net gain for China, for not only were the situations in Tibet and Taiwan left unchallenged, but US vulnerability rather than strategy was the express reason. "Those issues can't interfere" because the US assigned them negligible geopolitical importance; they were seen and duly exposed as secondary and subordinate. In contrast, as integral pieces of their "One China" policy, Tibet and Taiwan were seen by the Chinese as non-negotiable concerns.

The same year, however, the US showed itself capable of a more responsible and effective approach elsewhere in Asia. Having chosen in 1990 to impose economic sanctions on a repressive Myanmar, the US began lifting them after a policy review in 2009. In 1990 China was economically limited and other US interests in Myanmar were minimal, making sanctions a geopolitically sound policy. Two decades on, amid fast-growing Chinese influence in Myanmar, the sanctions had outlasted their debatable effectiveness and become counterproductive. The US's geopolitical calculus called for a more engaged and nuanced policy in Myanmar, as well as one in which democracy and human rights stood a stronger chance of progressing.

Thailand's place in that calculus has varied widely over the decades, accounting partly for the delayed and declining state of democracy and human rights there. During the Cold War, "the Free World" referred less to political rights than to capitalism, while economic, social, and cultural rights as often found champions in the communist bloc. With considerable US assistance, Thais successfully opposed domestic and encroaching communism throughout, but did not experience their "Thai Spring" until the Cold War ended in 1992. In fact, Thailand's anti-communist success depended upon dictatorship and political repression—also aided and encouraged by the United States.

Between 1992 and the 1997 financial crisis, Thailand's embrace of democracy and human rights coincided with only limited American engagement, as communism was by then long in retreat as an ideology for export. The US War on Terror was then a partial Cold War redux in Thailand, with democracy left alone but unlawful activity and rights violations otherwise characterizing bilateral engagement. And since Thailand's 2006 coup, US efforts in Thailand toward any end—much less toward promoting its "core foreign policy values" as elements of geopolitics—have lacked coherence and consistency.

Not so the Chinese. Contrary to conventional judgment, their approach to Thailand since the start of the Thaksin era has quietly accounted for governance and rights issues. It is true that China seldom criticizes other nations' attacks on democracy and human rights. Yet its silence is loud and clear and full of meaning. At the very least it speaks of implicit understanding and acceptance of authoritarianism; at worst approval and encouragement. More importantly, it is increasingly understood by other authoritarian nations (and likely intended by China) as an invitation for deeper engagement. China's repeated claims to the contrary notwithstanding, its silence on Thailand's coups and rights violations is the opposite of "non-interference in domestic affairs".

The geopolitical purpose this serves China is evident when placed next to America's more conditional relations with Thailand. In the words of former Thai Finance Minister Korn Chatikavanij, "The benefit to them of Thailand remaining under authoritarianism is that Thailand will have no choice *but* to befriend China because you can't befriend anyone else, and certainly cannot befriend the Western democracies. So that plays into China's hands."[8] US policy on Thailand since 2006 has been neither as resolute and pragmatic as its 2009 approach to China (engage at all costs), nor as principled as its pre-2009 approach to Myanmar (isolate at all costs). Nor should it be, for both divorce democracy and human rights from other geopolitical concerns.

For the US to regain and retain credibility abroad on its "core values", it must be consistent as well as effective. Its refusal to condemn Egypt's coup in 2013 was notably detrimental, not least in the eyes of Thais who have rightly criticized such "double standards" in relation to their own coups. Yet, except in the direst of human rights and humanitarian situations (when even military intervention might be justified), imposing a "democratic black hole" or "human rights vacuum" is equally ill-advised. When all other geopolitical concerns vanish pending a prescribed resolution by Washington, democracy and human rights themselves seldom emerge in stronger condition. Their forms are easy to satisfy—elections and laws—but their meaning and content languish. While China's insidious authoritarian influence in Thailand is already working to democracy's detriment, American dogmatism is not the answer. Given China's expanding global influence, a US policy of isolation in a world where few countries are actually isolated is doomed to failure.

To overhaul its political, diplomatic, economic, and military engagement with Thailand, the US must begin to *compete* with China for ideological influence. It must begin to see governance and rights in Thailand as the Chinese do: matters of real geopolitical importance. This means more than issuing critical statements, which are appropriate as tactics but do not count as strategy. More than just calling on the Thai leadership to adopt a democratic system and respect human rights, the US must *convince* and *demonstrate* that doing so is *in their interest.* The United States cannot persist, in the recent words of an American official, to "simply expect more of the Thais" than other crisis-prone countries.[9] In the 21st century, the Americans must expect more of themselves.

Part One

Chapter One:
The Fog of Peace (1945–1949)

Neighbors on all sides of Siam—Indo-China, Burma, India, and Indonesia—were deep in it. Siam, always wise or wily enough to retain her sovereignty from one monarch to the next, stood only in the shallows of the stream; but there was no doubt that this capricious Kingdom would one day feel the full force of the movement.[1]

Alexander MacDonald, 1949

So wrote the American ex-intelligence officer and founder of the *Bangkok Post* of early 1946 Siam. The half-century alliance between his home country and the country he called home was hardly foreseeable. The Japanese—to which the kingdom had been both friend and foe during the recent world war—were all but gone after four years of occupation. US history in Siam was neither long nor exacting; American missionaries would continue to outnumber officials through the end of the decade. In 1833, Siam was the first Asian country with which the US signed a Treaty of Amity and Commerce. In 1856, a Siamese official claimed, "We love the Americans, for they have never done us or anyone else in the East an injury."[2] The US was deft, however, in exerting influence surgically and strategically by offering a foreign policy advisor as early as 1903. In 1920, President Woodrow Wilson's son-in-law regained for Siam the jurisdiction it had previously forfeited to European powers over persons living there, earning high praise for his country.

This intimate US–Thai relationship would continue throughout World War II and greatly influence the immediate postwar dynamics. On the very day Japan bombed Pearl Harbor in Hawaii, its troops attacked Thailand in nine locations. While the US had recently canceled a sale of fighters to Thailand, Thai Prime Minister Phibun Songkram kept a promise and ordered courageous but short-lived resistance. Days later, Thailand's ambassador to the US, Seni Pramoj, declared himself independent of his government and announced the creation of a small Free Thai Movement in support of the Allies. He would later recall the response of a US official: "You are our first ally."[3] Seni further refused to deliver his country's declaration of war on the Allies to the secretary of state.

At the same time, one Pridi Phanamyong began organizing a separate and far larger Free Thai Movement in Thailand against the Japanese, while the US founded the Office of Strategic Services (OSS), predecessor to the CIA (Central Intelligence Agency). The OSS would provide structure, funding, training, arms, and operational relevance to Pridi's membership of up to 10,000 Thais. (The best known OSS officer, albeit for his later Thai silk business and mysterious disappearance, was Jim Thompson.) Neither Free Thai Movement was involved in a major operation or uprising, but their leaders would put their stamp on Siam's political direction after the war. Seni was made prime minister, while Pridi was regent for Siam's young king, whom President Harry Truman hoped would visit the US. In June 1946, however, Pridi fell under suspicion over the king's sudden death—shot by a pistol that had been given him by a former OSS officer.

ENTER THE CHINESE

At the root of the suspicion was a China at war with itself. A year after Pridi helped overthrow Siam's absolute monarchy in 1932, the kingdom passed an anti-communist law partly out of concern for his economic plans. It was to China that Pridi and the OSS sent contingents of Free Thai during World War II. Both Chiang Kai-shek and Truman, who hosted Pridi on a US tour in 1947, suspected him of communist leanings. And it was to China that Pridi would flee in 1949, just eight months before the communists prevailed in its long civil war. Living in Peking and placed by propaganda in southern Yunnan province, Pridi would later haunt his country and vilify its American ally from Chinese soil.

Since the late 19th century, the Chinese had been influencing Thailand more deeply, subtly—and despite Thai efforts—more irrepressibly than the Americans. Expressly excluded from political and military participation, and remaining socially apart save for their predominant role in the economy, over a million Chinese immigrants had entered the country by 1910. Sun Yat-sen had visited two years before and convinced most Chinese in Siam to support his nationalist cause against the communist challenge. Prior to a 1913 Nationality Act, Chinese could become Siamese citizens by registering as subjects, acquiring local names, and pledging loyalty to crown and country. But neither Chinese side favored a monarchy, while Siam's king described them as "every bit as unscrupulous and as unconscionable as the Jews ... aliens by birth, by nature, by sympathy, by language, and finally by choice".[4]

Racism aside, it was not entirely "by choice" but by law that the Chinese focused so much on money and markets. As a result, they recognized and sought to protect the advantage of their exclusion through underground societies and monopolistic practices. The last large wave of Chinese immigration occurred in the 1920s, consisting of roughly 100,000 per year. In 1921 a business known later as the Charoen Pokphand (CP) Group was founded. Destined to grow in size, economic reach, and political influence later in the century and well into the next, it began as a simple Bangkok seed shop.

Phibun Songkram changed the country's name to Thailand to reflect nationalist sentiment, after becoming prime minister in 1938. He instituted anti-Chinese policies to reduce economic power and increase assimilation, and imposed a raft of cultural edicts on Thais to set them apart from the Chinese. Remittances to China had become a significant drain on Thailand's economy, as had Chinese nationalism, since Japan (at war with China) was a major trading partner of Thailand. Chinese businesses were taxed or taken over—twenty-seven occupations were decreed for Thais only—separate schools were monitored, and Chinese newspapers were closed. Despite a letter from Chiang Kai-shek in 1940 asking for the protection of ethnic Chinese in Thailand, Phibun continued imprisoning and deporting leaders of both nationalist and communist causes.[5]

However, when World War II began favoring the Allies, Phibun gave way to sudden doubts and tacitly permitted Thailand's ethnic Chinese to assist the Free Thai and form a new Thai Communist Party. The partial shift was significant, for it was Phibun who had broken with Seni and Pridi and joined Japan in declaring war on the Allies in 1941. Finally, like Pridi, Phibun also reached out to Chiang Kai-Shek's forces abroad, and allowed the US to use northern Thailand for supplying nationalists in Burma with arms and assistance. By late 1944, Phibun's government, the Free Thai of Pridi and the OSS, and Chinese within and outside Thailand on both sides of their civil war, briefly cooperated in resisting the Japanese.

FAR-REACHING COMPROMISES

This partnership would hold for nearly three years. In addition to treating Thailand's declaration of war as having been made under duress, the US helped Siam establish diplomatic relations with China and gain membership in the newly formed United Nations, both in late 1946. To further avoid Siam being seen as a Japanese ally, the US not only allowed Phibun to be tried for war crimes domestically (rather than in Tokyo), but acquiesced to—and possibly influenced—the decision to acquit him; "Personal considerations took precedence over legal technicalities."[6]

More than any other, this single stroke of US policy in Siam during the heady months after the war helped determine the country's political nature and trajectory for the next half-century: military-dominated and pro-American. With brief exception, it would not be democratic and it would neither stand alone nor align itself with any other country or ideological bloc. The acquittal also ran against repeated requests for US support by Pridi, Thailand's elected and civilian prime minister. Phibun's rehabilitation not only helped return him to military prominence, but helped settle any question of the military's place in a Thailand no longer at war.

The Chinese nationalists (Kuomintang) disagreed with Phibun's acquittal, but resembled him in their wartime equivocation. Chiang Kai-shek announced in early 1943 that China had no territorial ambitions in Thailand and implored the Thais to join in defeating Japan. President Roosevelt endorsed this. However, when Pridi sent a delegation to southern China to meet the nationalist and Allied forces—none of whom yet knew of the Free Thai Movement in Thailand—the nationalists detained them. The main reason was that they harbored irredentist or sanctuary aims in Thailand depending on how the war ended, and thus did not want the Americans—then playing host to Chiang's wife in the US—to interfere. The delegates were eventually allowed to set up a Free Thai government in exile and meet the Allied forces, enabling the first contact between the two Free Thai factions. It also led to a firm commitment by Roosevelt and Chiang in 1944 to restore and protect Thailand's independence after the war.

Although Seni would use force to put down opportunistic nationalist "victors" in Bangkok (a witness recalled seeing Japanese trucks abandoned on Sukhumvit 19, one of the city's main roads), he also rescinded certain anti-Chinese laws and policies. In Siam's first Immigration Act, China's annual quota of 10,000 dwarfed that for all other nations of 200. The country also repealed the 1933 anti-communist law and legalized the Thai Communist Party. In 1947, Pridi was able to become a member of a new Thai–Chinese Friendship Society in Bangkok.

SETTING THE STAGE

In 1948, Phibun usurped power from the "pro-American" Democrat Party, followed by a communist victory in China the following year.[7] This again realigned the actors and interests at play, only this time settling them for the next half-century. The US protested Phibun's move on both principled and personal grounds, but it did "not waste its breath on moralistic foreign policy, not at a time when China was falling to Mao and the Thai military could actually control the country".[8] It fully recognized him as Siam's unelected prime minister in uniform, and immediately reconsidered his previous request for arms.

Phibun's return was greeted in Bangkok by both sides of China's civil war with "an almost visible, collective shudder".[9] While the nationalist embassy would remain for nearly three more decades, Phibun outlawed the movement outside its walls. Among the twenty-five official reasons given for the coup was that "the Chinese are above the law".[10] Planting seeds of both increased assimilation and fear of communist infiltration, some Chinese left Bangkok for Thailand's provinces. Conversely, Thais were not permitted to travel or study in China, and at least ten occupations were again reserved for Thais only. Phibun slashed the annual Chinese immigration quota to 200, outlawed Chinese associations, and closed all Chinese schools above the primary level. By mid-1949 the US asked the nationalists to support the new Thai regime.

US support for Phibun, however reluctant at times, was accompanied by an opposite relationship with Pridi, whose Free Thai missions to the nationalist Chinese acted as something of a political stain after the war. His closest companions, supported to the end by the fiercely loyal OSS, would all either be killed in police custody or imprisoned; like Pridi, they were deemed communist, republican, or both. In view of his real and imputed political leanings, the US simply did not permit him—as it did itself—to drop his support for "China" when the communists took over. The OSS would assist Pridi in escaping to Singapore before Phibun's power grab, only after the State Department denied him US transit. He returned in 1949 for a failed coup attempt of his own—aided by the nationalists but not the Americans—before fleeing a final time to Peking.

And therein lies the historical irony. The State Department's backing of Phibun would relegate it to the US foreign policy wilderness in Thailand. As successor to the outmaneuvered OSS, the CIA would emphatically assume a leading role in Thailand for nearly a quarter-century—aligning itself with another of Phibun's rivals. Alongside it would be the US military, which had advocated an arms deal with Phibun as early as 1947. Save for the US Agency for International Development (USAID), whose operations were thoroughly subsumed, infiltrated, and/or dictated by the CIA, the State Department would become negligible to the US–Thailand relationship. Decades of skillful, brave, even inventive diplomacy in both Washington and Bangkok had seen off challenges to the kingdom's sovereignty and prepared both nations for a long and durable alliance. But with Phibun back in power, its services were no longer required.

Chapter Two:
Means of Power (1949–1957)

Generally Americans in Asia are not effective. They are what I call the Intellectual Maginot Line. They feel that if the nice rich respectable people like them, they must be doing a good job. I can understand that. You look at foreign faces, hear strange languages—and you just feel more comfortable at the Press Club or the American Club or the Officer's Club.[1]

Ruth Jyoti in *The Ugly American*, 1958

Less than a year before Mao Zedong declared victory in China, a less recalled but equally lasting event occurred across the globe: the Universal Declaration of Human Rights (UDHR) was adopted by the UN General Assembly. Informed by the horrors of World War II, the UDHR was followed in 1949 by the Geneva Conventions on armed conflict and the Convention relating to the Status of Refugees two years later. Siam, the US, and China all signed the former; only China would eventually accede to the latter. Phibun hoped "a strong and effective Southeast Asian Alliance might be formed under United Nations auspices and with the United States an active participant".[2] In 1951, Thailand began supporting the US position that Communist China's treatment of its people violated the UDHR, and announced that "human rights covering bodily safety and property [of the Chinese] and other aliens would be fully protected" at home.[3]

Nevertheless, the rule of law had broken down in Thailand during the war, and the process of determining who would rebuild it was often a violent one. In the wake of the young king's death, Pridi declared a state of emergency and censored the press. Phibun dealt violently with Muslims on Thailand's southern border with Malaya, and stepped up targeting of the ethnic Chinese. Following Pridi's attempted coup, Phibun and his police chief, one Phao Sriyanond, had many of the Free Thai tortured, "reminding the people that disagreement with the police knights meant digging their own graves".[4] Over the coming decades, many of these rights violations would be repeated so widely and often in Thailand as to become, explicitly or effectively, state policy. Most enduring—the legacy of Phibun's walking away from war crimes—was a national commitment to impunity. "A free country was left after the negotiations", Seni later conceded, "A free country so that [Thais] can indulge in politics in the worst way they can, that's what happened.[5]

UNITED BY A DIVIDED CHINA

The chief cause for US interest in Thailand after the war becoming a bona fide alliance, was Mao's victory on the mainland. The Cold War's early drafts suddenly turned into alarming gusts of wind, as the Soviet Union was joined ideologically by an Asian giant of 500 million people. Both had been allies during World War II and both were fellow members of the UN's newly formed Security Council. From 1949 through 1957, US–Thailand dynamics were characterized by a shared belief that an alliance was advisable, yet not so imperative as to warrant either side taking the proverbial first step. No sooner did a conviction emerge that the relationship was mutually beneficial, however, than "escalation of commitment" concerns arose: was further investment of political capital (Thailand) and material resources (the US) being unduly influenced by that already invested? This tension would last a quarter-century.

The US and Thailand simply needed what the other had to offer and were unlikely to find it elsewhere. Phibun, as head of an army that lacked morale and materiel, needed to shore up the support of "those who originally established him".[6] As head of a government that lacked political legitimacy, he needed to see off his civilian challengers. He thus sought arms, aid, and access to assets seized or surrendered during the war. The Americans increasingly needed a political and military ally in Southeast Asia, preferably one motivated by conviction as much as calculation. Save that Phibun, like all his many successors, neither truly espoused nor opposed any political ideology, he and his rivals served the purpose. In 1949, the US released the wartime assets, and the following year made three requests that Phibun seized upon as opportunities.

The US urged him to recognize the Bao Dai regime in Vietnam, and to respond to a UN call for "every assistance" after North Korea invaded South Korea.[7] Overriding his foreign minister (who resigned—only to immediately become ambassador to the US), Phibun recognized Bao Dai and pledged 4,000 troops to the counter-invasion. Then in late 1950, a CIA plan to support a nationalist invasion of China's southern Yunnan province likewise required Thai quiescence, assistance, even direct participation. Phibun again ignored Foreign Ministry objections, agreeing not only to keep the operation secret, but to claim it as a Thai initiative if discovered. Preparatory success was due largely to Phao, who would quickly make his police invaluable to the CIA through most of the decade. He allowed CIA planes to refuel in Thailand, and personally transported the first shipment of arms to the nationalists in Burma, bordering Yunnan. Three invasions were attempted through August 1951, in the midst of which Phao flew to the US for briefings.

That the nationalists were routed each time was less important to the US than what "Operation Paper" signaled: Phibun lunging forward after a series of baby steps in the march toward an alliance. Initial hesitancy to assist the nationalists was to avoid communist ire—Radio Peking had called Phibun a "lackey of Wall Street"—a fear shared by US Ambassador Stanton.[8] Understanding what was at stake and setting a precedent, however, Phibun dismissed the advice of Thai and US diplomats alike. More broadly, Thailand's leaders supported the projection of American influence and power abroad in exchange for money and power at home. Thereafter Phibun was clear that, "in matters relating to China, the Government will act in accordance with the United States".[9]

RAISING THE STAKES

Phibun's newfound decisiveness would pay off. Long-sought US arms were promptly shipped. The US Department of Defense established a Military Assistance Advisory Group in Thailand, which envisaged a 60,000-strong army structured along West Point lines. A mere $4.5 million in 1951, military aid over the next two years would exceed $67 million. A Special Technical and Economic Mission was also set up to administer economic aid.

As evidenced by Operation Paper, however, the most consequential funds were covert, via a program developed and administered in 1950 by the CIA. Unlike the others, Congress was not involved. Already represented by many ex-OSS officers on the ground (and in Florida, site of a shipping shell company), the CIA was able to move fast and on the basis of personal relationships. This included a conspicuous number of marriages into Bangkok's elite families. Even US diplomats knew nothing of Operation Paper until an irate British ambassador informed them. "The Americans were the invisible hand in Thai politics, and your CIA operatives were very, very influential."[10] While the CIA directed its efforts mostly at Phao and his police, a steering committee also included Sarit Thanarat, head of the First Regiment of the army's First Division. As the police were soon a force larger than the army, it was the start of a politically consequential and often violent rivalry that persists to the present day.

An incident in 1951 illustrated to deadly effect the Americans' uncoordinated and incoherent build-up of Thailand's divided security forces. After Phao tried to appropriate coastal patrol duties for the police, the navy used a transfer ceremony of a US dredge (*Manhattan*) to attempt another coup. Phibun was briefly taken hostage aboard the dredge, after which three days of fighting resulted in over 3,000 casualties. The CIA supported the police and the navy was defeated, but the US embassy complained to Washington about the agency's covert and competing patronage.

Communist advances in neighboring Laos then caused the US to expand its approach to security, focusing on Thailand's northeast. The inaugural "hearts and minds" policy in Southeast Asia was thus underway: development projects, information campaigns, medical aid, infrastructure. When the US asked Phibun to appeal to the UN for assistance in Laos in early 1953, he had "no intention of disappointing the American government".[11]

Consolidation of gains and goals by the CIA and US military was achieved the same year by the arrival of an ex-OSS officer as ambassador, "Wild Bill" Donovan. A former Pridi supporter and the only person ever to be awarded all four of the military's medals, his appointment came over strong State Department objections. But as co-founder of the CIA, Donovan symbolized the US intelligence community's evolution and the fast-growing dominance of the security establishment in American foreign policy. Such would prevail for the next two decades in Thailand. Phibun created a high-ranking US–Thai psychological warfare team, and a new domestic intelligence agency headed by Phao. The CIA translated the *Communist Manifesto* into Thai to foster local fear of communist infiltration, and provided funds to the new Asia Foundation, which printed and disseminated anti-communist textbooks for Chinese schools. Within a year, a Border Patrol Police (BPP), a Police Aerial Reconnaissance Unit, and a Volunteer Defense Corps all followed, each with Phao as a central player.

After the fall of Dien Bien Phu in Vietnam in 1954, the US and Thailand discussed staging air strikes from Thai soil and deploying US troops to Thailand—both were agreed but delayed. Along with six others, the two nations then signed the Manila Pact creating the Southeast Asia Treaty Organization

(SEATO). Seni described it as "a happy consequence of the Free Thai Movement".[12] Assigned to the SEATO desk in Bangkok was one Anand Panyarachun, who two decades later would be made ambassador to the US and nearly four decades hence Thailand's prime minister. Despite wanting an even stronger pact, Phibun agreed to the Manila Pact unconditionally and was the first to sign it, and secured SEATO's headquarters for Bangkok.

Desiring to balance and even break the (largely illicit) economic bases of Phao and Sarit, as well the near monopoly of foreign investment by China, Phibun focused a new investment act on the US. When instability and corruption persisted in keeping the private sector away, however, US economic aid skyrocketed. At $9 million or less annually for four years before the Manila Pact, it increased to over $48 million the following year and would not fall below $26 million for the remainder of the decade. Phibun and Phao both traveled to the US in 1954 to compete for patronage. Although official military aid hit roughly $40 million that year, Phao lengthened his lead in the money game and was awarded the Legion of Merit. And if Congress's control of US funds remained the main challenge, Donovan also left as ambassador to act as Phao's lobbyist in Washington. By then, Thailand's Foreign Ministry resembled the Department of State in being merely "the executor of policies Phibun and the military had already determined".[13]

SECOND THOUGHTS

Neither Phibun nor Phao was anti-communist ideologically; they made an enemy of communism because it was politically expedient and personally lucrative to do so. By 1955, this was far less the case for Phibun, whose bases of power were shrinking fast. Not only was the lion's share of military capital from US largesse going to Phao, but even his smaller share was shifting to Sarit as head of the army's First Division. Ambassador Donovan had also fatally weakened Phibun's political support, as Thailand's opposition Democrat Party continued to receive what little attention the Americans had for soft power. Alongside growing concern that China might prove too much for a provocative and weak Manila Pact—a policy case of "buyer's remorse"—Phibun revisited his World War II equivocation. For the modern pioneer of Thailand's political philosophy, wherein power is to be obtained, retained, and as necessary recouped over all other domestic and international concerns, his overtures to China were almost automatic.

Phibun had refused to recognize China's new government in 1950. Originally saying he would wait for the UN to decide on China's status, he followed a faster, negative US decision. Following his bold move against China in North Korea, Phibun doubled down at the UN the next year by voting for a trade and arms embargo against it. Verbal attacks by Mao increased. And just as Thailand was helping establish SEATO, China was telling the world it would accept neutralism at face value, thus narrowing its focus on nations it would view as hostile. Two weeks after the Manila Pact was signed, China's premier railed against Thailand as a Southeast Asian "colonial" power in league with the US.[14]

Yet the most serious perceived threat to Thailand was the establishment in 1953 of the Communist Thai Autonomous Zone in China's Yunnan province. The Zone was announced by the Communist New China News Agency, attacking the US and the nationalists in equal measure. Indeed, though more propaganda than real cause for concern, Phibun believed that Pridi (who had fled to China in 1949) was "closely associated with this régime and have noted with concern his recent fulminations over the Peking radio calling upon the Thai people to overthrow the Government and drive out the 'American imperialists'".[15] His concern with Pridi's continuing influence and intentions bordered on the obsessive. The Zone was thus feared as a base for communist invasion and source of communist subversion, and only a lack of US support prevented Phibun from pursuing the matter at the UN.

In 1955, while the US was engaged in low-level talks of its own with the Chinese, Congressional and other civilian voices began criticizing Phibun's use of American arms. Feeling further exposed, Phibun publicly restated that recognition of the communist government would follow a potential UN decision to admit it. In fact, he had begun quietly reaching out to China several months earlier at a conference in Bandung, Indonesia, where he had met Premier Zhou Enlai. While he defended SEATO and declined an offer to discuss Thailand's treatment of ethnic Chinese, Phibun denied that Thais could never accept communism as an ideology. The means to power in Thailand were always open for negotiation. For its part, China explained its Five Principles for Peaceful Coexistence, assured that Pridi held no role in the Thai Autonomous Zone, and greatly toned down its criticism of Thailand's domestic policies.[16]

Phibun's wavering might have put him further behind Phao with the Americans, save that they still saw the two less as rivals than as sides of a single coin. Doubtless trying to exploit US displeasure, Phao sought help in moving against

Phibun in 1955, only to be roundly rebuffed in Bangkok and equally rejected during a last-resort trip to Washington. This forced upon him a virtual political imperative and presented the communists a rare opportunity: Phao would reach out to China as well—in turn causing Phibun to redouble his efforts at the same. And when a uniformly unpopular and ineffective US ambassador arrived later in the year, Thailand's opportunists predictably began coordinating a full-speed move eastward. Their representatives would twice meet Mao himself in as many months, the first time secretly, the second time openly and—for US consumption—"illegally". China gave more assurances regarding Pridi and delivered a formal invitation for Phibun to visit Beijing. The Thais lifted part of their trade embargo, and planned a secret (later canceled) stopover for Premier Zhou in Bangkok. Intriguingly, Phibun also allowed a close advisor to secretly send his two young children to live with Zhou, "intended as an offering to show China that Thailand was committed to building a strong relationship despite its deep ties with the US".[17] Formal relations were also discussed.

In late 1956, as Phibun coolly received an emissary from Formosa, Thai officials and ethnic Chinese welcomed Chinese diplomats merely transiting through Bangkok. Thailand also accused the nationalists—still assisted by the CIA—of illegally obtaining weapons and funds. The next two years saw more visits to both countries by business and trade representatives, monks, naval officers, journalists, entertainers, athletes; many were received at the highest levels and received strong publicity. As chair of the World Federation of UN Associations, Phibun's wife stated that China was welcome to join.

CHINESE ON THE HOME FRONT

Making matters worse for the US—and in retrospect more regrettable for China—the situation of communist-leaning Chinese in Thailand was modestly improving. In 1949, Phibun had publicly warned the local Chinese community to steer clear of Chinese politics, but Mao's victory made it more difficult for him to claim he wasn't specifically repressing communists. When they took control of the Chinese Chamber of Commerce, Phibun created a Combined Thai–Chinese Committee. He also deported fifty Chinese teachers for spreading communism, and ensured that election candidates had an ethnic Thai father. But pragmatism and placation in the face of continuous US pressure was key, as he repeatedly put off an anti-communism law but let the Americans lead on propaganda.

As US aid began rising steeply in 1950, however, Phibun and Phao saw a need to protect at home their anti-communist investments abroad. This was despite the fact that China's role in the Korean conflict, its domestic land policy, and its demands on overseas Chinese saw it drop in popularity among Chinese in Thailand. The Americans did not challenge Phibun's ban on criticism of his foreign policy and his deportation of Chinese communists. They welcomed his enlisting of labor leaders, civil servants, academics, monks, and merchants in the anti-communist drive. And they encouraged his efforts to censor, curb, and confiscate communist newspapers, reconsider an anti-communist law, and arrest errant journalists. Even communication between Chinese in Thailand and relatives at home was monitored, and the travel of Thai students to China controlled. Phao likewise felt little US pressure after a series of preemptive and extrajudicial killings of opponents.

Kraisak Choonhavan, who would cultivate Thai relations with China throughout his long career, recalled the era:

> My father was always saying that our contacts with China had to be hidden from my uncle, Phao. Obviously, as general of the police he was getting closer and closer to the CIA. Another contact that my grandfather kept close to him was a businessman named Luan Buasuwan. My father told me this since I was very young, openly, that this guy was our contact with China, an ethnic Chinese Thai. Even his son, Tee, would always come and spend weekends with me overnight. My father made sure we became friends, I could not understand why. Now that is something that has always been with me.[18]

A more comprehensive crackdown on dissent in 1952 was partly to satisfy US demands, and earned its praise for reversing "four years of hollow promises".[19] Phao banned the communist-controlled Central Labor Union, and ushered in a new Anti-Communist Act. He also arrested up to a thousand people: journalists, "Communist activists" (including Pridi's son), politicians, students, former Free Thai, anti-American leaders. Many were killed. Nearly all communist leadership in Thailand was pure Chinese and exclusively informed by Maoist ideology, but much of the rank-and-file were Thais of Chinese descent. The following year Phibun overrode a Chinese request and put an end to dual citizenship. Consistent with both its belief and propaganda, the US embassy claimed "that maps and information concerning military installations" in Bangkok were being sold to the Soviets, and "that plans were afoot to depose the King, overthrow the government and to set up a 'people's government'".[20] In early 1955, the nationalists sent a letter to SEATO claiming that most ethnic Chinese in Thailand supported Communist China.

But Phibun and Phao's cooperative turning to China meant again reversing course on anti-Chinese/communist activity. Phibun held press conferences to allow anti-American views, condemned coups, and welcomed new political parties. Phao released political prisoners and joined China in criticizing the legislation under which they had been locked up. A 1956 Nationality Law conferred nationality on all persons born in the kingdom. Remarkably, both leaders invited (unsuccessfully) Pridi back from abroad and invoked democracy in claiming that overtures to China were the will of the people.

Circular and self-serving, it backfired. The changes and rhetoric had come too late, allowing voters in a 1957 election to reject both Phibun as a US client and to blame vast vote tampering on the embassy. Phao was tarred by association. Only a consistently anti-American Sarit, head of the army's First Division, benefited. Protests by his supporters at the CIA and Standard Oil offices could have symbolized a profound turning point in Thailand's foreign policy and a vastly different trajectory over the coming decades.

Instead, the equally blundering Americans dodged a bullet and the Chinese squandered a unique and costly opportunity. The Thais were not for turning.

Chapter Three:
War Comes to Thailand
(1957–1973)

From the beginning of our relationship right up to the present time,
no conflict of any kind has arisen to disturb our cordial friendship and
understanding. On the contrary, there has been mutual good will and close
co-operation between our two countries—the time is ripe for even closer
co-operation. It will demonstrate to this world that we are one in purpose
and conviction and it can only lead to one thing: mutual benefit.[1]

King Bhumibol Adulyadej, June 1960

The Royal Thai Government has invited, and I have today ordered,
additional elements of the United States military forces, both ground and
air, to proceed to Thailand and to remain there until further orders. These
forces are to help insure the territorial integrity of this peaceful country.[2]

John F. Kennedy, May 1962

Military rule under Sarit Thanarat and his successor, Thanom Kittikachorn, lasted almost twice as long in Thailand as Phibun's administration. This was fitting, for US–Thai relations during those sixteen years were in every respect twice as deep, intense, and consequential to Thailand and the region. Fraught with tension and uncertainty in 1957, the relationship quickly took a series of turns linking the nations' aims and interests—only to once again abruptly falter in the early 1970s. It was never before, and has never since been, as strong as during the latter half of the 1960s. Where the CIA–police nexus dominated under Phibun and Phao, the US military drove policy in Thailand under their military successors. Indeed, thanks to Sarit's authoritarianism, domestic politics played less a role in Thailand's US policy than under Phibun; international events assumed a determinative place. War—in Laos, Vietnam, Cambodia—

manifested in refugees, insurgents, pervasive fear, and the second largest foreign deployment of American troops and materiel, came to Thailand. The People's Republic of China not only remained the bogeyman, but would again be the alliance's stumbling block. Thailand's ethnic Chinese—a formidable 16 percent of the population—were slowly assimilated if not yet accepted, as they ceased being the only appreciable communists and commercial engines. Replacing them as the primary target of persecution was anyone not seen as supporting the government absolutely; "Sarit's new regime was the most repressive and authoritarian in Thai history."³

Ending a leadership vacuum after the elections, Sarit staged a coup and purged the old guard. This included Phao's CIA benefactors, who burned their records as the tanks rolled, and were forced to transfer their police programs to USAID. For thirteen months, Sarit returned to the barracks and went to the US for medical treatment as the guest of President Eisenhower. Having pledged to abide by UN and SEATO commitments, he appointed as premier the man who had been foreign minister, ambassador to the US, and SEATO's secretary-general under Phibun. But in October 1958 he seized power again and dispensed with even a façade of civilian authority, deeply and successfully solicitous of US support both before and after. The Americans refused to label it a coup, while Sarit made Thailand's ambassador to the US his foreign minister. Although he had quietly favored his predecessors' previous visits to China, Sarit defended his coup in part as necessary to reverse such overtures, and he immediately banned Chinese imports. China responded vigorously but to no avail: "Thailand authorities have ignored China's hitherto friendly attitude" and "will have to take all the consequences".⁴

Indeed, the renewal and acceleration of the US–Thai alliance under Sarit was far more attributable to proactive moves by Thailand than to any action by the US or hesitancy by China. The Americans' reading of this transition in Thai power politics (and by extension its foreign policy) was consistently unsophisticated if not inaccurate. Their response was ponderous and unrefined. Much of this was the remit of the embassy in Bangkok, further lowering the standing and credibility of diplomats in the estimation of the US security establishment. The Chinese may have believed—not unreasonably—that Thailand was already clearly recalibrating in their direction, and thus saw no reason to further exploit the opening. They may have been preoccupied by Laos, Vietnam, the USSR, and even Tibet. Or they may have simply suffered an intelligence failure.

Whatever the case, Sarit's about-face—a fait accompli within weeks of the 1957 coup—was a stroke of luck for the US and a surprise to China.

"AN AMERICAN KING"

Why Sarit would stay the American course is equally difficult to surmise conclusively. Between 1961 and 1973, his decision would appear prescient at times, inevitable at others. But in 1957, the regional crises that would define the next decade had yet to fully materialize. Unlike Phibun, Sarit faced no credible challenger, and despite Phao's preponderant funding during the 1950s, Sarit's army was by then double the size of the police. Ideology also fails to explain, as it had and continually would in Thai politics and foreign policy: Sarit's bouts of anti-American, anti-Chinese, and anti-communist behavior were tactical, based on "the existing world power structure, not a common ideological commitment".[5] Finally, having worked his way up the army's chain of command while staying somewhat aloof from politics, Sarit was far more interested in domestic military affairs than foreign policy.

What Sarit saw was an opportunity to recast the US–Thailand relationship in a manner linking his army pedigree with the world's preeminent military power. In 1957 he partly justified his coup as necessary to protect the king, whom he visited on the day of the event, and officially renamed his former First Regiment of the army's First Division the "King's Guard". He also ensured that the constitution promulgated that year prohibited *lese majeste* as an offense against both monarchy and national security. In doing so, Sarit looked to Thailand's young king to confer a new "supra-political" legitimacy and purpose on the army, which would in turn look to the US for international patronage. On Army Day in 1959, he named Thailand's queen the honorary colonel of the 21st Regiment (thereafter the "Queen's Guard"), while the king presented personal flags to each of the army's regiments. In 1962, a member of the king's Privy Council resigned his post to head Sarit's National Security Council.

Representing a marginal power base since the absolute monarchy was abolished in 1932, King Bhumibol Adulyadej—born in America, educated in the West—was the perfect vehicle with which to augment US relations. Already united negatively against communism, the two nations would enjoy a positive source of unity in "an American king".[6] Moreover, by creating a symbiosis between the military and the young monarch, Sarit brilliantly turned the former from a political liability to an asset. This contrasted with Phibun, whose views of the monarchy ranged from ambivalent to adversarial. Sarit later changed Thailand's National Day from the date of abolition to the king's birthday, 5 December. Both king and queen presided at his funeral in 1963.

While Sarit conditioned a continuation of Thai cooperation upon US recognition of the army's new significance, the arrangement suited the Americans equally well. The CIA and the US Information Service (USIS) disseminated information that Thai communists were expressly opposed to the monarchy. It was not coincidental that Sarit's eventual successor and the young royal couple visited the US within nine months of one another in 1959 and 1960—or that the latter spoke of "even closer co-operation" in addressing a Joint Session of Congress.[7] President Kennedy would later send a letter to King Bhumibol conveying his personal commitment to the kingdom's security.

While Sarit had also pledged to "respect rights under the Declaration of Human Rights",[8] the new nexus among the military, monarchy, and the Americans afforded few grounds for protesting Sarit's violations against real or imagined communists. China's claim that his practices against the ethnic Chinese "violated internationally established fundamental human rights" was heard nowhere in Washington or Bangkok.[9] Where Phibun's restrictions on the press and peaceful gatherings had been acts of political desperation, Sarit's were in advance of domestic and foreign policy. Further, Sarit's initial failure to stamp out anti-Americanism caused Washington to instruct its embassy to act against such elements itself. It duly requested Sarit to arrest seventy-two named "Communists". According to an early 1960s US report on Thailand, "if we teach democracy at this time to the public it might boomerang".[10] Sarit declared martial law and promulgated a constitution that afforded him unlimited power. He banned all political parties, trade unions, and gatherings of more than five persons, and closed eighteen newspapers. The fortunate were charged under anti-communist legislation and given summary military trials; others were victims of extrajudicial executions, a practice Sarit not only made notorious in Thailand but bequeathed to his many successors.

DECLINING AID

Convinced by officials during his US hospitalization that diversified foreign investment would both spur domestic development and deter communist inroads, Sarit sought US experts to assist with Thailand's first economic plan of 1960. The US provided or facilitated over $100 million in World Bank loans between 1955 and 1957, and backed its effort to dismantle or privatize 150 state firms. A low point of $15 million in direct economic aid was reached in 1964, followed by a peak of over $60 million two years later when the nations signed a Treaty of Amity and Economic Relations. By 1968, the US was the top investor in Thailand's private sector.

Given that Sarit took power between US military involvement in Korea and Vietnam, military assistance to Thailand in 1957 dropped from $43 million the previous year to $26 million, before leaping to $88 million and $72 million in the two years prior his death in 1963. Coupled with transferring, diminishing, or eliminating many of the CIA's operations—US aid to the Thai police fell precipitously—Sarit's tenure was marked less by a build-up than by holding the line.

A US report in 1960 affirmed the prevailing and purposely ambiguous view in both countries that all American aid to Thailand was for "security".[11] A year later, with the situation in Laos fast deteriorating, a group formed by Kennedy recommended Thailand as one of twelve focus countries for still-new US counterinsurgency operations. Most aid was directed at transportation, infrastructure, and communications projects in Thailand's north and northeast. The poorest parts of the country, historically neglected by the central Thai leadership, and bordering Laos and Cambodia, they were the most prone to communist invasion or infiltration. Nearly all funds were administered by USAID and Thailand's Interior Ministry, pushing the Ministry of Foreign Affairs further outside of decision-making circles.

EASTERN NEIGHBORS AND THANAT-RUSK

Yet a downturn in aid hid as much as it revealed about the US–Thailand relationship under Sarit. Completed in 1960 under no written agreement—more legal ambiguity—was the construction of seven bases in Thailand: "That's a hell of a lot."[12] Indeed it was planes and not soldiers that defined the "Secret War in Laos" during the 1960s and early 1970s. The major exceptions were Thai Special Guerilla Units and ethnic minority Lao Hmong, both funded and trained by the CIA; the latter's plight would dog the Americans into the next century. Not since the days of the Free Thai Movement had the interests of the US and Thailand converged so completely as they did in Laos.

In 1961, following advances of the communist Pathet Lao, 200 Thai paratroopers were flown over the border by their CIA trainers. Kennedy also sent several hundred marines to the border, followed by his vice-president, who formally offered to station US troops in Thailand. All US forces in the Pacific were placed on alert, and the majority of the US navy's Seventh Fleet was dispatched to the South China Sea. Nevertheless, Sarit refused to host a SEATO military exercise and threatened to withdraw from the organization altogether. Not until the foreign minister returned from Washington in 1962 with a defense pledge signed with his counterpart, the "Thanat–Rusk memo", did Sarit desist: "[I]t is not so easy to find such a sincere friend who is as concerned about our own well-being as the United States".[13] With the Pathet Lao then advancing to the border, Secretary of Defense McNamara visited Bangkok and oversaw the first deployment of nearly 7,000 US soldiers to Thailand.

Common cause in Laos was not affected in 1963 upon the assassination of Kennedy and the death of Sarit less than three weeks apart; President Johnson and Prime Minister Thanom knew each other and continued seamlessly. Although not made public for another five years, a contingency plan was agreed in 1964 between Thanom and the US military, essentially a Laos-specific version of Thanat–Rusk. That year, approximately seventy-five planes and 3,000 US and Thai pilots were stationed at the bases, alongside a smaller CIA air operation. Within three years and remaining for the rest of the decade, those figures were a staggering 500 and 33,000. The number of flights also soared from perhaps twenty in 1964 to over 4,500 a year later. The cumulative total of reconnaissance missions, airdrops, bombing raids, and transportation runs would crest 90,000 in 1969.

Cambodia, also a source of tension between the US and Thailand during the 1960s, took longer to settle. Former Secretary of State Dean Acheson was well known to the Thais from his interaction with Phibun the previous decade, and remained an informal advisor to Kennedy. In a move that would come back to haunt the Americans literally a half-century later, however, in 1962 he argued on Cambodia's behalf in a dispute with Thailand at the International Court of Justice. Seni Pramoj, co-founder of the pro-American Democrat Party, led the Thai side. The court ruled that the Preah Vihear temple, of historical and cultural significance to both countries, was located in Cambodia. While Sarit faced down domestic anger and pledged to honor the decision, he felt betrayed. Adding to his pique was the provision of US arms to Cambodia, which despite Thai objections, continued for a year following the case. A public statement by the American ambassador that no US weapons would be used by Cambodia against Thailand proved insufficient.

VIETNAM

Triggering the very apex of the fifty-year US–Thailand alliance was President Johnson's decision in 1964 to begin bombing communist North Vietnam. Between 1965 and 1968, at least 75 percent of all air strikes in North Vietnam took off in Thailand, followed by B-52 bombers the next year. The latter half of the decade thus saw the two allies' policies on Laos, Cambodia, Vietnam, and indeed China—whose actual or anticipated exporting of communism was the basis for the alliance—in almost total harmony. It was a brief period for which the Phibun and Sarit eras had prepared the two nations, and to which the Americans would look back with certain longing and regret forty years hence.

Illustrating the extent of US influence in Thailand was that final approval of flights over Laos, including those with Thai pilots in the cockpit, rested with the US ambassador to *Laos*, Leonard Unger. He would become ambassador to Thailand in 1967, one of several appointed to re-inject competence and credibility in the embassy. However, much of this new-found authority in the State Department—gained with CIA backing—was cosmetic. The military (Joint US Military Advisory Group, JUSMAG; and the Military Assistance Command/Thailand, MACTHAI) stonewalled on nearly every issue and often won. Despite the ambassador's objections, it would deploy special forces to Thailand and file its own intelligence reports to Washington. Johnson's decision in 1966 to send a US troop figure exactly in the middle of those recommended by the State Department (lower) and the Pentagon (higher), suggested the former's limited authority. Moreover, analogous to the CIA in the 1950s, the Pentagon then pressed its advantage by sending a constant number of "temporary" troops to boost overall numbers. Finally, after the ambassador cut MACTHAI out of formal contact with Thailand's own counterinsurgency agency in 1966, the Thais similarly continued to place priority on informal meetings with the US military. Following a 50 percent cut in US military aid after Sarit's death, in 1965 and 1966 funding rose again to $59 million and $77 million.

The difference-makers were Secretary McNamara, whose influence in Washington was second only to that of the president, and Thanom. McNamara was clear: "Vietnam and Thailand are the immediate—and most important—trouble spots, critical to the US."[14] Thanom made the seven bases in Thailand available to some 50,000 (at its peak) US military personnel, accompanied by an enormous and controversial rest and recreation (R&R) program. This he did without so much as informing his foreign minister, chosen for his ambassadorial experience in Washington and the only civilian in his cabinet—until Thanom took over the job himself in 1971. The ministry was reduced to making "independent-sounding noises which served notice on the United States that the Thais were not to be taken for granted, and also eased Thai sensitivities concerning the presence of foreign troops".[15] In fact if not in form, both nations ceded the preponderance of policy authority to the US military: Ambassador Unger's required approval for flights to Laos often came after take-off.

COMMUNISTS AND CHINESE

Thailand's communist insurgency had been in the making since the early 1960s, but Sarit's speedy return to the American fold pushed it out of Bangkok into the countryside, delaying its organization and activity. Between mid-1965 and the end of the following year, more than 150 engagements occurred between an estimated 500 fighters and Thai troops. While most of the action was in the northeast, a separate communist terrorist organization staged attacks on the Thai–Malaysian border. As far back as 1954, US Ambassador Stanton had claimed that, "Communist agents have quietly organized many of the Chinese of the southern provinces of Thailand".[16]

With US encouragement, in 1965 Thanom created the Communist Suppression Operations Command (CSOC). To greater effect, after eight years of minimal presence and profile, the CIA was welcomed back by Thailand's leadership. It worked primarily and covertly with the Border Patrol Police, which by 1966 had twenty-three aircraft, the only M-16 rifles in Thai hands, and US special forces as advisors. US funds for Thailand's police also rose from $7 million to $17 million yearly from 1965 through 1969, up from just over half a million a year since the late 1950s. On a smaller scale, USAID increased work with Thailand's Volunteer Defense Corps and provincial police, while other programs were established or expanded: Village Radio Project, Village Security Force, Security Roads Program, Accelerated Rural Development, Mobile Development Units. The USIS and its new Mobile Information Team saw its budget expand to roughly $26 million a year through 1971. With most still based in the north and northeast, the programs constituted a second round of the 'hearts and minds' initiative of a decade or more earlier.

At half the population of Bangkok, Thailand's ethnic Chinese community was the largest in Southeast Asia in 1965. If Sarit saw such as less of a fifth column than under Phibun, overall policy still sought to ensure that Chinese money did not go toward funding communism at home or abroad. Formosa was assured that politics and not ethnicity was the basis of repression in Thailand, and the nationalists' embassy was afforded the highest treatment. Sarit decided against population control measures nationwide for fear that the Chinese would rebel and thus become a still larger demographic. He sought to dilute Chinese concentration and control of Thailand's wealth, by integrating Thais into traditionally Chinese industries and families via marriage. He also mandated that all schools teach the Thai language and took down Chinese-language signs in Chinatown. Most significant for the implications it would have on Sino-Thai relations beginning in the late 1970s, Sarit allowed the ethnic Chinese to enter the Thai military and civil service.

CHINA AND ASEAN

Sarit put a stop to visits with Chinese officials, reinstated a trade ban against China, and refused to repeal anti-communist legislation.[17] China thus returned to a more belligerent foreign policy, and criticized Thailand on Cambodia's behalf after the latter recognized the Beijing government in 1958. After losing the temple dispute in 1962, Seni believed that China had likely interfered in the decision. China's becoming a nuclear power in 1964 further raised regional fears, causing Thailand's king to remark that, "[w]hile millions of Chinese are starving, China has the luxury of the bomb".[18] And it was the New China News Agency that exposed the CIA's flights to Laos.

But the political bomb fell on 1 January 1965, when Thais in China announced the Thailand Patriotic Front. Created by the Communist Party of Thailand (CPT), with five years of propaganda behind it, the Front was a loose alliance of at least five groups, including the Thailand Independence Movement. Thailand believed that China was suppling weapons and money, and "there was evidence of a training camp for Thai insurgents in southern Yunnan province in Mengla, some seventy-five miles north of the Thai border".[19] The Thais cast a wary eye on China's continued construction of a railway in neighboring Laos, and worried about its reaction to the bombing of North Vietnam, with which it shares a short border. With Yunnan province only 100 kilometers from Thai soil, "The possibility of a Chinese Korea-style invasion, most probably knifing through Northern Thailand, was considered real in the 1950s and continued to haunt American and Thai policymakers as late as 1965."[20]

China's Cultural Revolution, begun in 1966, would disrupt its foreign policy and in some respects turn it "from a primary threat to a nonplayer in Southeast Asia".[21] At the same time, the Revolution included open and active support for local communist movements elsewhere in the world, including Thailand. In 1967, Thailand's King Bhumibol said that, "[t]he Chinese have always been a threat to Southeast Asia, because they are an expansive people".[22] It was against this backdrop that the Association of Southeast Asian Nations (ASEAN) was established in Bangkok the same year. Its declaration clearly stated its four founding members' desire to ensure "stability and security from external interference in any form or manifestation",[23] while Thailand's foreign minister called ASEAN "collective political defense".[24] The provision that "foreign bases are temporary and remain only with the expressed concurrence of the countries concerned"[25] was understood as only more boilerplate for public consumption. In fact, ASEAN would not affect Thailand's relations with China for another decade, coincident to SEATO's disbanding in 1977.

ROYAL ENDORSEMENT

The pinnacle of the US–Thailand alliance was captured in a series of visits by Lyndon Johnson to Thailand—the first for a US president—and by the kingdom's royal couple to the US. Although growing affection for the king and queen in Thailand did have a purely domestic element, their promotion by Sarit and Thanom was more a component of Thai foreign policy: pro-American and anti-communist. Such was equally true of their fast-unfolding royal development projects, in the same regions where US resolve was meeting communist resistance. More than simply afford the alliance royal cache, Thailand's king and queen were an indispensable and—as proven five decades later—irreplaceable piece of it. In October 1966, Johnson undertook a four-day state visit with the king and queen, seeking to clarify and affirm:"I think it is understandable why the people of Thailand should be puzzled by those who suggest that you are being 'used' or 'dominated' by Americans, or for that matter anyone else. The truth is that Thailand and the United States are going down the same road together. ... we act from a joint conviction of common interest".[26] Fourteen months later he returned to inspect troops in Thailand's northeast. In between, in June 1967, the royals undertook a second visit to the US lasting three weeks.

The most significant outcome was three months later in the first deployment of Thai military personnel to South Vietnam, the Queen's Cobra Regiment of

2,200 troops. Despite being critical of a pause in airstrikes in Vietnam and unsatisfied by assurances in the event that sending troops invited attack on Thailand, the king agreed to Johnson's request. Against an initial call for 20,000 troops, the Thais would deploy a total of 37,644 to South Vietnam, maintaining a division-sized unit of 11,000 from mid-1968 through 1971. This comprised 14 percent of the Thai army and the third largest contingent of foreign troops after the US and South Korea. Commanded by Thai officers along a strategic highway, they regularly engaged in combat and 539 were killed. They also carried out "hearts and minds" programs, often meeting with more success than their American counterparts on account of their ethnicity and better understanding of local conditions. Thus, "Washington could claim Thailand's entry as a victory in its efforts to recruit more Asian forces into the war",[27] while secretly paying Thailand $200 million,[28] and awarding the military a coveted anti-aircraft weapon.

If aspects of US policy and presence in Thailand were beginning to become unpopular with Thai officials and citizens alike, the deployment of local boys was not one of them. American commanders welcomed the Thai troops in Vietnam with great fanfare, and Bangkok-based diplomats attended their funerals back home. But royal endorsement was again the determinative factor. The queen, already an honorary colonel of the Cobra Regiment's parent unit, regularly visited wounded soldiers after they were flown out of Vietnam. Some were given a prominent place at her 36th birthday ceremony in 1967. That year, having said that the Regiment "cannot be ordinary Thai soldiers",[29] the king made them the focus of his all-important birthday speech: "It is heartening to see the large number who face the highest sacrifice by volunteering to fight."[30] He personally presided over send-offs, ceremonies, and funerals for Thailand's anti-communist heroes.

More than the Indochina equivalent of Thai troops to Korea in 1950, the Queen's Cobra Regiment was a major manifestation of Sarit's decade-old linking of military and monarchy. US critics would grow louder and more influential in the early 1970s, but Thailand's press, industry heads, religious leaders, and celebrities followed the monarchy and strongly backed the troops. This remained so after Thai society later turned on the Americans and the war itself, and even forestalled such hostility. Thai troops in Vietnam prolonged the lifespan of Thai military leadership and deepened its US alliance. A full twenty-three years later, the queen would dedicate the Monument to the Bravery and Sacrifice of the Thai Soldiers on the Vietnam Battlefield.

THINGS FALL APART

In contrast to 1955, when the Phibun/Phao rivalry put Thailand's relationship with the US at risk, in 1968 neither the king nor Thanom faltered. The Americans did, losing the war in Indochina and any semblance of policy coherence along the way. For the next five years, the level of congruity between the two countries would fluctuate wildly, finally giving way to a brief period of deliberate rebalancing. Just as it had triggered the apex in the US–Thai alliance, the bombing of North Vietnam—not beginning but being brought partially to a halt—prompted the decline. When Johnson subsequently announced that he was not seeking reelection as president, Thanom's concern deepened. By the time newly elected President Nixon began a partial withdraw of US troops from Vietnam—without so much as informing Thanom—Thailand's military leadership was outright panicked.

In 1969, finally accepting the American withdrawal and attempting to turn it to its advantage, Thanom recalled Phibun and Phao and reached out to China. His foreign minister was transparent: "Communist China will become pivotal to peace, security and freedom in Asia as it turns from internal preoccupations to outside interests and as the United States tries to sneak out of the Asian scene."[31] Nixon personally assured Thanom of US security commitments during a stopover in Bangkok, and via the highest sums yet ($105 million) in military funding in both 1969 and 1970. But coming just days after placing defense responsibility on allied countries themselves in his "Nixon Doctrine", the gestures meant little. The US Senate emphasized the point by exposing and casting doubt on US plans to defend Thailand, and referring to Thai soldiers in Vietnam as "mercenaries".[32] Thanom's foreign minister again replied in kind: "[I]mmature and irresponsible elements in the United States have shown persistence in persecuting and molesting such a loyal friend and partner as Thailand", which "has had to endure and suffer at the hands of those ugly Americans".[33] In 1970, the US refused to support Thailand's move to send troops into Cambodia but began training Cambodian forces on Thai soil. Budgets, personnel, and projects in Thailand were slashed, while US troop numbers—until then holding steady at about 48,000—were drawn down to 32,000 by 1971.

In the Thai countryside, the communist insurgency reached perhaps 3,000 fighters in 1968 and engaged Thai troops at least 370 times. The following year the CPT announced the People's Liberation Army of Thailand. By 1972 the insurgents numbered roughly 7,500, when Thailand's largest yet counterinsurgency operation involved 10,000 troops but yielded few gains. Ironically, it was against American advice. Thanom also gave support to residual nationalist forces "as a counterinsurgency pacification force in Northern Thailand".[34] Responsibility fell to Thanom's supreme commander, Kriangsak Chomanand, who would later become prime minister.

In July 1971, in one of the most consequential international developments of the 20th century, Nixon announced that he would visit Communist China. While en route to Beijing weeks earlier to advance the announcement, National Security Advisor Henry Kissinger had stopped in Bangkok to reiterate security assurances, but it was his silence on China—both his and Nixon's visits were secret—that later shocked and shook the Thais. Revisiting their overtures to China begun in 1969, they found the Chinese unresponsive. Thus when China again bid for UN membership, Thailand wished to have it both ways: vote in favor but join the US in voting separately to maintain Formosa's membership. With the questions combined, Thailand abstained. And when at the end of 1972 the US abruptly suspended its withdrawal of forces from Thailand, their hosts—despite having spent two years using the move to improve relations with China—did not object. US military aid to Thailand then reached an all-time peak of $128 million, before Thanom allowed the entire US military presence in Indochina to relocate to Thailand in 1973. "These were lost years for Thailand in term [sic] of adjustment", an unwitting ball in the "ping-pong diplomacy" between the US and China.[35]

But the death throes would not last long, as the conclusion in Vietnam was foregone and Congress finally firm in cutting its Southeast Asian ally loose. War had come and gone in Thailand, and the communists had won. The Americans, having taken a quarter-century to prepare for and prosecute the conflict, would occupy an equal amount of time in Thailand before realignment would occur. In the meantime, defeat would command a full accounting on all sides.

Chapter Four:
Experiments Interrupted
(1973–1980)

My grandfather had always had an affiliation with Zhou Enlai. My father kept repeating this over and over that they were in contact with each other. At the time of the Great Leap Forward there was huge starvation in China, and apparently my grandfather had sent fish that reproduces rapidly. That, he claimed, helped alleviate the famine in China. I don't know how true that is but he kept repeating it to me to instill how China was important to us, ever since I was very young.[1]

Kraisak Choonhavan, January 2015

The Americans were miffed that the negotiations for the retention of their forces in Thailand were not agreed upon. They had to leave. After that, America saw Thailand in a different vein. It used to be an important part of their Southeast Asian strategy, but in the 1970s we were nobody. Now did that pain us? No, it did not pain us at all. Yes, there was still some die-hard pro-American sentiment in Thailand, but taking a realistic point of view I think it did a lot of good for Thailand. My point is that we did not leave America, but you left us.[2]

Anand Panyarachun, January 2015

1973 is well known in Thailand for upending nearly all assumptions, authorities, structures, and alliances that had governed the country since the end of World War II, followed by their violent reassertion in 1976. If often described as an interlude or interregnum, these three years were envisaged and engaged by their protagonists not as a temporary period but as the start of a new and indefinite era. Like many nations before and since, Thailand experienced a popular if immature movement toward a more democratic society. To Thais who opposed the challenges and changes, however—more successfully than they realized— the mid-1970s were terrifying. After more than thirty years of military rule, Thailand's uniformed leadership was ill-prepared for and even less disposed to such a loss of power and prestige.

Among the many elements affecting and affected by Thailand's "democratic experiment" were its alliance with the United States and the alliance's primary basis, Communist China. If US–Thai relations under Phibun were driven by domestic Thai politics, and during the subsequent period by international events, beginning in 1973 both factors interacted equally. Having seemingly chosen the wrong patron, Thailand's military was at a loss to explain what the country, as opposed to itself, had gained. Even a moral victory eluded them, since their calculus was limited to political power and national security, and took no account of ideology. The alliance was thus doubted by the military and outright condemned by other Thai quarters emboldened by its failure in Vietnam.

The beneficiary, if only to a limited degree, was China. As recently as 1971, US moves toward the communist giant had given Thailand strong incentive to consider a delineated tactical shift. Two years on, defeat forced consideration of a wholesale strategic realignment. At play in Thailand, however, was a zero-sum logic that held no place for non-alignment or neutralism. Indeed, Mao had driven Thailand further into the US embrace by insisting until 1954 that the non-aligned were anti-communist. Thailand's king and America's war had maintained the status quo for nearly two more decades.

Dissident Thai students (and other civilian and labor leaders) hardly associated democracy with Communist China, but protested against the forfeiture of individual rights and national independence in exchange for American "protection". Rather than see the alliance as having championed their democratic rights and defended them from communist aggression, they saw it as precluding the former and substituting the latter for joint military domination. A certain nationalism thus pervaded the students' dissent; not the militaristic sort peddled by Phibun, but populist and infused with a sense of betrayal. Demonstrations against Nixon's policy shifts in both Vietnam and China expressed the view that the US had not so much lost as given up and left Thailand in the lurch. And if true that people did not vote in China, for twenty-five years Thailand's civilian leadership and constitutions had been engineered, ignored, or dispensed with altogether. Thanom's dismissal of both foreign minister and constitution in 1971 was especially galling. Communist sympathy among the students was never as strong as their opponents claimed (or their Mao suits would suggest), and fear of Chinese agents among them were wildly overblown. But that up to 3,000 fled to the insurgency's jungle locations after their protests were smashed did suggest a closer affinity to China's values (or propaganda) than America's.

Practically programmed to oppose any and all demands of a youthful (and sometimes inarticulate) demographic, the military held the students in contempt. Its regard for the Foreign Ministry, which "still regarded the United States as its closest ally" but generally favored the US troop withdrawal, was only marginally higher. Thailand's men in uniform simply could not envisage China ever backing them to the extent the US had and potentially still could: from 1957 through 1975 the US provided 60 percent of their budget.

CHINESE AND AMERICAN VIEWS

During neither Nixon's visit to China nor several by Thai officials in the early 1970s, was the US presence in Thailand discussed. During several subsequent Thai visits, however, the Chinese not only altered their position but strongly advised that the US military remain in Thailand. Underlying this—and adding irony to inconsistency—was the realization that China was essentially joining the US in defeat against victors it had backed throughout. While the Chinese and Vietnamese shared a contentious history, their mid-century communism had given them common cause against the Americans. Vietnam's siding with the USSR in a deepening Sino-Soviet rivalry, however, made quick enemies of erstwhile allies. Assumptions shared by Thailand, China, and the US since at least the mid-1950s were thus immediately made invalid: a victory for Vietnam was not a victory for China, and a US defeat did not mean Chinese communists would soon be crossing Thailand's borders.

On the one hand, this opened the door to improved relations with Thailand, even to the previously unthinkable point of providing security. On the other hand, fellow communists in Vietnam blocked China from pressing its strategic advantage in Thailand vis-à-vis the US. The Chinese could supplant the nationalists but not the Americans, whose presence was still needed for regional security—including China's. True that Beijing had always been far more interested in influencing Thailand's foreign policy than overthrowing its system of government, much less invading its territory. Preoccupation with US engagement, Soviet hostility, and a violent leadership transition from Mao to Deng Xiaoping might have also kept it from making Thailand's opening any less restrained than its own detente with the US. But the mere trading of status between Thailand and Vietnam hardly spelled a net gain for China, whose inroads into Thailand—if ground-breaking and real—would prove tactical rather than strategic; temporary rather than sustained. Indeed, in the recollection of a Thai negotiator, "the military void in Thailand left by the Americans was something that we did not want China to replace".[3]

The Americans claimed they would not entirely "lose" Thailand the way they had China and Indochina, but their actions throughout the mid-1970s gave their hosts reason after reason to dismiss them. They made no effort to support the Thai students and democratic rights they were demanding; the ambassador called them "neo-Marxist".[4] The embassy either lost or forfeited a canal initiative across Thailand's Isthmus of Kra, and likely sourced a fake news story of a road being planned from China to Thailand through communist Laos. All of these moves would resurface periodically into the 21st century to the disadvantage of the Americans, who failed even to limit the damage of their departure, much less capitalize on China's new vulnerability. If the Thais were surprised by the US withdrawal before embracing, accelerating, and maximizing it, the US initiated the withdrawal and then promptly lost control of it.

A coup in October 1976 brought Thailand's first experiment to an end and further handicapped the second, as the military violently put down the democracy movement, before reversing course on their outreach to China. At the same time, Thailand and the US moved cautiously but steadily to repair their alliance. In continuance of a pattern that would only change exactly thirty years later, the coup weakened Thailand's relations with China and strengthened those with the US. Events in Indochina two years later would turn China into a partner well into the 1980s, but any chance of a bona fide alliance was further delayed.

ROYAL PRINCIPLES

In 1973, a prestigious but only modestly powerful monarchy was thrust into a role it would occupy for over three decades: Thailand's political "king-maker" (and breaker). In October, following the arrest of twelve student activists, at least 200,000 people took to the streets calling for their release. In response, security forces and vigilantes wounded nearly a thousand and killed at least a hundred. Among those who fired on students from an open helicopter was Thanom's son, among the first Thai soldiers to have fought in Vietnam and been honored by the Americans. The generals' claim that the students were behind a communist plot fell flat, however, when staunchly anti-communist King Bhumibol called their bluff. Perhaps informing his verdict was his having witnessed demonstrations in Washington six years earlier, where he was also advised that further US aid would depend on Thailand improving its international image. Thanom was forced into exile (in Boston) and the military back to the barracks. Three years later, after Thanom's return sparked similar demonstrations, the military used vigilante violence to stage a coup. Officially forty-six and likely well over a hundred demonstrators were killed on 6 October 1976, before over 3,000 others were arrested. "Some were hung from trees and smashed with metal chairs."[5] Believing this time that communism was central to the demonstrations—US troops were gone and reports circulated of Chinese or Vietnamese infiltrators—the king endorsed the installed leadership of Thanin Kraivichien. That China's murderous "Gang of Four" was overthrown in a coup the very same day would only have affirmed for him that he made the right decision.

For King Bhumibol, the main priorities in the mid-1970s were preventing a communist invasion, eliminating the communist insurgency, and maintaining relations with an anti-communist United States. More than anything the Americans or Chinese did, it was he who cast the deciding vote on Thailand's alliances. Critically, he also ensured that any changes were modest in scope, qualified in content, and ultimately temporary. To the extent China was lessening as a communist threat, he had no objections to improved relations toward further lowering that risk. But the Soviets were increasingly backing communist forces in Indochina, two of which bordered Thailand and had recently lost their monarchies. The Americans' failure to prevent these events, as well as popular feelings of resentment, would have certainly influenced the king; that he led did not mean he did not listen. But if many Thais were beginning to believe Thailand had backed the wrong horse, the king disagreed. The US had lost but been right to oppose communism—and had largely succeeded in protecting the kingdom. In short, and in contrast to every Thai leader before and since, ideology played heavily in the king's thinking and decision-making. By 1976, with ongoing communist advances in the region and the Cold War still fifteen years from its conclusion, the king made clear his view that "you don't change horses in mid-stream".

Further, in both rupturing in 1973 the link forged by Sarit between Thailand's military and monarchy, and then reestablishing it three years later, the king reversed the primacy of the former over the latter. To this day, the military's mission and mandate—inculcated internally and publicly professed—is to "protect the monarchy". Thus what appeared to the outside world as a simple return to the *status quo ante* when the military regained control in 1976, disguised a fundamental shift in Thailand's power dynamics.

HUMAN RIGHTS

In the period's third and final experiment in 1977, US President Jimmy Carter introduced human rights as an official element of US policy on Thailand. That the agenda never took hold was for the same reason it hadn't for a quarter-century: (re)establishing the alliance was incompatible with a Thailand genuinely committed to human rights. While proactive violations were less imperative, resuscitation would require that the Thais not be held too strictly to fast-developing standards. The rate at which this realpolitik was accepted in both Bangkok and Washington was commensurate with how speedily and deeply the relationship redeveloped: initially slow and tentative, at full stride and strength when Carter left office.

One of Thanin's first acts, in patent violation of freedom of expression, was to increase imprisonment for *lese majeste* to fifteen years; forty-two Thais were arrested for the offense in 1977. He also allowed for the suppression of nine categories of citizens deemed "dangerous to society"—resulting in a warrant for Kraisak Choonhavan, the foreign minister's son, who had made a report to Amnesty International.[6] A US official responsible for human rights visited in 1978 followed by a Congressional hearing, but despite a decrease in military and economic assistance, "there was no evidence that such cutbacks were due to displeasure with the human rights performance of the Thai government".[7] Under Thanin's successor, violations against Indochinese refugees came to the fore, particularly the forcible repatriation of 45,000 Cambodians. Through 1980, restrictions on the media increased, enforced disappearances in rural areas rose, and a ban on gatherings of five or more persons was reinstated. A forerunner to three decades hence, 300 books were banned and jurisdiction over *lese majeste* shifted to military courts.

Consistent with the reaching out to China, no longer were Thailand's ethnic Chinese a target for persecution. To the contrary, with two global oil crises adding impetus, Thailand's political parties reached out to business and industry, long the bastion of the Thai-Chinese. It would take two more decades before they would dominate and largely define Thailand's "money politics", but shallow roots were dug into the country's shifting ground. The government also encouraged those who were not entirely or exclusively Thai citizens—including an estimated 300,000 nationalists—to sever ties of nationality with China. China assisted by adjusting its own citizenship law so that Chinese born in Thailand would no longer be considered Chinese nationals. A sizable number of Thai-Chinese partook in the tumultuous events of the mid-1970s, "but it was their views and not their national background or ethnicity that got them into trouble".[8] Some were communists, making the insurgency a natural refuge after the 1976 violence, but their focus was Thailand, not China. The post-coup government's strict control over Chinese language study proved exceptional and short-lived.

Organized vigilantes and paramilitary groups played a leading role in human rights violations. Most were formed expressly to protect the king against "communists" and, in contrast to the CIA's previous creations, most had US support but were otherwise indigenous. The Village Scouts were founded in 1971 by the Border Patrol Police—thus also obtaining royal patronage—and accounted for nearly 10 percent of Thai adults by 1976's crackdown. In 1974, a local CIA asset established *Navapol* (Power of King Bhumibol's Ninth Reign), which was likely behind the murder of twenty-one farmer leaders. Although civilian in make-up, both were assisted by the army's Communist Suppression Operations Command, which in turn founded the violent Red Gaurs after the 1973 demonstrations. The year 1978 marked the formation of Thailand's paramilitary rangers, who accelerated CSOC's practice of burning victims in oil drums; up to 3,000 such extrajudicial executions took place by the end of the decade. While the vigilantes would later disband or dissipate, the rangers' legacy would contribute to the resurgence of the southern Muslim insurgency in the early 21st century.

RECOGNIZING COMMUNIST CHINA

Thailand began making conciliatory statements about China as far back as 1969, but compromised its outreach with inconsistency; in 1970 the foreign minister *publicly* claimed that China was interested in "secret" talks.[9] Finally in late 1971, Deputy Foreign Minister (and future prime minister) Chatichai Choonhavan traveled to Beijing. While Nixon's ground-breaking announcement provided fresh air, Chatichai's authority was limited by the legal fiction "prohibiting" visits to China. For the first time, a Thai official referred to his host country as the People's Republic of China. Thailand and China's own version of "ping-pong diplomacy" began in September 1972, when another "private" visit of Thai officials accompanied the national table-tennis team to Beijing. Kobsak Chutikul was the desk officer assigned to the rapprochement and would make two more sports-related visits before mid-1975. According to him, the main issue for China was the nationalists still on Thailand's border; "What presence would the PRC countenance here?"[10] While neither side mentioned the American military presence in Thailand, reaching its numerical peak at the time, Premier Zhou Enlai did state the intention to continue supporting ideological friends around the region. The Chinese did not press Thailand on visas and trade with Taiwan, but made clear that they monitored relations down to the names of visiting officials and the placement of flags. Indeed, giving Thailand additional pause were China's association of UN membership with recognition of its "One China" position, and its growing hostility toward the USSR.

Following a Thai trade delegation in late 1972, a series of informal "corridor diplomacy" meetings took place between Kobsak's division chief, Tej Bunnag, and his counterpart in China's Foreign Ministry. Interpreting at these and even meetings with Mao, was the twenty-four-year-old daughter of the Thai advisor sent to live with Zhou Enlai in 1956. The nations' table-tennis teams exchanged visits in 1973, before China hosted Thailand's badminton team and delegates for seventeen days of sports and talk. Thailand closed the year by partially lifting its fourteen-year trade ban, resulting in a rise from $5 million to $136 million over the next three years. Believing that a cessation of Chinese support for the CPT would also deter Vietnamese aggression toward Thailand, in 1974 Chatichai undertook an early version of his strategy that would transform the region fifteen years later. In the words of his son, Kraisak Choonhavan,

> The knowledge that he had of the friction between Vietnam and China was something he truly believed in and others did not. I remember him saying that the military can only hold Bangkok for 48 hours. I asked him, "Literally, 48 hours before the Vietnamese take over central Bangkok?" and he said yeah. He said the only way out of this is diplomacy, and he explained to me—father and son dinner talk—that secretly he had met Zhou Enlai in New York. Now he didn't want Kissinger to know, or Nixon to know at all, and so he snuck out of the hotel's kitchen. He told him we want to normalize relations before the US does, before everybody else does. And of course he used his background as a descendant from China, from

a Chinese family on both sides of the family—even though it happened about 200 years ago actually. You know they often do that, brother and sister and brother and brother, China as the big brother. And all the time mentioning my grandfather's gesture with the fish during the Great Leap Forward as a very personal thing with Zhou Enlai and his wife.[11]

Indeed relations accelerated through mid-1975, including meetings in New York led by Anand Panyarachun, formerly on the SEATO desk and by then permanent representative to the UN. Thailand's defense minister admitted to having "spent more time discussing politics than sports".[12] China pledged to cease supporting communist insurgents and begin supporting Thailand's bids for a seat at UNESCO and detente with Vietnam. In "a dramatic turn of events in our relations",[13] China sold Thailand 125,000 tons of discounted oil during the global crisis and "recognized the need for a continued U.S. presence in Thailand".[14] Zhou Enlai, his language laden with significance, referred to his country as the "elder relatives" of the Thais.[15] By then Prime Minister Kukrit Pramoj—brother and political opponent of Seni—was ready: "this government will establish diplomatic relations with the People's Republic of China and will ask for the withdrawal of foreign troops within one year through friendly negotiations".[16]

In July 1975 Kukrit traveled to Beijing and made good on the pledge, reminding his hosts that "contacts between Thai and Chinese trace back to thousands of years".[17] With considerable historical irony, his counterpart outright warned of the danger that a vacuum left by the US could pose to the region, and asked Kukrit to normalize relations with newly Maoist (Khmer Rouge) Cambodia. A dying Mao met with him for an hour, reportedly quipping that to counter the communists in Thailand, the Thais should cease calling them communists. China would allow for continued party-to-party relations between communists in each nation, but otherwise formally agreed to cease government support for the CPT. Kukrit announced that SEATO would be phased out by mid-1977, and agreed to sever diplomatic ties with Taiwan. There was but "One China".

Each side got most of what it wanted from the other, and all concessions and gains came at US expense. American withdrawal was expressly linked to Thailand's new foreign policy, and it was China and not the US that would receive credit for fatally wounding the insurgency. The twenty-one-year-old Manila Pact would remain, but its chief proponent and purpose were no longer needed.

DISMISSING THE AMERICANS

In April 1973, Henry Kissinger instructed the Pentagon to cease all further planning for force reduction in Thailand, and envisaged a "substantial withdrawal" taking five to ten years.[18] Within six months, however, relations began a swift and fundamental restructuring. For the US, the three years preceding the October 1976 coup were a textbook in diplomatic incompetence and foreign policy sabotage. They also corresponded with a resurgence of the State Department in the development of policy on Thailand. Since 1949, the CIA and/or the Pentagon had won the internal battles in Washington and Bangkok, but had lost their wars in Indochina. Thus by the time the last Americans were evacuating Saigon in April 1975, Kissinger was on the defensive: "[T]he United States does not do favors to other countries by being in an alliance with them. Nor do other countries do us favors by being our allies."[19] The defense secretary confessed that he did not know whether the US remained legally bound to defend Thailand. Less than a year later, the Americans would agree to not only a "substantial withdrawal" from Thailand, but a total one.

Likewise, Thailand's Foreign Ministry, "in the years 1973–76 was allowed to play a leading role in the formulation of Thailand's policies toward the United States presence in Thailand and Thai–American relations".[20] It received rare backing from the National Security Council (NSC), a civilian advisory body that otherwise generally sided with the military. The Supreme Command was particularly resistant to an American departure. The internal debate was thus nuanced and contentious—not simply total retrenchment versus total withdrawal—and for the first time in decades its results were not preordained. Thailand's longest serving foreign minister, a civilian who had served military dictators, favored US withdrawal but feared that "if the United States can proclaim to the world that their withdrawal from Southeast Asia, namely Thailand, is because the Thai government has asked them to leave the scene, nobody would blame the United States".[21] The Americans' failure to identify the rise in civilian leadership, much less that its views might prevail, was partly to blame for how quickly and ignominiously they were marched off their Thai bases.

Underlying Thailand's democratic transition was of course a stronger citizen voice as well, which by the early 1970s was blaming the US military presence for uneven economic development, a rise in prostitution, and cultural insensitivity. Indeed, in the late 1960s the US military had been Thailand's second largest employer after the Thai government. But during the first half of the 1970s,

US economic assistance fell considerably, not least because of its express link to counterinsurgency and the war effort. In 1975, the total was $9 million, the lowest since 1964.

US troubles in Bangkok began with Ambassador William Kintner, whose CIA pedigree recalled "Wild Bill" Donovan of the mid-1950s. Arriving just before the overthrow of Thanom in 1973, he soon faced an elected premier who asked all government agencies to report on CIA activities and opposed construction of a US naval base in the Indian Ocean. The CIA then sent Thanom an obviously fake letter from an "insurgent leader" in the northeast, proffering a truce in exchange for limited territory but resulting in protests at the US consulate in Thailand's second city. Kintner immediately apologized to the prime minister and saw the responsible CIA officer removed, but the remarkably clumsy and duplicitous incident only added to rising nationalism.

The US withdrawal from Thailand began again a month later but would take over two years to complete. While the Americans reasonably cited logistical challenges, they also blatantly ignored Congressional directives to scale back, cease, move out. The year 1974 began with 600 planes and 35,000 American military personnel in Thailand, and ended with 350 and 25,000. Yet flights over Cambodia and Laos continued at the rate of at least thirty per day as late as early 1975, some still operated by the CIA. It took the fall of Saigon in April to put a stop to them—but also to start a year-long dispute with South Vietnam over the fate of the planes. Soliciting little input, the Americans would keep the best ones and leave the rest for their hosts, annoying both the Thais and the South Vietnamese.

In May 1975, the rescue of the *US Mayaguez*, captured by Cambodia's Khmer Rouge, marked "the lowest ebb in Thai–American relations since the end of World War II", highlighting how the US remained stuck in a recent but anachronistic past.[22] Prime Minister Kukrit told the embassy explicitly that he opposed the use of Thai bases and was given explicit assurances. But as with the CIA's Operation Paper in 1951, the embassy—much less the prime minister—was not informed that 1,000 marines were already on their way to Thailand. Inept and contemptuous of civilian leadership, the Americans had only informed Kriangsak Chomanand, deputy supreme commander (and future prime minister). The marines then complied with Kukrit's order to leave within twenty-four hours so as to avoid "serious and damaging consequences", only not to return to their bases but to recapture the *Mayaguez*.[23] Kukrit recalled his ambassador from Washington. Ambassador Kintner expressed "regret" and witnessed another round of anti-US demonstrations in which President Gerald Ford was burned in effigy.[24] More substantively, it "got Kukrit completely pissed off and to sign the paper kicking the Americans out".[25] He ordered an immediate review of all military arrangements and agreements, and stated his firm intention (six weeks before recognizing Communist China) to see a full US withdrawal within a year. The American military presence had become "a liability".[26]

As with Thailand's 1957 election that eventually saw Sarit come to power, US relations played a major role in the polls of April 1976. In January, Anand Panyarachun returned to Thailand from his post as ambassador to Washington, publicly lending Kukrit's withdrawal plans credibility. A month later he and Chatichai Choonhavan, by then foreign minister, presented a new US ambassador a set of Seven Principles relating to the Ramasun intelligence facility in northeastern Thailand. The deadline for acceptance was 20 March. Since his discovery of the secret 1964–1965 agreements establishing Ramasun during the previous year's *Mayaguez* fall-out, Kukrit had been privately telling the Americans that their "technical" personnel could remain behind and not be subject to Thai legal jurisdiction. He had also been saying publicly that the withdrawal deadline would likely be extended three months to June 1976. The Principles and their deadline—once made public—contradicted both of those pledges, stating that "American facilities and personnel shall be subject to Thai jurisdiction".[27] Kukrit had originally tried to use Ramasun as a bargaining chip for US hardware post-departure; his Principles were a power-play vis-à-vis the Thai military. They would backfire for everyone and spell the Americans' final miscalculation.

They "hit the Embassy like a bomb".[28] Deaf to repeated statements and in denial of recent events, the US was surprised by the Principles and objected most to the matter of jurisdiction. Consistent with most of the past three decades in Thailand, there was also considerable disagreement between a more accommodating Pentagon and a less flexible State Department. To no one's surprise, the former counseled delay in expectation of the supreme commander intervening; the latter left its embassy in Bangkok without instructions. The ambassador met with none other than the king himself in a desperate attempt to at least buy time. A final US proposal that it agree to the Principles for three months, at which point its own position would prevail, was outright dismissed. Just shy of the deadline and two weeks before the Thai election, the US was at last disabused of the notion that the Thais were bluffing—on democracy,

China, civilian leadership, and the complete withdrawal of US forces. In the words of a US citizen who has lived in Thailand since 1959, "the Americans found the door".[29]

Historical irony lay in the fact that, in 1920, the Americans had won favor in Thailand by acquiescing to the same jurisdiction over its nationals that it was disputing fifty-six years later. They had signed a treaty with such provisions and convinced European powers to do the same. Future implications were more serious, with the closure of a facility having the unique ability to spy on a poor but powerful China. Fearing it would fall into communist hands in the absence of its own personnel, the Americans dismantled Ramasun on their way out. While later negotiations with the US would secure minor consolation prizes for the Thai military, it essentially got nothing from either of Kukrit's Ramasun gambles. A pro-American Seni again became prime minister and expressed reservations about the totality of the withdrawal. But even he would reverse course on Ramasun, which by the 1976 coup was gone with the last American soldier.

FOREIGN POLICY COUPS

Thailand's military issued alerts on the day the Seven Principles were issued and two days before the 20 March deadline. Failing to prevent, slow, or limit the US departure, the generals at least ensured that Kukrit lost the election that followed, before seizing power themselves in October. Indeed, far less than his opening to China—which some in uniform thought inevitable if not advisable—Kukrit's handling of Ramasun and the US withdrawal more generally kept the military involved in politics. Thanin Kraivichien was installed as prime minister the same month that Mao died in Beijing, signaling an end rather than a new beginning to Thailand's men in uniform. "Anti-communism pervaded everything Thanin did", according to Seni.[30] A mere fifteen months after formal relations were established with China, he recalled Thailand's ambassador to inform him that "the relationship would not be the same as during the one-year honeymoon between 1 July 1975 and 6 October 1976".[31] He canceled two sporting events already scheduled in China, and despite purchasing Chinese weapons, called for a new military accord among non-communist Southeast Asian nations. Keeping a time-honored tradition but restating it emphatically, Thanin appointed as foreign minister another recent ambassador to the US, while Anand suddenly "became the target of the right wing in 1976 as the 'Communist in the Foreign Ministry'".[32] Having played an integral role in

Thailand's recent China *and* US policies, he and his colleagues "were all put in one room with no work to do".[33]

Thanin also hired two US firms to build local facilities for the production of arms, and deepened bilateral cooperation on illegal drugs suppression that had begun in the early 1970s. For over two decades the trafficking and sale of narcotics on Thailand's northern borders had been more than tolerated, having helped the CIA fund both the Chinese nationalists and the Lao Hmong and helped Thai security forces become rich. Beginning to see it as a threat to security and (licit) economic interests,[34] however, the US provided Thailand the fourth largest amount of anti-narcotics assistance in the world from 1973 to 1981. President Carter, elected one month after Thailand's coup, sent Thanin a letter of appreciation for his work in this area. One effect was a rise in membership of the communist insurgency to its highest levels, as people sought protection and ways to resist. Another was such discontent within elements of Thailand's security forces over their loss of revenue that they staged yet another coup against Thanin. But as further evidence of the monarchy's consistent anti-communist/ pro-American outlook, King Bhumibol immediately appointed him to his Privy Council.

General Kriangsak Chomanand, a veteran of combat in South Vietnam ten years earlier, took power in October 1977. Also anti-communist, he welcomed Carter's vice-president in 1978 and his reiteration of US commitments under the Manila Pact and Thanat–Rusk memo. Having been Thanom's man in northern Thailand supporting residual nationalist forces, he also put an end to any last-ditch, latent notions of violence. Yet Kriangsak also recognized China's usefulness in improving Thai–Cambodian relations against a saber-rattling Vietnam. Signaling a kind of "restart", he sent Kukrit back to Beijing and finally consummated his original visit by appointing the first ambassador to China. Kriangsak also helped resuscitate those banished within the ministry the previous year, and continued to avail himself of Chinese weapons at "friendly" prices.[35]

Thailand's insurgency hit its numerical peak in 1977 with perhaps 14,000 insurgents, well over half in the northeast. According to a Thai general, Thanin had been "completely lost" on the insurgency, endorsing the violent and unsuccessful "body count" approach of the US war in Vietnam.[36] Yet having publicly blamed the monarchy for the previous year's crackdown before downing a helicopter containing an aide to the queen, the CPT was suddenly ripe for a steep decline. As Chinese supplies continued to dwindle, an amnesty initiative under Kriangsak resulted in roughly 400 defections in 1978 alone.

Kriangsak met Deng Xiaoping twice that year, discussing the insurgency, further economic ties, and especially their expectation that Vietnam would invade Cambodia. As the second meeting was in Bangkok, however, Thailand's queen threatened to visit Taiwan at the same time in an unmistakable anti-communist statement. There was even brief talk of merging the Ministries of Defense and Foreign Affairs to ensure a more uniform approach to China. Yet, in a deft display of diplomacy and strategy—whose fruits would take several more decades to fully ripen—Deng managed to meet the king and even attend the ordination of Thailand's crown prince. Accounting for the palace's about-face was Deng's recognition that China could simply no longer afford any association with a CPT targeting the monarchy.

CROSSING BORDERS I

On Christmas Day 1978, Vietnam invaded Cambodia. The next month the United States and China established formal relations. And the next month China responded to Vietnam's aggression—as well as a Thai request—by invading Vietnam. The Chinese "shared Thailand's interest in curbing growing Vietnamese (and Soviet) influence in the region. Hence, Thai Prime Minister Kriangsak essentially viewed President Carter's move to normalize relations with China as a 'positive contribution'".[37] The US was fast regaining its alliance status with Thailand, while China had yet to fully cede its gains from earlier in the decade. The result was a rare and short-lived convergence of security concerns among the three nations, before a return to previous bilateral dynamics.

Before the first invasion, Deng told the Thais he expected the Khmer Rouge to succumb and that China would respond with a strike of its own against Vietnam. He was clear, however, that China anticipated a protracted conflict in Indochina and that Thailand's security would thus be at risk. He proposed mutual support in defeating the Vietnamese. Kriangsak demurred on a formal partnership but did agree to allow Chinese planes to fly over Thailand to supply Cambodia. Sixteen days after the invasion during a pre-scheduled trade mission to China, Deng upped the ante and pressed Kriangsak's deputy for use of Thai territory for the same purpose. Just before or just after the trip—accounts vary—Colonel (and future prime minister) Chavalit Yongchaiyudh and Kriangsak's foreign minister (yet another former ambassador to the US) were sent to Hong

Kong to deliver the same message for Deng: arm the Cambodians. During a mid-January visit of a Chinese military delegation, Kriangsak's briefing officer flatly informed his guests that Thailand would be no match against Vietnam, and likewise requested assistance. According to the briefing officer's retelling, this contributed substantially to the Chinese decision to invade Vietnam a month later on 17 February. Ultimately, Thailand agreed to Chinese use of all transport facilities and territory for supplying the Khmer Rouge. China made public statements after April 1979 "that it would stand on the side of Thailand in the case of a Vietnamese attack".[38]

That Thailand believed Vietnam's claim that it could cross the Thai border in the morning and "reach Bangkok in time for lunch" is not in doubt. The Vietnamese advised the CPT that they were "well-equipped by the Americans whom they had driven out", and so "could fly American F-16s one hour from Cambodia to Thailand and seize the country in three hours".[39] Whether, however, in the words of the briefing officer, "China saved our asses" is debatable.[40] Deng had been explicit that Cambodia would not be able to repel an invasion and that China would invade Vietnam only briefly—"teach it a lesson" rather than fight until the Vietnamese left Cambodia. True that China had to watch its long northeastern border with the USSR, and that it did maintain up to twelve divisions of troops on its border with Vietnam to both deter and draw away Vietnamese forces from Cambodia. But it is eminently possible that Deng sought to draw Thailand into the situation so as to cast China as its new chief guarantor of security, and thus slow or even neutralize its return to the American fold. Remarkably, neither then nor since has a single prominent Thai leader publicly mooted this possibility. Despite increased suspicion by the mid-1980s, Thais uniformly credit China as having plainly come to their rescue in 1979.

Colonel Chavalit, who steadily became Thailand's primary emissary to China over the next decade, was invited to fire the first symbolic cannon shot at Vietnam. He also renewed Thailand's request that China put a stop to the CPT's Yunnan-based broadcasts, which had only slowed since bilateral relations were restored; China did abandon the CPT's bases in Laos and Cambodia. In 1979 regular military exchanges also started between the two nations: the deputy chief of the People's Liberation Army (PLA) traveled to Bangkok, the Thai navy's commander-in-chief to Beijing.

CROSSING BORDERS II

If the two invasions placed China front and center, new leadership in both Bangkok and Washington since the defeatist days of 1975–1976 ensured a US return in other ways. Despite their differing policies on human rights—but also to overcome them—the two nations found common cause in a growing regional refugee crisis. After the fall of Saigon, Phnom Penh, and Vientiane, security in Thailand would be symbolized and partly measured by the number of refugees crossing its borders. Moreover, for the first (and last) time, the Americans would appreciate the strategic advantage to their Thai relations of deeper engagement with ASEAN.

By end of 1976, some 64,000 refugees from Laos alone had entered Thailand (alongside 10,000 from Cambodia and 2,600 from Vietnam). The same year, Kukrit described ASEAN as a "pillar of Thai foreign policy" on account of communist aggression in Indochina and the people it was displacing.[21] In light of his previous pledge to disband SEATO in 1977 and the two invasions a year later, Kukrit's emphasis on ASEAN would fast become a security imperative for his successors. Indeed, Thanin visited other ASEAN leaders soon after becoming prime minister, and attended the first US–ASEAN meeting in late 1977. By that time, 1,700 refugees were fleeing Vietnam each month, including roughly 500 "boat people" by sea. Carter's decision to fund their basic needs and a resettlement program to the US served simultaneously as humanitarian assistance, a contribution to Thailand's security, and a point for his human rights agenda. The 15,000 refugees resettled to the US in 1977 nearly tripled the next year as the numbers coming to Thailand each month continued to rise: 4,500 in January 1978, 6,000 by August. Roughly half were from Laos. A former American aid worker recalled being asked by a Thai official if the US would have a similar program "if Thailand fell".[22]

Following the invasions of Cambodia and Vietnam, Thailand's refugee population literally doubled. This spurred Carter to back ASEAN at the UN and during a visit to Washington by Kriangsak in early 1979. Despite unlawful push-backs and border closures, a staggering 65,000 refugees arrived in May 1979 alone, causing the vice-president to meet with ASEAN the following month. Another 500,000 would arrive by the time First Lady Roslyn Carter visited the camps in November and announced $60 million in humanitarian aid; the US was covering a third of the costs associated with refugees in Thailand. The Americans also raised military aid to $37 million and agreed to scale up arms sales, which had slowed considerably since 1972. Kriangsak even expressed openness to the return of US troops and planes. A Thai general recalled US military contributions as being "merely symbolic", however, for which "to add insult to injury, they sent a bill".[23] When the US army attaché was asked by a Thai commander where the reinforcements were if the Vietnamese should cross the border, he pointed at his assistant and replied, "He's here."[24] For its part, China supported Thailand's move to have Pol Pot replaced as the titular head of the Khmer Rouge, and likewise backed most ASEAN–UN efforts. But its diplomatic role was roughly equivalent to the minimal military investment by the US, as both countries' recent experiences and perceptions in the region placed limits on what they could do.

In his last State of the Union address in 1980, Carter said that the US was attempting to "deter Vietnamese attacks on Thai territory".[25] Six months later the first such attack occurred. Thirty years since Thailand had begun fearing a communist invasion, forces it had assisted the US in fighting briefly crossed its border. The Americans suddenly faced the possibility of having to defend an ally no longer playing host to their men and materiel; Carter tacked on another $17 million in military assistance. But more than anything else, the attack assumed a disproportionate importance in returning US–Thai relations to their pre-1973 levels of understanding. The era's experiments were over.

Chapter Five:
Policy Drift (1980–1988)

Let me reassure you that the United States stands with you as a partner and as a friend. Our common commitment to freedom and friendship has served us well in the past, and I believe the shared values that link us across half the globe will continue to help promote the well-being of both our nations.[1]

Ronald Reagan, 1982

As a great power with an obvious and visible role to play in the region, the United States has suffered notably from vacillating tendencies which are attributable to a lack of clear purpose. One the one hand, it is perceived that American vital interests in the region provide a legitimate basis for strong American action, but these vital interests are never singularly defined and focused so as to produce a unified pattern of action.[2]

Sarasin Viraphol, 1982

The names Prem Tinsulanonda, Ronald Reagan, and Deng Xiaoping are virtually synonymous with the 1980s in Thailand, the United States, and China. Until the disruptive events of Tiananmen Square in 1989, Thailand's interaction with the two powers was uniquely aided by the continuity and consistency of leadership in all three nations. It is axiomatic that personal relationships between and among policy-makers can influence decisions. American–Thai relations had benefited from many strong individual connections since the early 20th century, while changed Sino-Thai relations over the previous decade had likewise been partly due to personal bonds. Reagan was known for his charisma with foreign leaders; Deng put a new face, literally and figuratively, on Chinese diplomacy. While Mao cast a long shadow even after his death in 1976, Deng's reform agenda included putting the Five Principles of Peaceful Coexistence into practice. Prem and Reagan were s/elected eight months apart in 1980, and led their countries through 1988. Deng preceded them by two years and succeeded them by four. Assisted by the previous decade's trilateral detente and common cause in Indochina, the views and visions of all three governments would be largely known commodities to one another for eight years.

The views and visions were not the same, however; nor were Thailand's relations with the US and China of equal strength. When the political dust of the 1970s finally settled, the Americans and Chinese found that their positions vis-à-vis Thailand had once again begun to shift, just as they had briefly if firmly done during the dust-up itself. The US had gone from strong and strategic ally to non-ally, before beginning a swift and steady return. At the same time, China had gone from enemy to tactical partner, and was set to begin a slow but steady move to non-ally status. These trends for both countries would deepen considerably over the course of the 1980s. By the time Reagan left office and Chinese tanks rolled into Tiananmen, Prem's successor would again see the Americans as Thailand's closest ally in the world and the Chinese as an uncertain threat. In the words of elder statesman Seni Pramoj in 1989, "American participation in our country is a consequence of the Free Thai Movement— we've got to rely on someone."[3]

However, it was telling that a conservative Republican successor to Democrat Jimmy Carter would intensify the latter's liberal initiatives. For US national security—Reagan's primary calculus and compass—simply had no obvious or imperative interest in the region in 1980, even under a conception including natural resources, new markets, and more than 500,000 refugees in Thailand. The Vietnam War and its Chinese specter, as a "hot" manifestation of the Cold War, had been an arguable case of *force majeure* for US regional involvement. It had also made obvious that involvement's military and ideological nature. In the mid-1970s, however, the Americans lost in quick succession its war in Vietnam, its diplomatic monopoly on China, and its troops in Thailand. Realistically, China's own invasion of Vietnam then rendered communists less threatening to Thailand than in the three years since the Americans left, as it drew 700,000 Vietnamese troops away from Cambodia's border with Thailand. More damningly, it "provided incontrovertible evidence that only China was willing and able to expend blood, treasure, and international goodwill in order to protect … Thai national interests".[4] Vietnam was going to remain communist for the foreseeable future regardless. Globally, Reagan would back a host of unsavory governments, become open to multilateralism, and raise foreign aid to record highs. But in inheriting the Khmer Rouge, ASEAN, and the "boat people", why should he have done any of those things in Southeast Asia? With an outsized embassy and a dwindling core of JUSMAG advisors (just thirty in 1980), the US mission in Thailand seemingly lacked a mission.

Reagan's primary reason for continued engagement in Thailand was a post-Mao China. Anxious over how the Cold War's Southeast Asian template might shift yet again, the US was far less interested in the ongoing partnership in Indochina than on where it might lead. The American national security interest in Thailand was thus to *determine* its national security interests vis-à-vis the Chinese. While not inconsistent with the previous thirty-five years—Thailand as more means than end—it was born not of a certain Chinese threat but of an uncertain one. The Americans would use refugees and ASEAN as "wedges issues" through which to diversify intelligence and interaction with China, as well as arrest its filling of the void they had left in Thailand. Refugees had already provided an entrée to an uptick in US money, manpower, and assistance. That the ostensible focus was humanitarian was ironic, for with it came the backing of a genocidal regime: classic realpolitik, with costs paid in millions of lives. Several more attacks by Vietnamese forces on Thai soil helped justify a disproportionate spike in US military aid—and thus deepen and diversify proximity to China—but refugees were the central issue throughout the decade.

A secondary factor in renewed American engagement during the 1980s was certainly on the minds of policy-makers but likely seldom voiced: a desire to win back regional credibility after an ignominious defeat in Vietnam and undignified exodus from Thailand. One of the few remaining JUSMAG officers was charged solely with locating American and Thai soldiers still missing. Reagan exemplified in Thailand the effect of past policy failure(s) in the later design and management of foreign affairs. Mao's shadow reached as far as Washington. This is even plainer in light of the greater financial and political resources than Carter probably needed to meet basic policy objectives. Rather than scale them back, Reagan scaled them up. Consider Carter's genuine humanitarianism and Reagan's cuts to other human rights initiatives, and the corrective impulse looms larger still. Like the airstrikes on Iraq ordered later by four consecutive presidents, two from each major party, US involvement in Thailand during the 1980s transcended partisanship and was driven by recent history as much as future contingencies. The US had witnessed anti-American protests in Bangkok, the fall of three capitals in Indochina, and Thai recognition of Communist China. Eight months later, its last soldier left the region. More broadly, over three decades the US had invested untold amounts of real and political capital into defeating armies and the ideology they championed. All had prevailed. Some were thriving. Although pockets of "Thailand fatigue" existed in Washington and "Vietnam Syndrome" would long work against US military involvement abroad, the Americans were simply not prepared to walk away from a botched job.

ECONOMIC TIES AND TENSIONS

During the 1980s, the scope of US–Thai relations broadened significantly, ensuring that the overall scale remained large even after the US military's recent departure. Where through the mid-1970s American economic assistance had simply been one element of Thailand's national security equation, economic relations soon transitioned into its own business. Trade initiatives and foreign direct investment (FDI), replete with their own experts, rules, and priorities, began occupying a parallel track to political and military affairs. This was in keeping not only with the substantial shift in regional geopolitics, but also with a slow but sure global process: optimally, economic affairs between and among states would be largely divorced from the vagaries and ideologies of politics. Between Thailand and the United States, they became detached from the rebuilding of their alliance and subject to only their own norms and standards. In the few and exceptional instances in which economics did become politicized, they never threatened to cause the alliance lasting harm.

In 1980, Thailand's trade with the US exceeded $2 billion as compared to only $300 million a decade prior. In 1984, as Thailand became the first Southeast Asian country to receive a Structural Adjustment Loan ($200 million) from the US-dominated World Bank, the US became its second largest trading partner. Yet by the end of 1986, the US trade balance with Thailand had shifted from a considerable surplus to a $1 billion deficit. The chief culprit was a protectionist US Food Security Act of 1985, to which the Thais attributed their lowest sugar prices in years and lowest rice prices in a decade. In the words of a former ambassador to the US, "[b]ecause of several recent economic measures taken by the U.S. government ... the Thai public's view of the United States has never been so negative".[5] Three letters from Thai House leadership to the US Congress in 1986 went unanswered, causing further frustration. Thus, despite having been supported by the US in its bid for a non-permanent seat on the

UN Security Council, Thailand voted with China and the USSR to condemn it for recent military action in Libya.

While the Thai economy rebounded quickly, hitting 10 percent and Newly Industrialized Country status in 1987, its relations with the US did not. In what would become a longstanding bugbear, the US Omnibus Trade and Competitiveness Act of 1988 resulted in Thailand being designated a priority country for intellectual property rights violations. Despite domestically unpopular concessions by Prem, Reagan revoked valuable trade privileges for Thailand on his last day in office. That the foreign minister chaired the US–Thai subcommittee on the issue spoke to its importance; he resigned the chair over Reagan's parting shot. A future foreign minister confessed that, "[w]e are confused about the role Congress now plays in foreign policy", and again Thailand responded via attention to an unrelated issue.[6] In what would otherwise have been a matter handled between cultural attachés, Thailand accused the US in the global press of having stolen an artifact in the 1960s. The item was returned and Thailand's priority status on intellectual property was dropped in 1989.

If the economic drama was sincere, then unlike a genuine crisis to come a decade later, it was more a reflection of "growing pains" between the countries than a serious injury to their relations. The structures of modern global trade were fast evolving in the mid-1980s, with developing nations like Thailand just beginning to play an active role. In the words of a senior Thai official, "You cannot invoke old friendships. From the U.S. perspective the relationship has to be short-term and on the basis of dollars and cents. That is a realistic approach and Thailand has to accept that."[7] To be sure, the US was wrong on the Farm Act and Thailand on intellectual property, but both were taken as correctable mistakes rather than alliance-breakers. That the disputes arose at the same time as the two countries were strengthening security relations on account of China only reinforced the point.

PREM

The 1980s marked the first time since the end of World War II that Thailand could assume a level of cooperation and agreement between the Americans and Chinese. Thais were still paying a security price for regional conflicts they had played no role in starting and had only directly engaged on their margins. Refugees and the insecurity they brought with them were problems that Thailand could not address without help. The US and China, both UN Security Council members and newly engaged with ASEAN, were not unwelcome benefactors. And the fact that they were not overtly adversarial toward each other—much less to Thailand—afforded Prem an unfamiliar but welcome degree of flexibility in foreign policy. "China is no longer seen as an Asian bully", said future premier Anand Panyarachun in 1985, "The United States retreats from its 'world policeman' role."[8]

Prem was a rare military figure to take and retain power in Thailand via constitutional means, despite remaining army chief until late 1981. His nine-year tenure was equal to those of Phibun (post-war) and Thanom, but despite several coup and assassination attempts, it was far more stable than either. The primary reason was the new post-1976 dynamic between the Thai monarchy and military, of which Prem was an almost custom-made personification. Garnering the palace's attention in the late 1970s by advancing the defeat of an increasingly anti-monarchical CPT, he would take office one day after an audience with King Bhumibol. Kriangsak, also in the meeting, resigned. When a group of the army's "Young Turks" attempted a coup a year into his administration, Prem left Bangkok in the company of the royal family. A message of support from the queen was promptly broadcast over the radio, and Princess Sirindhorn let it be known on television that she was spending her birthday with the prime minister. Two days after the soldiers moved, Prem was back in Bangkok and even more firmly in power.

The Young Turks were not against Prem himself and certainly not against military rule; one Chamlong Srimuang, a staunch opponent of democracy before and since, was his office's first secretary-general. They had also mobilized troops and vigilantes against the US withdrawal the previous decade. They opposed the continued predominance of the First Region (including the King's and Queen's Guards) in the army and of the ethnic Chinese in the economy, as well as Thailand's recent partnership with Communist China. Despite their progressive name, the Young Turks sought a return to the old order of the late Phibun era. Their defeat at the hands of royal disapproval rather than armed defense ushered into Thailand the first halcyon days of what scholar Duncan McCargo famously deemed "Network Monarchy": "a form of semi-monarchical rule ... as a para-political institution".[9] Before a second coup attempt in 1985, and rendering its failure a foregone conclusion, the palace hosted Prem for an extended period. His retirement from the military was delayed after the queen backed a petition circulated by officers that he remain "active".[10] The Queen's

Guard had played a role in quelling the second coup attempt months before and had grown under his leadership. Less than three weeks after his eleven years in Thailand's top military and government posts came to an end, Prem would be appointed by the king to his Privy Council.

Prem engaged considerably with both the US and China, undertaking a state visit to the former in 1981 and to the latter in 1980, as well as a trip to the US for health reasons in 1984. He also kept in place Kriangsak's foreign minister who had been a part of the changing relations with both countries for nearly forty years. Before joining the ministry, he had headed the National Security Council, a post many felt he never truly left. "With the NSC controlling the Foreign Ministry … it was only concentrating on Vietnam as a threat, and the closer we got to China the more disturbing things became."[11] He would travel to both the US and China, initially to Beijing in 1980, and enjoyed good relations with excellent US ambassadors, particularly Morton Abramowitz (from mid-1978) and John Gunther Dean. Abramowitz was the first since 1961 to be later designated a "Career Ambassador" for distinguished service over a sustained period. Directly under him served one J. Stapleton Roy, who would also achieve the honor and later become ambassador to China. The embassy would not again be led by a career ambassador until 2011 (with much different results).

The foreign minister also facilitated visits of the queen and crown prince to the US in early 1980 and late 1981, where the former collected a number of awards and honorary degrees and the latter received flight training. Upon his return, the crown prince was granted his own flight unit in the air force—another nexus between Thailand's monarchy and military. Following the advice of a "special link and friend" to China (and the first Thai to visit Tibet post-1959), Beijing invited the king's sister to visit.[12] Having just tacitly helped defeat an anti-Chinese coup attempt earlier in the month, Princess Sirindhorn took her first of a series of trips to China over the decade in 1981—after which she was given an open invitation. The king bid farewell at the airport to the visiting Chinese president in 1985, while the crown prince visited China on the king's behalf in early 1987. In 1991, Prem's foreign minister would join him on the Privy Council.

SINO-THAI SITUATIONS

Recognized by the UN (replacing Taiwan, 1971), Thailand (1975), and the US (1979), China's international relations in the 1970s had been truly transformative, conferring a legitimacy it had long sought and was poised to leverage. By the time Deng, Prem, and Reagan were all in power, its slow but sure instrumentalization of ASEAN was underway and its military was being viewed by others primarily as protection. With Indochina the main focus, China could also take credit for imposing enforceable limits on at least one (fellow) communist country, and provisional order on the region. And unlike the US, it shared borders with both. All of this was to Thailand's security benefit and to Prem's political advantage at home.

It is therefore significant that Sino-Thai relations were not set for another fillip during the 1980s. Greatly strengthened connections between China's leadership and Thailand's monarchy were investments set to return enormous political rewards after the turn of the century, but their contemporary value was limited. China's status as partner would remain steady during the early years, before wavering in 1982 due to its reconciliation with the USSR. By the middle of the decade, with Indochina settling into another war of attrition, China was no longer a clear contributor to Thailand's overall security. Weapons deals with Thailand beginning in 1985 were welcome, but even larger deals China struck with neighboring Burma after a coup there in mid-1988 finally tipped the balance. Rather than transform its partnership with the Thais into a bona fide alliance, China remained limited in its aims and interests. Its mostly low-grade weapons could be transshipped through Thailand and purchased by Thailand, but unlike US military men and materiel pre-1976, they would not be *based* in Thailand. China did increase its economic activity with Thailand (and ASEAN) in the mid-1980s, and its Four Modernizations drive announced in Bangkok in 1988 was well-received. Overall, however, while Thailand's disputes with the US caused many Sino-Thai businesses to desire deeper Chinese links, it was Thailand's economy and not China's that was growing rapidly.

Thailand's ethnic Chinese were increasingly seen as its most valuable economic resource, and in 1980 were beginning to extend their reach. Remarkably, the Charoen Pokphand Group had established a presence in China's food industry in 1949, at the same time that Phibun was demonizing China at home and Mao was winning its civil war. Having fast become its largest foreign investor writ large, CP was tapped by Prem's foreign minister and General Chavalit to assist with introductions to senior Chinese leaders. Thailand wanted Deng's help in Indochina. CP's founder—whose Chinese accent was no longer a hindrance at home—proved so instrumental that his company directors were thereafter appointed as advisors to Thailand's foreign ministry. Indeed, "money politics" hit its stride in the 1980s via the modern incarnation of Sino-Thais' early 20th century triads and societies. Groups and individuals leveraged their private business connections and acumen to influence politics, but also to become politicians. It is ironic that military figures like Chavalit were usually the linchpins of the deals, donations, and transitions, since they had previously been placed in boardrooms precisely to curb the clout of the Chinese merchants.

This is what the Young Turks opposed in their 1981 coup attempt, for it brought Sino-Thais into Network Monarchy rather than forcing them to compete for an alternative base of power. This would prove critical to the network's thriving during the 1990s as well as its foundering in the new century. A Sino-Thai businessman educated in Hong Kong secured leadership of the royalist Democrat Party. Record sums of money to the palace and royal projects more explicitly ensured entrée. Thus was a powerful demographic seen since the early 1900s as a potential republican threat, co-opted and subsumed to a greater extent than anywhere else in the region.

HUMAN RIGHTS

President Reagan significantly downgraded and politicized human rights as an element of foreign policy, while China viewed international human rights as a foreign concept. Limited attention to Cambodia's genocide did exist within ASEAN, with which Reagan briefly met in 1986, but it too was compromised by US and Chinese support for its perpetrators. A number of other factors and developments notably contributed to Thailand's human rights situation in the 1980s. Removing a major theatre for abuses, Thailand's communist insurgency was essentially over by the middle of the decade. Its gamble to target the monarchy with words and weapons had come twenty years too late in the national psyche, and caused turmoil between the insurgency's more educated and urbane elements and the older Sino-Thai leadership. By the time Prem took office, the insurgency numbered around 10,000 but only two members of its central committee were Thai; all others were ethnic Chinese. An unpopular CPT report of a royal US visit and a series of battlefield losses turned the tide in 1981. With considerable assistance from nationalist troops still residing in the area, the army overran the CPT's headquarters in northern Thailand. Against a backdrop of an extended amnesty program and efforts to bring the country's economic growth to the countryside, the insurgency dropped to perhaps 1,200 members by 1984. Prem lifted martial law in twenty-nine provinces the following year. The CPT was barred from elections and a number of alleged communists were held without trial, but the insurgency was history.

In contrast and not unrelated, Muslim discontent in Thailand's deep south dating back eighty years (and partly subsumed by the CPT) emerged again under Prem as a separate and separatist insurgency. Before the term assumed new meaning two decades later, in 1981 the State Department referred to their actions as "terrorist".[13] The Thai government admitted in 1986 that police "death squads" were committing extrajudicial executions of real and suspected Muslim insurgents and supporters.[14]

Away from the north and south, the main area for rights violations under Prem was on Thailand's eastern borders with Laos and Cambodia, and involved refugees rather than rebels. Carter's resettlement program resulted in roughly half of the half-million refugees who entered Thailand during 1980 leaving for the US. Seeing this as a "pull factor" adding to the "push" of conflict across the borders, in 1981 the Thais substantially worsened camp conditions to discourage all but the most desperate. When more and more just disappeared into the Thai countryside, the authorities resumed unlawful "push-backs" on both land and sea. Nonetheless, hundreds of thousands more Cambodians and one in every ten Laotians would enter Thailand by the middle of the decade. A Thai policy of "humane deterrence" failed in both nature and intent. Cambodians were tortured, Lao Hmong were blocked at the border, Vietnamese were pushed back at sea. Host to over a million displaced Indochinese in 1988, Thailand closed its entire east coast. American and Thai attitudes were best captured by a former foreign minister: "[A] U.S. Senator, perhaps believing that Thailand lies in his own state, saw fit to express his concern over the alleged decision of the Thai Government to turn away Laotian refugees."[15] By then the US was itself home to some 400,000 refugees, reminders and representatives of American regional involvement.

GOLD VS. STEEL

When in 1981 Vietnam threatened to fight the Khmer Rouge on Thai soil if Cambodian refugees were repatriated, Reagan's secretary of state reaffirmed the Manila Pact. That he did so at an ASEAN meeting sent an even wider signal of commitment, for which Thailand reciprocated by obtaining ASEAN's endorsement of a boycott of Vietnam. Reagan himself referenced the Manila Pact during Prem's visit to Washington, and promised to lobby Congress for more aid. The following year, Thailand and ASEAN added their voices when the end of the China–USSR rivalry threatened to soften China's resolve in Indochina. The US thus introduced a surface-to-surface Harpoon missile system, sped up artillery deliveries for border defense, and substantially increased military funding to $81 million. Prem and Reagan also agreed to a joint air/sea surveillance program to combat piracy against Vietnamese "boat people"; up to a quarter died of piracy or storms en route to Thailand in 1982.

If the US scored a signal achievement in its relations with Thailand during the Prem–Reagan era, it was the commencement in 1982 of yearly joint military exercises. Coinciding with the China–USSR detente and Reagan's express pledge to expand the US navy's Seventh Fleet to 500 ships, the timing could not have been better. "Cobra Gold" marked the first time since the early 1970s that US personnel worked on a large scale with their Thai counterparts in situ. While Indochina gave the exercises an immediate context for planning and cooperation, they went well beyond the current conflict in their potential objective. Most importantly, Cobra Gold confirmed that the US military—the institution most readily associated with US–Thai relations since World War II—was not only welcomed back but wanted. The following year, in a move smaller in scale but not significance, Thailand allowed the US military to use U-Tapao airbase for the first time since the war for which it had been built. The Americans agreed to make repairs, stock aviation fuel, and station an air force refueling specialist at the base full-time—US boots on the ground. Summing up official Thai sentiment was the head of the NSC: "Everybody would like to forget the Vietnam War. Alright. But don't go away."[16]

After Vietnamese forces twice attacked refugees on the Thai–Cambodian border in early 1983, the US immediately sent missiles to Thailand. Military assistance crested $100 million in each of the next two years—not least due to more fighting on Thai soil in 1985—before dropping in 1986. That the crest was only about $25 million less than the all-time high in 1972 showed the level of US success in returning relations to pre-departure conditions. Much of this was used to purchase American weapons and materiel: tanks and armored personnel carriers (APCs), howitzers and anti-tank missiles, helicopters and F-16 fighter jets. Logistical cooperation through JUSMAG increased as well, with Thailand becoming the first country outside of NATO and South Korea to secure a US war reserve stockpile in 1986. Ammunition and other gear would be kept in-country to ensure readiness and sustainability in the event of armed conflict.

With the Vietnamese laying mines two kilometers into Thailand and more intermittent border combat, the preparation was well-founded. By then there were over 1,000 Thai casualties. Finally, "We were there in a big way with the CIA" and other intelligence cooperation.[17] An army intelligence officer found villagers on the border acting suspiciously and uncomfortably, only to learn after departing that Pol Pot was living minutes away.

Following the first Vietnamese attack on Thai soil in mid-1980, China gave security assurances to Prem and his foreign minister during visits in Beijing. While its approach concerned a more conciliatory ASEAN—which began to see Thailand as part of a larger Chinese design to utilize or neutralize it—China agreed the following year to support a possible Indochina federation. After Vietnam's attacks in 1983, China's army chief both visited and hosted Thailand's supreme commander. Beijing would also undertake limited infrastructure and communications efforts. The same US intelligence officer surprised the CIA with photographs of a Chinese-built pier in a coastal Thai province, extending 200 meters into the sea and wide enough for two-way truck movement. In 1986, the PLA in Yunnan province established a communications link with Thailand's Supreme Command, and at the end of the decade put a final end to the CPT's radio broadcasts there.

In 1985, General Chavalit facilitated the first transfer of Chinese weapons to the Thai military: anti-aircraft and anti-tank guns and T-59 battle tanks. Often at half-price and low interest, China would sell Thailand munitions, APCs, surface-to-air missiles, and three F-17 fighters until the end of Prem's tenure, and late in the decade would build Thailand's first warship. But while its quality increased over the years, the majority was "absolute rubbish".[18] The different calibers, non-uniform shells, and constant need for parts induced dependency and new facilities in Thailand for maintenance and production, and Mandarin-only manuals had to be translated. In contrast, the US provided large sums of military aid with which to buy high-grade hardware; US tanks and APCs were superior even to the USSR-supplied equivalents used by the Vietnamese. Those sold and sent by China were "tin cans on wheels".[19] For decades the Thai military had been familiar with US weapons and equipment, and JUSMAG had been present since 1950. When the border battles finally came to an end, the Thai military was larger and stronger far more on account of American kit than Chinese—much of which was used up, broken down, or in Cambodian hands. During a visit to the US as late as 2000, Prem would voice "his 'heartfelt' appreciation".[20]

Chapter Six:
The Thai Spring (1989–2001)

Right in the middle of the 1997 financial crisis, I go in to see Chuan
Leekpai, who leans across and says, "Karl, let me get this straight. We were
your ally during the Vietnam War, weren't we? And now we're in a pinch
and you can't come to our assistance? Do I understand you correctly?"[1]

Karl Jackson, April 2015

It was a sign of things to come for both countries in 1997 that China
would take the opportunity it had to be seen to be different in its approach
to Thailand as compared to the United States. The signal coming out of the
United States was that now that the Cold War was over, we weren't really
on their radar screen.[2]

Korn Chatikavanij, May 2015

The long decade in Thailand between Prem and Thaksin Shinawatra saw trends
set under Prem continue, with Thailand more able to determine its political and
security relations with the US and China and less able to do so economically. The
trends also broadened in scope, as the kingdom's choices vis-à-vis its neighbors
increased, and the "globalization" originally applied only to economics included
other elements of Thailand's foreign affairs. A negative "equidistance" espoused in
the late 1970s had evolved into more outward policies of "omnidirectionality" and
"constructive engagement". As the end-game became increasingly clear for both the
Cold War and the conflict in Indochina, Thailand entered its most independent
and proactive foreign policy period since before World War II. The "New World
Order" of President George Bush was presenting it a unique set of opportunities and
challenges. Continuing initially to maintain strong ties to the US and arm's length
from China, Thailand would be fertile ground for change by the end of the 1990s.

Prime Minister Chatichai Choonhavan took over from Prem, wishing to
"turn battlefields into marketplaces" in Indochina.[3] Opposed at first by the US

and China, the transformative initiative was eventually welcomed by both. Successor Anand Panyarachun would join him in regaining the Americans' personal trust after their joint role in the Seven Principles departure drama of 1976. But it was the two internationalist administrations of Chuan Leekpai that would most impress the Americans and make the subsequent geopolitical changes so regrettable. Chuan's foreign policy was formulated over three years beginning in 1992 and fully implemented over three more ending in 2001. It was intelligent and progressive during his first term, principled and courageous during his second; Chuan remains the Thai premier closest to having espoused a political ideology. Careful to guard against over-investment in a US ally and to maintain even relations with China, on balance he conducted Thailand's foreign affairs much more in conformity with American views and values than those of Communist China. Chuan looked to the US as a "countervailing power to an ambitious and expansionist China" experiencing unprecedented economic growth.[4] During his first term, China was also transitioning from Deng Xiaoping to a confident Jiang Zemin, whose rise to power had begun with the fallen in Tiananmen Square. While Chuan would considerably increase links with China late in his second administration, this was driven by prudence and ever-changing regional circumstances rather than principle.

Coinciding and consistent with the US presidency of Bill Clinton, Chuan also allowed additional interests to compete with the national security imperative. "The Chuan administration found its security in an intimate alliance with Western powers, and thus tightly bound Thainess with international norms … such as respect for democracy and good governance."[5] Clinton visited Thailand during the brief term of Chuan's first successor in 1996, twenty-seven years after Nixon had come in 1969. But it was Chuan who had laid the visit's political groundwork and it was Chuan whom Clinton would host two years later. On account of what transpired in between his two terms, Chuan's policies would also inadvertently contribute to Thailand's realignment in the 21st century at the hands of his second successor.

That event was a financial crisis that originated in Thailand in 1997 and spread throughout the region. Chuan's first-term policies did not precipitate the crisis; Prime Minister Chavalit of military and "money politics" notoriety presided over the fiscal mistakes and mismanagement. But once returned to office, Chuan persisted with a policy that was—in the simplified discourse of electoral politics—equated with the "international" solution imposed on

Thailand by the IMF and its chief patron, the United States. By the end of the decade, the Americans had once again placed their hard-won allied status in jeopardy, for failing to appreciate that alliances are more than a military concern. Unlike the economic "growing pains" of the previous decade that had caused more drama than damage, the financial crisis spoke to the "fulcrum" of the relationship and thus posed a real threat.[6] It also presented China an opportunity in Thailand to pledge seed capital toward far larger political dividends after the turn of the century.

THE THAI SPRING

Chuan's progressive foreign policy was founded in domestic political developments. During the twelve years between Prem and Thaksin, Thailand saw six men account for eight total premierships, the first of which was overthrown in a February 1991 coup. Publicly citing Chatichai's corruption, coup leader General Suchinda Kraprayoon recalled Sarit in claiming that democracy needed specific recalibrating for Thais. Within two weeks, he pushed through the then-largest arms purchase in Thailand's history and placed Anand in power. A year later, this counter-intuitive use of military means toward civilian leadership was reversed, as Suchinda took power for himself after another round of elections. On 4 May 1992, 80,000 people took to the streets in protest; by 17 May there were 200,000. "[W]ith the knowledge and consent of Prime Minister Suchinda", an order to "destroy the enemy" was given. Distinguishing themselves were two veterans of Thailand's troop deployments to Vietnam in the late 1960s. Major General Chamlong Srimuang, retired but still scheming with the Young Turks, invented a cynical relationship between Thailand's military and democracy. Although a distant second to the military's main mission since the late 1950s to defend the monarchy, "defending democracy" commenced its political usefulness in May 1992. On the other side of the demonstrators—most of whom were genuinely pro-democracy—was General Surayud Chulanont, in command of soldiers who killed at least 100 and wounded many hundreds more. At least 200 protesters went missing. In a meeting with the US embassy, former prime minister Prem "affected to be out of touch with the situation, and revealed little of what was going on".[7] Hours later, however, he facilitated a call for both Chamlong and Suchinda to report to the palace, after which the latter resigned and left the country.

Thus, for the first and only time, a majority of Thais rejected actual or de facto military rule and a "Thai Spring" finally blossomed. It would last five years, half with Chuan as premier, and culminate in the passage of Thailand's most progressive constitution. Chamlong therefore succeeded in ways he could not have expected and certainly not have wanted—dissent's poetic justice. And as the king had sided with the demonstrators, and not with either of the two military factions, Network Monarchy was compromised. In its place, however briefly, was a more democratic network of palace, Chuan's Democrat Party, and people, as Thais turned anger into activism and gave birth to modern Thai civil society. "The press was celebrated as among the most free and feisty in Asia … Economic planning was reoriented from growth to social goals. Reforms in education and health care were plotted by private initiative and forced upon a reluctant officialdom".[8] Most effective was an Assembly for the Poor opposing environmental degradation.

ROYAL GUIDANCE

Following the 1991 coup, the palace sent immediate assurance to the US via a visit by Queen Sirikit and Princess Sirindhorn, hosted by President and Mrs. Bush. Not having traveled to the US since her childhood, the princess unveiled a plaque at King Bhumibol Adulyadej Square in Cambridge. In a 1994 reminder not only of Thailand's military–monarchy nexus but its link to the US, Princess Chulabhorn's husband was appointed military attaché to Washington. Even after the financial crisis, a visit by Princess Sirindhorn to the Kennedy Space Center in 1998 symbolized the king's ongoing commitment to the US. Though an internationalist by birth, experience, and inclination, the king was mindful of the disproportionate US role in globalization, and cautioned against being swept into its thrall as in an earlier era. Some of his rural development projects not only complemented new grassroots networks and NGOs, but further indigenized progressive trends. But rather than cause an ideological conflict of interest with the US, the turmoil of 1997 simply confirmed the king's distaste for the risk and greed inherent in the global market. He agreed with the US on the need for "austerity" and sustainability in the kingdom's fiscal and economic policy.

The king also remained unconvinced that China had no geopolitical designs on Thailand. While Princess Sirindhorn was the first person of her stature to visit Beijing after Tiananmen, by then her travels there (sometimes monthly) had been routine for a decade. In 2000, she would receive China's inaugural Language, Culture, and Friendship Award. Even Queen Sirikit's visit as late as 2000 was merely consistent with the higher profile China was beginning to assume. The only regional disagreement with the US concerned Myanmar. Assuming they were "to report everything to the embassy", representatives of Georgetown University were told by the king in 1994 that US economic sanctions would only lead to problems on the border.[9]

HUMAN RIGHTS

The events of 1991–1992 did not so much close the door on human rights violations as open a wider one to exposing and addressing them; Thailand saw 988 public protests in 1994, up from 170 four years prior. However, Prime Minister Anand granted amnesty to all involved in the May 1992 violence, denying accountability and redress. This included Sonthi Boonyaratglin, who would stage the 2006 coup, and General Surayud Chulanont, who would become prime minister after that coup. Having lamented the previous year that "it may take another fifty years" before the military accepts its proper role in Thailand, Anand thus helped fulfill the prediction.[10] In 2000, the Ministry of Defense finally released its (non-independent) report on the crackdown, including no acceptance of responsibility or wrongdoing on the part of the security forces.

The US protested at an American's death in custody in 1994, reporting that a "climate of impunity is the single largest factor militating against any significant change in police behavior".[11] The police acknowledged practicing torture, and killed 359 suspects in 1995 alone. Forced repatriation of refugees remained rife throughout the decade, and conditions in immigration detention centers constituted abusive treatment. In a practice they would repeat several times in the 2000s, Thai authorities chose the December 1995 Western holiday period to forcibly return Hmong asylum-seekers to Laos. Lacking formal citizenship, nearly 900,000 "hill-tribe" Thais faced draconian restrictions on movement, labor, education, and health. In 1996, roughly eighty police stopped two Amnesty International delegates from delivering a report on China's human rights record to its Bangkok embassy. They also issued sixty spurious warnings to media and academic publications in 1997, although the Anti-Communist Act was finally repealed a year later.

In both its positive and negative aspects, Thailand's 1997 Constitution was the single most representative element of the Thai Spring. Inclusive drafting ensured grassroots credibility and genuine progress, but resistance from conservative interests kept many reforms and voices in check. Many rights (on gender, information, criminal suspects, local communities, the environment) were codified, while new commissions and courts focusing on elections, corruption, human rights, the media, and governance were established. Eligibility and selection criteria, however, placed progressive actors at a disadvantage, and the military defeated inclusion in the constitution of the right to resist coups.

In the words of Chuan's foreign minister, "It is not surprising, therefore, that democracy has found its way into our foreign policy."[12] Before Chuan left office for the second time, Thailand had signed or ratified UN treaties relating to children, civil and political rights, torture, economic and cultural rights, and the newly established International Criminal Court (ICC). It also finally made official the UN Refugee Agency's presence in "temporary shelters", most by then housing refugees from Myanmar.

AMONG THE TOP 10 PERCENT

Thailand's citizens of Chinese ancestry, still at least 10 percent of the population, took major strides in the "money politics" they had helped create and into the civil service and all-important military. In essence, the Sino-Thai advanced in prominence and power in Thailand just as China was doing so in the world outside. Socially it became fashionable to be *lookjin* (born of a Chinese) or even the previously pejorative *jek*. Chatichai was president of the Thai–Chinese Friendship Association. In 1990, the rich and well-connected CP Group assisted General Chavalit in his formation of a new political party. Three years later he founded the Thai–Chinese Cultural and Economic Association. When he lashed out during the financial crisis at "Those others who came to settle in this land … destroy this land", the irony was surpassed only by the political injury.[13] His successor Chuan proudly stated that "my ancestors were Chinese, and there is a special kind of feeling between our nations and peoples due to ethnicity".[14] And a decidedly Thai-Chinese Thaksin would use the financial crisis as his electoral point of departure.

That the crisis hit Sino-Thai companies particularly hard attested to their growth and ambition (and over-exposure) earlier in the decade; the CP Group was by then the only foreign company to have investments in every Chinese province. This was the "ground floor" of China's sharp and sustained economic growth. Sondhi Limthongkul was a Sino-Thai business mogul who rose and fell financially during the 1990s. He claimed that connections (*guanxi*) with fellow Chinese in China were key to his initial success, more reliable and lucrative than American contracts. Indeed, 86 percent of Southeast Asia's billionaires in

1994 were of Chinese descent, a "borderless Chinese Overseas Network" whose economy was said to be the third largest in the world.[15]

A 1999 visit by China's President Jiang Zemin was strongly welcomed by the Sino-Thai community, but "sparked a mild controversy when some perceived his trip to Bangkok's Chinatown as an overt appeal to his ethnic brethren".[16] At the same time, the community supported Chuan's refusal of Jiang's request to ban a meeting of Falungong practitioners in Bangkok. The Falungong had been active in Thailand since the mid-1990s, practicing in the cafeteria of CP's main office building. A senior manager was a member himself and welcomed its Chinese founder to Bangkok in 1996, two years before China's campaign against the practice commenced and use of the cafeteria ceased.

CHATICHAI/TURNING THE MAJOR POWERS

1989 was a significant year in Thailand's foreign policy. The focus was Indochina, but success would turn in large part on the United States and China. Prime Minister Chatichai did not begin on favorable terms with the US, however, for "He was the deputy foreign minister and foreign minister successively in the days when the United States abandoned us to face the big and hostile outside world, and he had not forgotten that."[17] Neither had the Americans. He had kept Thailand outside the US-led oil boycott in the Middle East and engaged the Palestinians. Via one Pansak Vinyaratn, he had secretly reached out to Vietnam in 1973, a personal response to the "Nixon Doctrine" not well received later by the US. And in the 1980s he had scored political points vis-à-vis China by taking a public stance against US trade penalties. Said his son Kraisak, "Talk was that he would be untrustworthy as a leader."[18]

Moreover, Chatichai began to supplant the Foreign Ministry as the leader in Thailand's international affairs. While he retained Prem's foreign minister, he marginalized some of Thailand's more experienced policy hands in favor of six trusted aides. He also alienated the military, which managed to see off one advisor, an independent-minded relative of the royal family. His son and chief advisor explained:

"Hey Kraisak, you know all these communists, you've been to Vietnam, Cambodia, Laos, come work for me." I was drinking with Pansak and some others. We didn't care about the government and who was going to come and go at that time. We didn't even know the old man was going to take over the next day. He walked in and said, "Look, it's a fait accompli that I will become PM, so I want all of you in this room to become my advisors." And that's how *Baan Phitsanulok* started, red-faced academics in the middle of the night.[19]

Chatichai's determination to seek peace in Indochina thus caused apprehension. "The Americans were pro-Chinese at the time and were suspicious of me as chief advisor, thinking I was pro-Russia and pro-Vietnam. I had to maneuver the American embassy close to my chest."[20] As during the previous four decades, however, personal connections served US–Thai relations: the embassy's political counselor, Ralph "Skip" Boyce, had gone to graduate school with Kraisak at George Washington University. "I let Skip in on every detail and told him, 'You must trust us. There's no way we would abandon the US for some stupid cause. I am no longer the communist you think I am.'"[21]

In early 1989, Chatichai met President Bush in Tokyo (without consulting the Foreign Ministry), and gave him a letter explaining his views and vision; "Bush, being an old CIA guy and having dealt with China directly, will understand if we explain everything."[22] He hosted Bush's vice-president in May and scheduled a working visit for the next month to Washington, where he sent two of his advisors in advance. Citing Japan's interest in potentially large oil deposits in Vietnam, the advisors invited the secretary of commerce to visit the region. They also emphasized to Congress that a peace process would free the US from the politics of backing a genocidal government in Cambodia. Surakiart Sathirathai, one of Chatichai's advisors (and future foreign minister), would spend considerable time in Washington as part of a US–Thai policy "basement team", liaising with Bush's chief of staff.[23] After meeting Chatichai again and overriding objections from the State Department, Bush came on board.

"The Chinese were much more difficult."[24] On the one hand, Chatichai partly owed his premiership to army chief Chavalit, who had worked quietly to assure Prem's departure. With military links to China dating back a decade, Chavalit was a natural and trusted liaison and a counterbalance to Chatichai's team of whizz-kid advisors. Heavily discounted weapons and materiel thus continued; Thailand ordered six *Jianghu*-class frigates in 1989. On the other hand, Chavalit had backed Chatichai because of his Indochina policy, which he firmly—if only privately—welcomed. Thus China's most consistent Thai interlocutor was compromised and "unable to deliver the process".[25] The result was that the Chinese "were surprised, they were at a loss, they were angry—because we hadn't consulted them. Typically, Chatichai made the announcement before he had worked it all out".[26] Consistent with power and purse over any political ideology in Thailand, the "battlefields" which Chatichai wished to turn into Indochinese "marketplaces" were at the heart of Chavalit's support. So long as Chinese weapons sales continued—also motivated largely by the lucrative concessions they included—Chavalit simply saw Indochina as a better deal. If Chatichai possessed a genuinely diplomatic impulse, Chavalit and the "whole train-load of Thai politicians who controlled the North and Northeast and Central Plain" saw dollar signs.[27]

Indeed, the Americans and Chinese were not the only parties to resist the new policy, as a decade of tepid partnership with China had also engendered economic interests in Thailand.

> CP was the only company that stood to gain from our close relations
> to China. It recruited the best brains. Diplomats were working for CP,
> everybody was working for the China lobby. It became very disturbing
> to the old man that these Chinese experts instantly called to question
> him on television, and that a barrage of attacks would come whenever he
> mentioned more balanced relations with the neighbors. Control was via
> Prem or remnants of Prem in the NSC, the Thai academe, CP, and the
> Foreign Ministry.[28]

Beijing was even more abuzz than Washington about the policy change, with the Thai embassy being constantly queried for consultation and clarification. As recalled by a senior diplomat posted there, "At one session, the Chinese vice-foreign minister said to me, 'Your prime minister says one thing, your commander-in-chief says another, and you're saying something else. Whom are we to believe?"[29] As for chief advisor Kraisak, "the Chinese didn't come near me because they really thought I was the enemy. Why? Because our policy coincided with Tiananmen and Tiananmen came right after the visit of Gorbachev to China—and the Chinese connected the two".[30] As with the Americans, a visit by Chatichai himself in March 1989 would help turn the tide.

> The first sitting with Deng Xiaoping was the worst session we ever
> confronted. From the first minute we sat down he was so undiplomatic
> you would not believe. He started lecturing the old man on Soviet

imperialism, on and on. After about 15 minutes, the old man said, "Mr. Chairman I am the prime minister of Thailand, please stop lecturing me. I am here on the relationship between Thailand and China and on regional peace and economic development. It has nothing to do with Soviet imperialism. Who was the first man who came to see Zhou Enlai and Mao Zedong? Who brought the first Thai prime minister to recognize you even before Kissinger came? I remain your partner, your friend."[31]

With nuts-and-bolts operational issues on the next day's agenda, the outlook was poor.

That night the first real thing happened. My father said I had to go meet Deng's patron, an 80-year-old man by the name of Wang Zheng who apparently had controlled the army since Mao. "What the hell?" But he said that's the way China is. So at about 11pm I was taken out of the kitchen exit of this huge hotel and taken inside a Mercedes 500 to the old part of Beijing. Now the guy was alert, a skinny man who lived in an old brick house, not very well lit. All he wanted to hear from me was that we remain friends, that we were not betraying them for the Soviet Union. He gave me a red vase, which he claimed is the most difficult to make because the color can go off—I laughed to myself thinking that Red is indeed very difficult to make. The next day the atmosphere changed completely, nearly 100 percent. No more lecturing. One of the officials said, "You asked us to support the Khmer Rouge, so we did for the past ten years, and now you tell us to stop. How come you didn't tell us before you came?" Chatichai said he didn't have time, that he had only been made prime minister a couple of months ago. The Chinese said that we are friends and will do whatever you ask us to do.[32]

Back in Bangkok, Boyce at the US embassy and his Chinese and Thai counter-parts formed a "Cambodia cabal" to build trust at the working level, although China's commitment would waver. Chatichai abandoned one proposal after Premier Li Peng criticized it during an August 1990 visit to Bangkok. Others he tried to keep from both the Chinese and his own pro-China Foreign Ministry altogether. But by the time of the 1991 coup, the "graceful exit" his policy afforded all in the region had led to peace.

Away from his signature policy, Chatichai moved closer to the US and further from China on neighboring Myanmar, set to replace Indochina as the region's problem patch. Less than a year before Tiananmen Square, Myanmar had carried out a similar crackdown on pro-democracy demonstrators. Four months after Tiananmen—about which Chatichai was publicly silent—Myanmar signed a major arms deal with China. This concerned Thailand not only for its timing but for growing tensions with Myanmar's military government. While Thailand would not experience the same levels of violence and refugees with Myanmar as it had with Indochina, the 1990s would see its military attention shift from its eastern to its western border. The difference was that China's involvement was no longer welcome and supportive, but instead gave rise to "an element of competition and suspicion".[33]

Suggesting the end of the Cold War, in 1989 Chatichai quietly accompanied the army's Surayud Chulanont to Beijing to say goodbye to his dying father. Surayud had fought communists in Vietnam and Thailand and would play a starring authoritarian role in Thailand for decades to come, but his father had been a senior leader of the Communist Party of Thailand. They had fought each other. "Surayud has two facets in him", noted Kraisak, "An excellent record as a suppressor of Communists, and yet he would tell me that he has nightmares of killing his own father."[34] According to a US army officer who served alongside him in 1968, other Thai officers "shunned him".[35]

Finally, forgotten amid the peace process but no less visionary, Chatichai pursued a "Growth Quadrangle" where northern Thailand, Myanmar, Laos, and China's Yunnan province intersect. The goal was increased trade with China via an east–west corridor spanning four river basins, and a 25-kilometer road from Yunnan through points further southwest. The latter recalled the US embassy's fake news story from the mid-1970s, but its future realization would hold real consequences.

ANAND/BREAKS AND BONDS

Fortunately for the US, the first Gulf War in Iraq concluded in February 1991, for the same month saw Chatichai overthrown in Bangkok. For several months, the Americans had utilized Thailand's U-Tapao airbase—one of seven they built in the 1960s—to fuel and fly jets to the Middle East. Chatichai had been "out of the loop" on the airbase and coup leader Suchinda had delayed approval for its use.[36] In the wake of the coup, the US summarily suspended military aid and assistance to the Thais.

Three points must be made. First, in the Gulf War the US commenced a preoccupation in the Middle East that more than any other single factor would account for its progressive disengagement with Thailand over the following decades. The operation, "not well-received but well-understood" by the Thais, was the initial piece of a desert backdrop to US–Thai relations ever since.[37] Second, there is considerable irony in the war and the coup overlapping for five days. The former occasioned the same bilateral cooperation that had characterized the previous forty-five years; the latter presaged future conflict and drift. While U-Tapao was less critical to the operation than other bases in central Asia, its speedy fall from grace penciled writing on walls in Washington and Bangkok. And third, starting well before the turn of the century, the US policy of reviewing military relations with coup governments in Thailand (and elsewhere) would result in only brief and minimal fall-out in 1991. The country would not only recoil from military rule but renew itself via the Thai Spring thereafter, before the US and Thailand commenced new Balance Torch joint exercises for special forces.

Indeed, installed as premier for a year after the coup, Anand looked back on "even keel" relations with the Americans:

> Fortunately, in my many previous years in the US I had made many good friends, especially President Bush. America and western powers decided not to treat me as a legitimate government, and I did not get an invitation to visit those countries officially. But partly because of the Americans'—shall we say—larger vision of the world and my personal relations with President Bush, I was invited for a working visit to Washington, and the program was comparable to official programs. I was received in the Cabinet room and Bush showed me his private quarters. We had a good lunch and a good meeting, and I spoke to the National Press Club and appeared on TV. So treatment was practically the same, and I do not recall any conflict or any particular event or episode that damaged or jeopardized our good relations.[38]

This is not to say that differences did not exist. In response to persistent economic disputes, Anand stated, "I do not believe the approach by the United States Government in its attempt to resolve trade issues that it has with foreign countries, particularly its unilateralist attitude, is the correct one."[39] Thailand was again penalized for intellectual property violations. Anand also accused the US of "double standards" in its criticism of "constructive engagement" with Myanmar, correctly citing a similar American policy toward China after Tiananmen.[40]

In 1992, the US publicly announced it had denied a visa on drug trafficking grounds to Suchinda's initial pick for premier in the run-up to elections. In turn, Thailand did not act on a US request to investigate a particular Thai for drug-related activity. When Suchinda then seized power and ordered the deadly crackdown in May, the US suspended the Cobra Gold joint military exercises already underway for the first and only time. "State was all spun up" and told Karl Jackson at the National Security Council to recall the US ambassador in protest. Aware that it was past midnight on Saturday in Bangkok, however, Jackson treated the cable like Thailand's declaration of war in 1941: "I did a Seni Pramoj, I put it in my drawer." King Bhumibol flexed his muscle over the weekend without Jackson having "gotten around to it".[41] Further, those attacked on the streets "came to us, they didn't think of going to the Chinese for help".[42] Undeterred by the CIA's refusal to assist its long-time asset and by Washington's counsel that no legal basis existed for keeping a Thai from the authorities, US diplomats hid him. Even a student recalled being told by protest leaders that if things deteriorated further she could go to the embassy; "affected by Tiananmen Square", she wanted "US-style democracy".[43]

On the China side, while Anand hosted President Yang Shangkun in Bangkok in 1991, relations had lost their security imperative. Thus "it was not a choice that was forced upon us, America or China. Definitely at that time America was still *the* power".[44]

CHUAN I/CHINA RETURNS TO FORM

Emboldened by election victories just six weeks apart, Chuan and President Clinton got straight to work. In 1993, the two nations signed a logistics agreement at a bilateral security forum in Bangkok, and resumed Cobra Gold. Chuan scored US praise, and a point against the military, in allowing eight Nobel Peace Prize laureates to visit and advocate for Myanmar's Aung San Suu Kyi. Upon joining the WTO in 1994, Thailand agreed to an exceptional ten-year extension of investment privileges for US companies. Both leaders were at cross-purposes with the Thai military's two-way involvement on the Myanmar border, which featured ethnic insurgencies, a lucrative drugs business, and 75,000 new refugees. In contrast, Chuan backed the military in their continued support for the

Khmer Rouge, refusing a US request for use of Thai airspace to spy on them in 1993. A former American ambassador counseled "continually reminding the Thais that they are undermining a neighbor and the costly work of the world community".[45] After a truly puzzling decision to join the anachronistic Non-Aligned Movement, Thailand also registered a rare criticism of the US for a missile attack on Baghdad.

A request by Clinton that the US be allowed to pre-position naval ships in the Gulf of Thailand—"floating bases"—was extremely significant.[46] Chuan was concerned with the "highly influential role in Myanmar for Beijing", less on the border than on the coast: the Chinese navy.[47] Several years after the large China–Myanmar arms deal in 1989, China sold it fast-attack patrol boats and physically assisted in the construction of facilities. Myanmar's naval capabilities would remain limited, but the presence of Chinese ships in the Andaman Sea and growing interaction between two neighbors he distrusted signaled a new security concern for Chuan. Compounding the matter was that the army had opportunity and incentive to see it differently, as Thailand's own navy and air force had condemned the 1992 crackdown and distanced themselves from their counterparts in China and Myanmar.

At the same time, across the country in the Gulf of Thailand, Thai and Vietnamese ships arrested a number of each other's sailors in maritime claims disputes. The latter's assertiveness stemmed from similar Chinese action in the South China Sea further to the northeast. In 1994 China constructed structures "for fishermen" on the aptly named Mischief Reef. Unlike six other Asian nations, Thailand had no maritime claims there, but the saber-rattling between China and Vietnam had a cascading effect on interests closer to home. With the Thai economy racing ahead, fish, natural gas, and the freedom of navigation needed to transport goods and resources were increasingly part of Chuan's security calculation. Rewarding the navy and air force with budget increases thus served both domestic and off-shore purposes; an order was placed with the US for a squadron of F-16s.

The linchpin in these concentric geopolitical circles was the narrow Straits of Malacca, connecting the Andaman Sea on the west with the Gulf of Thailand on the east. The former leads to the Bay of Bengal, the latter to the South China Sea. The US Seventh Fleet had been patrolling it for a decade and shared Thailand's apprehension regarding China's projection of power on either side. The result was two-fold. First, after two proposals over as many decades regarding a canal across Thailand's Isthmus of Kra, Chuan commenced instead an easier Highway 44 "land bridge".[48] Hardly replacing the Straits, it would still provide a more direct alternative for connecting the gulf and the sea. While Chuan claimed in retrospect that the highway was simply the east–west half of a purely domestic transportation plan, that could only be half-correct. Doubtless it was "less controversial than a canal or the north–south ideas".[49] But that he "went ahead with it to at least ensure that the waterways would be connected" speaks to a larger geopolitical picture.[50] The second result was an up-tick in Thai military relations with the US, and a defensive policy toward China euphemistically referred to as "balance of power".

In view of this, Chuan's decision to refuse Clinton's request for "floating bases" would seem inconsistent, even self-defeating. What better way to balance a Chinese naval presence in the Andaman Sea than with the US navy in the Gulf of Thailand? And how better to defuse tensions in the South China Sea than by placing the world's only blue water navy on the literal horizon? Yet it was because of Chuan's security concerns and not in spite of them that he turned Clinton down. With the Seventh Fleet already present outside the gulf, he saw ships closer to Thai shores as upsetting a delicate balance rather than correcting an imbalance—potential escalation rather than a calming of the waters. Chuan twice informed Panitan Wattanayagorn, a security advisor, that his real concern was ASEAN and an overall regional security balance. The foreign minister told him that US ships could "complicate matters with other nations".[51] Thus Chuan's own recollection that "It had nothing to do with China" was accurate only in the most technical sense, for everything concerning US–Thai military relations for four decades had implicated China.[52] Closer to the mark was his conclusion that Thailand had simply passed the period in which a foreign military presence was acceptable domestically or advisable in security terms.

In a similarly tactical decision two years later, the US withheld advanced missiles from Thailand for fear of a regional arms race. President Clinton made a state visit to Thailand in November 1996 during the brief premiership of Chuan's first successor, signing a bilateral tax treaty. Another agreement, obligating Thailand to allow the US use of its facilities for training during crises or conflicts, further put the "floating bases" in perspective.[53]

Chuan conceded that "we did sometimes honor China's requests in deference to the relationship", but overrode its objection to including the Dalai Lama among the visiting Nobel laureates in 1993. "We also saw ourselves as a potential bridge between China and Tibet."[54] The same year Chuan visited Premier Li Ping in China and welcomed the head of China's National People's Congress, given assurances that Beijing's "regional policy was one of peace".[55] The following year, however, saw Bangkok host the first ASEAN Regional Forum (ARF), including the US and China, in the midst of the Mischief Reef crisis. ASEAN warned that "further aggressive action might force Southeast Asian states to look to extraregional actors for protection".[56] After Vietnam became a member in 1996, Chuan worried that it "was all too eager to use ASEAN as a club against China".[57] He again visited Beijing in 1996, accepting $3 million in military assistance. Yet in keeping with his mediatory approach, he also informed his hosts that their crisis with Taiwan at the time "has created tension and caused concern to countries in the region".[58]

CHAVALIT/THE BEGINNING OF THE END

By the time General Chavalit Yongchaiyudh was elected prime minister in November 1996, he had been commander-in-chief, minister of the interior, and twice minister of defense. He had served under three premiers representing two political parties. He had fought in the Vietnam War, becoming Thailand's closest liaison with Communist China. Despite or because of his large role in the amnesty program for the CPT, he had been suspected by friends and opponents alike of harboring communist leanings. However, he had also founded Thailand's paramilitary rangers in 1978, and would later resurrect two vigilante groups of 1976 infamy—all rabidly anti-communist. He gave speeches against money politics and political parties, despite having helped build the former and founded his own party. He would later serve as defense minister a third time under a third party, as well as *deputy* prime minister under Thaksin Shinawatra. Perhaps more than any other leader in modern Thai history, Chavalit exemplified the land without ideology.

As prime minister, Chavalit was reflexively opposed to the internationalism of President Clinton, who had just visited his brief predecessor. He did not overtly look to provoke the Americans but was cavalier and careless, publicly siding with Myanmar and challenging China for its attention. Among his early acts, he removed the US air force refueling specialist who had worked at the U-Tapao airbase for fourteen years. He again scored discounted Chinese weapons during a visit to Beijing in early 1997. Alternately claiming that the US was a threat to ASEAN or somehow threatened by it, he was integral to its acceptance of Myanmar and Laos in 1997. As ASEAN became the world's fourth largest trade bloc, he was most concerned with ridding it of outside scrutiny. Most potentially significant, Chavalit sought to go beyond Highway 44 across the Isthmus of Kra and reconsider a canal.

But by then he was on borrowed time; the country was nearly broke. Since 1959, Thailand's GDP had increased at an average of nearly 8 percent a year. Since 1984, the Thai baht had been pegged to the US dollar to attract investment. High-interest foreign loans had allowed Thailand's economy to skyrocket, while Thai banks were lending large sums of money domestically with little collateral. When the dollar began to appreciate in early 1997, the baht became overvalued, such that Thailand's $38 billion in foreign currency reserves were worth less than $3 billion by June. Exacerbating this was that only 200 companies accounted for 62 percent of Thai GDP, and just thirty companies for almost 40 percent. Most were owned by Sino-Thai capitalists or the Crown Property Bureau; those with the ability to borrow abroad in US dollars. While the public sector was actually running a surplus, private debt tripled between 1992 and 1996 to $92 billion. Interest payments on debt, having also tripled, suddenly became impossible. Chavalit let the baht float free of the dollar, only to watch it plummet by over 100 percent against it. This caused widespread bankruptcy in Thailand in a matter of hours. And because other regional countries were dependent on Thai companies and interest payments to finance their own projects, the crisis spread.

Chavalit threatened to proclaim a state of emergency to stay in power, but resigned in November. Despite negotiating a deal with the IMF before he left, he would later attack his successor for having "allowed the United States to impose its will on the country".[59] He rightly believed that the US favored Chuan, wrongly that the US had orchestrated his demise. Chavalit's rancor notwithstanding, through the rest of the decade American politicians and policy-makers did provide ample reason for Thais to question their alliance.

First was that the US had disproportionate power within the IMF. Thus, as a precondition to IMF involvement, in August 1997 the US demanded that Thailand disclose the status of its foreign currency reserves and the extent of its lending. "Once this information was out, the currency speculators knew they could hammer the baht with impunity, and foreign creditors rushed to withdraw their loans as rapidly as possible."[60] As Thailand's own speculative and corrupt practices became clear, the crisis deepened. Led by Chavalit, Thai leaders repeated the nationalistic and injured slogans of the previous decade's economic disputes, while ordinary Thais—devastated—were equally angry with leaders from both countries. Sarasin Viraphol of the Foreign Ministry recounted a pivotal meeting:

> The US sent the deputy secretary of the treasury. He didn't say much, he simply had three conditions that Thailand would have to accept. He put it very bluntly. It was more like a surrender. One, put everything under the IMF. Two, listen to what the IMF tells you. You must quickly deflate your economy. We were growing at zero at that time, at the outbreak of the crisis, and he said the economy must deflate very quickly to minus nine the following year. And three, you must clean up all of your troubled financial institutions.[61]

The second reason for growing anger at the US was that it did not contribute to the IMF's original loan of $17.2 billion to Thailand, the second largest ever up to that time. Three years previously, Clinton had used "exchange stabilization funds" to assist Mexico in a somewhat similar crisis. In response—and explained to the Thais at the outbreak of their own troubles—Congress placed a moratorium on the option through November 1997. Congress could make an exception only as a matter of US national security. Concerned as to whether they could make such a case to Washington, the US ambassador and his deputy, Skip Boyce, approached the Thai finance minister for "ammunition".[62] To their surprise, he told them that while Thailand needed $3 billion more, all it asked from the US was a favorable vote at the IMF. Looking back, Boyce regretted that "neither one of us took into account what this was going to mean not being part of that package, the enormity. I blame myself. It didn't have to be a large sum, we should have tried".[63]

Third, the IMF package was economically inappropriate and punitive, a fact known even at the planning stages. In addition to the enforced deflation, Thailand received a mere third of what the organization had itself loaned Mexico three years before. Given the large percentage needed to resuscitate the economy's big players, too little was left for the millions of others. In Washington's view, the IMF was the blunt "stick" with which Thailand would have to suffer before receiving any bilateral "carrot".

Finally, arrogance and opportunism on the part of IMF and US officials, including President Clinton, damaged the American image and brand substantially. Thai legal expert Bhokin Polakul recalled pushing back against the dictatorial tone of the IMF, resulting in a "clarifying" phone call from its vice-president.[64] Adding insult to Congress's moratorium on aid and undermining any suggestion that Clinton's "hands were tied" was the Treasury's deputy secretary: "Thailand is not on our border."[65] And when the moratorium finally expired in late 1997, Indonesia—which had actually contributed to the IMF package—was the first nation to receive US assistance. American funds reached Thailand in April 1998, a "too little, too late" $1.7 million.[66] While US officials tried to explain that Indonesia was simply the worst hit by the crisis, it was hardly on America's border either. "The main thing here", recalled Sarasin, "is that America didn't lift a finger ... did not even mention or refer to Thailand's status as an ally of the United States, but only geography."[67] In its own assessment, the US "made real progress in furthering some key American values"—namely increasing market access.[68] Thailand would experience record FDI, much of it by the US, "to buy up the wreckage of bankrupt companies".[69] However, losing investment ground in Thailand and political ground within the WTO, in both cases to Japan, the US blocked Japan's efforts to establish an Asian Monetary Fund in late 1997 and Thai efforts to head the WTO the following year. Also in 1998, Thai senators were rebuffed on a visit to Washington over eleven bills in Congress, and informed that, after leaving Thailand three years earlier, USAID would be back with a new agenda devoted to "good governance". In the words of Thailand's ambassador to Washington in 2015, "the US gave Thailand a reason to look East".[70]

China took a different approach. "We went to China and they said, 'What can we do for you? You are asking for $17 billion, we would be happy to extend the first $1 billion.'"[71] Although the money never materialized beyond a pledge and was hardly a tidy sum relative to the crisis, its political impact was considerable. It was to be a grant and not a loan, and differed not only from the American response but also the Japanese, a staunch US ally with greater economic interests in Thailand than any other nation. Most importantly, the Chinese offer came *first* and a full nine months before any American money materialized. While Chuan recalled that "China has also always been a true friend, has always been a nation to respond quickly to us",[72] another senior politician saw the nuance: "The Japanese were upset and approached me and asked why the Chinese were getting all the credit, because in the initial package of assistance the Japanese put in a lot of money. But not the Chinese. Somehow,

I don't know whether it was clever marketing or whatever, everybody was saying 'Oh, thank you, China.'"[73]

Coincidentally, prior to Chavalit's departure in November 1997, two tropical storms caused deaths and damage in Thailand. Boyce presented the Thais with $50,000 in relief money from the US embassy; China gave $5 million. Finally, China chose not to devalue the renminbi (yuan), which would have exacerbated Thailand's currency situation, and quietly encouraged Sino-Thai companies—hit hard by the crisis—to invest. Sarasin Viraphol of the Foreign Ministry would leave to join the CP Group, which in turn helped smaller Sino-Thai companies survive. In April 1999, Premier Li Peng would also suggest that his country's trade deficit with Thailand was "another means of help" toward the kingdom's economic recovery.[74]

CHUAN II/THE END OF THE BEGINNING

In late 1997, Chuan returned to power in Thailand for over three years, replacing Chavalit and preceding Thaksin. He could not avoid the US heavy-handedness and its local effects—hundreds of farmers protested at the embassy in 1998—much less the crisis itself. But his Democrat Party, having enjoyed a strong relationship with the US for a half-century, was a welcome return for the Americans even as it led to further accusations of bias. Rather than resist international involvement in Thailand's recovery, Chuan engaged the process toward regaining the nation's credibility more broadly. "The US underestimated the depth of the crisis and had other interests at the time, but there was no intention to turn away from Thailand. For me, it was about maintaining a long-term friendship."[75] Indeed, Chuan was Thailand's last pro-American prime minister. The US, later assessed to have "crawled two-thirds of the way back", was equally keen to regain credibility on the ground.[76]

Ambassador William Itoh had been appointed on the directive of the First Lady, with his only previous posting abroad as head of a small consulate in Brisbane. His initiation of thematic cluster meetings in Bangkok was soon deemed best practice within the Foreign Service, and the embassy, despite its enormous size, among its most efficient. In 1998, Itoh received the Cobb Award, "awarded annually to the career ambassador who best leads U.S. trade policy".[77] An admirable tribute, the award was also an unfortunate coincidence to the economic advantages secured by the US in response to the crisis. Itoh was thus the right man at both the right and wrong time. He continued to be assisted substantially by Boyce, who had eight years' experience in Thailand by late 1998 and was long since fluent in Thai. Ambassador Richard Hecklinger, who took over in 1999 having never been posted to Asia, was chosen for his technocratic approach to economic policy in the wake of the crisis.

Chuan's finance minister went to Washington in early 1998 and had an exceptional meeting with President Clinton. Henry Kissinger visited Bangkok to announce new business and investment initiatives. In preparation for a visit by Chuan himself in March, Boyce partially redeemed himself for his IMF "own goal" the year before. When Thailand could no longer afford to pay for F-18s previously ordered from a US company, Boyce suggested that the US government simply purchase them instead. He recalled that Clinton "botched the roll-out", failing to elicit the desired reaction and attention and misspelling several Thai names on the White House place-cards, which "just showed where they stood".[78] Yet Chuan recounted his meetings with the president, leaders of both major parties, and the secretary of defense with satisfaction:

> On the F-18s, all paperwork was done and construction had begun.
> The Americans waived the fine, completely nullified the order, and made
> themselves the buyer. Clinton noted that it was the first time this had
> been done and mused that he hoped it would be the last. I apologized
> in advance to Secretary Cohen for being so greedy in asking him for the
> down-payment back too, explaining that our financial situation was that
> dire. But he said he understood and returned the payment in kind.[79]

According to his security advisor, Panitan Wattanayagorn, the move "shows you how close the relationship was. More than $150 million if I am not mistaken was returned, which the country used to purchase used F-16 fighters a few years later".[80] In a speech to the Council on Foreign Relations in New York, Chuan then placed his own cards on the table for Americans and Thais alike: "Our relationship with the International Monetary Fund is key to the revival of market confidence and economic recovery." Listing seven mistakes made by Thailand, he was clear that "there is immunity in success" but not in failure. Chuan concluded—credibly for the final time—that Thailand and the US shared a "friendship which has withstood the challenges of time, distance and differences".[81]

There was more to Chuan's second term than economic recovery and US relations. Revisiting his previous administration, he pledged that "the participation by Thailand on the international stage in the protection and promotion of democratic values and human rights" was a priority.[82] Hence, Thailand increased protection for over 100,000 refugees from Myanmar and cooled relations with their government. Democracy there and at home was Chuan's stated policy aim. In 1998, he welcomed the US establishment of an International Law Enforcement Academy (ILEA) in Bangkok, for countering illegal drugs and other crimes in the region. Led by an ambitious minister who sought a "sea-change in diplomacy", the Foreign Ministry regained some of the influence it had lost as far back as Chatichai's government a decade before.[83] Chuan also reversed gains made by the military under Chavalit by making himself defense minister, marking only the second time that the men in uniform were brought under civilian control. He made General Surayud army chief, either accepting his denials of ordering the 1992 crackdown or co-opting a potential opponent. And in sending troops for a US-backed peacekeeping operation in Timor Leste, Chuan provided an insular military with a new outward-looking purpose.

* * *

By the time Chuan returned to power, just two and a half years after his first term, China had changed markedly. Despite commissioning four more frigates, Chuan remained wary of Beijing from a security standpoint; in 2000 it voiced its displeasure about US military exercises with "regional countries".[84] Yet China's economic growth to nearly pre-crisis Thai levels presented Chuan with a unique challenge and opportunity: "The main thing at the time was economic expansion for both nations, us in recovery and the Chinese in the first instance."[85] While Thailand's exports faced sudden competition, China reduced import tariffs on 136 Thai products by almost 50 percent to smooth its own WTO membership. By 2001, "China had invested $233 million in more than 230 joint ventures and enterprises in Thailand, while Thai companies had directly invested over $2 billion in some 3,000 projects in the PRC".[86] Chuan also returned China's generosity from nine months earlier by donating $10,000 in the wake of its own massive flooding. Their differences on Myanmar notwithstanding, Thailand and China found common cause in combatting illegal drugs trade via a 2000 agreement.

Finally, initiated by Thailand, a comprehensive Sino-Thai "Plan of Action for the 21st Century" was agreed in February 1999. The first such plan China signed with any ASEAN nation, it would appear almost prophetic in its name and content fifteen years hence. "[W]idely recognized as Chinese code for 'a desire for a decline in American power', it outlined cooperation in trade and investment, defense and security, judicial affairs, science and technology, diplomacy and culture."[87] The latest sign that both nations prioritized one another over their other Southeast Asian neighbors, it also formalized Thailand's role as a Chinese link to ASEAN, despite no written corollary within the regional body itself. In the hopes of a Thai Foreign Ministry official, the plan would "remind China of the commitment to Thailand when it becomes the centre of world attention".[88]

Much of this was achieved through intensive personal relations, which unlike those with the Americans, were unburdened by any redemptory element. In April 1999 Chuan visited China for the second time as prime minister. Five months later, President Jiang Zemin flew to Bangkok and delivered a major foreign policy speech in which he characterized Thailand as "one of our most important cooperation partners in the region".[89] Li Peng also returned to Thailand in 1999, this time as Chair of the National People's Congress. Over 1,500 more Sino-Thai exchanges at all levels—the most Thailand had with any nation—took place between 1998 and 2000. Despite borders only 100 kilometers apart, proximity could not fully explain the flurry between capitals separated by a nearly five-hour flight. In Chuan's words, "China would invite me to even minor events, such as on forestry in Yunnan. Relations in this region are about keeping our word and not promising what we cannot deliver. China asked for land to grow trees for paper, but I had to be honest with Premier Zhu Rongji that our law prohibited foreigners from owning land."[90]

In addition to the US and China, Southeast Asia required considerable attention. In moves supported by Washington, Chuan resurrected his critical "flexible engagement" on Myanmar and agreed to a maritime border with Vietnam in 1999.[91] He hosted Myanmar's prime minister in Bangkok but was the only ASEAN leader not to visit Yangon. China participated in a raft of post-crisis regional economic initiatives, including "ASEAN Plus Three" (China, Japan, and South Korea), the first meeting of which was held in Bangkok in mid-2000. It also agreed to help Thailand realize a broad "Mekong Development Decade", beginning with a pledge in 2000 to make the river navigable for larger ships. Although neither the US nor China showed interest in his government's reluctant reconsideration of a canal across the Isthmus of Kra, a wider and deeper Mekong would prove a factor in that equation in the century ahead.

Likewise, neither welcomed discussion in 2000 of recalling a symbolic number of troops Thailand had maintained in South Korea for fifty years.

* * *

In fact and fairness, Thailand's financial crisis had roots far older and deeper than Chavalit, and neither he nor Chuan had much choice but to comply with the IMF/US package. Moreover, the worst was past: after two years of zero growth, Thailand's economy grew by 4 percent in 1999. But just as Chuan benefited from his predecessor's fury and resistance, so did his successor benefit from Chuan's accommodation. Where Chuan was returned to the premiership as an enlightened technocrat, his successor would redefine the required profile as that of a nationalistic entrepreneur. In 2000, and with an election approaching, the opposition moved to censure Chuan for being more responsive to international institutions and the US than to Thais. Months later, the country at large would do the same, electing Thaksin Shinawatra and profoundly altering the kingdom's outlook and orientation.

Interface

Dates:	1972, 1985, 1989, 1997, 1999
Location:	The Isthmus of Kra, southern Thailand
Project:	A canal of 50–100 kilometers linking the Gulf of Thailand in the east with the Andaman Sea in the west.
Purpose:	A canal would provide vessels with an alternative to the Straits of Malacca. Increasing amounts of global trade traverse the Straits, including all-important oil and liquefied natural gas. A canal would afford a more direct and faster route between the waters on either side, as well their maritime extensions in the South China Sea to the east and Bay of Bengal to the west. Its ports would rival Singapore and Malaysia's Port Klang and thus create considerable economic opportunity for Thailand.
Status 1972:	Prime Minister Thanom contracts US engineers to conduct a feasibility study. They propose a canal from eastern Songkhla province through western Satun province, wide and deep enough to accommodate ships carrying up to 500,000 deadweight tonnage. The Americans propose ports and industrial development on both sides. Mooted as the US grants its largest amount of military aid to Thailand, and a year before moving its entire military operation from Vietnam to Thailand, the proposal becomes a victim of backlash and defeat in Southeast Asia.
Status 1985:	Prime Minister Prem welcomes a Japanese institute's proposal for a canal from eastern Surat Thani province through western Phang Nga province, blasted through the isthmus with nuclear

power. The proposal is the result of over five years of renewed interest attendant to Thailand's economic boom. Tabled as the US passes its Food Security Act, equally damaging to Thai crops and the American image, the proposal neither attracts nor welcomes US support.

Status 1989: Prime Minister Chatichai ignores a report, The Kra Canal and the Future of Thailand, produced by the Science Society of Thailand under the patronage of His Majesty the King. Already skeptical of Chatichai's "battlefields into market-places", the US shares his approach to the report.

Status 1997: Prime Minister Chavalit revives interest in a canal amidst growing maritime tension in the region and Thailand's meteoric economic growth. An alternative Highway 44 ("land bridge") across the isthmus, begun four years earlier by a predecessor, remains incomplete and adds political and economic incentive. Thailand's devastating financial crisis, to which the US responds dogmatically, immediately removes the project from the national agenda.

Status 1999: Prime Minister Chuan is forced to order new feasibility studies, after opposition leader Chavalit persists with the idea as a means to economic recovery and establishes a parliamentary subcommittee. As a canal of the Japanese design is calculated to cost $25 billion, Thailand's banks, business leaders, and military get behind the project. NGOs counter with concerns over soil displacement, environmental impacts, and effects on local livelihoods and culture. Despite Chuan being predisposed to American interests, "there is no foreign influence one way or another in the initiative", which does not advance.[1]

Result: During five distinct periods in the late 20th century, the US misses an opportunity to actively support, if not sponsor, a maritime route through a treaty ally. The US is the world's largest economy and effectively controls the Straits of Malacca throughout. China's energy and trade interests are second only to those of the US by 1997. The Straits' high level of importance during the Cold War only increases with the triumph of capitalism and commerce. China's regional presence is assured, while its designs for the next century remain unclear. A canal would anticipate a foreseeable desire in Beijing to diversify maritime options. It would thus afford a degree of strategic control over the Straits by Thailand and its American ally. But in 1997 and 1999, the US does "not take it very seriously".[2]

Part Two

Chapter Seven:
A Thaksin for Turning
(Thailand and China, 2001–2006)

Symbolic of our deteriorated public image in southern Thailand—when compared to the PRC—the former US Consulate General in Songkhla now belongs to the Chinese.[1]

Alexander A. Arvizu, July 2006

You don't need to have democracy to have economic growth and lift at least 400 million people's lives up from the shithole—this is the Chinese view. The West should say that democracy is a function of qualitative change in risk-taking for economic growth, instead of saying that you use democracy as an end in itself as an abstract good. Do not think that the Communist Party of China is so stupid. They are debating and thinking about this all the time, about democracy as a possible utility to sustain the economy of the country. I talked to them.[2]

Pansak Vinyaratn, January 2015

In the gradual, geological movement of the continents across the earth's surface, known as continental drift, an equally constant movement of tectonic plates occurs far below the surface. Most of the time, such movement on either level is unfelt. Sudden and occasional shifts of the plates, however—along fault lines in the earth's core—cause earthquakes and tsunamis on the surface. In a few violent moments, entire physical, political, and psychological structures can come into existence, change, cease to exist. In 2001, the party of Thaksin Shinawatra received 41 percent of the vote in Thailand, resulting in 248 of 500 parliamentary seats—the largest electoral victory in Thai history and a minor political earthquake. Eight months later, hijacked airplanes brought down the World Trade Center and put a gaping wound in the Pentagon, triggering an

American tsunami that would soon become the world's. A year on either side of those events, China's economic growth steadied at 8 percent before climbing to nearly 10 percent the next two years. Growth hit 11.5 percent in 2005, nearly 13 percent in 2006, and an improbable 14.5 percent in 2007. Within and among the three nations, the year 2001 was a fault line.

It was fitting that Thaksin was elected at the turn of not only a century but a millennium. For better or worse, few Thais have ever changed their country as much as Thaksin has—as much in exile as in power. Initially one of the most unifying politicians of the modern era, collecting voices and votes from the most disparate quarters, he would tear the Thai body politic in half both electorally and geographically. A court that saved his infant premiership in 2001 would void a later victory at the polls, both times under dubious legality. After being elected twice consecutively, Thaksin would be overthrown in the nation's first coup in fifteen years. In between, he ran the nation as a self-described "CEO", consolidating power and enacting major structural changes. He embodied, as a billionaire businessman *and* a lieutenant police colonel, the predominance of Thailand's ethnic Chinese in all sectors of society. Hailing from the north, he effectively enfranchised and empowered whole regions of the country that had previously been neglected. He was notably corrupt, even if the "real crime was rather that Thaksin no longer really needed to buy votes to win elections".[3] He purposely and implicitly threatened Network Monarchy in a way political protesters never had or could. And he did such violence to rights and the democratic process as to usher in authoritarianism on a scale not seen since Field Marshal Sarit four decades before.

Perhaps most importantly, Thaksin Shinawatra altered the orientation and trajectory of Thailand's foreign policy. In a manner more subtle but more serious than "turning battlefields into marketplaces", Thaksin began moving Thailand away from the American sphere of influence and toward the Chinese. Unlike his domestic policies, the effects of this were not immediate or immediately appreciated at home, for he was working against a half-century of history. Yet once underway, the force and momentum of the shift worked directly against any reversal. A Sino-Thai free trade agreement did not assist similar American efforts but made them more difficult; a zero-sum dynamic in play since the Cold War was its clearest in decades. Nor was the US War on Terror a valuable counter-stroke, but fool's gold; evoking its Manichean predecessor in Indochina, the US would pay for dubious short-term security gains with its long-term "values".

"Behind the curtain there was nothing" in Washington supporting its embassy, while Beijing began appointing Communist Party operators.[4] Aged seventy-four in 2001, Thailand's King Bhumibol—America's single most steadfast ally in Southeast Asia since World War II—was finally beginning to show his age. Although Thaksin lacked an advocate in the palace, his Chinese orientation was less unwelcome there than at any point during the previous century.

In 1998, Thaksin had founded his political party, *Thai Rak Thai* (Thais Love Thais), named in response to Chuan's imputed foreign allegiances. According to his deputy prime minister, "Thaksin was not a true believer in anything."[5] Ideology is not required for vision, however, and Thaksin had it in spades. Having become the world's 421st wealthiest person via questionable dealing, considerable risk-taking, and deft management, he was interested in changing not only policy but the process by which it was made. His chief political advisor was Pansak Vinyaratn and his foreign minister Surakiart Sathirathai, both core members of Chatichai's personal think-tank. Surakiart was clear that Thailand's affairs would not be "ideology driven" but "business driven" in every respect.[6] Thaksin implemented a "CEO ambassador" program, whereby Thailand's envoys were to focus on economic interests and procedural efficiency as chief executives. By his last year, many in the ministry wore black in opposition or displayed the yellow paraphernalia of a fast-growing street movement dedicated to his departure. Again recalling Chatichai, Thaksin appointed General Chavalit his first minister of defense, as few Thais could boast his networks in Beijing. Thaksin also initially agreed to General Surayud—a key member of Network Monarchy—staying on as army chief. In 2003, however, he replaced him with his own cousin, passing over the Network's choice of General Sonthi Boonyaratglin; Surayud was immediately appointed to the king's Privy Council. In 2006, Sonthi would overthrow Thaksin, Surayud would become the junta's prime minister.

EAST ASIAN ARCHITECTURE

Asia was at the center of Thaksin's foreign policy. Just after the election, Surakiart gave a major speech pledging to advance Thailand's role "between ASEAN member countries and countries in East Asia".[7] "Prosper thy neighbor is the right approach", said Surakiart, a veteran of Indochina's transition, in 2015. "And after the neighbors, Asia was the next concentric circle, a natural outgrowth, the expansion of the same principle. Asia had been divided for too long."[8] The CP Group's Sarasin also briefly joined Thaksin's team:

Thaksin said, "This is a new era, Asia for Asians, and I am going to be the leading voice." This was driven not by ideology but opportunism. He was one step ahead of others all the time. It was his advisors in the ministry and his foreign affairs circle who proposed this idea, but he immediately seized it. Put not only his stamp of approval on it, but his brand.[9]

Consistent with this, Thaksin pressed both China and the US in 2005 to support Thailand as a mediator in bringing North Korea back to the Six-Party talks on its nuclear program. Surakiart's successor traveled to Pyongyang and Beijing several times and reached out to Secretary of State Condoleezza Rice. Concluding that Thaksin "wants to firmly establish Thailand and himself as Southeast Asia's undisputed leader, and a force in Asia writ large", the Americans joined China in being open but skeptical.[10] They also saw the initiative as closely related to Thaksin's nomination of Surakiart to become the next UN secretary-general. The same month his foreign minister was in North Korea, Thaksin expressed confidence in China's support for Surakiart and solicited that of the US throughout. China did not oppose but welcomed other Asian candidates as well. Surakiart withdrew from the race after Thaksin was overthrown, and South Korea's Ban-ki Moon was selected.

Team Thaksin's collective vision also included new regional architecture, and accounting in large part for its effectiveness and durability was the People's Republic of China. The Chiang Mai Initiative (CMI) was first mooted at a 2000 "ASEAN Plus Three" meeting, before Thaksin became its self-appointed representative. A bilateral currency swap for alleviating liquidity problems after the 1997 crisis, it attached its label to an early $2 billion credit line to Thailand from China. Abhisit Vejjajiva (future prime minister) recalled that, "China, especially on the CMI, was also playing on the sentiment that, 'If you are going to look after yourselves and not need another IMF or World Bank, then we'll support.'"[11] Team member Sarasin was succinct: "A friend in need is a friend indeed."[12] In 2003, Thailand hosted an ASEAN meeting on the regional SARS pandemic and the only meeting of a "Bangkok Process" on Myanmar, both of which China joined. Thaksin conceived and led Cambodia, Laos, and Myanmar in co-founding the Ayeyerwady–Chao Phraya–Mekong Economic Strategy (ACMES), to facilitate and manage inevitable Chinese riparian interests in the region. China also "got the point that it was to their benefit to engage with the Mekong countries beyond the Greater Mekong Sub-region group, which had existed for a long time".[13] Late in the year, Thailand hosted the annual Asia-Pacific Economic Cooperation (APEC) gathering, for which Thaksin assigned the Ministry of Commerce rather than Foreign Affairs to take the lead.

Most far-reaching was the Asia Cooperation Dialogue (ACD), based on an idea developed by Surakiart in 2000:

> Asia is very divided and has all shades of ethnicities, religions, systems of governance, values and cultures. If you were going to create an organization like the EU or even the AU, it would break. So it had to be as loose an organization as possible—that is why a "dialogue". It had to be inclusive, based on comfort level and voluntary participation. All major countries were not sure what Asia meant and who should be included, whether some countries would serve their interests. But I convinced them by saying that it was not a forum for bi-lateral conflict, but to talk about positive things such as road linkages. Asia had so many sub-regional and inter-regional organizations but nothing pan-Asian.[14]

Indeed, Thaksin conceded that while they "welcomed my initiatives and leadership ... the Chinese were really reluctant in the beginning" toward the ACD.[15] The reason was Japan, a Chinese rival and American ally.

> India's prime minister had just agreed on condition that it include Pakistan. So I went to the Boao Forum in 2002 and sat between Japan's premier and China's Zhu Rongji. I said that I had just come back from India and they both fully support the ACD. So when Zhu Rongji said China would support, Japan said it would also support.[16]

Sarasin, who would leave Thaksin's team shortly thereafter, had a different explanation:

> Thaksin's voice stood out with his advocacy of the ACD. What he could have done was court China and then offered it the leadership, instead of saying, "I am the architect and I am going to lead it." You can say you are the architect but then, "China, please, you are the big brother here in Asia." It did not affect relations in a big way, as it was all in that early period when China was emerging.[17]

The first ACD was held in a Thai seaside province in mid-2002 with eighteen foreign ministers, including China's. The second was in Thaksin's hometown of Chiang Mai, with "several of the activities conducted at the PM's private home … since it was meant to be informal".[18] Indicating China's full endorsement was its hosting of the third gathering in 2004 in Qingdao. Months later, Thaksin and Chinese premier Wen Jiabao had a private breakfast at an ASEAN summit. According to his spokesperson, "Thaksin asked that if China was determined to be the new economic hub for Asia, could Thailand be first among equals. Wen said yes. On the plane home Thaksin told me, 'It's time to reunite Asia.'"[19] The ACD was held each year of Thaksin's tenure, alongside a litany of area-specific meetings, including two in China. ACD foreign ministers met at the annual UN General Assembly in New York, and Thailand's Foreign Ministry hosted yearly retreats for its envoys in ACD member countries.

Finally, Thaksin's foreign policy was equally defined by the demotion of two erstwhile pillars: ASEAN and the United States. Surakiart noted that, "ASEAN is the most difficult organization in which to initiate anything new, wait for this, wait for that."[20] Its secretary-general and national chair both rotate on five- and one-year bases, respectively, and are charged with guiding, not leading. Thaksin was impatient and wanted to lead. Most importantly, China's formal involvement via ASEAN Plus Three was already established, and Thailand had already solidified its place as an informal ASEAN–China nexus. The former was thanks to Chavalit, his subordinate; the latter to Chuan, his opponent. Particularly through the ACD, Thaksin could simultaneously subsume and "leap-frog" ASEAN Plus Three en route to both expanding and recasting it. Redundancies of membership and mission were secondary to a new grouping initiated by Thailand and featuring China.

Similarly, Thaksin did not intend to ignore the US, but to move beyond his predecessors' decades-old economic reliance on the US (and Japan), and deliver on the anti-IMF sentiment that he rode to election. The US had been a driver of ASEAN's establishment, was a founding economy of APEC in 1989, and had been a member of the ARF since its inception in 1994. Despite China's view—backed by Thaksin—that it should not be a founding member, its participation in an East Asia Summit (EAS) was also never in question (except by the Americans). That China was also a member of these forums was to Thaksin largely offset by American participation. Conversely, while the US was not part of the China-led Shanghai Cooperation Organization (SCO), nor was Thailand;

Thaksin's interest in 2005 would thus be significant. Thaksin thus saw his ACD as "the missing link" on account not only of China's centrality but of America's absence.[21] In describing the ACD's principle of inclusion, Surakiart mused that "Asia is in the eyes of the beholder", before stating plainly that "the US is not in Asia".[22]

FOLLOWING THE CHINESE STAR

Assisting Thaksin's vision and ambition and ensuring that "Asia" read "China" atop his foreign policy agenda, were two other factors: Thaksin had a pre-existing relationship with China, and a critical mass of Thai Rak Thai and Team Thaksin was made up of old or new Sino-Thai elite. Thaksin sold his first satellite to China in 1996 when he was deputy prime minister under Chavalit. "On every official visit to China, government leaders always brought up the satellite issue for discussion, since this was considered important to bilateral relations."[23] When a new Thaksin satellite in 1999 showed far more promise, China became his company's top priority. Politically, Thaksin spoke to the Chinese about how to establish and run a political party, and told Premier Zhu Rongji that if he won Thailand's election, "Asians should rewrite the rules of the game and give preferential treatment to Asian businesses and investors".[24] China was no exception to Thaksin's non-ideological rule, however. According to a Foreign Ministry official who worked on or in China during Thaksin's entire tenure, he simply "followed where the money was to the new frontier; it was like the Gold Rush".[25] His dual market-seeking motive was better served by pragmatism than a principled approach.

Thaksin was also gifted a perfectly timed domestic phenomenon: following four decades of upward mobility within and across all sectors of Thai society, the start of a new century saw the Sino-Thai ready to lead the nation. If not all were movers and shakers, it was increasingly rare to find those who considered themselves "pure Thai" among the kingdom's elite. As one Foreign Ministry official quipped, "Who cares if your grandfather was an immigrant if now your daddy's rich?"[26] Thaksin himself was descended from a Hakka Chinese great-grandfather from Guangdong province, who immigrated to Siam in the late 19th century and married a Thai. Thaksin also symbolized Sino-Thai success outside of Bangkok and the economic sector; a northern son who finished first in his class at Thailand's police academy. Nor was he alone, as over half his cabinet and as much as 90 percent of parliament in 2001 was of Chinese ancestry. Thailand was not just "the only nation in Southeast Asia to have solved its Chinese problem", but to have turned it into an unlikely success.[27]

Alongside this was a commensurate if less quantifiable shift in sentiment among the Sino-Thai, and Thais more broadly, toward China. Where the past two decades had seen the Sino-Thai accepted and embraced in Thailand, the 2000s would see them announce and embrace themselves. Many would begin using their Chinese surnames alongside their Thai ones, and "frequent inter-marriages among the ethnic-Chinese and the ethnic-Thai do little to dilute their sense of ethnic-Chinese identity".[28] According to a 2005 poll commissioned by the US embassy, the number of Thais believing China would soon become their most important external influence had risen from 12 percent in 1998 to a majority, and 83 percent had a favorable opinion of the Chinese. Bangkok's large Chinatown began celebrating not only Chinese New Year, but King Bhumibol's birthday. Dancers, fireworks, and Chinese flags encircled portraits of the monarch, and were visited by relatives of the royal family. Both private and government-funded Chinese celebrations increased among Sino-Thai communities outside of Bangkok too, where authorities began putting up Chinese street signs. In 2004, the US embassy observed that, "Thai sports fans openly pulled for Chinese athletes in the Olympics in ways they've never supported Japanese or other Asian competitors in the past".[29] More significantly, at a function including hundreds of Sino-Thais, a Chinese diplomat quietly remarked that, "ten years ago this would have been Taiwan's crowd".[30]

A lingua franca had never existed among the largely illiterate and diverse Chinese immigrant community of the last century. But by 2000, those who spoke Mandarin began using it, while others promoted or learned it. Minister of Education Chaturon Chaisang did both, hiring a personal tutor and announcing that any school could teach the language. One southern province alone had thirteen Chinese associations by mid-2006, each corresponding to the Chinese province of its members' ancestors; all opened their own language schools. Finally, a new trend developed among Sino-Thais of visiting their ancestral land. Thaksin himself visited his mother's resting place there in 2005: "When Chinese people see a Thai leader and so many entrepreneurs coming to China to pay homage to the place where their ancestors had lived, they will understand that Thais and Chinese are from one family, and they are relatives."[31] Also commemorating the 30th anniversary of bilateral relations, Thaksin told his hosts that there were more Chinese in his cabinet than Thais. The number of Thais overall traveling to China rose by over 60 percent between 1997 and 2003, as Thailand likewise began welcoming Chinese tourists in large numbers.

Despite the new reality, Thaksin "had to be careful with China, as many accused him of being Chinese himself".[32] During the 2001 election in which the financial crisis still loomed large, Thaksin leveraged his Chinese ethnicity and connections: who better to promote and protect Sino-Thai capital and companies than one of the most successful Sino-Thai entrepreneurs? His own companies were damaged far less than most others, and one of his early advisors was the head of the powerful CP Group. Both the Crown Property Bureau and the same Sondhi Limthongkul who had previously extolled Chinese business practices backed him as well. Once in power, however, Thaksin had access to top political leadership, Communist Party operatives, and industry bosses, and so was able to advance not only Thailand's economic prospects, but also his own. Sarasin of the CP Group explained:

> Even without invitations, Thaksin would seek them out, and he had a good agent in China, still working for him today, Yan Bin. An entrepreneur who has a share in the Red Bull energy drink business, he is one of the richest men in China today and served as a kind of political power broker on the side. You know, in China you need that, the *guanxi*, the relationship—through the back door, through the front door, whatever. So it's a more personal kind of thing, and Thaksin has been very good at it, even up to today.[33]

Yan Bin was a Sino-Thai and the fourth wealthiest person in China in 2012. In his second visit as prime minister in 2001, Thaksin raised the satellite issue last discussed when Chavalit was in power. In 2003, China Railway Communication Asia Pacific became the first customer for his new satellite, and a deal with the China Satellite Communications Corporation was signed the following year. At the same time, his finance minister reportedly blocked a Chinese state enterprise from bailing out the company of one of Thaksin's opponents.

Thaksin thus collected enemies as quickly as dividends, including several private Sino-Thai banks that had either applauded or avoided his anti-IMF campaign; Bangkok Bank housed Thailand's consulate in Shanghai. Sondhi Limthongkul would also turn on Thaksin and lead the royalist street movement that ushered in the 2006 coup. Yet the ethnic element he put into play was negated (and mocked) by his own Chinese ancestry. The grandson of a Hainanese immigrant and son of a nationalist colonel, Sondhi essentially proclaimed that he and his followers were "better Chinese" than Thaksin. His call to arms, *Lookjin Rak Thai* (Children of China Love Thailand)—otherwise so similar to Thaksin's Thai Rak Thai—gave pride of place to China over Thailand. In mid-2006, he would lead a rally of a thousand people in front of the *Chinese* embassy, turning a century of perception and persecution of the Sino-Thai inside out. In the intra-elite political conflict just underway, the Chinese of Thailand would constitute both sides.

PRESSING HOME THE ADVANTAGE

Sino-Thai predominance was welcomed by the Chinese in Beijing no less than by those in Bangkok. Not unlike the way the US capitalized after 1949 on Thailand's growing anti-Chinese sentiment to further its anti-communist crusade, China was able to exploit the consummation of the opposite experience in the person, party, and policies of Thaksin Shinawatra. Although Phibun and Sarit had been nationalistic Thais, they saw themselves and were seen by the US as American allies in Thailand. To a lesser degree, China could say the same of Thaksin a half-century later. For the six years he was in power, bilateral relations increased in quantity and quality on every front. In May 2001, between two trips by Thaksin to China the same year, Prime Minister Zhu Rongji described his time in Thailand as a "family visit to a relative" and quoted a song written by Princess Sirindhorn: "China–Thailand friendship is like a friendship between brothers, which will last thousands of years and beyond."[34] Rhetorical flourish notwithstanding, the ethnic connection between the two nations' leadership—subsuming cultural similarities, shared history, and geographic proximity—had real meaning. On Thaksin's second trip that year, he and Zhu determined "to consolidate the traditional ties of friendship, and work for the first time on a strategic partnership".[35]

Like some of their American counterparts, Chinese ambassadors to Thailand historically spoke fluent Thai, many having been translators at the Foreign Ministry or held lower posts at the embassy. According to a Thai academic who has known nearly every Chinese ambassador for three decades, in about 2000 Beijing began "upgrading" its chief envoy to Bangkok with individuals who had spent their careers as Communist Party operators. Ministry stand-outs, fluent in both English and Thai, were made numbers two and three at the embassy.

The ambassador thus had more authority and influence in Beijing, while the overall diplomatic team on the ground was strengthened. The Chinese themselves told the US embassy that their Bangkok-based diplomats were their best in ASEAN. In 2004, Skip Boyce—by then US ambassador—noted that his counterpart was "a veteran of two previous tours to Bangkok", a member of the Communist Party's Politburo, and reportedly a protégé of China's former vice-premier.[36] Fluent in Thai, he did a "masterful job of reaching out to Sino-Thais".[37] He and Boyce would appear together on a famous and friendly Thai television program, where the Chinese was judged as the more fluent. Likewise, the Chinese defense attaché was "a vast improvement over the previous", and the political officers conversant on the US, Southeast Asia, the Middle East, ASEAN, and the EAS.[38] Finally, a long-time Thai ministry official confirmed the trend: "The Chinese have an approach that is better received in Thailand than the US approach. Chinese diplomats mingle with the Thai and they know officials better. The embassy will call and speak Thai to us. That means they took the effort of getting someone here who studied Thai."[39] As far away as Washington, Thailand's ambassador (and future foreign minister) "saw a lot of" his Chinese counterparts, two of whom would go on to become foreign minister.[40]

A former US diplomat claimed that Sino-Thai relations also benefited from "superficial engagement", for which the Thais had a penchant and the Chinese a tolerance. A shared ethnicity and physical proximity, with cabinet-level Chinese officials "stacked like cordwood", were given as reasons.[41] Boyce recalled Surakiart being unable to provide much reason for a "global meeting" in Bangkok after the 2004 tsunami, but where the US sent the president's low-profile science advisor, China sent its foreign minister. "Every visit by a senior American official", said Boyce, "is countered by multiple visits by Chinese."[42] Beijing sent a tooth of the Buddha for display during King Bhumibol's 75th birthday in 2002, and began "panda diplomacy" in cooperation with Thai zoos.

As part of its effort to make Mandarin an official ASEAN language, China facilitated construction in 2004 of a $1.5 million language center at a northern Thai university. It linked a northeastern university with another in China toward establishing a Confucius center for language and cultural studies. A Confucius institute was likewise established at Bangkok's historically prestigious Thammasat University. The Chinese consulate in southern Thailand—which physically replaced a US consulate in 2005—oversaw the placement of hundreds of Chinese professors. By 2006, plans were underway between the two governments to standardize a Mandarin curriculum, causing the US to remark that the "competition between Beijing and Taipei to influence Thailand's Chinese educational system may be coming to an end".[43]

Through its Propaganda Department, China greatly increased its media presence in Thailand during Thaksin's tenure, and developed relations with Thai outlets: "Thai journalists are regular beneficiaries of Beijing-funded junkets to China."[44] In 2004, the English-language China Central Television (CCTV) was "very popular in Thailand and Mandarin broadcasts on CCTV Channel 4 are readily available".[45] It secured direct feeds each morning on a channel owned by Thailand's military, and collaborated on "special focus" programs, including one on the king's sixty-year reign. CCTV also traveled with Chinese delegations to cover major events. While the state-owned *Xinhua News Agency* had been there since 1975 and had offices elsewhere in ASEAN, the English-language *China Daily* established its regional hub in Bangkok in 2005. Joining them were the *People's Daily News*, the *Guangming Daily Media Group*, the *China News Agency*, and *China Radio International*. By 2006, as *Xinhua* was producing and feeding hard news to the other outlets, the newer *Guangming* and *People's Daily* were pressured by Beijing to avoid being "misconstrued as official PRC views".[46]

MADE IN CHINA

Surakiart claimed in retrospect that "We did not intend to be closer to China, but it was because of our focus on neighboring countries and on Asia, and how China responded."[47] Thaksin's economic outlook alone renders the claim untenable. Surakiart proposed a free trade agreement (FTA) in Beijing two months after the 2001 election. A month later, Thaksin referred to the US, Japan, and the six "Asian Tigers" as having failed economic models for their slow growth or recovery. Who was left? Thaksin's second visit to China in 2001 was as head of a trade delegation. In 2002, China was headed for its third consecutive year of remarkable 8 percent growth, having *declined* to that level for eight years previously. By then, Thai exports to China were set for a year-on-year increase of 54 percent, with imports declining by 4 percent. A deputy prime minister recalled that "Thaksin didn't see shame in being part of the Chinese supply chain management, it was realistic."[48] Chief advisor Pansak agreed: "We moved with that reality. Notice the terms of trade, the trade relationship between us and the Chinese, it was becoming bigger and bigger and bigger."[49] In Thaksin's own recollection: "Sooner or later integration would happen, so why don't we go first? If we don't do it, someone else will do it and we will lose competitiveness, so we had to do it now. I looked at the economy like business, we needed to be there first."[50]

Yet Surakiart was not wrong to emphasize China's responsiveness, for the FTA with Thailand was indeed its first with any ASEAN nation. Beijing had been looking at Thailand's north and northeast, seeing commercial advantage in the familiarity many Thais and Yunnan Chinese had long had with one another. As China was prepared to allow province-to-province deals in addition to those negotiated by the ministries of commerce, Yunnan Communist Party representatives visited Thailand to create a working group in 2002. Thaksin's expansion of rubber production in the region further impressed the Chinese, before resulting in a ten-fold increase of shipments between 2003 and 2005.

Thailand and China signed the FTA in October 2003, exactly half-way through Thaksin's time in office. Of its provisions, 87 percent pertained to produce and agriculture, with a more comprehensive agreement deferred to 2010. In the twelve months following the deal, the value of Thai fruit and vegetables exported to China increased by 37 percent and 73 percent respectively, and bilateral trade hit $12 billion. China rapidly moved into second place behind Japan on Thailand's list of trading partners. By early 2005, China accounted for 7 percent of Thailand's relevant export market, up 4 percent since 2000. In 2006, Thaksin's finance minister—tellingly dubbed "Mr. China"—and the Chinese vice-premier pledged to increase bilateral trade to $50 billion by 2010. "We were quite proactive", confirmed Surakiart's successor at the Foreign Ministry, "because we didn't want to be on the receiving end. We could actually be partners with China and have a win–win situation."[51]

Half the figures told only half the story, however, as overall growth could not obscure a new and deepening trade deficit. In the twelve months following the FTA, imports in Thailand of Chinese fruit and vegetables increased by roughly 123 percent. Non-tariff barriers against other Thai imports were erected, and an estimated 40 percent of Thai garlic and onion farmers were put out of business. Other problems involved poor communication between capitals and provinces, absentee officials, different banking practices, unreliable insurance, and an impoverished consumer base in Yunnan. With an eye on his electoral strongholds, Thaksin had foreseen some of this during negotiations, but had simply seen the advantages as greater: "I said there is no country with which we can have full advantage or full disadvantage, it's give and take. But the government must have help for those who are disadvantaged. So this was the way I moved."[52]

Having bypassed parliament and signed the FTA via executive decree, however, he did admit to a letdown in process:

> Sometimes I moved fast, too fast, and when you are a leader you must be a guru-master at explaining. But when you don't have time to tell the story, people don't understand. When they have doubt they think negatively, this is the fact. I was moving quite too fast and then domestic politics created turbulence, so I had no time for explaining.[53]

"Policy corruption" would also dog Thaksin throughout and partly underlie his overthrow. A Thai Foreign Ministry official cited "less rules and transparency" in China and greater profits in explaining both good deals and deals gone bad.[54] Senator Kraisak Choonhavan investigated the disappearance of 50,000 tons of fruit, yielding crates of empty Red Bull bottles in Thailand and a Chinese national executed for corruption: "Over-priced interests and cheated, so there you are."[55] But given the attributability of fraud to low-ranking individuals and China's lopsided economic gains, there was no evidence of the issue adversely affecting bilateral relations.

Thaksin sought to encourage investment with China as well, which in contrast to trade was heavily imbalanced in Thailand's favor. Following Surakiart's first trip to China in 2001, a Thailand–China Business Council was established and headed by a vice-chair of the storied CP Group, before opening branches in eleven southern Chinese provinces. The next year, China's Ministry of Commerce set up a Chinese–Thai Enterprises Association within the Bangkok embassy. In 2003, Thailand's Board of Investment (BoI) created a China desk headed by a "veteran China hand", and aimed to increase Chinese investment by 30 percent for the year. The actual figure proved a whopping 300 percent, with projects valued at $115 million and aided greatly by Beijing's underwriting of low construction bids. In 2004, the two nations founded the Thailand–China Joint Committee on Trade, Investment and Economic Cooperation, with Thaksin's "Mr. China" chairing the Thai side. A Thai–Chinese industrial estate in northern Thailand was planned in 2005, in which China would invest in pharmaceuticals, electronics and textiles. By then it had 154 projects in Thailand worth $773 million. "Bilateral trade is ballooning, and investment is likely to follow directly in its path", opined the US embassy.[56] The China State Construction Engineering Corporation and two other state-run entities were set to receive 20 percent of the contracts on a $24 billion infrastructure plan in 2006.

As with the FTA, however, both sides encountered obstacles and repercussions. The industrial estate was stalled, as lower Chinese labor costs began to harm Thailand's competiveness and its firms changed terms of payment. Both investors and their foreign partners struggled with the other's arcane ministries and regulations, and a lack of access to supply chains. The Worldbest company, despite arriving in 2001 and accounting for a quarter of all Chinese investment by 2006, continually complained of unreliable networks. Further, if stability and a consistent economic message attracted initial Chinese investment, tension in Bangkok and violence in the deep south acted as a brake later in Thaksin's term. Premier Wen Jiabao canceled a 2006 visit in which he had planned to announce $5 billion in loans to assist with Chinese investment.

Nevertheless, China invested more in Thailand that year than in any other ASEAN country. That it accounted even then for only 1 percent of Thailand's net foreign investment, in contrast to ten times more valuable Thai investment in China, showed how great the original imbalance was. But it would also make China's meteoric rise on Thailand's list of FDI over the next decade even more remarkable.

GATEWAY POLITICS

On the occasion of the FTA's signing in 2003, Thaksin's deputy prime minister stated that Thailand would continue to play a mediatory role between China and Southeast Asia. On its face, the issues were totally unrelated: one a formal trade agreement between two countries, the other an informal pledge by an ASEAN nation to facilitate relations between its fellow members and a rising global power. Yet the deputy spoke to a larger scene on which the FTA was just the latest window: both nations saw Thailand as a "gateway to ASEAN". The deep trade deficit with Thailand made any economic gains for China of an FTA far less certain and immediate than the political inroads it would afford. The same was true of the FDI imbalance, only more so. Partnered with an enhanced diplomatic approach, increased economic integration was measured by Beijing in geopolitical terms. And in Southeast Asia, Thailand was at the center of the geography and the politics.

In 2001 and 2003 respectively, Thaksin and Chinese President Hu Jintao each placed the other's country first on his foreign travel schedule; Thaksin would travel a second time to Beijing the same year. In his initial trip to China in 2001, Foreign Minister Surakiart met not only with Prime Minister Zhu Ronji—who pledged to reciprocate in Bangkok—but also with the Communist Party's head of foreign relations. In 2002, former premier Li Peng made his second visit to Thailand in three years as chair of the National People's Congress. Premier Wen Jiabao made a visit of his own in 2003, while Thaksin traveled back to Beijing once each year in 2003–2005. Senior Thai military and government officials attended PRC National Day in 2004. China's vice-premier visited Thailand in 2005 to discuss economic issues. That year, US Ambassador Boyce said that Thaksin "believes he has become a more important player on the global stage and, like other national leaders, responds favorably to suggestions or proposals pitched personally by prominent leaders such as Vladimir Putin or Hu Jintao".[57] A former Thai foreign minister went further, describing Thaksin's relations with the Chinese as "very intimate", leading them to believe "we can do anything with the Thai".[58] In China, according to CP's Sarasin: "Once the top decides, it cascades down to the bottom. Where in America it doesn't work that way, right? It is a different system. So if you have Hu Jintao agreeing with the Thai prime minister, then something happens, there will be a lot of interaction subsequent to that."[59]

Indeed, preceding the bilateral FTA, China signed a framework agreement with ASEAN in 2002 for a trade deal that would come into force three years later. Along with increased FDI, this was consistent with President Jiang Zemin's 2001 pledge to Surakiart that China would work for regional development. Surakiart characterized Zhu Ronji's subsequent visit as "testimony" to China's desire to "enhance Thailand's role as a gateway to southern China".[60] Thailand was the first country to agree to the ASEAN–China FTA, and began advocating use of the Chinese yuan as a regional currency. The Ministry of Commerce saw Chinese FDI as "an extension of its 'Go West' policy, opening up economic opportunities in China's western frontier and taking advantage of their southern provinces' relative proximity to Thailand".[61] Adding weight was the policy's exclusive focus on state-owned enterprises, which could win access, contracts, and market share through bids that otherwise made little economic sense. In Southeast Asia, this commenced in Thailand but was not designed to stop there.

Shovels were ready and jointly financed by China. A rudimentary and fragmented road linking northern Thailand via Myanmar with China's Yunnan province was significantly upgraded in 2003. Beginning the following year, the

Thai portion of another road was upgraded and a new section built, which linked a large town with a new port on the Mekong River separating Thailand and Laos. A bridge and road through Laos to Yunnan were planned for completion by the end of 2007. Thailand and China would thus be connected. Two new railway options for northern Thailand were also considered in 2004, both of which would run from the Mekong to a deep sea port in Bangkok. One would be built through Laos as another means of linking Thailand and China. In 2006, China's Guangxi autonomous area mooted road and rail proposals extending all the way to Thailand through Vietnam.

Thailand's Foreign Ministry was clear in 2004 that, both literally and figuratively, "Hu [Jintao] is building bridges … to ASEAN in a way Jiang never did".[62] By then, China had signed a separate agreement on the Mekong with Thailand and two neighbors, a China–ASEAN Joint Declaration on Non-Traditional Threats, and a regional agreement to combat piracy. It joined a major drugs raid in Myanmar, mediated a brief but violent dispute between Thailand and Cambodia, and pledged $85 million for the nations affected by the Boxing Day tsunami (sending two medical teams to the Thai coast). It also held the first annual China–ASEAN Expo and Business and Investment Summit. Most importantly, in 2003 China signed the ASEAN Treaty of Amity and Cooperation, and agreed to a regional "strategic relationship".

Tension over Chinese expansion arose within ASEAN, although concerned voices in Thailand were generally quiet and took a long and wide view. Senator Kraisak Choonhavan remained an early and consistent critic:

> The flooding of cheaper Chinese products in the north was unchecked because of the dams and the shipping. The water was set for ships to come in and deliver their goods, and after the sluice was cut for producing electricity for China. All of this manipulated the river itself in China's interest, while the locals were suffering from the unseasonable rise and fall of the river. The riverbanks were vulnerable, dirt collapsed, fish started to disappear. But China never carried back heavy loads upstream because the shallowness of the water could not carry the weight. So it was only a one-way ticket.[63]

China did not join the Mekong River Commission (MRC) and seldom consulted with its downstream neighbors. In late 2004, by which time the fish catch in northern Thailand had declined by half, Thailand's National Defense Studies Institute cited Chinese dams as a source of future tension. The National Intelligence Agency rightly assessed that they afforded Beijing greater influence over politics and security in ASEAN. More broadly, sources in the Foreign Ministry, National Intelligence Agency, and military all told the US that Beijing sought a "China-centric" ASEAN.[64] In turn, regional nations were cooperating because Japan was in decline and the US was "preoccupied in the Middle East and with the War on Terror".[65] ASEAN did resist Chinese pressure in 2003 to sign a Southeast Asia Nuclear Weapons-Free Zone protocol, but the Thai military was correct in predicting "that China's growing role in ASEAN will not allow the organization to act contrary to China's wishes ten years from now".[66]

HARD POWER

Within ASEAN, China's military links with Thailand under Thaksin were second only to those with Myanmar, which in contrast to Thailand's treaty ally status, was under US sanctions. Thaksin and the army proactively deepened "mil-to-mil" relations with China, partly as a hedge against inevitable but unforeseeable regional changes. To the extent he could anticipate advantages and preempt problems, Thaksin emulated China, which he described as "very calculating" in its military decision-making.[67] He likewise understood that although bilateral relationships require certain disaggregation to move forward, their constituent parts are never entirely independent of one another.

In a 2004 assessment of Thailand's National Defense College, "China says it does not want to be a superpower, but it seems to be moving in that way by acquiring better defense technology, improving its space program and modernizing its military."[68] A Thai diplomat was more specific: "Everyone is scared of the China threat, but if you can't fight it, you must accept it and become its friend. Build ties with that threat so that if they ever do hit you, they hit their own interests."[69] The prevailing view was that any optional Chinese military objective would be secondary to growing its economy, making Thaksin's primary emphasis on economic ties well-placed.

His recollection—"business as usual, with the Chinese wanting to sell weapons to the armed forces"—was on account of having had General Chavalit as his first defense minister.[70] It was also only partly accurate, as business was better than usual. In 2001, China extended $200 million in credit to both Thailand's army and navy toward the purchase of arms, waiving any interest for two years. It also sold Thailand rocket-propelled grenade launchers, and over the next five years would refurbish tanks and air defense equipment it had provided in the late 1980s. Evincing the interplay of Thaksin's foreign policy priorities, the Chinese would also consider a barter proposal involving armed vehicles for Thai fruit. China sold the Thai navy two missile-armed offshore-patrol boats in late 2002, and agreed to plans for two more. Affording the army and navy equal attention actually signaled growing emphasis on the latter. "Usual" however, was that the quality of most materiel remained low and most "commissions" high. The US remarked in 2004 that "Chinese defense sales delegations visit Bangkok frequently", referencing the remilitarization of Thailand's southern provinces.[71] Yet "[e]ven in southern Thailand, troops complained about the quality of Chinese gear that could not really protect them from anything, even something so simple as goggles".[72]

Four months after Thaksin was elected, Chavalit traveled to China and established annual defense meetings, enabled by his personal friendship with the defense minister. In 2004, Thailand's military noted, "For every one officer we send to Beijing for training, we send 400 to the United States."[73] But two years on the gap was closing, with most studying at Chinese defense colleges on scholarships provided by Beijing. A major Chinese ship visit to a port on the Andaman Sea took place in 2005, facilitated by a defense attaché described by Ambassador Boyce as "[e]ngaging, intelligent and well-informed".[74] In 2006 he would conclude that China wanted "more regular high level military talks, more Thai students at the PLA Command and General Staff College, a better international military education and training program, and subject matter expert exchanges".[75]

For the first time in 2002 and through to the end of Thaksin's term (save for 2004), China observed the Cobra Gold exercises on a limited basis. In turn, Thailand observed the PLA's "Northern Sword" exercises in 2003 and 2005, and "Iron Fist" in 2004. That year, the first Sino-Thai naval exercises were held in the Andaman Sea, followed by similar "China–Thailand Friendship" drills in the Gulf of Thailand in 2005. A joint search and rescue exercise took place in 2006. These were the first military exercises of any kind between China and a Southeast Asian country.

ONE CHINA AND BEYOND

A strategic partnership between Thailand and China (about which more in the next chapter) was mooted in September 2001 and launched four years later.

Yet for Beijing it was as much about the US as it was about Thailand; the one was a partner, the other the focus of its geopolitical strategy. As early as 2003, a Thai security advisor saw Hu Jintao's outmaneuvering of President Bush on a currency dispute as contributing to a "regional shift" already underway.[76] "China is trying to be the center of economic power in Asia, and it has demonstrated to the US that it has its own agenda."[77] Moreover, the Thais were not unwilling to state—or demonstrate—their position on China's rise; the Americans were informed. Exactly half-way through his tenure, Thaksin expressly told a group of Thai officials that he was emphasizing China over the US.

"During my administration we were strict on the One China policy", Thaksin recalled.[78] More than a half-century after the Chinese civil war and twenty-six years after Thailand formally recognized China, Surakiart committed to the policy during his 2001 visit to Beijing. Each of the next two years his ministry denied visas to Taiwanese officials. Thaksin further recalled that, "We could connect with Taiwan on trade, not politics", but alongside a US he deemed "not in Asia", he excluded a squarely Asian Taiwan from his Asia Coopera-tion Dialogue.[79] In 2004, the National Intelligence Agency said that China was using FTAs with ASEAN nations to "cut Taiwan out".[80] Yet even before its FTA with Thailand, the value of Thai exports to Taiwan versus China dropped from 67 percent to 46 percent between 2001 and 2003. Although FDI was markedly different—Taiwan remained Thailand's third largest source in 2006—it was becoming increasingly difficult to resist Chinese pressure to dismiss Taiwan's project bids. Beijing's invocation of One China also masked a still larger geopo-litical calculation: Taiwan was a mutual defense treaty ally of the US, which was in turn allied with Japan. The US and Japan were Thailand's top two trading partners, and the latter its largest source of FDI. "Cutting out" Taiwan was thus not "irrational" as described by the Thai military, but spelled a zero-sum gain vis-à-vis larger rivals.[81]

Another early announcement of a shift in Thai policy and Chinese power was the neutral response by Thaksin to a collision between a US intelligence aircraft and a Chinese interceptor fighter in April 2001. Long sensitive to competing territorial claims in the South China Sea, China was just beginning to assert and defend its own. Pending greater leverage, the next year it would sign a Declaration on the Conduct of Parties in the South China Sea. Thailand was never a party to the historical disputes, and saw no advantage in becoming one to this latest partial-proxy incident. That it took place above China's exclusive economic zone under disputed factual and legal circumstances assisted Thaksin's neutral response. At the same time, he would have known that neither party was going to see it that way. A cabinet minister confirmed in 2015 that Thaksin consistently used the South China Sea as "leeway to gain favor from the Chinese".[82] While he did have a relationship to maintain with the US—not a claimant beyond rights of flight and navigation—Thaksin had far more to gain by not siding with the Americans.

After Thaksin irritated Beijing in 2005 by backing Japan for a permanent seat on the UN Security Council—pressure from Tokyo was intense—he quickly compensated by equivocating on India's similar bid. A Foreign Ministry official suggested that the US encourage greater Japanese leadership in regional fora as a balance against China, adding that it "would be good for U.S. interests".[83] That he did "not see this as a zero sum game", however, betrayed a naivety shared by the Americans and only ensured that Thaksin would not repeat his mistake.[84]

RIGHTS REVERSAL

By a coincidence, the same month that Thaksin was elected, Thailand was elected a member of the UN Commission on Human Rights. Surakiart told the Commission that his country was "conscious of the sensitivities involved in blending international norms with national values", and that "We are ready to listen more. We are ready to understand more."[85] Yet, often citing or soliciting national support, Thaksin would preside over Thailand's worst human rights record since that of Field Marshal Sarit in 1957–1963. In the course of several brief years, the "Thai Spring" was cut down and trampled. It would not return. And his response in 2003 alone to UN concern was anything but to listen: "The UN is not my father" (February); "The UN does not give us rice to eat" (May); "We are not a UN lackey" (August).[86] Although Surakiart had personally told President Bush that Thailand wanted to see a credible body, it "expressed the view that human rights could be better promoted through positive reinforcement, rather than by 'publicly shaming' individual countries".[87] The same year, citing domestic sensitivity, it refused to vote with the Americans on criticizing grave violations in five Muslim-majority nations. Ever sending mixed human rights signals in Thailand, the US would support its second and unsuccessful bid for a seat in 2006, largely due to the even worse records of other candidates.

Consistent with a cabinet minister's explanation that Thaksin "didn't have a real concept of what human rights should be", he pressured Bangkok embassies to stop funding Thai NGOs.[88] He bought, threatened, and attacked media and journalists, beginning a steep decline in freedom of expression. In 2003, drawing comparisons to police general Phao from the 1950s, Thaksin waged a "War on Drugs" that killed over 2,500 people. At least half were victims of extrajudicial executions in what constituted a crime against humanity. He blocked the UN refugee agency from screening refugees in 2004, and despite considerable effort by the US embassy, repatriated twenty-six ethnic minority Hmong children to Laos. However, Thailand did approve a long-term US resettlement program, and worked with the embassy and Congress on cases of North Korean asylum-seekers. Its suggestion that the US involve Beijing in resettlement was a non-starter, however, as the North Koreans were also fleeing detention and repatriation by China.

Among the reasons given for the 2006 coup was Thaksin's handling of Thailand's southern Muslim insurgency, which reignited dramatically in 2004. The insurgents' escalating war crimes notwithstanding, Thaksin responded in kind: enforced disappearances, arbitrary detention, systematic torture, more extrajudicial executions. Explaining in 2015 that his plan was "to help the good people, get tough with the bad people", he complained that the military had its own rules of engagement and was difficult to "pull back".[89] Casting this deflection in its deadliest relief was a standoff ending in eighty-four dead protesters, most from suffocation in the back of a military truck. "I was very angry", Thaksin said, "But the military said they were afraid they would jump off because the truck was not meant for transporting prisoners."[90] Supporting the operation was a Vietnam War veteran who had earlier ignored the defense minister's order to deescalate another confrontation: thirty-two Muslims were gunned down.

* * *

According to historian David K. Wyatt, in the late 1950s Field Marshal Sarit "had been ruthless, grasping, arbitrary, and authoritarian. He had turned back the clock on parliamentary democracy and human rights, he had hitched Thailand's international position to the brightly blazing American star, and he had mortgaged the nation's future".[91] Thaksin's turn toward China was more measured than Sarit's toward the US, and China's geopolitical interests in

Thailand required less abuse for their protection. But Beijing's influence on rights under Thaksin was strong and growing. While Thaksin's interior minister recalled with satisfaction that China "never, never, never" commented on the deep south, in 2004 the Thais did begin consulting the Chinese on internal security matters.[92] The commander in charge of China's Xinjiang Uighur Autonomous Region met with the defense minister. The Uighurs shared an Islamic identity with most southern Thais, and those resistant to Beijing's domination had been deemed "terrorists". Thaksin was also interested in the counterterrorism efforts of the Shanghai Cooperation Organization, run by China and excluding the US. Reciprocally, Thaksin acted in Beijing's interest with regard to "splittists" it saw as threats to national security. Chinese media in Thailand was—rightly—permitted to run all order of propaganda on Beijing's policies in Xinjiang and Tibet, while domestic papers ran similar stories after China sponsored a trip to Tibet for Thai reporters in 2004. The following year, Thaksin reversed Chuan in accepting China's request to deny entry to the Dalai Lama. "We could connect with the Dalai Lama on culture and religion but not as head of state or government."[93]

In April 2001, pressure from both countries forced the Falungong to abandon a meeting in Bangkok. After initially repeating Chuan's citation of domestic law allowing the peaceful expression of beliefs, Thaksin ordered that the gathering not be used as a forum to criticize China. Demonstrating their political evolution in just the two years since Chuan departed, this time Sino-Thai groups vocally supported the hardline approach. Thailand's police chief was clear: "We want to keep good relations with China."[94] Similarly, the expulsion of Falungong adherents from the city before a 2003 APEC meeting was directly due to pressure from Beijing. However, the US embassy saw "no reason at this point to think the Thai will object to U.S. resettlement of the Falun Gong case" it urgently processed in 2005.[95] In Thaksin's words, "We cooperated but we never deported them because they had not really committed any crime. They may have some different ideology but we just stopped their activities—'Please don't do it, we don't want to hurt the relationship with China, don't do it'—and they said OK. But we never sent them back to China."[96]

But they sent others back, namely Chinese dissidents the US lost in a political tug-of-war. The Americans maintained a slight edge under Thaksin, but that China was even flexing its muscles on the issue was a new development and it would gain the advantage over the coming years. In 2001, China requested that Thailand investigate a man it claimed wanted to bomb its embassy. The Thais found no evidence of the specific claim, but said they found a letter from him to Taiwan's minister of defense about attacking China. Lacking grounds to bring charges, Thailand deported him and barred him from reentry, before he was promptly imprisoned in China. A US senator pressed the Thais for more information, even as "PRC officials in Bangkok were actively pressuring" them—generally via cash transfers.[97] An officer told the Americans he "did not want himself or the RTP [Royal Thai Police] to be a tool for the political agenda of other nations", but that was precisely the case.[98]

In 2004, however, human rights prevailed twice. First, Surakiart asked the UN to assess a well-known Chinese dissident's asylum claim, and the US to resettle him in seven days. Second, when two members of a Chinese rock band arrived after a pro-Taiwan performance, "high-level Chinese officials subsequently requested Prime Minister Thaksin during a visit to Beijing to deport the pair to China".[99] Although Thaksin ordered their arrest, the authorities turned a blind eye when they were quickly and quietly smuggled to Cambodia and into the hands of Swedish officials. How much interference there was from US diplomats was unclear. The UN also had records of at least 100 less prominent Chinese asylum-seekers, some of whom it was able to resettle to the US or elsewhere. In Thaksin's words, "We never wanted to send back women or children, we had to be cautious."[100]

Between *refoulement* and resettlement was involuntary removal across a border. After the "Chinese had leaned on them", Thai authorities pressured a dissident to accept this move in 2005, assuring him that neither side would interfere in a discreet reentry into Thailand.[101] Resisting the idea, he was sent nonetheless. After news of another dissident's arrest appeared on US websites, Thailand refused to send him back without an official extradition request, but allowed Chinese officials to visit him in detention. Telling the Americans they were trying to balance humanitarian considerations, sustainable policy, and relations with Beijing, the Thais then pressured the dissident to accept deportation across a border. They also claimed they could not be seen as "doing whatever the United States wanted".[102] The dissident likewise refused the offer but was still removed. Thaksin's conclusion was thus not entirely consistent with the record: "We only sent back those who really committed a serious crime—not like in the War on Terror, but not for ideological differences."[103]

THE CHINA MODEL

Four months after his election, Thaksin said that Thailand would not interfere in neighboring countries, "but we will convince them that democracy is better because we are now tasting the good food of democracy … Instead of trying to force them to change their eating habits, we could persuade them to taste some democracy".[104] Six months before the 2006 coup, his ideologue Pansak would tell the US deputy assistant secretary of state (and future ambassador to Thailand) that he wished to "export" democracy: "After Rangoon, we go to Beijing … if successful, we can export to your guys in Latin America".[105] The historical irony in these statements was that, within Sino-Thai relations under Thaksin, the governance imbalance was entirely in China's favor. Bangkok imported from Beijing an authoritarian capitalism it had not so embraced since the days of Sarit, who was the first to speak of a "Thai way of democracy".[106] Like Sarit (but not like China), Thaksin, his opponents, and his successors would all evoke democracy in their undemocratic pursuit of political power and economic gain.

The foremost factor in this was Thaksin himself. According to early team member Sarasin, "Thaksin was very clear: 'I am going to use democracy as the means to my end', and that is authoritarianism."[107] Assisting him was a 1997 constitution designed to increase executive power, and whose "infrastructure" for checks and balances he neutralized. During his 2005 reelection campaign, he criticized democracy as getting in the way of "working for the people".[108] Indeed, accounting for both the indisputable legitimacy of the Thaksin government and a cognitive dissonance that attends any analysis of his actual governance, was the huge majority of Thais who consistently voted for him. Having put him in power, they readily accepted his authoritarianism: an estimated three-quarters of the population supported his War on Drugs.

Conversely, Thai civil society proved unworthy as a political factor outside of niche issues. Born of the "Thai Spring" and a beneficiary of the financial crisis, it had not grown large or strong enough to withstand Thaksin's demonization. Thailand's praetorian history, culture of hierarchy and patronage, and educational system of rote learning and hostility to critical thinking also conspired against it. As "[a]ll the Thai translations of 'citizen' are words invented by the state to enforce duties on the people, not rights", non-governmental organizations were easily tarred as non-representative, non-useful, non-Thai.[109] Further, when such outfits finally rose to the challenge in 2005, they did so as founders, members, and supporters of the People's Alliance for Democracy (PAD), dedicated to

Thaksin's departure. Since the premier had twice won the popular vote and the PAD sought to replace democratic elections with selected leaders, only the third of its name claiming an alliance was accurate. It also argued that coups should be expressly provided for in the constitution. Joining Sondhi Limthongkul at the top of the PAD leadership was Chamlong Srimuang, the army's "Young Turk" who had likewise parroted "democracy" in continuing his power-play after Suchinda's 1992 coup. Notably, the PAD enjoyed the support of the Democrat Party—which had not won an election since 1992—and important factions of the military. While backing from the palace was initially tacit at best, the PAD evoked a royalism from the beginning as a rhetorical means to its own ends. Thus was Network Monarchy not only pitted against Thaksin, but assigned a set of reactionary characteristics and aims for the new century.

According to Human Rights Watch's Thai specialist, the PAD saw Thaksin "as an authoritarianism that could be brought down by corruption. They saw this with nostalgia for the 1970s when they went to the jungle and most of them adopted Maoist ideology. They still had this nostalgia about China. They admired Mao's authoritarianism".[110] To be clear, despite their affinity for the Chinese, neither side of Thailand's new political divide was advocating to expressly adopt China's system of governance. The form alone—an all-important Communist Party overseeing both the PLA and the economy—was vastly different from Thailand's praetorian Network Monarchy and globalized nouveau riche. And as late as 2006, a small minority of rank-and-file PAD members still harbored truly democratic motivations. But each side increasingly believed that the level and nature of its support—the monarchy and the electorate, respectively—gave it the right to govern exclusively and unquestionably. The political opposition became the enemy, media and NGO criticism lies, the rule of law subjective, respect for human rights conditional. That is, in spirit and substance, China's model of an authoritarian government backed by a market economy was gaining hold across the board. "The Chinese dynamo affects Thai politics", Pansak told the Americans in 2006, "and the old elite don't even know it."[111]

COUP

On the evening of 19 September 2006, tanks rolled through Bangkok in a swift and virtually bloodless coup. It was the country's first in fifteen years and the eleventh since 1932, in addition to seven failed attempts. Thaksin was in New York to deliver an address to the UN General Assembly the following day.

Instead, across the globe in Beijing, a spokesperson for China's foreign minister gave a brief comment:

> The changes taking place inside Thailand are its domestic affairs. The Chinese Government consistently pursues the principle of non-interference in internal affairs of other countries ... We wish Thailand harmony, prosperity, peace and stability. We hope to see constant development of the friendly relations between China and Thailand.[112]

Premier Wen Jaibao would send a widely reported letter to Thailand's Ministry of Foreign Affairs, stating that the "traditional friendship between China and Thailand dates back to ancient times" and that the countries "are like each other's relatives with friendly feelings".[113]

Within China's own ministry, however, its top diplomats to Thailand "lost credibility with the Chinese leadership for failing to predict the coup". The ambassador was temporarily recalled to Beijing, as the *Guangming Daily*'s Bangkok-based reporter was tapped to brief officials. This was inconsistent with the embassy's reputation, demonstrated the level of expectation placed upon it by Beijing, and spurred a redoubling of attention and activity. "Working through the night of September 19 ... their initial focus, after reporting on breaking events, was to provide analysis to Beijing on whether China's close relationship with deposed PM Thaksin Shinawatra would hurt bilateral relations".[114] The ambassador would return in time to meet Thailand's new military premier before he chose a cabinet, an opportunity provided first and otherwise only to the Americans.

Despite losing its most engaged Thai partner in modern history, Beijing had nothing to fear. Its embassy rightly "advised Beijing that China's influence in Thailand remains strong for a variety of reasons: growing commercial links, cultural ties, collegial diplomatic relations, and growing military cooperation programs".[115] In late 2006 this was due as much to Thaksin's efforts as anything else, but it was certainly not confined to one man or even two nations; the Americans would continue their unwitting assistance. "The Chinese are about institutions, not about democratic values, so the Chinese were business as usual" after the coup, according to Thaksin.[116] The Chinese offered him a house on the outskirts of Beijing and promised to send a high-ranking official to the airport whenever he visited the country—"Every time", he confirmed in 2015. "They never forget their old friends."[117]

Chapter Eight:
Another American War
(Thailand and the US, 2001–2006)

I don't care. Because nothing happened. We felt proud we had been granted major non-NATO status because we supported in Iraq after the war, but nothing happened really. I still don't know even now what is the benefit of major non-NATO ally status.[1]

Thaksin Shinawatra, August 2015

And then there is China. Some are concerned about Chinese inroads into Thailand and indeed the region as a whole. The Thaksin government seems to be embracing the Chinese wholeheartedly. Thailand is being portrayed as the gateway to China. Is this a concern for the U.S.? With the benefit of three months' reflection, it seems to be less of a zero-sum game than might appear. The Chinese are indisputably very active ... But is every Chinese gain necessarily at our expense? ... This is China's neighborhood, and while they were out of the picture for fifty years after the end of World War II (precisely the period when U.S. presence was paramount), they are back, and they are bringing the A team. For reasons of geography, we cannot realistically match the Chinese visit-for-visit. But we are capable of directing more high-level attention to the region, and we should.[2]

Ralph "Skip" Boyce, March 2005

The ways in which the terrorist attacks of September 2001 altered the trajectory of American relations with Thailand are cause for regret and reproach. While stipulating Thaksin's Asia-centric nationalism and the geostrategic element of China's nascent rise, nothing accounts more for the decline in US–Thai relations under President Bush than his reaction to "9/11". An unwelcome if undeniable catalyst for renewed engagement was seen by Washington as a license to dictate

Bangkok's policies abroad and its unlawful practices at home. Recalling another ideological war a half-century before, the US learned none of its lessons in the War on Terror. Continuing a single-minded focus on security that even 1997 had failed to broaden, it approached relations almost entirely through the laws, language and logic of force. Moreover, rather than leverage this perspective to its political fullest by invoking time-honored security pacts, the Americans regarded their treaty ally as any other nation: "with them or with the terrorists". They took Thaksin's initial hesitation as betrayal and his reversals for granted. And just as the US had undermined its similar Cold War message of freedom by helping suppress democracy in Thailand, after 9/11 it imitated its attackers by attacking their human rights. By the time Thaksin wrote to Bush complaining of his opponents' "threat to democracy" three months before they overthrew him, Thailand was not the only country lacking the genuine interest and credibility to do anything about it.[3]

Even more consequential than the War on Terror's Manichean prosecution was its preemption from the US agenda of a situation actually warranting a zero-sum approach. Between 11 September and the war in Afghanistan twenty-six days later, Washington began a dramatic pull-back from a Southeast Asia in which Beijing was increasingly engaged, allowing the region's geopolitics to advance without its interest or participation. Save for the continuance of certain 20th century agreements and activities—signaling stagnation more than strength—the US did not match Chinese efforts in growing its relations with Thailand or ASEAN. Indeed continuance spelled the exception; in most areas the Americans fell even further behind by downgrading, scaling back, or deemphasizing their engagement. Most damningly, this American retreat was pursuant not to a policy calculation but to a policy vacuum, created by a War on Terror that sucked up monetary and military resources, career ambition, and political will at a rate not seen since the height of the Cold War.

Foreign Minister Surakiart explained and complained: "My first year was 9/11, the second year Afghanistan, my third year Iraq, my fourth year still Iraq. And then between the war, weapons of mass destruction, anti-terrorism dialogue, intel cooperation, the sale of this and that, the arrest of Hambali—where was the economic approach? Where was *China*?"[4] While it had been fashionable since the start of the modern relationship six decades prior to complain of American heavy-handedness and inattention, growing frustration with a blinkered ally was both justified and communicated. Even Thai leaders uneasy with Thaksin's prioritization of China found in the US a largely unavailable and uninterested alternative. Quickly ceding ground regained after their bungled response to the financial crisis, the Americans simply left the regional reins to a China engaging the whole region. In that respect, the Thaksin era resembled that of General Prem twenty years earlier, only in reverse. China was becoming the ally deepening ties across the board; the US—recalling Chinese belligerence with Vietnam—offered only security alongside a primary focus on its own.

TERROR AND TORTURE

Thaksin joined the War on Terror in stages, attempting to balance relations with the world's only superpower with qualitative gains for Thailand. By his own admission he was largely unsuccessful, winning only cosmetic, unfulfilled, or self-defeating concessions. Among the latter was a freer hand in dealing with the issue he repeatedly cited as the reason for withholding assistance: Thailand's small but sensitive Muslim population. Also influencing him would have been the establishment of a US–Thai regional Counter-terrorism Intelligence Center in Bangkok several months *before* 9/11, and a new draft security bill (to replace the 1952 Anti-Communist Act). Seemingly ahead of the curve, Thaksin was clear that his country would be "strictly neutral" in the newly declared war, unmoved by Surakiart's pledge two weeks after the attacks to "render all possible assistance to the United States".[5] He rejected a US request—last made seven years earlier—for permission to position ships in the Gulf of Thailand for its campaign in Afghanistan and, until duly reminded of relevant 1993 and 1996 agreements, "dithered" in allowing use of a Vietnam-era airbase for the same.[6] More seriously, he refused to contribute Thai troops to the effort. Thailand did assign its Internal Operations Security Command (ISOC; successor to the anti-communist CSOC) to lead anti-terrorism efforts, and sign a fifth (of twelve) terror-related treaty in December 2001. But a "perceived lack of support at the United Nations" threatened to derail Thaksin's visit to Washington the same month.[7]

Surakiart recalled that Secretary of State "Colin Powell understood us very well but the National Security Council was very upset. They almost did not receive Thaksin on an official visit, so I sent Nitya Songkram to talk to many of our old friends—Wolfowitz, Jackson, Armitage—and try to overrule it."[8] Nitya was the son of dictator Phibun Songkram, who had ruled Thailand on and off through 1957, while Paul Wolfowitz and Richard Armitage were second in charge at Defense and State, respectively. Karl Jackson "protested that I didn't work for the NSC anymore, but said I would do what I could".[9] Having already warned Thaksin of a "truly disastrous visit to Washington", Jackson received a call at home "about 48 hours before Thaksin was supposed to land in DC: 'I've changed the policy 180 degrees, can you get the American government in line?'"[10] Having just replaced his ambassador in Washington, Thaksin effectively had no one on the ground, while Jackson had to contend with US holiday absences. Two days later, the ambassador accompanied Thaksin en route to the Pentagon "trying to explain that only Wolfowitz and not Defense Secretary Rumsfeld would be meeting him, when they pulled in, an automatic door opened up, and just behind the Marine guard came Rumsfeld running down the ramp for a just-in-time delivery".[11]

As the visit's joint statement noted a "mature partnership" and a pledge to contribute to Afghanistan's reconstruction, Thaksin would join Bush in reversing their predecessors' commitment to an International Criminal Court, and deploy 130 troops (mostly engineers).[12] As it also would the following year, Thailand hosted US-led "Ellipse Charlie" counterterrorism exercises in 2002, and contributed several experts to a UN team looking for weapons of mass destruction in Iraq. Washington began referring to Bangkok as an "ally" in its efforts.

*　*　*

The most significant aspect of US–Thai cooperation in the War on Terror was never intended to become public. It was also indisputably unlawful under international, US, and Thai law, and constituted a crime against humanity for which officials from both nations should be held accountable. Surakiart's words in 2002 were thus as patently inaccurate as they were ironic in their selection: "We are fully committed to *render* all possible support to the international fight against terrorism, in accordance with international laws" (emphasis added).[13] Thailand was one of at least fifty-four nations to participate in the CIA's program of "extraordinary rendition", wherein at least 136 terror suspects were sent to "black sites" for interrogation and torture by Americans. Thailand was one of eight nations to host at least one such site.

The program was rooted in a 2002 memorandum by President Bush, informed by an agency charged with testing interrogation techniques considered unlawful under the Geneva Conventions. Despite characterizing his response to 9/11 as a war, Bush decided that the Conventions—the laws of war—did not apply to detainees suspected of terrorism. They protect prisoners of war from techniques "based, in part, on Chinese Communist techniques used during the Korean war to elicit false confessions".[14] The techniques constituted torture. Two months later, a Pentagon expert in torture's "reverse engineering" proposed that an "exploitation facility" be established, off-limits to all but an interrogation team.[15] In consultation with the White House, the Department of Justice issued three legal opinions. One defined torture in such a way as to exclude the techniques considered unlawful under the Geneva Conventions. Another listed ten techniques it explicitly deemed lawful, including waterboarding. It also determined that the techniques would not come under the jurisdiction of the International Criminal Court, which had come into effect the previous month and covered torture. Thus for the next several years, Americans tortured detainees under "legal" cover invented for the purpose.

The third legal opinion pertained specifically to the first time the torture was used—in the Kingdom of Thailand in June 2002—prior to the opinion itself. Captured in Pakistan, Abu Zubaydah, a Palestinian, was rendered to a black site in Thailand, likely the original "exploitation facility" and the same U-Tapao airbase US planes were using for flights to and from Afghanistan. After three months of lawful treatment, a former US air force psychologist and agents of the US Federal Bureau of Investigation (FBI) and the CIA began torturing Zubaydah. One CIA official unwittingly spoke to the legal prohibition against torture as treatment or punishment, in describing their techniques as "coercive" and "corrective".[16] Zubaydah was stripped naked, bombarded with loud music, deprived of sleep, and subjected to frigid temperatures. Known to have a great fear of insects, he was threatened with having one placed with him in a box. By both design and default, his treatment was experimental, coming not only before "legal" guidance but ten months before the CIA's medical guidelines. Although the CIA had told the Department of Justice that Zubaydah would be tortured "up to thirty days ... in some sort of escalating fashion, culminating with the waterboard", two months of unauthorized escalation had already occurred.[17]

The torture then intensified. "Interrogators wrapped a towel around Abu Zubaida's neck and slammed him into a plywood wall mounted in his cell. He was slapped in the face. He was placed in a coffin-like wooden box in which he was forced to crouch, with no light and a restricted air supply."[18] Over four days, he was waterboarded at least eighty-three times, an average of almost twenty-one times per day. Unconvinced that he was fully cooperating, more CIA officials flew from the US to witness a final waterboarding themselves.

Zubaydah was detained in Thailand through at least April 2003, seven months after Congress was briefed on the unlawful action, before a tour of other black sites ended in Guantanamo Bay in 2006.

Ramzi bin al-Shibh of Yemen and Abd al-Rahim al-Nashiri of Saudi Arabia were also captured abroad in 2002, and rendered to a facility called the "Cat's Eye" in Thailand's northeastern Udon Thani province.[19] Its previous *nom de guerre* was the "Elephant Corral"—the Ramasun intelligence station shuttered in 1976 and occupied by the Voice of America radio station since 1994. Although the *New York Times* exposed the black sites in June 2003, two months later Mohammed Nazir bin-Lep of Malaysia was apprehended in Bangkok, where he alleged he was kept naked and denied solid food for several days. Three others were captured in Thailand in 2002 and 2003 and wound up in Guantanamo. Finally, Fatima Bouchar and her husband Abdul Hakim Belhadj of Libya were apprehended in Malaysia in 2004, rendered under false pretenses to Thailand on a commercial flight, and allegedly "abused by the CIA for several days in a special room in the airport".[20] This was most likely Don Muang airport located in north-central Bangkok. The couple were reportedly beaten and chained to a wall, their legs resting in an ice container, and deprived of food for five days. Bouchar was nearly five months pregnant.

According to the director of the CIA's Counter-terrorism Center, Thailand was "promised three things: our gratitude, a sizable amount of money, and our assurances that we would do everything in our power to keep their support secret. We were eventually able to deliver only two out of the three".[21] US Ambassador Boyce, admittedly not on the ground until late 2004, stated that, "I don't know anything about black sites because there weren't any on my watch—if there was such a thing going on. If there were sites there were people running them obviously and who knew about them. But I didn't need to know because there weren't any there when I was there."[22] However, an official who served under Boyce claimed to know where ninety-two interrogation videotapes were kept inside the embassy. According to the CIA, the tapes were "to ensure a record of Abu Zubaydah's medical condition and treatment should he succumb to his wounds and questions arise about the medical care provided him by the CIA".[23] It ordered their destruction in November 2005, along with those of al-Nashiri.

Thai officials denied press reports, pledged to investigate, and even briefly considered suing the *Washington Post*. Following news of the "Cat's Eye", Thaksin's spokesperson and the Foreign Ministry immediately contacted the US embassy for "assistance in denying the allegation".[24] The embassy referred them to the CIA, before granting a request by the district governor and the local press to briefly visit the facility. Boyce recalled Surakiart worriedly asking if he knew anything about the sites, afraid that Thaksin had made a secret deal. Looking back, Surakiart simply emphasized "deep intel cooperation",[25] while Pansak was characteristically cryptic: "Never mind, that's a silly thing."[26] In 2010, a civilian government led by Thaksin's opponents denied the sites' existence to the UN, before the NSC protested: "The CIA is capable of running its own operations without having to ask for help from Thailand."[27] Thaksin himself "issued heated denials" of the reports,[28] and in a meeting with Boyce, "chuckled at how the Thai media had gotten the mistaken idea that VOA's Udorn facility was one of those 'black prisons'".[29] He also pled ignorance in retrospect:

> I don't know but I heard that there was cooperation between security officers at that level, that they allowed the CIA or FBI to investigate, to interrogate those we arrested. I really don't know what was going on, but after I left office I heard that there was some cooperation at the working level, at the official level, that never came up to me at the political level.[30]

* * *

2003 saw more pirouettes. In the run-up to the March invasion of Iraq, Surakiart told Secretary of State Powell "that we can help you more by not joining the Coalition of the Willing, and we did help them more. But they were not very happy with Thailand".[31] The Thais ordered Iraqi intelligence officers to leave the country, but again noting their own Muslim minority, initially refused permission for the use of U-Tapao. "We said, in 200 years of our diplomatic history, we have never joined a war with anyone but have helped in post-conflict reconstruction—we did in Afghanistan."[32] Triggering protests at both the US embassy and northern consulate, Thailand soon succumbed to the pressure and opened the airbase, but it refused to be publicly identified as supporting the invasion.

Bouts of political quid pro quo followed. Before Thaksin was to meet Bush in Washington in June—the same month the *Times* exposed the black sites— he agreed to exempt US personnel in Thailand from the ICC's jurisdiction, which was to commence on 1 July. The Thai black sites were closed the same year, but the CIA's rendition program would not officially end until 2008.

Reportedly in exchange for the agreement, Bush announced at the meeting that, "the United States is actively considering Thailand's designation as a Major Non-NATO Ally".[33] Although the status afforded access to special arms purchases and training, it was largely "cosmetic" for a Thailand party to both the Manila Pact and Thanet–Rusk memo.[34] Not to be outdone, also on the day of the meeting Thai authorities detained three Thai Muslims in the deep south, allegedly connected to bombings in Bali the previous October. Two reportedly confessed to a bomb plot against the American and four other embassies during an upcoming APEC meeting Bush was planning to attend. All would eventually be released two years later due to lack of evidence, but the political benefit until then was considerable. Thais demonstrated outside the White House but were not heard by either party inside.

Also in mid-2003, Thaksin arrested the leader of the Bali bombings three days before issuing two executive decrees against terrorism. Having ordered the arrest on immigration grounds, he cited the decrees "as the legal basis for placing Hambali in U.S. custody".[35] In between, the suspect was tortured for several days—stress positions, nudity, food deprivation—although it was not clear by whom. Thaksin thus remained one step ahead of domestic law and well behind international rules. Moreover, by choosing executive decree over parliament, he caused "fear that the United States has abandoned its policies of the 1990s to promote due process and transparent government in favor of urging Southeast Asians to adopt stricter internal security laws".[36] Thaksin's summation in 2015 was revealing: "We had to consider case by case, not just anyone that they wanted and then send him. We had to be sure that he was a real culprit, a real terrorist. The case of Hambali was quite clear, he was a high-ranking member of al-Qaeda. So if we didn't cooperate it would not be good for us."[37]

Finally, due to a "long-standing Thai fear that if we didn't do it relations with the US would be damaged",[38] Thailand sent 423 troops to Iraq in September 2003.[39] Billed as a humanitarian and peacekeeping mission, it suffered two fatalities but was replaced by 443 new troops after six months. At the time, Thaksin said that "Thailand and the US are allies. When the US requests help from us, we respond. It is a gesture of hospitality."[40] In retrospect he said, "We cooperated because we regarded that issue as for the whole world, not only the US. If we didn't cooperate, we would feel like we were not a good world citizen. But we had to cooperate in our way that was acceptable to our own citizens as well."[41] In between, however, after the US requested troops in 2004 for another year,

Thaksin was less sanguine: "You will get no cooperation, assistance or dialogue with the US if you refuse to talk of cooperation to suppress terrorism."[42] His second foreign minister recounted the dilemma:

> The generals and most people were uncomfortable, feeling that it would aggravate the already bad situation in southern Thailand. The ideal situation would have been not to send any more troops to Iraq. But the generals and everyone were saying that we don't want to but we have to because the US would get angry and we'll have to do it.[43]

In Washington, however, he met with Rice and Rumsfeld:

> I explained to her that we would like to do that for our friends, but that the problem is the southern part of Thailand, and it's very difficult for us. How about another way? We could help with training, with medical assistance, but no troops. And she accepted it. Rumsfeld asked the same thing, but I explained in the same way and no problem. So this fear was unfounded.[44]

Yet in 2005, the US Joint Chiefs of Staff sent a letter to Thailand's commander-in-chief seeking officers for a multinational headquarters in Baghdad; "Thaksin has shown the capacity to make a tough decision and we want Thailand's renewed support for Iraq operations."[45] Although Thailand issued a public statement of support for Iraq's new transitional government, Boyce's response was "that to be an active member of the coalition, presence on the ground was the proof. We left it at that".[46] After the defense minister received a direct query from Secretary Rumsfeld and the rotation of troops was missed, the foreign minister reiterated his offer of training and assistance but was otherwise clear: "The Thai government would continue to work with the U.S., but a future deployment of Thai troops to Iraq or Afghanistan was out of the question due to sensitivities over the situation in southern Thailand."[47]

RIGHTS GONE SOUTH

The reigniting in 2004 of Thailand's southern Muslim insurgency both caused and coincided with growing suspicion and frustration at American interference in the kingdom. More than the use of U-Tapao, the CIA's rendition program, domestic legal action, or even the deployment of Thai troops—all clearly pursuant to another American "war"—the insurgency was a Thai problem on Thai soil. And although its historical roots predated new US interest, the south appeared ripe and ready-made for the same US exploitation that had attended its communist analogue decades before. Three conclusions are in order. First, the perception of many informed and interested Thais was that the Americans were fomenting and funding the southern violence. Second, while the US was far more involved than leaders of both countries stated, the perception of purposeful manipulation or exploitation was unfounded. Third, Washington's unlawful policies and practices in the War on Terror were factors in the escalation of violence and rights violations in the deep south.

However politically expedient the perception was for some, its expression in Thailand's parliament and press had penetration nationwide. Thai Muslims both in and outside the south (less than 10 percent of the population) were particularly suspicious of US moves and motives. In 2003, Islamic committees of the five southernmost provinces described the US as a "terror state", and protested at the conferral of major non-NATO status on Thailand.[48] A southern senator stated in 2004 that "Local people believe the CIA has played a role in what's happening here."[49] Even the Cobra Gold military exercises were "interpreted negatively in the South".[50] Moreover, before its center of gravity moved to the northeast, Thailand's Communist Party had been strongest in the same provinces bordering "Malaya". The US had consistently overstated that threat to get Bangkok more firmly onboard with its anti-communist crusade. If the enemy of "freedom" had merely changed its name, it was not unreasonable for Thais to perceive its self-appointed champion as remaining the same as well.

In 2005, General Surayud and Ambassador Boyce discussed "rumors" that the latter's predecessor had visited the south three times and offered indeterminate US assistance.[51] Anand not only cited "pervasive" rumors of US links to officials involved in extrajudicial executions, but intimated he believed some to be true: "I'm concerned the CIA is talking to the wrong people."[52] Chuan's former foreign minister—a southern Muslim himself—told a visiting US Senate staff member that "the entire South could turn against the U.S. if the rumors continue".[53] After two Americans were injured by an explosion in the south, Thai senators said that "the Pentagon orchestrated recent bombings".[54] Boyce told Washington that such claims were "widespread and widely accepted",[55] "hurt the bilateral relationship",[56] and "are variations on two conspiratorial themes: 1) the U.S. Military is inciting Muslims to violence in order to justify establishing bases in the region; 2) the CIA is funding the insurgents in order to justify an expanded U.S. presence in the region for the Global War on Terror".[57]

As for American and official Thai assessments, Boyce and Army Commander Sonthi concurred that the insurgency was driven by ethnic and not religious tension. The US noted that Thailand had not co-sponsored any designations of terrorists to the UN committee on the same[58], and "does not have any indigenous terrorist groups".[59] A deputy secretary of state remarked that Thaksin "clearly doesn't understand what he's up against. I think that's the real problem ... he will find his way to the answer down there. But it is very distressing for all of us who consider ourselves friends of Thailand to see this playing out so painfully".[60] Both countries initially agreed that the insurgents were acting without influence or involvement of regional or global terrorist networks. Yet the United States Pacific Command (PACOM) warned that the south could "become a staging ground from which outsiders could launch terrorist acts".[61] Thaksin said the insurgency was "an issue that potentially reaches beyond Thailand's borders".[62] Going further, his defense minister surmised that insurgents had met terrorists while studying abroad or even received training in Indonesia, Pakistan, or Afghanistan. Most strongly, the NSC noted that a prominent southern Muslim leader had met the Bali bombings' Hambali before his capture in 2003.

Perceptions and public relations aside, it was simply not in the interests of the United States to place the insurgency in the context of the War on Terror; Thailand sent troops to Afghanistan and twice to Iraq only before its own insurgency reignited. The US provided extensive assistance to be sure, but it went to unusually coordinated lengths to exclude Thai insurgents from "the terrorists". To the extent it was in Thailand's interests to cooperate, either toward avoiding American "anger" or securing its largesse, Thaksin was attuned and decisive. For the most part, however, Thai leadership genuinely believed that US involvement in the south would do far more harm than good.

The US urged Thaksin to shore up security as early as January 2002, two years before the situation reignited and the Counter-terrorism Intelligence Center shifted its focus to the south. US Special Forces began training Thai soldiers, and Thaksin's interior minister recalled receiving "top information" from the US on the insurgents.[63] A PACOM intelligence program for the south was denied in 2005—prompting an embassy cable, "US Assistance in the South, Thanks but No Thanks"—but it carried out a Military Support to Public Diplomacy program to clarify and reinforce US policy.[64] In response to a journalist's question on potential US involvement, Anand suggested he "Tell them to stay the hell out of here."[65] Yet a US general invited Thai army officials to visit Joint Forces Command in Virginia to explore "inter-force" possibilities in the south.

On the diplomatic side, before a 2005 meeting with Bush, Thaksin determined that "if he doesn't raise the issue, I will".[66] Bush commended a National Reconciliation Commission chaired by Anand. Thailand's NSC asked Boyce to talk with six Muslim leaders, and embassy officials traveled regularly to the south to oversee "a vigorous outreach program".[67] This included "American corners" at universities, in-kind donations, English language instruction, media programming in the local dialect, International Visitors and Fulbright educational programs, an embassy speaker program, and an Ambassador's Fund for Cultural Preservation. The US also proposed programs in partnership with southern civil society, including a study on anti-terrorism movements, democracy programming for community radio stations, and empowerment of Muslim women. USAID administered a $500,000 program implemented by the Asia Foundation, focusing on citizen engagement and the media. Although the Foundation's former director described it as "heavy-handed" and "lacking the right people",[68] he also recalled the Thais not wanting even the "right" Americans in the south—"It hurt the relationship."[69]

Tensions continued into 2006, by which time over 2,500 Thai soldiers had been trained by the US and Army Commander Sonthi was directly involved. Both sides agreed that all assistance would be located and labeled without any express link to the insurgency, as the training facility previously proposed for counterterrorism exercises was revisited for counterinsurgency operations. US marines taught rules of engagement, Joint Combined Exchange Training (JCET) focused on information warfare, and PACOM expanded its efforts to counter ideological support and increase area-specific sensitivities. Anand asked the State Department to issue a statement in support of his commission's report, but to avoid a "kiss of death" by ensuring that the south was labeled a purely Thai issue.[70] The embassy proposed a "bold, new inter-agency plan to refocus our assistance, combat Thai shortcomings, and help the government reverse some of its losses in the South".[71] Legal advisors would focus on improving police and prosecutorial performance, while the International Law Enforcement Academy would train "Thai agencies—including the military—in everything from basic investigative techniques to more advanced counterterror strategies".[72] The embassy also urged Washington to fund the border control computer system for southern crossing points. The US Bureau of Alcohol, Tobacco, Firearms and Explosives analyzed improvised explosive devices (IEDs), finding that a "handful of individuals are producing the majority of bombs", thanks to "a single Chinese industrial supplier on the internet".[73]

* * *

Unlike its 20th century antecedent, Thailand's insurgency largely garnered constructive American input and assistance. US diplomats, generals, and politicians all made human rights a priority, and intensified their efforts after a series of deadly incidents in 2004. Moreover, Thaksin and the military excepted, the Thai leadership readily accepted the message and training, agreeing that rights violations were exacerbating the situation. A member of Anand's commission encouraged the US to translate its annual human rights report into the southern dialect. In Washington, Thai Ambassador (and future foreign minister) Kasit Piromya, having long since turned against Thaksin, voiced concern. The embassy monitored the trial of a prominent Muslim lawyer who was forcibly disappeared, while the US Defense Institute of International Legal Studies ensured "more comprehensive human rights training for military forces before they deploy to the South".[74] Most of this was via JCET in Thailand and International Military Education and Training (IMET) in the US. Pursuant to a US law conditioning military assistance to foreign units on human rights compliance, the embassy vetted all those selected for training. In 2005, it received "recent information indicating that 7 individuals from the 2nd Cavalry Division and 11 persons from the Special Warfare Command have links to human rights abuses".[75] PACOM's team for public diplomacy and counterterrorism also had a human rights element.

In the run-up to his 2005 meeting with Thaksin, the embassy advised the president to ask that a new emergency decree "not be used to justify human rights abuses in the south".[76] Boyce then followed up in a meeting of his own with the prime minister:

> I told him that we had heard disquieting rumors that lists of suspected
> militants had been drawn up by authorities—to be targeted for
> extrajudicial killing … If any official took it upon himself to "unilaterally"
> commit an extrajudicial execution, even in the face of official RTG
> [Royal Thai Government] policy to the contrary … there would be a risk

of serious damage to our bilateral relations, and to Thaksin's personal reputation. Thaksin said that he understood.[77]

High-level visitors in 2006 from the State Department, Pentagon, and Congress spoke with one voice: "I urge all senior U.S. officials visiting Thailand to ask the Thai to conform with international norms while working in the South and warn them what might happen to important programs like IMET should they resort to extra-judicial means."[78]

Yet if the south was exempt from the War on Terror, so was the promotion of human rights, and the inconsistency undermined US efforts to influence the counterinsurgency. Although Thaksin's War on Drugs was a crime against humanity, its timing amidst black sites and US planes at U-Tapao cost him only paltry US funding cuts to the provincial police. Torture in Thailand continued well into 2004, when the south reignited, as did widely published photos of US abuse at Abu Ghraib prison in Iraq. It was unclear whether Bush and Thaksin explicitly traded violation vouchers, but the premier would have at least assumed greater license and leeway in the south. According to Kraisak Choonhavan, then head of the Senate Foreign Affairs Committee, "In return, Thaksin complemented this by being very heavy-handed with the southern Muslims, which showed an alliance."[79] He asked the government, "Because you signed up to an agreement to become closer friends with the US on the War on Terror, what did Thailand get in return? Was it to set the bar a bit lower on human rights?"[80] It was ironic on several levels that in 2006 the US counterterrorism coordinator would discuss human rights at all in Thailand, much less in the deep south. And while US diplomats in Bangkok rightly protested at Thaksin's approach, they also recalled their Vietnam-era predecessors in being among the last to know and the least listened to in both capitals.

One of the king's privy councilors told Boyce he believed Thaksin knew in advance of the enforced disappearance case the embassy was monitoring. An ex-cabinet minister told him that "Policemen carried out killings ... and the perpetrators received promotions, as if as a reward".[81] More chilling for the potentially implicit reference to the black sites, Thaksin "boasted several times that he had personally interrogated some of the captured militants ... that under questioning the captured militants readily confessed their involvement in the insurgency and that harsh interrogation techniques were not required to obtain information".[82] The military was also compromised: three years into

Thaksin's government in 2004, those who cooperated with the Americans on anti-terrorism were the same who worked with them on the south, well aware of the contradictory messages they were receiving. Hypocrisy aside, it was clear that the ends justified the means in the US War on Terror; it was only reasonable that some of Thailand's soldiers would follow the example.

That included the justice system as well. In 2005, Thaksin's second foreign minister told the US that, "Like your situation at Abu Ghraib, a few individuals went too far."[83] Others asked "how the USG dealt with American officers who had been found guilty of misconduct at Guantanamo".[84] The answer could only have been that American officers were not held accountable for "going too far" in torturing detainees anywhere under the CIA's rendition program; rights violations were not only planned and perpetrated, but protected. Not surprisingly, nor would any Thai official be convicted of a human rights violation in the counterinsurgency. An emergency decree enacted by Thaksin codified immunity from prosecution for violations "rendered in good faith".[85] The misgivings of a Foreign Ministry official recalled similar minority voices in the US on the post-9/11 Patriot Act:

> security forces had seized upon the general sense of alarm … to force through a poorly conceived edict providing them greater power … far more draconian than what was needed to respond to the violence … rushed through the Cabinet while everyone was anxious to do something … and passed before many of those gathered even had an opportunity to read the text.[86]

DIPLOMATIC FOOTNOTES

A half-century after its founding, the Asia Foundation said in 2002 that "anti-Americanism is at an all-time high".[87] The following year, an American lawyer who has lived in Thailand since 1955 wrote that, "xenophobia in an anti-western, anti-American form is increasingly in evidence … given impetus by the perceived unilateral approach and economic and political predominance of the U.S. … Thailand has to bear the cross of a recent past marked by decades of a close alliance and special relationship with the U.S."[88] These assessments were particularly arresting given the long memories: the US was hardly popular in Thailand in 1956, 1972, 1985, 1997. Chuan Leekpai, born in 1938, was a lonely voice under Thaksin in asking the US to retain the Voice of America and commemorate the centennial of an equally pro-American Seni Pramoj. Rather than lay the foundation for more balanced, advanced, and mature future relations, as the American crusade against communism had imperfectly done, the campaign against terrorism was a bilateral house of cards.

Just before deploying to Thailand in late 2001, Ambassador Johnson told the US Senate that "vigorous public diplomacy" was needed to strengthen bilateral cooperation, and that the US was "doing everything we can to assist the Thai in solving the serious problems that affect their country and society".[89] Yet he was sworn in a mere three months after 9/11, and despite experience in Hong Kong, China, and "East Asian and Pacific Affairs", had little leeway to expand the scope of relations. This was especially unfortunate given his Peace Corps service in Thailand during the mid-1960s. Among the last senior US officials to bring a cultural understanding of the kingdom to his responsibilities, Johnson was hamstrung by an agenda on which anything not related to terrorism was a footnote. At the same time, his appreciation for increasing Chinese power was surprisingly limited. That the Bangkok embassy remained among the Americans' largest but their consulates in the northeast and south had been shuttered the previous decade further displayed the Americans' centralized and myopic approach. While Thaksin once complained that Johnson had "talked down to him" and vowed not to meet him again,[90] he greeted his successor by "recalling how they had talked about the country's future during the Ambassador's previous assignment to the Embassy".[91] Skip Boyce first met Thaksin in 1994, and enjoyed eight years of Thai experience and an "off the scale" command of the Thai language.[92] "The White House relies on the US ambassador", he said, "And Boyce had a good relationship with me, but at the same time had a good relationship with my opponents as well."[93] Indeed, with strong connections to the military, Privy Council, business leaders, academics, and politicians from all sides, "Skip was the most knowledgeable person on Thailand in the United States government, period."[94]

That was, however, part of the problem: two months before a pro-China Thaksin was reelected, Boyce embodied the sum total of Washington's interest in Thailand. Such was the State Department's confidence in him that it simply left relations in his hands and directed its attention elsewhere. Upon his arrival, Boyce later confessed he felt the relationship was "on fumes", adding that CIA station chiefs and military attachés confirmed the conclusion.[95] An early cable to Washington was more measured but equally clear:

The real challenge for us, and increasingly for the Thai, is to resist relying too much on the mantra of the "historic relationship." Instead, we need to bring this important partnership into the 21st Century, and channel our long-standing influence in positive directions ... Here in Thailand, we can have our cake and eat it too—by mixing classic "realpolitik" (which Thaksin understands and responds well to) with principled interventions.[96]

Unclear from a hugely symbolic episode in 2006 was exactly when and whether the department appreciated its lack of institutional investment. A week before the coup, Secretary Rice would request a meeting with Boyce in Washington, planning to reassign him to none other than a vortex of US foreign policy, Afghanistan. "I'm not going to tell you that Thailand is as important to the United States as Afghanistan is, or even close", he protested, "But it's a country that's on the brink of some serious stuff and I know what I'm doing there."[97] Wrong on his first point but right on his second, Boyce stayed.

None of this was lost on Team Thaksin. If many Thai Rak Thai politicians were "unfamiliar with the United States",[98] the premier "told President Bush that more than half of my administration are US alumni".[99] Chief advisor Pansak had escaped to the US for five years during the 1976 pro-democracy protests. Both of Thaksin's commanders-in-chief had received military training in the US. Thaksin himself had studied at two American universities and remained an active client of several high-end Washington consultancies; Thai Rak Thai was ultimately based on the American party model. He claimed a strong rapport with President Bush, referring to himself as a fellow Texan (via Sam Houston State University), and "was even invited to golf putt in the Oval Office".[100] In his first meeting with the president in late 2001, Thaksin recalled saying "that it seemed to me that the US was taking Thailand for granted even though we are the oldest treaty ally in the region".[101]

Displaying how widely this view was held was Thaksin opponent Panitan:

You saw a generation gap, whereby your diplomacy was not able to connect, explain, and push a complicated set of interests, rather than only the security interests shared during the Cold War. So the relationship with Thailand as a whole was falling, slipping, slipping without any good coordination or good sense of direction. It was like on automatic pilot based on the old map. Thaksin came in and said we need to get control of that. Yes we will help you in Iraq, but you need to help us in much better ways too. Thaksin was supported more or less by the majority of the people on this new kind of relationship.[102]

In 2015, a US army colonel agreed that the "weakening of our relationship began maybe 10 or 12 years ago ... While we still had people at the embassy and at JUSMAG, we weren't devoting the same amount of energy and attention we should have been to the relationship".[103] Similarly, early Thaksin supporter Sarasin saw personnel as the problem:

> You had very good people in Washington but they always said access to the White House is not so simple. You had the National Security Advisor who could go next door to the White House, but they also claimed they had very little access. So it was the feeling that Thailand was really very down on the priority list. They didn't have to do anything with Thailand, Thailand was manageable.[104]

Thaksin and Bush met in Washington in December 2001. Foreign Minister Surakiart met the president at the UN and the secretary of state in Bangkok in mid-2002. Thaksin and Bush would meet again at APEC in 2003, and twice more in Washington that year and in 2005. Prior to the final meeting, Thaksin told Boyce he had just been asked by the press what he wished to discuss. "I told them that I have no 'issues,' only areas of cooperation. We are two friends catching up."[105] However, "he hoped to leave Washington by noon on September 19 in order to meet with the PRC vice-premier in Chiang Mai on September 21 and wondered whether his meeting with the President could take place in the morning".[106] The position of vice-premier is senior, but several large steps below the Chinese—and American—head of government.

* * *

The record of political setbacks under Thaksin and Bush began with the former's signature piece of East Asian architecture: "I informed President Bush that this is not Asia for Asia but Asia for the whole world. Because now we are very fragmented, we have conflicts here and there. If we can prosper, we have more purchasing power, which is good for the whole world. So it does not mean that we want to isolate ourselves from anyone."[107] A cabinet member recalled that the Americans tried to join the ACD, having determined that

Asia's expansion was somehow not within the US's interest. The formula of ASEAN plus dialogue partners was tolerable, but the permanent and equal membership group of Asia seemed not. "The rise of Asia", a concept Thaksin was very much involved in, was highly relevant. US paranoia only increased when China agreed to host the third meeting. Some believed this was one of the reasons the US's opposition to the 2006 military takeover was not exactly enthusiastic.[108]

In 2002, Thaksin replied to an embassy query on the threatened expulsion of two American journalists by citing national security and sovereignty. When the 2003 State Department human rights report criticized the police, of which Thaksin remained a lieutenant colonel, he replied that "For a country that likes to talk about peace, it sure doesn't practice it much … We are a friend. But we are nobody's lackey".[109] Following his War on Drugs, Thaksin said: "If you are telling me that someone will cut off aid because of what we are doing, I will say directly that I don't care."[110] In 2004, a US Congressional representative-*cum*-presidential candidate concluded that, "Thailand is no longer the most democratic, open and free partner of the United States in Southeast Asia that it once was."[111] After the 2005 human rights report, the Foreign Ministry summoned Boyce to tell him it "hurt bilateral relations", before agreeing to help limit the damage.[112] In contrast, future premier Samak Sundaravej challenged him to a televised debate ("Why does such a good ally accuse a close friend?"[113]) and called for a protest at the US embassy. Boyce assumed that Samak's "vehement criticism could not have been made without a green light from the current government".[114] Reaction to the last report under Thaksin would become the tired mantra of all post-coup Thai governments: it was "missing the real situation in Thailand".[115] Although essentially a theatrical distraction from all-important anti-terrorism cooperation, US criticism was no less valid or Thaksin's replies any less sincere.

After policy overlap on Myanmar during Chuan's premiership, disagreements reemerged under a Thaksin far more committed to business dealings than democracy across the border. In 2003, the Americans showed little interest in his "Bangkok Process", and criticized his weak response to another round of repression in Yangon. In retrospect, Surakiart explained that the US took the same approach to Mexico: "It was not that I liked Myanmar leadership or did not like Myanmar leadership, that is not the question. The question is that we have 1,700 kilometers of common border and I cannot move Thailand to anywhere else."[116] Refugees remained an area of concern for both the US and the Thai military, which occasionally acted contrary to Thaksin's policy. Surakiart's successor in 2005 would recall Rice urging Thailand to adopt the US policy of sanctions and isolation. "I explained to Rice, we have the same goal. We want to see Myanmar come out from the situation, but we have alternative channels for the same goal. She accepted it and said we could work together."[117] He added that she appreciated his quiet diplomacy in 2005 toward Myanmar's postponement of the ASEAN chair, which would have been "very bad for relations with the US".[118] On the other hand, a press interview suggested that "Thailand was backtracking on various assurances on Burma given during Prime Minister Thaksin's meeting with the President".[119] He telephoned Rice directly to explain, but also hosted Myanmar's foreign minister the following month, regarded by the US as unwise and unhelpful.

The NSC told Boyce it was embarrassed at Thailand's image vis-à-vis Yangon, while Supreme Commander Surayud said that Chuan's policy had been more effective. The latter also confided that after initially agreeing with the military's border policy, Thaksin altered his view at "about that time the Shin satellite deal with Burma was being fixed".[120] Indeed, in more ways than one Thaksin was conflicted on Myanmar, telling the US in 2005 that neither its sanctions nor Thailand's constructive engagement had worked, and actually suggesting "regime change".[121] He assured President Bush four months later that he would be more critical of Yangon publicly, but demurred when pressed by visiting members of Congress. He then traveled to Myanmar without advance planning or informing most of his team; the purpose and message were unclear. In 2006, Thailand refused to support a US-led effort to bring Myanmar before the UN Security Council, referencing ASEAN and border problems, and "citing the Human Rights Report and Burma as examples" of a fading US image in the region.[122]

* * *

One area in which the Foreign Ministry identified a shift in US diplomacy during the War on Terror was in negotiating agreements: "It was not really whether you had a treaty, the shift was whether you could have cooperation without a treaty … political commitments rather than legal. So a treaty no longer mattered if you had enough power to say we made this agreement."[123] Designed by the US to stop the spread of weapons of mass destruction, the Proliferation Security Initiative (PSI) was a product of the Iraq invasion predicated on their existence; talks with Thailand started in 2004. "They were saying forget the treaty, those treaties don't work anyway, the Nuclear Test-Ban and those treaties are kind of defunct and have not had proper ratification and entrance into force. They were saying let's do it differently, by-pass all the treaty obligations and ... work around the laws that you have and just do more practical cooperation".[124] In 2005, Surakiart said he would personally work on getting the PSI endorsed, but that no fewer than nineteen agencies had concerns, the Defense Ministry in particular. Having agreed to attend a related meeting in the US, the Thais canceled just days before when the Americans asked for a public commitment to signing on. Just as Defense Secretary Rumsfeld got involved, Thaksin said that the PSI could aggravate Muslims in the deep south, resulting in Bush raising the issue during their September meeting in Washington. His government came to an end before any progress was made.

Surakiart was replaced in 2005 by a foreign minister who sought to make global issues a central part of Thai policy, "so that our relationship with the US could improve".[125] He had enjoyed a "very close" relationship with Rice since 2004, when he shared information from a trip to North Korea (including that his hosts attributed the invasion of Iraq to its *lack* of weapons of mass destruction).[126] Upon being invited back to Pyongyang in 2005, he "thought I would do telephone diplomacy, so I called Rice and Ban-ki Moon, the Chinese, Russians, Japanese".[127] Helping convince North Korea to return to the Six-Party talks, he was asked to meet with Rice in New York during the UN General Assembly, "so the relationship became even closer".[128] In 2006 he met with her in Brazil after being told by Boyce that it would not be possible, and traveled to Washington to see her again later in the year. "From then on Skip was a bit unhappy with me."[129] He also established a relationship with Iran, which also interested Rice. The US embassy reported that Thailand was looking "for all of the Muslim friends it can get to assist in dealing with the Southern insurgency", and complained of its signing a lucrative rice agreement with an Iran seeking nuclear weapons.[130]

Among the final diplomatic acts during Thaksin's tenure, "the US eventually rejected Surakiart's candidacy" for UN secretary-general in late 2006.[131] Two years before, he had opposed US use of U-Tapao for the relief mission after the Pacific tsunami. The next year, Boyce had asked Anand about possible repercussions if the US backed another candidate: "None."[132] Thaksin lobbied on the grounds that Surakiart was "obedient",[133] and the candidate himself said he "could be counted on to take US interests into account".[134] His campaign plainly claimed he was not "too close to China".[135] It was an open secret that the US would have preferred Chuan's foreign minister of the more pro-American Democrat Party. It was telling that it had to reject—rather than back—a candidate from a treaty ally to prevent a pro-China orientation at the top of the world's largest multilateral forum. That Ban-ki Moon also represented an Asian ally provided certain political cover, but the decision could have been between two equally pro-American candidates. Surakiart's career paid a price, but the US had already absorbed the far larger cost.

FREE TRADE DISAGREEMENT

If Washington's War on Terror produced a single casualty in its relationship with Thailand, it was a free trade agreement. A chance to finally put to rest lingering scar tissue from the 1997 financial crisis and take advantage of the most pro-trade prime minister in Thai history, the FTA instead reopened old wounds and went down with Thaksin's ship. The Thais made inexcusable errors in process and procedure throughout the talks, but ultimately dooming the deal was a lack of political will in Washington and another uncompromising campaign. Two weeks before 9/11, a Thai official met with the acting US trade representative, who "said US policy was to have no more FTAs with any country at all".[136] Although this was reversed after the attacks, it "was a global thing, not focused on Thailand".[137] And therein was the problem: the US did not prioritize one of its two Southeast Asian treaty allies for an FTA, but, as in all other post-9/11 policies, treated it as any other nation. Rather than couple anti-terrorism and pro-trade policies in a manner befitting a genuine and holistic alliance, Washington saw progress on the former as reason for downgrading the latter. "I think part of it was the US's lack of energy on Thailand, the US was looking everywhere", recalled the Thai official.[138] Congressional authorization to commence negotiations with Thailand passed by a single vote. Two years later, the FTA appeared above only air transportation, ASEAN, and infectious diseases on a ten-point joint statement after Thaksin and Bush met in Washington.

It is true that Thaksin went after an FTA with China first, and that controversy over the process and initial results worked against him. It is also true that in October 2003—the month the China deal was inked and a US deal initiated—the US was already Thailand's leading trading partner. Exports to the US increased by 2.5 percent in 2003, and were expected to rise by nearly 5 percent annually under an FTA. Yet China had also prioritized Thailand over other ASEAN nations, while Thaksin again bypassed parliament in negotiating with the US, showing his will to get it done even at political cost. He even contravened Thai law placing trade responsibility squarely with the Ministry of Commerce, by assigning US negotiations to the Foreign Ministry—tapping into 170 years of diplomatic relations that had seen thirteen ambassadors to Washington become foreign minister. Laying the groundwork during a December 2001 visit to the US, Thaksin watched Surakiart sign a Memorandum of Understanding on the Framework on Economic Cooperation, and announced Thailand as host of the US Trade and Development Agency's regional office. Most tellingly, Thaksin established a team of trade representatives (including his eventual second foreign minister) to mirror the American negotiating structure. He appointed a full-time negotiator for the US in mid-2004, none other than Nitya Phibunsongkram, son of Phibun and a former ambassador to Washington. Surakiart would state that, "one of the most important, if not the most important, FTAs we have embarked upon is with the United States".[139]

Politically, in 2002 the candidate whom the US had blocked to lead the WTO finally assumed the post, while Thaksin and former US president Clinton—among the villains of 1997—talked enthusiastically together about globalization. By the time Thailand paid back the last of the IMF's loan two years early in mid-2003, the financial crisis was no longer an issue for the prime minister. To the contrary, large US banks would be welcome in breaking up dominance of the local money market by (Sino-Thai) banks beginning to turn against him. And as an agreement with Australia was signed a month before US negotiations began, the "the assumption that if we negotiate an FTA with a developed country we will always lose", was no longer valid.[140] In principle, Thailand was ready for the US.

It was in practice that Thaksin erred. To the US embassy's disappointment, he initially designated Nitya as an advisor to the foreign minister—"not a very powerful position"—before giving him cabinet-rank status.[141] Like the Americans, Nitya favored a comprehensive FTA but had no previous trade negotiation experience, and had even told colleagues it was the only role he did not wish to play. Alongside his main ally Surakiart, he was not a member of Thaksin's inner circle. At the same time, Thaksin made his powerful finance minister chair of an FTA Oversight Committee in late 2004, and assigned chief advisor Pansak to join him. Both were proponents of a narrow, incremental agreement, and "found common cause in blocking Nitya's plans for the FTA".[142] Thaksin consistently backed Nitya and his approach with the Americans—including President Bush in their 2003 and 2005 meetings—but privately seemed to back the others. In early 2005, Thailand's commerce minister told Ambassador Boyce that real responsibility for the FTA lay with Pansak's team, even as Nitya continued on and made no headway. In early 2006, "owing to his inability to exert authority on FTA matters over the various ministries involved, as well as his inability to recruit the assistance of the Prime Minister", he resigned. The rival finance minister told Boyce that Nitya "hadn't made the transition from being Thailand's Ambassador to the US and this makes him much too nice to the Americans".[143]

In addition to decentralization, neither of the two Thai camps was well-versed or briefed for comprehensive negotiations with the US. The Oversight Committee ordered agencies to provide recommendations, slowing the process considerably and allowing for an anti-FTA movement to grow. In 2005, a team assigned to one particular discussion with the Americans failed to even show up, before the finance minister "indicated that he would fully engage in our FTA 'now that I have time'".[144] Thaksin made the same pledge to Bush in Washington. Another confusing press interview by Thaksin's foreign minister muddied the waters again, but all parties claimed optimism in the run-up to a sixth round of talks at the end of the year. Nitya told the US "that a certain amount of preliminary 'dancing around' was necessary for the real talks to begin".[145] While the Americans rightly saw Thaksin's dual-track, "learn as we go" approach as scattershot and inefficient, it was likely a misguided tactic designed to increase rather than decrease the odds of a deal.

* * *

In 2004, US Ambassador Johnson asserted that an FTA "will effect a transformation within the Thai economy, by moving it towards a more rules-based, transparent way of conducting commerce … serving as a positive precedent for the many other developing economies which are weighing economic development and trade policy options".[146] The grandiose vision did not explain why only an "all at once" approach (contra "piece by piece") would yield the desired outcome. In words characterizing the US approach to Thailand writ large, Johnson added that "Usually, an FTA is designed to take bilateral relations to a new level. In the case of Thailand, however, much of our motivation is the preservation of our current position."[147] Preferential treatment for US investors under a bilateral Treaty of Amity and Economic Relations (AER, 1966) was set to expire, and "Our best hope for continuing our preferential rights in services investment in Thailand is the conclusion of an FTA."[148] Yet again he did not explain how taking relations "to a new level" and retaining privileges were mutually exclusive aims. Two months later, Thailand's finance minister said that "the FTA is *not only* about reducing tariffs and taxes, but also about pursuing activities of mutual support … the agreement should *not only* be concerned with trade liberalization, but with cooperation in trade and in investment" (emphasis added).[149] Both he and Thaksin urged the US to refer to their negotiations as discussions, and to the FTA as an economic partnership, "because it carried more of an image of equals working together".[150]

This was not all symbolism and semantics. Thailand was concurrently "discussing" an "economic partnership" with Japan, likewise under exceptional (and illegal) Foreign Ministry leadership but progressing far better. The finance minister offered two reasons. One, anathema to the comprehensive approach of the US was an incremental agreement of "early harvests", leaving more difficult areas for later. The second was "negative Thai perceptions of U.S. investors, another hangover from the 1997 crisis".[151] The US agreed to exclude one contentious topic from a round of talks and consider "phase-in periods",[152] but refused to consider "early harvests".[153] It also "explained that despite this perception, American investors bring more into Thailand than the Japanese"—a highly debatable claim given that Japan was Thailand's largest foreign investor.[154] What the Americans did not say was that they were set to cede their top trading status to Japan the following year, precisely on account of the latter's FTA with Thailand. In their own hangover from 1997, they remained dogmatic, arrogant, and wrong. It was not surprising that Thaksin's express desire to conclude an "open skies agreement" before his 2005 visit to Washington was not latched on to by the US as just the sort of deal Thailand wanted to complement the FTA. The agreement was focused on "promoting increased travel and trade, enhancing productivity, and spurring high-quality job opportunities and economic growth".[155] It did appear in the post-meeting joint statement, but was inexplicably and unnecessarily separate from the FTA.

The Treaty of Amity and Economic Relations referenced by Johnson both encouraged and discouraged the Thai side of the talks. Although it provided for reciprocal preferential treatment on visas and temporary entry, the US had never honored that provision to the extent Thailand had. Nitya made clear that "the RTG's basic position on somehow addressing temporary entry is inflexible, and as such is probably one of a handful of issues that falls outside the normal give and take of the negotiating process".[156] The embassy remarked that insistence "comes directly from the PM".[157] On the other hand, concerned that the AER would place them in violation of WTO rules on investment privileges—and aware of the rare leverage it afforded them—the Thais agreed to extend the privileges for a year. They continued to do so in exchange for assistance against any legal challenge, and "pending successful completion" of an FTA including temporary entry privileges.[158]

* * *

A Thai trade representative recalled an early meeting between Surakiart and Rice before formal negotiations began, in which the "atmosphere was very cold … a frank exchange of views" on "trying to get Thailand to open up certain aspects" of its economy.[159] Negotiation then featured a range of disputes, several of which would prove persistent. After Thailand's Bankers' Association and Chamber of Commerce raised FTA concerns on rice, silk, financial services, and telecommunications, the deputy secretary of state spoke to a parliamentary group in 2005. Thaksin agreed twice that year to lift a health-related ban on US beef in Thailand, both times during meals with Ambassador Boyce. After a final request in 2006, he pledged it "would be topic number one in his weekly Cabinet meeting".[160] In the wake of the Pacific tsunami in late 2004, the US agreed to conduct a "changed circumstances review" of its tariff on shrimp. A year later, with the review ongoing, industry representatives held a press conference outside the US embassy and Pansak challenged Boyce: having heard the US on beef, "what will you do now about our shrimp?"[161] Some Thais were even "comparing the need for US understanding of Thailand's position to the situation during the 1997 financial crisis. PM Thaksin raised this issue with the President in their September 19 White House meeting".[162] When the review resulted in no change in 2006, Thais staged another protest and filed a complaint with the WTO. Pansak told a visiting State Department official "that as an ally the U.S. should be 'fair and equitable'".[163]

The Americans were not wrong in 2005 to conclude that "overall IPR [intellectual property rights] protection in Thailand remains woefully inadequate", and to recommend that it remain on the US watchlist for violators.[164] At first glance, the nature and content of the largest FTA dispute recalled the economic drama between the US and Thailand during the mid-1980s. But where that had been mostly about the latter's initiation and integration into larger markets, this concerned a bald US attempt to win greater concessions from Thailand than rules required. Thus 1997 would again prove to be the apposite specter, as the IPR negotiations revealed two things, one old and one new. First, long apparent in the War on Terror was that the US perceived no drawback from engaging Thailand in the way it had throughout the 20th century. If 9/11 changed Washington's outlook on the world and caused it to renew bilateral trade efforts, it did not change its view that Thailand could be ordered into line. Second, negotiations showed that Thailand could *not* be ordered into line in the 21st century. It could not be moved at all. From long-time American friend Nitya to the FTA Watch group shouting outside the venues, the kingdom finally had the wherewithal not only to complain but to refuse. The FTA would officially founder on Thailand's political crisis, but Boyce's admission that "That may not be all bad" hinted at a growing realization: the US was driving the FTA to failure.[165] Unlike competing Thai teams, the AER, or a jumbo-sized shrimp dispute, intellectual property was "the one issue that has the power to kill the FTA".[166]

In early 2005, diverse and increasing anti-FTA critics began to coalesce around a US demand for twenty-five-year patents for pharmaceuticals, rather than the twenty years under WTO rules. The US also wanted to restrict the use of "compulsory licensing", whereby governments could break laws protecting patented drugs toward producing cheaper generic versions to meet public health crises. In a nation that had seen new HIV infections drop from a 143,000 peak in 1991 to 19,000 in 2003, compulsory licensing was as much about life as about law. Thailand had begun producing generic AIDS drugs the year before for the more than one million Thais living with the disease. During a visit to Thailand in early 2005, none other than former president Bill Clinton told Thaksin he would "explore having his foundation purchase drugs from Thai firms" producing them more cheaply than in the US.[167] That the current president's policy stood to price Thai patients out of life-saving drugs added an emotive and ethical element to the FTA debate.

Following the third round of FTA negotiations, Nitya "told the Thai media that Bangkok would not cave in to Washington's demand".[168] By then, FTA Watch had collected over 50,000 signatures demanding public and parliamentary access to the negotiations. There was no contradiction in Thais protesting against both the US and Thaksin, for it was Washington's position on pharmaceuticals in particular that made them wary of Thaksin's lack of transparency. Before the sixth round of talks in early 2006, Thaksin told business leaders: "On the Thai–US FTA … We will be at a huge disadvantage to others if we lose our access to the US market, as other countries will pursue their own deals. We need to move now, before we have no more room to move".[169] Protesters then tried to storm the venue[170], contributing to Nitya's resignation and his parting words to Boyce on the deal and its dogmatists: "Nobody likes it, and nobody likes you."[171] Senator Kraisak said he would ask the Americans to suspend the talks and a Thai court to rule on their constitutionality.

In response, the US released a statement that the two countries had agreed to cut tariffs on 200 industrial goods, and prepared a public fact sheet in cooperation with pharmaceutical representatives. This was despite its express belief "that if the FTA formally excluded all HIV/AIDS medicines from its provisions, better than 90 percent of the anti-FTA demonstrators, and much of the anti-FTA public commentary in Thailand, would disappear".[172] Moreover, by 2006 narrow opposition to an FTA was expanding into a general anti-Americanism, expressed by more than AIDS activists and FTA Watch. Sondhi's People's Alliance for Democracy, never bound by logic or principle, saw an opportunity to expand its economic nationalism cloaked in the red, white, and blue of not only the Thai flag but the American one as well. And with China's FTA a done deal, opposition to a US agreement furthered Sondhi's Lookjin Rak Thai (Children of China Love Thailand) image and agenda as well. Indeed, what made Ambassador Johnson's claim that the US was merely seeking "the preservation of our current position" even more astonishing was what followed: "The relentless rise of China's economic profile in this region represents a challenge to the U.S.'s trade and investment leadership."[173]

Once the numbers were crunched in mid-2006, the statements were even less reconcilable. Lost US agricultural and industrial exports alone were projected to total more than $60 billion over the next decade—most via trade diversion to Chinese suppliers that had already negotiated much lower tariffs into the Thai market. "US suppliers will face average effective tariffs of 16 percent for agricultural products, and 23 percent for industrial products, versus mostly zero tariffs for our competitors."[174] As 75 percent of US exports to the kingdom overlapped with products covered by Thai FTAs with other countries, they would be placed at a huge disadvantage across the board. According to Boyce, "China will, of course, elbow the US out of some business; the question is just how much."[175] Some answers were already available: Thai imports of Chinese fruit from 2000—even before their FTA was agreed—through 2005 had risen from $19 million annually to $63 million. Fruit imports from the US of a comparable $18 million in 2000 had not budged for six years.

Further, a pending decision by the US to eliminate Generalized System of Preferences (GSP) benefits for nine of Thailand's top exports meant that both Thai exporters to the US and the US itself stood to lose considerable market share to China. Bangkok's power to negotiate improved market access to China would be hindered, as the US insisted upon yet another self-inflicted wound. The man Thaksin had dubbed "Mr. China" in chairing the Thailand–China Joint Committee on Trade, Investment and Economic Cooperation was the same finance minister also chairing the FTA Oversight Committee. Generally at loggerheads with the Americans, he could only have been at a loss by their admission of "an even wider trade deficit with China and a smaller trading relationship with our long-time key ally in Thailand".[176]

Finally, a Congressional Research Service report in mid-2006 flatly stated that the main purpose of FTAs for the US was to advance IPR protection rather than promote free trade. This was hardly new to Thailand's negotiators and protesters, but it was news. The US then successfully pressured the World Health Organization (WHO) to replace its representative in Thailand, a US national who had openly advocated the Thai position on compulsory licensing and generic AIDS drugs. In his recollection, "their attack on me was rather crude and out of line with norms of the UN system. It worked in the short term, but government officials in India, Indonesia, Thailand and elsewhere took note, and it was just one more little thing contributing to the re-set of SEA countries towards China".[177] A Foreign Ministry official concurred: "We didn't trust the US. Look at the FTA, it didn't come through basically just because of trust."[178]

Political turmoil in Bangkok had by then reached a tipping point; suspended in March 2006, the talks would not resume in June as hoped. "Political uncertainty came in", the foreign minister recalled. "And so the negotiations kind of stopped to wait for more clarity and it never came."[179] The coup would claim the prime minister, but it did not claim the FTA; that distinction belonged to a distracted and dogmatic superpower.

WE WERE SOLDIERS

In 1972, during the final and floundering years of the American war in Vietnam, US pilot Robert Hymel's B-52 was shot over Hanoi and crash-landed into Thailand's U-Tapao airbase. He and a comrade were rescued, but Hymel was so badly burned that last rites were administered. He not only recovered but flew during the first Gulf War in 1990–1991, again taking off from U-Tapao. On 11 September 2001, while relocating his office from the area struck, Hymel was among the 125 personnel to perish in the terrorist attack on the Pentagon. While in no way reducing his service and sacrifice to symbolism, Hymel's story was a window into how US–Thai military relations survived and even thrived after the alliance-rupturing 1970s, only to falter needlessly at the turn of the century.

On its face, the War on Terror marked precisely the opposite: a significant uptick in "mil-to-mil" cooperation between treaty allies, on bases, agreements, troops, training. As late as 2004, Thai military officials stated that "we are cordial with China, we are allies with the United States, and that's not about to change".[180] Yet it also revealed chinks in the armor that the coup would widen into outright fissures. Alongside the mutual exclusivity—more for counterterrorism spelled less for other military activities—demographics was also at play. It was generational, even personal. According to a former long-time head of JUSMAG, historically the Americans saw 15 percent of the Thai military leadership as their counterparts. While prone to business, intra-military, and even extra-constitutional machinations, this contingent was professional, well-trained, and serious about national security and international relations. With few exceptions like General Chavalit, most were not closely linked with China. These leaders were close to the US because they were close to Americans. They were close to the soldiers with whom they had fought in Indochina or studied at Fort Leavenworth, and were close to the CIA and US embassy even if they came from a different place and pedigree. The father of Prem's foreign minister had sent his son to a US university in the 1940s "because this century is going to be an American century".[181] And they were close to many US nationals who had served in one capacity or another in Thailand since the 1950s, before choosing to remain or come back—often with Thai spouse and family. In the words of a US diplomat, "Whether they were US or Thai generals, their first combat tour was side by side with each other, and they drew on that web of connections. So what you had when they came home, was a whole generation of officers whose defining early adult experiences were fighting literally in the combat trenches."[182]

It worked in the other direction too among Americans who continued their careers in the US. The diplomat who split his first seven years in the foreign service, working on Thailand in Washington and Bangkok, was witness:

> When I first got into government, all the people who followed Thailand at the Office of the Secretary of Defense, at the CIA, at PACOM, were people—many of whom draftees, not even officers—who had done their service, fallen in love with Thailand, and then gone to work with the US government as civilians. They spent 30-plus years as people who cared about the relationship, who understood a strategic commonality and were willing to invest personally in the relationship.[183]

In 2006 a future Thai ambassador to Washington "observed that US–Thai relations are solid, but not sufficiently understood beyond the Department and DOD. He stressed that the strength and longevity of this relationship requires nurturing, particularly within the US Congress".[184] This was only a recent reality, as Senators (and future presidential candidates) John McCain and Jim Webb were two of many US legislators who had taken a piece of Thailand with them upon leaving the region decades before.

Through the mid-1970s, of course, US influence was hugely detrimental to Thai military leaders' commitment to human rights, democracy, and the rule of law, resulting in their forceful and harmful entry into politics over the next three decades. Chavalit was one of the earliest Thai soldiers to study at Forts Monmouth and Leavenworth in the early 1960s, a decade and a half before his reaching out to China. A main factor toward at least slowing this, however, was the International Military Education Training program, established in 1976. Directed by the State Department and administered by the Pentagon, IMET allowed foreign military personnel to participate in some 2,000 courses at over 150 US military schools. In the thirty years before the 2006 coup, Thailand was among the largest contributors, with over 1,700 participants from 1998 through 2004 alone. This was quite distinct from the many civilian Thais, including Thaksin, who had simply studied in US schools; IMET was not just education in the US but *American education*. Given that one of its main purposes was to prepare fully professional soldiers—via courses in international law, rules of engagement, human rights—IMET was partly to credit for Thailand's experiencing only one successful coup between 1977 and 2006. Further,

> IMET graduates helped us to convince civilian leaders to make Thailand
> a regional training center for peacekeepers ... in winning Thai support to
> deploy to Afghanistan and Iraq ... to make PKO [peacekeeping operation]
> deployments to East Timor, Cambodia, Aceh and elsewhere ... to making
> Thailand a more effective and reliable coalition partner that has joined us
> in making the transformation from the cold war era to the new security
> challenges of the present—and future.[185]

Yet in the early years of the 21st century, the generations of close Thais and Americans were retiring, and "by 2005 most were gone".[186] General Surayud was among the last, having not only attended the US Army Command and General Staff College (CGSC) at Fort Leavenworth but become a member of its Hall of Fame. His "presence in senior military leadership positions was, according to one US diplomat, a factor in Washington's 2003 decision" to confer major non-NATO status on Thailand.[187] Others still in uniform or influence in late 2005 were four senior members of the Defense Ministry and six senior members of Supreme Command, including a Leavenworth graduate who had overseen operations after the Pacific tsunami the year before. Two senior members of the army, air force, and navy were also IMET alumni, including the commanders-in-chief of all three forces. However, this would not prevent army chief Sonthi from overthrowing Thaksin the following year, assisted by the NSC director and approved ex post facto by Prem, both CGSC graduates. The former had also attended infantry school at Fort Benning in the late 1960s, where he delivered difficult news to a US officer just ten days back from Indochina: his friend and counterpart had just been killed, the senior-most Thai to die in the Vietnam War.

IMET itself suffered a setback in Thailand when in 2003 Thaksin stated that officers had to complete the entire curriculum at their military academies to become commander-in-chief, supreme commander, and permanent defense secretary. According to a US officer in charge of IMET in the mid-1980s, this put a "tremendous blanket of distrust on the whole idea of going abroad, which

Thais had traditionally always looked upon as for the best and brightest and gave people a leg up in their career".[188] The embassy confirmed that top graduates were "recruited by senior officers as staff aides or placed into other positions of authority because they are deemed to have the most current understanding of U.S. military doctrine ... this 'Leavenworth pipeline' has been invaluable in ensuring we have access at the highest level of the Thai military".[189] The policy trickled down to cadets with lower prospects and ambitions as well and would have negative effects in the post-Thaksin years. And while it would have technically affected studies in China too, courses there were generally geared to those having completed their Thai academies, creating a zero-sum effect in China's favor. Suggesting disagreement, in early 2005 the defense minister asked Ambassador Boyce about increasing IMET participation and "heartily endorsed" his offer to raise the matter with Thaksin.[190] Thailand's own budget for co-supporting the program was also diminishing, even as it remained the fourth largest recipient in IMET dollars globally. Officers also asked about raising Thai numbers in the prestigious US military academies and at the Asia-Pacific Center for Security Studies; "Thai alumni return better informed about vital issues of mutual concern and better prepared to work with American counterparts."[191]

* * *

Procurement also experienced a significant challenge under Thaksin. Mid-2001 saw the US allow Thailand to purchase advanced medium-range air-to-air missiles (AMRAAMs), on condition that it do so only in response to comparable missiles appearing elsewhere in the region. This was a first for a Southeast Asian country and reversed a 1996 decision by President Clinton. Two years later, and coinciding with the delivery of previously purchased F-16s, the US sold eight AMRAAMs to Thailand after Russia sold similar weapons to China. The Bush administration told Congress that Beijing's ability to relocate the missiles "creates an imminent threat justifying AMRAAM deliveries to Thailand".[192] Procurement in 2004 totaled $179 million, including thirty refurbished UH-IH helicopters and seven UH-60 Blackhawk choppers. It totaled $92 million the following year, when the Thais requested that private companies be permitted to bid on US defense contracts "as a tangible way to demonstrate benefits of Thailand's designation as a Major Non Nato Ally".[193] In turn, the US asked to modify an existing deal to allow the continued transfer of excess defense articles to Thailand. According to the embassy, the Thai navy "does not have a long-range vision of what Thailand's maritime security needs are, what threats Thailand might need to counter … As a result, its inventory includes a wide variety of equipment of questionable utility".[194] It would opt for six Sikorsky MH-60S Naval Hawk helicopters in 2006 for a whopping $246 million, while the army purchased over 70,000 rifles and machine guns alongside goggles and sights.

If Thailand still harbored ill-feeling over the US response to the 1997 financial crisis, it had forgotten altogether its unprecedented buying back of pre-purchased F-18s a year later. Thaksin summarized and sanitized: "When the military wanted to buy jet fighters, the F-16 was already outdated so Rumsfeld came and offered to retrofit them, and offered to do barter trade. So we agreed. They did not want us to use the Russian planes. At that time we used only American planes."[195] Indeed, with interlocutors ranging from senior military to the foreign minister, Pansak, and Thaksin himself, Boyce repeatedly urged Thailand to fill its bid for eighteen new fighters with the F-16. In early 2005, Secretaries Rice and Rumsfeld weighed in. All emphasized interoperability, knowledge and experience (Thailand had fifty-nine F-16s already), and Thailand's express goal of buying into the US Joint Strike Fighter program. Adding to the Americans' urgency—but tellingly not the Thais'—was China's increasing missile capability, as the AMRAAMs recently sold to Thailand were designed for the F-16. The Thais cited Russian and Swedish willingness to accept chicken stockpiled during a recent avian flu scare as an offset for their fighters. "Thaksin said the priority is not so much on the aircraft itself as a policy to 'expedite exports'."[196] The US defense contractor then offered a 100 percent countertrade deal; the Thais responded that Russia and Sweden were offering more than 100 percent. Thai military sources advised that US officials speak out "to counter recent statements of support the King of Sweden and President Putin have made".[197]

After Thaksin said he might prefer retrofitting existing F-16s to purchasing any new jets, the matter reached President Bush himself in their September 2005 tête-a-tête. Bush encouraged the latter, but was most focused on ensuring a purely American solution. No sooner did the Thais commit to retrofitting worth $650 million and suggest that any new aircraft would be either F-16s or Russian *helicopters*, than Thaksin announced that new aircraft would be Russian jets after all. Having gone to its commander-in-chief, the US was essentially out of ammunition. It argued that Thaksin had "left a clear impression that he would not procure Russian planes … that fighter aircraft purchases by treaty allies are a 'hot button' issue for us … that Thaksin find other ways to improve his relationship with Russia that would not come at the expense of his relationship with the United States".[198] He in turn denied giving Bush a clear answer and "believed the purchase of Russian aircraft should not affect cooperation with the U.S."[199]

Within months, the premier would change his mind and stay his hand at retrofitting, and the Americans would thus score a draw. Ultimately they would lose, however. In the meantime, Thaksin had clearly learned something from his American "ally" about leverage and loyalty. Pansak ruefully recounted the visit to Washington to meet Bush, when "we were briefed by the Pentagon on our cooperation. As we walked downstairs from the briefing room, around eighteen Vietnamese generals in full regalia were walking the corridors of the Pentagon as guests. Give me a break. You guys are not dumb, you know, you guys are very good".[200]

* * *

Counterterrorism and counterinsurgency training dominated military relations in the wake of 9/11 and the south's reignition, respectively. In 2001 Thaksin also agreed to semi-permanent participation by US special forces in a new counter-drugs task force in northern Thailand. Otherwise, Thailand staged some forty joint or combined exercises under Thaksin, even if most were small and non-integrated. Cobra Gold continued to evolve, but having symbolized the US return to the region two decades before, it was starting to signal "business as usual". The same was true to a lesser degree for Cope Tiger, the largest US–Thai air exercises, and the Cooperative Afloat Readiness and Training (CARAT) exercises with the navy, both established in the mid-1990s. In the words of an early Team Thaksin member, Cobra Gold "did not reflect really what was going on in the White House in terms of its perception of Thailand. It had become an annual thing, a regular thing for the military to do".[201]

China joined other nations in observing Cobra Gold in 2002, save for large 2004 exercises (13,500 US and 6,000 Thai forces) focused on anti-terrorism. Smaller iterations in 2005 and 2006 focused on disaster response and peace-keeping, by which time at least twenty other nations were observers. The former was influenced by the Pacific tsunami the year before, the latter by Thailand's membership in a Global Peace Operations Initiative (which also saw Thailand participate in US–Mongolia peacekeeping drills). The Thai air force viewed Cope Tiger as offering "training opportunities for Thai and American pilots unavailable elsewhere", regularly declining an invitation to join Cope Thunder in Alaska.[202] It convinced the US to reconsider combining Cope Tiger with Cobra Gold, saying it would "even invite a third country" to keep the exercises separate. In addition to CARAT, US navy SEALS trained their Thai counterparts in the protection of oil and gas platforms. Other cooperation included construction projects, the US Defense Resource Management Studies program, and annual talks between Supreme Command and PACOM. The former wanted more "strategic" use of an Interagency Intelligence Fusion Center in northern Thailand, and appreciated US action against Somali pirates who threatened a Thai fishing vessel in 2005.[203] The US sought an increase in ship visits (twenty-four in 2004 alone), as one carrier strike group in 2006 received high-level media coverage in Thailand.

* * *

On 26 December 2004, less than two weeks after Boyce was sworn in as ambassador and Thaksin's first term was ending, the Pacific tsunami struck hard and fast, claiming 250,000 lives globally and perhaps 8,000 in Thailand. Secretary Powell was the first foreign official to call and offer assistance, as the US navy's Seventh Fleet and other forward-based resources were immediately mobilized: "nearly 11,000 servicemen afloat aboard 19 navy ships and a coast-guard cutter, and nearly 1,800 on the ground".[204] In Thailand alone, they

> distributed over 660,000 pounds of supplies within Thailand including medicine, food, dry ice and body bags. Teams made up of medical specialists from the CDC [Center for Disease Control], the Armed Forces Research Institute of Medical Science and the Joint POW/MIA Accounting Command in Hawaii were also deployed to Thailand to assist with victim identification. U.S. Navy SEALS and a representative from the Office of Foreign Disaster Assistance worked closely with Thai military units to search for the remains of American and other victims of the disaster.[205]

Once again, Thailand's U-Tapao airbase was front and center as host of Combined Support Force 536, out of which the entire US regional effort was planned and staged. Thaksin approved blanket overflight less than twenty-four hours after the wave broke, leading to thousands of flights from U-Tapao and the *USS Abraham Lincoln*, *USS Essex*, and *USS Bonhomme Richard* aircraft carriers. It was the largest international response to a natural disaster in history, and the fastest that PACOM's commander had ever seen.

As evidenced by expressions of gratitude through the remainder of Thaksin's tenure, the Americans experienced a modest "bounce" in popularity. Surakiart said they had "won the hearts of Asians".[206] Thaksin was shown on television personally thanking SEALS on a devastated beach. He "said that the Thai people were deeply touched that President Bush and former Presidents Bush and Clinton had all personally visited the Thai Embassy in Washington to sign the book of condolences".[207] A month later the former leaders visited Thailand in a bipartisan show of support. While several Thai papers speculated that the US was using the disaster to establish a more permanent presence, most troops redeployed in March 2005, as relief gave way to recovery projects under JUSMAG. Secretary Rice would tour the beaches in July, a month before an early warning system was launched with critical US effort and expertise.

The problem with the US response was the disproportionate effect it had on policy-makers in Washington. Despite improvement in the US image, its pre-tsunami "starting point" in late 2004 was low, while the rise in goodwill in Thailand was less than Washington believed it to be. Moreover, rather than build upon this narrow opening, the US cashed in its reputational chips and returned to the lackluster status quo. Aside from agreeing that decades of Cobra Gold had greatly assisted the response and that lessons should be incorporated into future exercises—right but hardly revolutionary—the Americans limited themselves to chest-thumping: "[N]o other country could have responded to the tsunami the way that the United States has ... Many who questioned our extensive military exercise program with Thailand and our frequent use of Thai military facilities now understand clearly that our 50 year-old military alliance with Thailand is needed as much today as it ever was."[208] This was even more unfortunate for the fact that allowing US ships in Thai waters pursuant not to strategy but sympathy was a costless political win for Thaksin vis-à-vis both China and at home. Without disputing the unqualified good done from a humanitarian standpoint, the tsunami was more an opportunity missed than seized by the US in Thailand.

TURNING ASEAN INSIDE OUT

The tsunami was an unforeseeable event; the US could not have planned for it. The size and swiftness of its response befitted the most powerful military in the world, as its generosity did a values-based foreign policy. But after moving their boats and boots to Southeast Asian shores, the Americans could not and would not adjust their singular aim of fighting real and imagined terrorists. The US so narrowly defined its post-tsunami objective and so quickly declared "you can manage" to its regional hosts, because it was fully committed elsewhere and unmoved beyond humanitarianism.[209] What the Americans might have seen during their command performance was that China was changing the region as drastically, if more subtly, as the US was the Middle East. A belated wake-up call to continental drift geologically in Southeast Asia, the tsunami might have been the same geopolitically as well. Underway since 1997 when disaster of another kind had struck, this movement was increasing rapidly under a Thaksin who saw himself and his country as regional leaders. As early as his first meeting with Bush in 2001, he said, "You engage in so many things but not in ASEAN. I tried to convince him that ASEAN was important for the US. If the US cannot align with ASEAN, well, the Chinese are gaining importance, China is getting bigger, China is closer."[210] Instead, the Americans would further indulge their self-satisfaction: "*Prior to the tsunami*", wrote Boyce in 2005, "a number of analysts in the region concluded that the United States was preoccupied with other parts of the world and would likely be supplanted by others, perhaps China, as the most influential nation in Southeast Asia" (emphasis added).[211] The wave had altered little more than coastlines.

In 2002, Bangkok hosted a workshop on terrorism prevention under the yearly ASEAN Regional Forum (ARF), which included the US. As Thailand took over as coordinator for ASEAN–US relations in 2003, the US introduced the Secure Trade in the ASEAN Region (STAR). In 2004 there was a joint workshop on counterterrorism and anti-piracy, and the signing of a Joint Declaration on Counter-terrorism. Thailand's foreign minister recalled 2005:

Suddenly Condoleezza Rice said no to the first ARF that I was attending. She gave us about four days' notice and appointed her deputy to come. Frankly everyone was upset because it was noted as a downgrading of ASEAN. But it so happened that a few weeks after that, Rice came to Thailand regarding the tsunami. I decided to bring this up. She explained that some urgent things came up, she did not specify what, but said they looked at the situation and felt that the deputy secretary of state was an expert on Asia and so felt he would be the best person to come. I said that we enjoyed him a lot but there was another aspect to this, the symbolic aspect, as it was all foreign ministers. If the US only came as a deputy, many of my colleagues felt it was downgrading ASEAN, even that we were being taken for granted. I was quite frank with her, and she promised me she would go the next year and she did.[212]

ASEAN's economic integration by 2015 was discussed with Rice later in the year in New York, but "the US was preoccupied with something else", according to Surakiart (retaining a role in foreign affairs). "It did not look at Southeast Asia as their kind of backyard to counter the influence of China. They forgot to look at ASEAN as an economic hub of 600 million people. Even after 9/11, ASEAN went ahead with the ASEAN community with a clear roadmap for economic integration, but the US was still not interested."[213] Thus at the end of 2005, the US told an ASEAN gathering in Bangkok that the "ARF needs to be strengthened as a forum for discussing serious security matters".[214]

An "Enhanced Partnership" with the US was "at the forefront of Thai ASEAN policy" during the 19th ASEAN–US Dialogue in 2006.[215] Not unlike Cobra Gold, the Dialogue generally represented more of the same rather than forward movement, and was not even held annually; the first was in 1977. The US sent an assistant secretary of state and his deputy, the next ambassador to Thailand. In the US view, "while the United States welcomes growing integration within Asia, we need to work to ensure that regional institutions such as APEC, ARF, EAS, ASEAN and others work in concert rather than in competition with each other".[216] An otherwise reasonable concern, it came from a nation that had barely engaged any of the institutions in recent years. The assistant secretary also noted "key areas of common interest, such as counter terrorism, maritime security and non-proliferation", all security-related. His briefings—on Iraq, Israel–Palestine, Iran, Libya, and North Korea—were similar in that regard, and save for Thailand's minor role in Pyongyang, none was directly relevant to ASEAN. The US did continue cooperation on public health and environmental initiatives, in addition to urging reform in Myanmar, long a wedge between the US and ASEAN. It also pressed the body to complete its governing charter. In response, Thailand's representative hoped that the US would appoint an envoy to ASEAN, and endorse its Treaty of Amity and Cooperation, a thirty-year-old document China had signed three years previously. ASEAN would sign its charter the following year, but the US would not meet ASEAN's requests until 2008 and 2009.

The Americans' main economic message at the 2006 Dialogue was "to move the process forward across the entire Doha agenda" of WTO negotiations.[217] Not a US–ASEAN free trade agreement or bilateral FTAs, but the WTO. In late 2002 the US had established the Initiative for ASEAN Enterprise toward reaching FTAs in the region, and otherwise outsourced economic discussions to the US–ASEAN Business Council. The former resulted in a single agreement with Singapore, while the Council not only favored a US–ASEAN FTA, but was "looking to … the USG for ideas on how to move ASEAN forward on a range of economic and trade issues".[218] With such disconnect within and among US parties and interests, the most agreed in 2006 was a Plan of Action for an Enhanced Partnership, and a vague and vacuous ASEAN–US Trade and Investment Framework Agreement (TIFA).

The Americans made no reference to China's decade of progress with ASEAN, including its strategic agreement in 2003. "Because of that feeling we had in ASEAN and in Thailand that the US was focusing its attention elsewhere", recalled Thailand's foreign minister, "it was an opportunity for China."[219] Surakiart concurred: "We had been calling on the US to use its economic might to engage Southeast Asia, to engage Thailand as you used to. All the headquarters of your multinationals were still in Bangkok compared to other countries. You could use Bangkok as a hub. China got that and moved in."[220] The US had led in the establishment of ASEAN in 1967 to counter the ideology and approach of the Chinese, and supported the ARF's creation in 1994 with similar if updated concerns in mind. By 2006, however, the US had all but forgotten their purpose and forfeited their allegiance. ASEAN was being turned inside out.

THE STRAITS OF MALACCA

In 2004, two-thirds into Thaksin's tenure, US Ambassador Johnson sent an astounding cable to Washington, "China's Rise Coming at Whose Expense? Peaceful Coexistence—Are Thais Naive?" Of the seven observations he made about Thailand, six were far truer of the United States. In a kind of reverse narcissism, unwittingly self-admonishing rather than self-admiring, Johnson said that the Thais:

hope that problems associated with China's growing strength will either fix themselves or be mitigated by other powers … discount notions that China will jeopardize its generally good relations in the region in the near future by pressuring ASEAN nations to support Beijing on political or strategic issues ... view China's growing role as either not affecting the influence of other countries or as coming at the expense of Taiwan and Japan rather than the United States ... seem unable to consider moves a struggling China might make that could jeopardize regional security .... seem unable to gauge the impact of many of Thailand's recent trade deals with China ... seem overly sanguine about the effect China's rise will have on the security situation in the region.[221]

The cable's title, tone and tenor implied that the US did not share in Thailand's (debatable) naivety, despite years of policy and practice that insisted that it did. Indeed, the most crucial observation was demonstrably false, for earlier that same month a Thai general told the US that China's aim was "to emerge as a long-term counterweight" to the US, and ideally to "replace the United States as the strongest power in the region".[222] The ambassador's overall conclusion was, "While Thailand's desire to see China emerge in the future as a responsible member of the international community is in line with our objectives, Thai analysis of the ramifications of China's growing influence seems inadequate and overly optimistic."[223] One fuller of irony and consequence could scarcely have been offered.

The Foreign Ministry told the US in 2004 that China's efforts to reach the Andaman Sea through Myanmar would adversely affect Sino-Thai relations. As far back as 2001, Beijing had ignored pleas for assistance after a large militia in Myanmar moved from the Chinese to the Thai border. The military likewise said that Thailand's "gateway" interests would collide with any diversification of China's geopolitical strategy. Given that China's main point of reference was the United States, however—not Thailand or ASEAN—Thailand's assessment spoke as much to zero-sum Sino-*American* dynamics as it did to Sino-Thai relations. Myanmar had been under US economic sanctions since 1990 and none of Thailand's immediate neighbors had strong relations with the US. Thus, even as Thaksin was turning Thailand eastward, China would naturally play to its pre-existing geopolitical advantages by ensuring *multiple* Southeast Asian outlets to the Andaman Sea. Thailand was playing a delicate game in complaining to the Americans about Chinese inroads elsewhere, while simultaneously rolling out the carpet for Beijing in Bangkok. Yet if Thaksin was powerless to stop China's diversification, the US would choose not to exercise its power at all, leaving its "ally" little choice but to accept both realities and focus on being "first among equals" with Beijing. America's loss was China's gain.

As had been the case for a decade, China's main concern in Southeast Asia was the US-dominated Straits of Malacca. China now also had a fast-increasing appetite for oil, gas, and trade outlets—and a growing capacity to satisfy it. Seldom recalled is that Thaksin had been foreign minister for five months during Chuan's first term, just after Chuan commenced the "land bridge" across the Isthmus of Kra. In 2002, Thaksin briefly considered seeking Russian assistance in completing it. He and General Chavalit then revisited the latter's 1997 and 1999 initiatives, setting up a National Committee on the Study of the Kra Canal Project to Alleviate the Economic Crisis. Chavalit chaired the committee, while the Thai-Chinese Culture and Economy Association he had founded provided membership and expertise. It is also often forgotten that Thaksin had been Chavalit's deputy prime minister and placed in charge of the initiatives. Eight years later their roles were reversed when the committee's report was released in 2005. It recommended a 120-kilometer canal from eastern Songkhla province to western Trang province. "We came to the conclusion that the project would be beneficial in many ways", Chavalit recalled in 2015, but the newly rekindled conflict in southern Thailand caused second thoughts: "We had to suspend the project, even though we wanted to proceed, because we have to take national security into consideration."[224]

The Thais were not the only ones who wished to proceed; China was "very calculating" in its pursuit of energy, according to Thaksin.[225] By mid-2004, having had to import oil for seven years, it was considering as many as ten projects in the region to secure more resources. "[T]he one from Thailand has gone the furthest and received enormous support from the Thai government."[226] Thailand's PTT energy company and China's Sinopec announced that they were considering a pipeline across the Isthmus of Kra, already host to Chuan's unfinished highway. Expected to cost $880 million, receive a minimum of 1.5 million barrels of oil per day, and cut transshipment time by a week—bypassing the Straits—the project would include tank storage and terminals on both coasts. Although NGO opposition kept this project at bay as well, it would—like a canal—merely be shelved and not discarded. Indeed, in 2005 Thai security specialist Panitan told the US that China had begun purchasing land in the south.

The embassy would tell Washington in 2006 that the pipeline project was "not expected to go forward".[227] Yet the China National Offshore Oil Corporation, likely seeking the assets of America's Union Oil Company of California

(UNOCAL), was working with PTT on joint oil ventures. PTT also began working with Chinese Petroleum Pipeline Engineering Corporation on a 70-kilometer pipeline near Bangkok. China signed an agreement with Thailand, Laos, and Myanmar that allowed it to transport greater amounts of oil up the Mekong River—having first deployed engineers in 2004 to make it feasible. As the Mekong empties not into the Andaman Sea but where the Gulf of Thailand meets the South China Sea, it did not implicate the Straits. It provided another route for getting oil to China's landlocked southwest and to its coastal Guangxi autonomous area, which also extended sea links in 2006. The aforementioned first Sino-Thai naval exercises in the Andaman Sea and Gulf of Thailand in 2004 and 2005 were partly meant to protect these investments.

This was the geopolitical context in which Ambassador Johnson sent his cable and the US agreed to a bilateral "Strategic Dialogue" with Thailand in 2005. Pursuant to efforts with all permanent members of the UN Security Council plus Japan, the Dialogue was entirely Thaksin's initiative. The purpose was to develop action plans to "enhance bilateral relations and Thailand's stature in the region".[228] "In practice", according to Boyce, "these plans seem to be virtually anything the two countries want them to be."[229] Two days after escorting Secretary Rice to Thailand's battered beaches, he announced the goal of a US action plan on national radio. At Thai insistence, however, "strategic" was dropped as an early descriptor, as it "might have unwanted connotations within the Thai media".[230] No similar concern had attended Thailand's plans as far back as 1999 with China, which was likely much more to account for the government's decision than the press. Talks with the US did not even begin until after Thaksin's third and final visit to Washington in September 2005, such were the exigencies of the War on Terror. They lasted two days. While including representatives from five US defense agencies, the US side was led by the same mid-level deputy assistant secretary of state who had attended the US–ASEAN talks. In contrast, Thailand's permanent secretary of the Foreign Ministry led the Supreme Command, Ministry of Defense, NSC, National Intelligence Agency, and the military services.

On the agenda were "China and India's roles in the region, regional group-ings, promoting democracy in Burma, the Korean peninsula, Indonesia, Avian Influenza, trafficking in persons, maritime security, educational exchanges, mil-mil cooperation and exercises, the Proliferation Security Initiative (PSI), and the continuing unrest in Thailand's far South."[231] Regarding the change in nomenclature, it was hardly clear that the Americans saw China and the Straits of Malacca as strategic and related concerns. A summary's only substantive mention of China was that, "*On the margins* of the meeting, several Thai officials indicated a willingness to work with the Chinese PLA in future GPOI or peacekeeping events" (emphasis added).[232] A US brigadier general lamely suggested "that the next US–Thai Strategic Dialogue should include a full day devoted to discussion of Thailand's special position with regard to China".[233] In contrast, China's action plan with Thailand was already nearly seven years in progress and doubtless undergoing regular revision and refinement. And the Sino-Thai Strategic Partnership, formally launched in 2005, followed not two days but *four years* of dialogue. Both were motivated more by the US than any other factor, with the US-controlled Straits of Malacca utterly central. The chief US delegate concluded his summary and presaged his ambassadorship by claiming that "the rise of China was not a zero sum game and could benefit both the U.S. and Thailand".[234]

The Thais presented a six-page draft and suggested it be concluded in three months. The embassy offered that it "may have some utility in helping us promote key U.S. objectives"; the Foreign Ministry that it would assist in bureaucratic turf wars. Mention was made in the joint statement after Thaksin's meeting with Bush in September 2005.[235] In 2006, Rumsfeld's office gave a briefing on US efforts to improve relations with China, which the Thais described as "a relief for us smaller countries in the region".[236] The Seventh Fleet discussed China's "future role" with Thai leaders, as Congressional delegations asked about its recent military buildup.[237] Thaksin told them that Sino-Thai relations were "very close, particularly under his administration".[238] The final word before the coup was that "Post seeks guidance from Washington on whether to proceed with the Action Plan."[239] Thus Thaksin's recollection of US engagement generally also applied to his effort to facilitate an exception: "Every time there was a visit at the secretary level, even the presidential level, they would come and just do one thing and go. Then some assistant secretary would follow up and the next visit it would have to be redone."[240]

* * *

Under the prevailing counterterrorism rubric in 2003, Thailand implemented a Container Security Initiative on both coasts. The next year, under a program whereby US states are linked with foreign nations regarding security cooperation, Thais participated in exercises off their own shores and those of Washington State. In 2005 and 2006, ports were the focus of programs designed to stem the shipment of materials used in weapons of mass destruction, and to improve the security of Laem Chabang port on the Gulf of Thailand. Given its "capacity to support large USN ships visiting Thailand—including U.S. aircraft carriers—making sure the port was secure would enhance our force protection capabilities", according to the embassy.[241] The US "Eyes in the Sky" initiative consisted of a single patrol flight from each of three countries in the Straits of Malacca, Malaysia, Singapore, and Indonesia. As an observer in 2005, Thailand was unimpressed with this "token" effort, but backed Indonesia's "Combined Maritime Patrol" program of ships reporting to regional port stations.[242] Not only was one such port slated for Thailand's Andaman coast, but with focus on the Straits, it could potentially "provide tactical feed from all of the stations into a Thai–U.S Maritime Operations Intelligence Fusion" plan.[243] It was clear, however, that US interest in maritime intelligence was not related to China, since the US Joint Inter-agency Task Force assigned to it focused exclusively on illicit trafficking. This was consistent with their queries on international crime and "a terrorist link to piracy in the Malacca Strait".[244]

A Regional Maritime Security Initiative (RMSI) was endorsed by Thailand and the US Congress in 2006, "to secure Thai territorial waters in the Andaman Sea ... provide radar coverage of the northern entrance to the Strait of Malacca ... provide coverage of the entire western side of peninsular Thailand down to Sumatra ... give the RTN a coastal interdiction capacity, enhanced communications and improved aerial observation radar".[245] Indeed, "the heart of the initiative" was a high-frequency radar covering 200 nautical miles to the northern Straits, linked to a Maritime Operations Center. Six Boston Whaler patrol boats, three search and surveillance aircraft, and ground sensors would

> curb gun running between the South and Aceh, thwart smuggling, protect fisheries, and rescue sailors ... Half the world's oil tankers and a third of the world's waterborne commerce pass through the Strait—this initiative could be instrumental in protecting that commerce ... monitoring the movements of suspected terrorists ... furthering the Proliferation Security Initiative.[246]

Cooperation and coordination with Malaysia, Singapore, Indonesia, the Philippines, and India was expressly noted. Yet, in hailing this "ambitious project aimed at promoting domain awareness in the Andaman Sea", the embassy seemed unaware of the one nation most interested in the domain.[247] China, with its insatiable appetite for tankers and trade, eluded US diplomats with front-row seats.

Conversely, it was not China's absence but its inclusion that skewed the design of joint US–Thai military exercises. In 2006, the embassy was "convinced that we can continue to modify Cobra Gold and other exercises to meet our regional security objectives—including an ability to establish a near-continuous presence in the region".[248] Growing participation of Singapore, Japan, and Indonesia in Cobra Cold was rightly welcomed as both evidence and promise of greater US influence in "Asia". But what of China's limited observation from 2002 onwards (save for 2004)? On the one hand, its rise to that point had been primarily economic, lending real if short-lived validity to claims of "partnership" with Beijing. And as the direction and implications of China's growth remained unclear, Cobra Gold could be seen as the operational analogue of IMET training. On its face this was not unwise. Yet, given the near-total absence of the predominant regional power from US regional thinking, it was only half the equation. Inviting China to observe parts of Cobra Gold without making it an express subject of "observation" during the majority part was strategically naïve—even in 2002. A cable to Washington betrayed an eastern blind spot:

> Given the wide range of U.S. security interests in East Asia—ranging from counterterrorism and counter narcotics to non-proliferation—there may be other key foreign policy objectives we could support through our exercise program in Thailand of which we are unaware. Post welcomes any suggestions or guidance from addressees about ways we can shape our program in Thailand to advance our interests in this region.[249]

Similarly, in 2005 the US focused the CARAT naval exercises on issues pertaining to the Regional Maritime Security Initiative, and increased their "regional flavor" the following year.[250] Claiming that the Thai navy was "searching for a mission", the US also saw the Initiative as a means of extending and exerting influence.[251] After the Pacific tsunami destroyed half the Phang Nga naval base on the Andaman Sea, Thailand readily welcomed an offer to assist in rebuilding. In the Americans' estimation, it was "the only strategic naval facility on Thailand's west coast".[252] Across the country's narrow isthmus was the U-Tapao airbase on the Gulf of Thailand, leading to the South China Sea. It was little known outside of military circles that it belonged to the Thai navy, not the air force. Although it continued to see over 420 US military aircraft each year, "we cannot take for granted the access we have enjoyed to date. Despite the high tempo of U.S. activity in Utapao, we have offered very little in the way of lasting facility improvements or maintenance that would provide mutual benefits and be supportive of our strategic objectives regarding expanded access and influence".[253] Thailand asked for such assistance in 2005, which JUSMAG and PACOM duly provided.

Underlying the focus on U-Tapao were two determinations. One was Thaksin's decision in 2001 to reject a second US request to pre-position ships, "floating bases", in the Gulf of Thailand. Unlike a similar decision in 1994 by Chuan, for whom he had briefly been foreign minister, Thaksin did not see the matter as simply maintaining the right balance of power in the region. He did not share Chuan's pro-American outlook and was unmoved by post-9/11 pressure. If the balance was set to shift in China's favor—however slowly on the military front—he was at the very least unconcerned; more likely he approved. Thaksin's decision would have been far less complicated and nuanced than his predecessor's, and even more consistent with his foreign policy vision and orientation. The Americans, whose request was driven by an entirely unrelated crusade, had no appreciation for this in 2001 and little more four years on.

Second was that in 2005 the US judged U-Tapao the "most important Cooperative Security Location (CSL) we have in all of the Asia-Pacific region".[254] Identified pursuant to the Pentagon's Global Posture Review in 2004, CSLs hosted few or no permanent US military personnel but could be used for counterterrorism training, interdiction, and contingency access to areas removed from actual US bases. U-Tapao had historically proven itself in these respects, most recently after the tsunami, and had been the subject of a 1996 agreement allowing its use for training during crises or conflicts—likewise after "floating bases" were denied. Despite or because of its location in the gulf, Boyce acknowledged its "key role" in Straits-related operations.[255] However, reminiscent of the informality that pervaded the US military during the Vietnam War, there were "no formal agreements with any level of the RTG regarding the establishment of CSLs in Thailand. The access that we currently enjoy is solely the result of our traditional alliance and military-to-military partnership that has been sustained over many years".[256] "Hosting" a CSL was also consistent with the express view of the Thai navy that its forces were meant to protect the Andaman Sea and the Gulf of Thailand only and not "blue water" areas.[257]

In view of the expansive region noted by the US (the Asia-Pacific) and the narrow zone delineated by the Thai navy (excluding the Bay of Bengal to the west and the South China Sea to the east), it could be inferred that China factored into both nations' CSL calculations. But such would assign far more concern than either genuinely felt; the Thais by policy design pre-dating 9/11, the Americans by a dearth of policy since then. Moreover, cooperating with US-funded initiatives cost Thaksin as little politically as it did financially— precisely because it cost China nothing at all. To the contrary, Beijing only benefited from others' efforts to secure the passage upon which its exports and energy currently depended, for it was by then concerned less with passing through the Straits of Malacca than *bypassing* it. As the Americans continued to see the maritime region largely through the myopic lens of counterterrorism and transnational crime, the Chinese were investing in a future in which the security of the Straits would hardly matter. Thaksin thus played it expertly, cooperating dutifully with a US "ally" that refused to see "the Straits for the sea", while being the "gateway" for a China playing the long game.

ALL THE TEA IN CHINA

Described by Ambassador Boyce as "part of post's effort to monitor more closely PRC relations with Thailand and ASEAN",[258] in 2005 he initiated "regular tea meetings with the Chinese"[259] and hosted large dinners on "many nights together".[260] Similar to his Cambodia "cabal" in the late 1980s, the effort revealed a greater appreciation in the embassy than in Washington of Chinese ascendency. Reciprocating, China's delegation invited the Americans to a Chinese New Year reception and "suggested that Thailand provides a convenient venue to discuss regional issues".[261] Indeed, Boyce rightly assessed that "Chinese diplomats are rarely interested in the minutiae of Thai politics and are much more interested in US involvement."[262] China's ambassador said that their nations could cooperate on security in the Straits of Malacca. Referencing the 2001 mid-air collision over the South China Sea, the military attaché said, "It is our job in the field to find ways to build trust."[263] An expert on counterterrorism, Central Asia, and the Shanghai Cooperation Organization, he had also been briefed on recent high-level visits by US defense officials to Beijing. China believed it could "share a vast array of developmental experiences from which the ASEAN nations can learn and benefit", and encouraged the US to join the EAS.[264] Informality worked both ways, however, as China offered that it "does not invade" other nations[265] while "neither ... mentioned our differences over Taiwan".[266]

Entrepreneurs and journalists from China were also a source of information for and about both powers. In 2006, local Chinese businessmen told the US that they blamed Thailand's southern insurgency on a corrupt Thai government and "US interest and involvement".[267] One asked plainly, "first Iraq and now North Korea, why should anyone listen to you (the US)?"[268] Friendlier but no less ominous was an influential Taiwanese businessman:

> China is seizing the opportunity to expand and cement existing influence in Southeast Asia "while the U.S. is tied up in Iraq and Afghanistan" ... Chinese leaders look at foreign investment as a political tool ... China's more active and collegial participation in ASEAN in recent years is yet another indicator of China's policy of expanding its influence in the region ... Thaksin Shinawatra has facilitated China's policy.[269]

A *Guangming Daily* reporter asked the US embassy not to disclose their meeting to anyone. He confided that China's main goal in Thailand was to "keep a close eye on the US", believing the ASEAN–US Enhanced Partnership was designed to "counterbalance the PRC".[270] Yet he argued that Beijing's "double insurance" of economic links and powerful Sino-Thai would spell continued advantage.[271] In addition, "PRC reporters swarm to US military functions ... six reporters from Xinhua showed up for the opening of the Cobra Gold exercise last year despite Xinhua only having three reporters on staff in Bangkok ... focused on taking photographs of the machinery and headshots of US officers".[272]

THE LAST AMERICAN COUP

That the Chinese did not anticipate Thailand's 2006 coup was partly because related announcements and activity had existed only in the extremes. Whispers behind closed doors alternated with megaphones at PAD street rallies. And although both gave rise to daily speculation starting in late 2005, rumors are notoriously fickle harbingers. At that time, Thaksin and privy councilor Prem tangled over the annual military reshuffle, resulting in eventual coup-maker General Sonthi remaining as commander-in-chief. While he reportedly set up a team devoted to uncovering any plots against him, Thaksin told Boyce that he had "a uniformly good relationship with the Palace".[273] At the end of the year, General Surayud, by then retired and a fellow privy councilor, asked the PAD to cease calling on the monarchy to act. Instead, in February 2006 it publicly delivered a petition to Prem, not royalty per se but long-time head of Network Monarchy. Surayud told the Americans that "there had been 'some talk' within the military about the option of a 'one-day' coup which would turn power over to the King", but that General Sonthi "absolutely did not support such a move".[274] Nevertheless, that same month planning for a coup within the next two to three months began.

In March, Boyce told Washington, "Thais tend either to look to the US for leadership or blame the US for what goes wrong. That said, it is particularly striking that neither side is asking for the US to take their part in the ongoing struggle ... everyone wants to know what we know—but no one has asked us what to do".[275] He would meet three times that month with the king's principal private secretary, a former ambassador to the US, who said that both sides were dragging the palace into the fray and described Thaksin's relationship with the king as "correct".[276] Boyce gave him an advance copy of the already controversial *The King Never Smiles*, a book by a US journalist to be published later in the year. Tej Bunnag, former ambassador to both the US and China and assistant to the secretary, complained to Boyce that the press was turning a regularly scheduled Privy Council meeting into a political event. General Sonthi told the embassy that the situation was different from 1992, when the king had stopped violent demonstrations, in that the army lacked a "vested interest" in Thaksin's fate. The Americans were "struck by how tepid the senior Army leadership's support for Thaksin seemed to be", although "Sonthi gave every appearance of being a measured professional who is committed to keeping the Army on the sidelines".[277] Another of the coup's planners told Boyce that the military was "firmly on the sidelines".[278] Prem said outright that Thaksin should "go now", and that the embassy should try to influence his more amenable advisors.[279] Even Surakiart—still in Thaksin's government—confided that someone "with the Palace's authority" should make the premier step down.[280]

Thaksin reportedly learned of a coup plot for the run-up to April elections, likely influencing his decision to take a "break" from the premiership after the polls.[281] Surayud told the Americans that Thaksin had met the king beforehand but had not been directed in any way. Chief advisor Pansak, however, accused a "small cabal of advisors in the palace of interpreting the King's words and actions to force Thaksin's resignation".[282] Neither mentioned a coup, but Prem was again central. While Boyce was more persuaded by Surayud—Thaksin "sees no irony in comparing himself to Aung San Suu Kyi"—Pansak urged the US to issue a statement.[283] In May, still worried about the PAD, Surayud made two other meaningful points with the embassy. He "expressed concern that the ongoing political stalemate would likely cause budget woes for the armed services".[284] Although Thaksin had raised the budget to minimize opposition, it had fallen greatly since the "Thai Spring" a decade before—and would sky-rocket after the coup. Surayud also said that "contacts within the judiciary expected it would take at least two or three months ... to render decisions in all of the cases having an impact on the political situation".[285] Four more months would pass before the army intervened, but not all such decisions had been rendered.

Thaksin sent a letter to President Bush in June. He claimed that his government was being "repeatedly undermined by interests that depend on creating chaos and mounting street demonstrations in Bangkok as a means to acquire political power that they cannot gain through winning elections ... my opponents are now attempting various extra-constitutional tactics to co-opt the will of the people".[286] The "interests" were understood as Prem and Network Monarchy. Belying a lack of interest, Bush's reply that "the Thai people are resilient and the Thai democracy is strong", was open to positive interpretation by both sides. Indeed, Senator Kraisak and the Foreign Ministry protested about Thaksin's letter in the media, while the PAD marched on six embassies—including China's—and delivered an open letter to the US:

> We reaffirm the Thai people's determination to carry on the equal, sincere and mutually beneficial relations of friendship between our two countries that the kings of Thailand have forged with the presidents of the United States of America over centuries ... This is why we must apologize to the United States government for the head of Thailand's caretaker government breaching protocol by bypassing your ambassador here ... seeking personal friendship over and above the friendship between our two countries.[287]

General Sonthi called the situation "untenable" in July, but claimed to have the military firmly under control.[288] Boyce replied that the military's remaining on the sidelines "can largely be attributed to Sonthi himself",[289] but also reminded

Washington that "one can never completely rule out the potential for military intervention in Thailand".[290] Prem told Boyce he had advised Thaksin to clarify his letter to Bush, and that he "needed to learn that he was the manager of the shop, not the owner".[291] In his own meeting with Boyce, Thaksin freely admitted he was referring to Prem and recounted a recent trust-building meeting with General Sonthi, who assured him that, "as a Muslim and therefore a moral person, he would never condone a coup".[292] Thaksin also met with long-time US contact Karl Jackson, telling him he would not return as premier after new elections and placed the crisis in "a 30-year cycle in Thai politics: 1946, 1976, and now 2006".[293] Predicting that it would be resolved within forty-five days, Thaksin told Jackson that, "there are only two ways out of this, assassination or a coup". Jackson joked that he should "Take the latter", although fifty-one days later a car bomb narrowly missed him.[294]

A former cabinet secretary told the embassy "that he believed that Thaksin's family members might also become targets for Thaksin's opponents".[295] Conversely, he said that the premier had long become paranoid, tapping his ministers' phones, having aides test his food, intimating consequences for resignation. Pansak protested that Thaksin had tried to protect the Crown Property Bureau from economic harm, and the palace from *The King Never Smiles*. Finally, Boyce met twice more with Surayud, the last time on 1 September 2006: "Surayud told the Ambassador he considered Sonthi as a solid professional and an unemotional person—not the type to carry out a coup. When the Ambassador remarked that, given Thai history, it might be unwise to think a coup would be impossible, Surayud simply laughed."[296]

* * *

On the afternoon of 19 September 2006, Ambassador Boyce was in the northern Thai province of Chiang Mai on leave, riding elephants with his family. Before flying back to Bangkok, his deputy called him to ask whether there was "any unusual military movement at the airport".[297] Thaksin was in New York, but "there were rumors that the Thais might do an Aquino on him"—kill him on the tarmac the way former Philippines senator Aquino was shot dead in Manila in 1983.[298] As Chiang Mai was Thaksin's home province, speculation was that he might land there instead of Bangkok. Boyce then got a call from Senator Kraisak, who requested that he keep his phone turned on all evening; he would later explain that his concern was for Thais possibly needing protection inside the embassy or ambassadorial residence. At that point, Boyce called Surayud, who said he had heard the same rumors but doubted that anything would happen "tonight".[299] A week later, he told Boyce he had been "in his pajamas" just after 9:30pm when royal songs interrupted a broadcast from Thaksin's hotel room.[300] "He maintains that when we spoke, he was on his way home from a palace religious ceremony … After returning home, he had turned on the TV and saw Thaksin's attempt to declare emergency rule and fire Army Chief Sonthi. At that point, Prem called and instructed him to 'come to the palace'."[301] General Sonthi later said that the army needed two days' lead time for the coup, making Thaksin's trip abroad the ideal opportunity. "All along I had advised Thaksin not to go to the UN at that time because it was too unstable", recalled his foreign minister.[302]

The coup was unique in Thai history in featuring the Second Army Division's 11th and 21st Infantry Regiments, the latter being the Queen's Guard. Retaining area responsibility for Bangkok, the First Regiment of the army's First Division—the King's Guard—was hardly marginalized, but it did not dominate the leadership as it had in most previous coups. Soldiers wore royalist yellow ribbons on their uniforms, while the leadership promptly branded itself the Council for Democratic Reform under the Constitutional Monarchy (CDRM). In a late-night call from Boyce, Thaksin's explanation did not contradict the imagery: "I said they allege me of not being loyal to the king and they think I was the one who sponsored *The King Never Smiles*. I have never known Handley. He was very critical of me although I have never met him in my life, I didn't know who he was. Pansak told me who he was. And that was the allegation."[303] He would add later that, "Boyce may have written not a good report about me to Washington, because he had a one-sided view from the Yellow, especially those who criticized me, former CIA staff".[304] The junta's first announcement was to cancel national elections scheduled for October. The State Department said it was "monitoring the situation with concern".[305]

The next day, after Thaksin canceled his speech to the UN and prepared to leave for London, President Bush took the podium. "I was still at the UN", recalled Thaksin, "and George Bush delivered a speech about democracy in the General Assembly. But he never mentioned the coup d'etat in Thailand. It looked like the Americans felt good that I had been ousted. Never mentioned it."[306] The US embassy also noted that the omission was "widely commented upon here".[307] While Bush was probably and rightly waiting for guidance from that same embassy, a "mention" of the coup as at least a factual occurrence would have been welcome and wise. A democratically elected government had just been overthrown by its military. A formal ally by no fewer than three measures had just been rendered uncertain. And in front of the US president sat not the White House press corps or Congress, but representatives of literally every nation in the world, including the People's Republic of China. As far as Thailand was concerned, it was a foreign policy concession speech.

Nothing formal came out of the State Department that day either, a delay Boyce would later attribute to the coup's timing relative to Washington's 12pm press cycle—"bad luck".[308] On Washington's clock, the coup occurred less than three hours before noon on 19 September; the embassy would forward a draft statement at 6.55am on the 20th. During those twenty-two hours, the embassy focused primarily on what action the US should take, sending those proposals over an hour *before the draft statement* and recommending that a statement wait until the proposals had been reviewed. Further, while the draft statement was still sent a full five hours before the next press cycle, its language would appear only piecemeal for a *week* as press quotes. It read in full:

> In response to the military coup in Thailand, the United States is
> suspending assistance to the Thai government in a variety of areas,
> including military assistance. We note the stated commitment of the
> Council for Democratic Reform Under the Monarchy (CDRM) to set up
> a civilian government within two weeks. We urge that democratic elections
> be held as soon as possible. We believe the Thai people are capable of
> resolving their political differences in a peaceful manner and in accordance
> with the principles of democracy and rule of law.[309]

Yet far from needing specific determinations, the draft statement did not so much as require agreement in principle in Washington to suspend "military assistance". For it was not a matter of discretion but of law: Section 508 of the US Foreign Operations Appropriations Act obligated the government to implement military sanctions against Thailand, as a nation that had just experienced a coup. US diplomats in both countries were right to favor substance over speed, but the law left them little initial discretion, leaving them even less excuse for delay. Thirty-four minutes after cabling the draft statement, Boyce unwittingly expressed the law's inspiration and intent: "A coup is a coup is a coup and we believe a strong U.S. statement … is entirely warranted".[310] He would later rue that "we were the last country to criticize".[311]

Boyce was, however, rightly credited for his balance of prudence and principle on the ground. "He played it the right way", recalled his political counselor in Bangkok. "He played it with integrity but he also played it with understanding. He was able to deliver a tough message without needlessly offending."[312] Karl Jackson contrasted his response to that in Washington: "His real skill was in handling DC after the coup, for many here wanted to pull the ambassador, break relations. And it was across the aisles."[313] While former Thai premier Anand was "quite flabbergasted" with US press quotes two days after the coup, he also recalled the State Department "prevailing" over a "childish" NSC.[314] Boyce was at the center of that. Indeed, the embassy engaged a flurry of meetings after the coup, including with General Sonthi within hours of the event; it sent six detailed cables to Washington on 20 September alone. Sonthi said that while Thaksin had "not done anything legally incorrect", the "people requested us to act".[315] Others included Prem, the architect of an interim constitution, Democrat Party leader Abhisit Vejjajiva, the central bank governor, the Foreign Ministry, numerous academics, other party leaders, and various business representatives. Boyce also spoke by telephone with the Thai ambassador in New York. Two Thais delivered a letter for President Bush to the embassy, asking that he oppose the new "dictator committee of Thailand".[316] In northern Thailand, US diplomats found themselves under heavy surveillance and their contacts reticent to discuss the situation.

Two overall points for each side were constant but complementary. For the US, military assistance would be suspended, and timetables for both the return of civilian leadership and new elections should be set and kept. For the Thais, Thaksin had left them no other option for ending his undemocratic government, and thus they fully intended to restore democracy as soon as possible. "I told him that I warned him and so now we have to cut off assistance", recalled Boyce on Sonthi. "He understood."[317] The Foreign Ministry acknowledged "the legitimacy of USG statements expressing disappointment",[318] while a fellow junta member agreed that "military force to bring about political change had damaged the country".[319] Only a few Thais claimed a "double standard" in the waiving of US sanctions against Pakistan after its 1999 coup.[320] If there was basic disagreement over the coup's effects—Sonthi claimed that "Thailand is 100 percent democratic now"—the immediate future was in general accord.[321]

The Americans were even willing to "take an encouraging tone to help Thailand set itself back on a democratic path".[322] Despite having claimed that 1992 "convinced me that the army should never be involved in politics", General Surayud was quietly tapped to be Thailand's "civilian" prime minister eight days after the coup.[323] In a meeting with Boyce, he "shared a laugh over the frustrating nature of the position: a difficult job for 8–10 months that angers many people and then you get kicked out".[324] Put simply, both sides well understood the other. Important enough in the short term, this mutual understanding was even more notable for having viability *only* in the short term. As cast in strong relief eight years later when the two nations would hardly speak to each other, much less listen, 2006 marked the final time they would so much as attempt to find common ground.

As Surayud's official appointment was slated for the day before Boyce was due in Washington, he chose to be the first ambassador to call on the new premier, rather than repeat the "bad luck" of being last. Surayud practically preempted Boyce's main message of returning Thailand to democracy within a year via free and fair elections. Surprised but pleased, Boyce then suggested they announce it jointly to a waiting press corps outside; the US could assume a degree of credit, the Thais credibility. As he ruefully explained, however, attracting the most attention was a photograph of the two appearing "buddy-buddy" as they exited the building; "That picture has not been useful to me over the years."[325] Indeed, in the words of a Thaksin cabinet member, "Boyce immediately went to see the generals and that sent a different message, the message that who is out of power is out; who is in is in. I think it was his initiative, and that message was taken negatively by Thaksin."[326]

Noting the perception challenge presented by Surayud's Privy Council membership and military pedigree, Boyce did not favor the royalists over a Team Thaksin seen by many as harboring republican sentiments. But he did understand two things: first, that the monarchy had been inseparable from the military since Field Marshall Sarit in 1957, and had been tied even closer in 1976. While the CDRM would drop the "M" (monarchy) to prevent "damage to the King's reputation" abroad, it was in fact a non-issue.[327] So long had Thailand's military pledged the monarchy's defense as its primary purpose that hardly anyone assigned significance to the junta's names. True that General Sonthi had noted "offenses to the Thai monarch" among his reasons for the coup,[328] but as Boyce explained, this was "not unexpected or atypical".[329]

Thaksin's mistake was in offending not the monarchy as such, but Network Monarchy and Prem in particular. The junta's final name change to the Council for National Security (CNS) elicited far greater comment for its elimination of the truly conspicuous "D" (democratic). Second, Boyce understood that the largest foreign policy element of Thailand's military–monarchy union had long been the United States. Sarit had joined his American patrons with the Thai patriarch, and the king himself had demonstrably restated his pro-US position during the experimental mid-1970s. Generals Sonthi and Surayud were active then and throughout, fighting communists, suppressing the "Thai Spring", commanding the army, advising the palace. Prem was active as well, running the army, nation, and eventually the Privy Council. All had helped make the US a kind of member *ex officio* of Network Monarchy.

What is not clear is whether Boyce fully appreciated the changes underway within Network Monarchy, beginning with the nuanced shift in the units and uniforms that led the coup. That the Queen's Guard was at the forefront, having previously played mostly a defensive role in the failed coups against Prem, held a significance that would become more apparent over the ensuing years. Among the leaders of both Queen's Guard and coup, although not of the CNS, was one General Prayuth Chan-ocha. Commanding a new unit dedicated to repressing dissent and eventually becoming army chief in 2010, he would go on to stage Thailand's 2014 coup. Another would become army chief between the two coups. To be sure, both the King's and Queen's Guards were favored by the palace and had far more in common with one another than with less famed units or those led by Thaksin loyalists. Moreover, both were created during the American era in Thailand and were to a degree American creations. This did not make any of Thailand's coups attributable as such to the US, but it did implicate the US in a tradition of extra-constitutional changes that were often to its benefit. Yet where the King's Guard maintained its US pedigree, the Queen's Guard was evolving, and thus causing a subtle evolution within Network Monarchy.

The result in 2006 was limited, with both units returning to the barracks and a premier with a King's Guard background coming to the fore. Although the generational shift felt most keenly within the Thai and US militaries had an obvious impact on the coup, its aftermath marked the old guard's last stand. In Boyce's words, Surayud's "appointment would be a very positive development for Thailand internally, as well as for Thai–U.S. relations, and we should welcome it".[330] It was notable too that Prem, by then eighty-six years old, was the other main consideration for prime minister. The WTO's former director-general was reportedly blocked for the post after asking to name his own cabinet, but his previous rejection by the Americans (for the WTO) likely also played a role. The new foreign minister was Nitya, who despite late-game FTA differences, had favored the US approach to the deal and had a pro-US history going back a half-century. His "acceptability to the Network seems to have grown out of his American wife's service as Prem's English-language tutor".[331] A graduate of the prestigious US Army academy was named Supreme Commander, and a former Cobra Gold chief remained in charge of border affairs. The simmering kinetics within Thailand's bastions of power would mean a very different dynamic eight years later, but in 2006 the center held. In 2006, Thailand experienced its last American coup.

* * *

The US suspended $29 million in military aid to Thailand. Approaching the minimum required under the relevant US law, it was far more than necessary to "send a message" to the Thais but far too little to ensure it would be received. As indicated by a cable he sent the day after the coup, Boyce understood this; Washington did not. In addition to the stipulated sanctions,

> Post further proposes that those military programs that are similar to initiatives subject to Section 508, but not part of the Foreign Operations Act, also be suspended … It will likely be months before Thailand will have a democratically elected government and we can lift 508 sanctions. In order to give us intermediate measures to encourage the Thai to respect democratic norms, we propose also suspending other military programs, the suspension of which will not jeopardize vital U.S. national interests, until the Thai install an acceptable interim civilian caretaker government.[332]

Despite agreement with Surayud on Thailand's democratic plans, Boyce knew that to make—rather than just state—the point that coups are unacceptable, more than the minimum would be needed. A coup after fifteen years of democratic activity warranted an equally unexpected and exceptional response. Boyce proposed that the US cease "all planning and execution of military exercises, including Cobra Gold", which had not been affected since the last coup in

1991. While appreciating that this would "place a tremendous burden on exercise planners", he rightly concluded that it would "demonstrate to the Thai military the consequences of their actions".[333] Less dramatically, "[a]lthough not subject to 508", Boyce also proposed that no new Thai students be admitted to the prestigious US military academies.[334] Ignoring a request from the junta "that the USG not push the Generals into a corner, but rather help them to create a democratic government", he correctly believed that the best way to accomplish the latter was in fact to do the former.[335] Washington did not agree. Continuing to call for a constitution, elections, and civil liberties, it "tarried on decisions whether to scrap a joint memorandum on military-to-military logistics, an arms-procurement program ... continued use of U-Tapao Air Force Base, and the annual Cobra Gold joint military exercises".[336] In late October, Boyce told Prem—"sensitive to the international implications and especially to the US angle"—that it would "reassess in early November the degree to which progress was being made ... Possible further actions we might take in the absence of progress or if things got worse could include canceling Cobra Gold, suspending ship visits, limiting senior military interaction and cessation of commercial sales of military equipment".[337] These would soon expire without Washington's support.

IMET, Foreign Military Financing (FMF), and the Economic Support Fund (ESF) were not negotiable under Section 508. However, Boyce successfully advocated that Thais already enrolled in IMET and the Counterterrorism Fellowship Program be allowed to complete their studies, pursuant to discretion allowed by law. As he would rightly say in 2015, given its purpose and products, it would have been ideal to "double IMET, it's the gift that keeps on giving".[338] Boyce also subtitled a cable "Programs We Want to Shield", correctly naming the Global Peace Operations Initiative, "discreet bilateral training to assist Thai soldiers rotating to the South to identify and disarm IEDs", and the joint civil affairs/PACOM team countering ideological support for the southern insurgency.[339] General Sonthi had been in direct command of the latter. Yet Boyce erred in advising that regional maritime security programs not be shielded. Despite their lack of focus on China, they were still the US initiatives most closely approximating a geopolitical move; suspending them would allow the Chinese to project even more power and influence. To no one's surprise, the joint Counter-terrorism Intelligence Center was fully maintained.

Ultimately, as a Thai general explained, since Thailand's annual military budget was roughly $2 billion, the $29 million cut by the US barely caused it to "feel the pinch".[340] And pinch was operative, when what was called for as both a punitive and preventive measure was a punch. The US response irritated and annoyed but did not *hurt*. The Thais knew the US law and had been warned, and so were able to simply factor sanctions into their calculation. It is unlikely that they were prepared for a suspension of "all planning and execution of military exercises, including Cobra Gold". That would have forced a post-coup recalculation. When there was none to fear, the US "cried wolf"; it should have given itself reason to shout.

A NEW CHESSBOARD

Citing their own "different standards" after the coup, the Chinese told the US embassy that Thais' "Buddhist philosophy of accepting fate enabled them to easily accept political contradictions like a 'democratic coup'" and a prime minister whose father had led the CPT.[341] They "had urged Beijing to make a quick show of support".[342] More clearly and significantly, the army attaché said that he "looks at U.S. military sanctions as an opportunity to expand influence", and that "his approach of telling the Thai that 'China is your neighbor, we will be here long-term, we will not interfere in your internal affairs,' will give him a leg up on his American counterparts".[343]

That Washington was unmoved by any of this, despite regular dispatches from Bangkok, was telling and consequential enough. What made it truly transformative was its inextricable connection to the shifts underway within Network Monarchy. Tapping into the very foundation of the kingdom's power structure—one the US had helped establish—China was supplanting the Americans in Thailand where it mattered most. According to a Thaksin cabinet minister, President Bush "did not understand the monarchy at all".[344] Relations between the palace and Washington atrophied considerably in the early 2000s, due to the same realities that defined relations more broadly: a war that, unlike its Cold War predecessor, did not feature a central role for the king; and a generational shift coinciding with the twilight of his sixty-year reign. The most the Americans could muster was a US–Thai Education Roundtable, symbolically founded by Princess Sirindhorn in 2001. Royalty still visited the US, including the crown prince in 2003 and the queen in early 2005, but their frequency and profile were declining fast. In contrast to the aura that attended such visits during America's own "Camelot" years, four decades on "the Americans didn't care".[345]

Moreover, royal news from the US was often negative, as in a controversy in 2005 over an ancient headdress at a San Francisco museum. Three times in a single week, Thais protested in front of the US embassy, alleging the piece had been stolen during the 1950s. The first time featured 200 people and six elephants. "Interestingly, the controversy in Thailand was stirred by Prime Minister Thaksin himself."[346] An associate of Princess Sirindhorn asked the embassy to ensure that the item be returned to the palace rather than the government. "He expressed his hope that the matter of the headdress would not spark a major 'diplomatic incident' between the U.S. and Thailand."[347] Six months later, the Foreign Ministry informed the embassy that someone had delivered flyers to the Thai Consulate in Los Angeles, criticizing both the consul general and the royal family. It asked that the FBI investigate; the embassy contacted diplomatic security. In the coup's immediate aftermath, the ministry's main concern was about a US reporter who had asked a disparaging question about the king during a press briefing.

To be sure, the Americans did keep abreast of royal news and views to the degree possible, largely through the Privy Council and others close to the palace. Nearly everyone with whom Ambassador Boyce spoke for eight months before the coup offered a different perspective on how the king, queen, or "the palace" was positioned. Credibility varied as widely as the perspectives, however, as some contacts were genuine insiders, others had the occasional royal audience, and a few were divining tea leaves. Each had personal and political agendas to advance. Worst of all, just fifteen days after the coup, all of these private and personal conversations would become public with the founding of WikiLeaks.

In contrast, two weeks after the coup China's ambassador told the US that Princess Sirindhorn was "our special Ambassador in Thailand".[348] This was no mere platitude: in 2004 the Chinese People's Association for Friendship with Foreign Countries had awarded her the title of "friendship ambassador".[349] She had been visiting China for over twenty years, including for two weeks annually in April for her birthday, and spoke Mandarin fluently. Princess Chulabhorn had also become a frequent and extended visitor, engaging in teaching and other activities. According to a Foreign Ministry official who worked extensively in Beijing under Thaksin, "The Chinese really cherished that even more than the government, because they knew governments come and go, but that royalty does not go. The Chinese were willing to go an extra mile to receive our royals. Whatever we asked it was always given."[350] Chinese visits to Thailand likewise "touched all the bases"; Hu Jintao's welcome dinner on a 2003 state visit was held at a royal palace.[351] The official further recalled Thaksin getting upset when a Chinese leader asked to call on Prem, "an old friend".[352] He posited that in China's eyes, and accounting for the understanding and respect, Thailand's monarchy was akin to its own Communist Party. Not of course in ideology—the root of their deep enmity for decades—but in standing and influence. A cabinet minister had a simpler assessment: "The Chinese *got it*."[353]

Chapter Nine:
China's Pivot (2006–2014)

In many ways, the story of Thailand is the story of this region … And when a new occupant moves into the White House next year, America's alliances in Asia will be the strongest they have ever been.[1]

George W. Bush, August 2008

Initially, we held out hope that—as happened with the 2006 coup—the military would move relatively quickly to transfer power to a civilian government and move towards free and fair elections. However, recent events have shown that the current military coup is both more repressive and likely to last longer than the last one.[2]

Scot Marciel, June 2014

When China emerges because of her size, because of history, some other countries start talking about a China threat. But for Thais, because we are so close by blood, we are naturally more at ease in engaging with China. You would be surprised at how many Western delegations came through that used the term "China threat" or "Chinese threat", and my response was always, "Well, what threat?" We didn't see China as a threat. We obviously saw her as a major power and therefore maybe having a lot of influence, but we didn't have this feeling that she would be a threat.[3]

Abhisit Vejjajiva, February 2015

In a late 2011 article in *Foreign Policy*, articulating a vision first mentioned two years earlier, Secretary of State Hillary Clinton began: "As the war in Iraq winds down and America begins to withdraw its forces from Afghanistan, the United States stands at a pivot point."[4] The pivot in question was away from a decade-long policy of reactive and bellicose anti-terrorism in the Middle East, toward one proactively focused on peace and prosperity in Asia. She went on to state, "Our treaty alliances with Japan, South Korea, Australia, the Philippines, and Thailand are the fulcrum for our strategic turn to the Asia-Pacific."[5] Yet in the preceding three years, Clinton and her boss in the White House had done little to make such a pivot possible, and as subsequent years would show, none was forthcoming. The result was not regional inertia, however, or even continuance of the status quo in which Sino-Thai relations grew at US–Thai expense, but an acceleration of that trend. Despite its sound conception and calculated introduction, the pivot had the innate capacity to alarm the Chinese. The Americans knew this, and rightly judged it unavoidable but manageable: it was natural that one global power would react to a major policy change of another, and an actual pivot could present as much opportunity as challenge for Beijing. It was, after all, a belated response to China's powerful rise. The problem was that the US announced its plan but failed to carry out more than preliminary steps. Where the US response to Thailand's coup had been welcomed and taken advantage of by China, its plan to pivot was unwelcome, spurring still more engagement in Thailand, Southeast Asia, the Asia-Pacific. US policy was finally spot-on, but its architects and agents could not get out of their own way. Causing China to pivot even further into the country and region, America's non-pivot would backfire.

In Thailand, if the eight years following the 2006 coup recalled the "Thai Spring" of the 1990s in the succession of premiers, they were its opposite in policy orientation abroad and at home: China and the China Model would increasingly flourish in Thailand. Even with their most notable representative in exile, the Sino-Thai would consolidate their control among all governments, groups, fighters, and factions. Network Monarchy would remain Thaksin's political enemy, but prove—through governments both military and civilian—his fellow traveler on rights, democracy, and the rule of law. In 2007, the government disavowed Thaksin at every turn, but could not and would not turn back or away from the China he courted so strongly. The 1997 Constitution, opus of the Thai Spring, was jettisoned for one designed to disempower parties and disenfranchise voters. A new "Red" movement opposed this and everything else the "Yellow" PAD publicly espoused, but otherwise shared its antipathy for democracy; its United Front for Democracy Against Dictatorship (UDD) was also not what it claimed. China itself, busy cutting opportunistic military deals, feigned indifference. The Americans, in self-imposed political exile, could do little more than "urge", "warn", and "encourage".

In 2008, two Thaksin nominees took office via popular vote, before having it taken away by court decisions referred to by both sides as "judicial coups". An increasingly violent and reactionary PAD again led the charge for Network Monarchy, albeit more and more as a rogue member. It occupied Government House and Bangkok's two airports, as the army commenced a six-year stretch in which it forgot, refused, or failed to keep order. Concerned with stability above all else, China kept a close watch, but managed to stage its first joint military exercises in Thailand and ensure a repressive running of the Olympic torch through Bangkok. The US literally praised the Thai army for its "restraint", while surrendering the top spot among Thailand's trading partners to China.

Abhisit Vejjajiva was prime minister in 2009 through mid-2011, representing a Democrat Party with a long US history. Coinciding with the election of President Barack Obama, relations would enjoy their most constructive and balanced period since the late Clinton–Chuan governments of the 1990s. Encompassing the largest share of Thailand's eighteen months as ASEAN chair, 2009 also saw modest advances in US regional relations. Yet casting a long shadow over Abhisit's government was Thaksin Shinawatra, by then living abroad. Many of his initiatives remained or returned, while Thailand's human rights record changed in color but not in tone. Abhisit's foreign minister could reconcile his pro-American sentiments with neither China's inexorable march nor his personal endorsement of the PAD. Indeed, indicative of Network Monarchy generally, the Democrats spent most of their energy reacting to real, anticipated, or imagined actions by Thaksin, rather than developing original policies. The courts confiscated more than half his wealth in 2010, triggering the most deadly protests-*cum*-crackdown in modern Thai history. Reminiscent of Pridi, who had likewise fled to China under a cloud of royal suspicion a half-century before, Thaksin remained a specter hanging over the country. Unlike Pridi, he remained the most influential Thai in the world. China's concern for stability heightened, but for the second time in three years over 70 percent of Thais ranked the Middle Kingdom as Thailand's closest friend; Princess Sirindhorn had visited over thirty times. The US, despite a global financial crisis of its own making, could not get FTA talks restarted with Thailand and lost a tug-of-war with *Laos* over Cold War refugees. Visits to Bangkok by Bush (mid-2008) and Obama (late 2012) on either side of Abhisit's premiership would demonstrate how great the gap between the two "allies" had become, and how little and late were the efforts to close it.

Finally, a decade after he first took office, Thaksin effectively became Thailand's premier for a third time in 2011 via Yingluck, his sister and proxy. At the same time, King Bhumibol, America's single most steadfast Southeast Asian ally over three generations, was in declining health. With evidence mounting that elections had become merely another means of deciding the color of authoritarianism, Yingluck also focused on the China Model's economic element: Trade with the Chinese grew 21 percent in 2011 compared to 9 percent with the US. As China's premier became the first foreign national ever to speak in the Thai Parliament, the US fumbled the diplomatic football with an ambassador more interested in Washington than Bangkok. What limited common ground had been found under Abhisit was ceded by the Americans, transferred by the Thais, claimed by the Chinese. Recalling China's embassy eight years before, this would culminate in US surprise at the 2014 coup, and in the amateurish response it managed at record speed. Having consistently misinterpreted the Thai army's incompetence and calculation as forbearance or professionalism, the US was not only back-footed but knocked over. China, as it had since the start of the century, stood firm—a new ally in all but name. In being overthrown, Yingluck thus unwittingly finished what Thaksin had begun years before in being elected: regardless of who held power moving forward, they would look first and foremost to Beijing.

SURAYUD/BACK TO THE FUTURE (2006-2007)

The US response to Thailand's coup and the military-installed government blurred the lines between political and military relations over the next sixteen months. Wasting no time, Chinese Premier Wen Jiabao met with Surayud during an ASEAN–China meeting in October 2006 in Beijing. The PLA's chief of staff met in Bangkok with the Thai supreme commander and defense minister. Indicative of Beijing's ability to hedge its political bets, was its granting Thaksin entry six weeks after the coup, despite not being informed of his arrival in advance. After attempting to meet Surayud at the ASEAN gathering, he traveled south in December without incident. General Sonthi visited China in January 2007, meeting not only the defense minister but the vice-president, about which "the Chinese made a great production".[6] Although he told Ambassador Boyce that little of substance was discussed, the Chinese embassy announced that increased military exchanges and procurement would be forthcoming; both sides publicly pledged closer "friendly" relations.[7] March saw a Chinese state councilor visit Prime Minister Surayud, and, in a "meeting between old friends", General Chavalit.[8] Surayud visited China again in May. In the words of a Thai official whose assignment in Beijing staggered the Thaksin and Surayud governments, the Chinese maintained a "foreign policy of convenience, not based on any virtue".[9]

In February 2007, a full year before the US would renew its aid and assistance, China gave Thailand $49 million for military use. Seven months later, the Thai navy would spend all but $1 million of it on Chinese C-801 anti-ship missiles. More momentous was the May signing of a security joint action plan—pursuant to the broader Strategic Partnership agreed two years before—covering cooperation in fifteen areas through 2011. Among them were the first joint military exercises with any nation involving China's special forces: "Strike 2007" featured marksmanship, hand-to-hand combat, jungle warfare, and hostage rescue for thirteen days in Guangdong province. Thailand observed several exercises China conducted with other nations, and the Chinese continued to send observers to Cobra Gold. The number of exchange students at each other's staff colleges also rose. In addition, the action plan addressed terrorism, trafficking, money laundering, cyber-crime, and piracy.

Military-political complex

The US spent most of its energy after the coup advocating a progressive constitution and lifting martial law; the Thais demurred and deferred. According to the supreme commander, "martial law in Thailand was much less draconian than what was perceived in the United States".[10] Democrat Party leader Abhisit advised maintaining pressure "without giving the impression the USG wanted to alienate Thailand".[11] Thus following a decision to partially lift martial law in November, the Americans allowed a visit by former President Bush to proceed the following month. That they also agreed to hold the annual Cope Tiger air force exercises, however, was remarkably ill-advised. Moreover, the leading advocate was not Washington but the embassy in Bangkok, judging the move on martial law sufficient to protest at an initial cancelation by the Defense Department. That is, two months after rightly favoring a "carrot and stick" approach, Boyce saw it as having already worked: not participating "will be sending the Thai mixed messages, and this will not enhance our ability to encourage a quicker return to democracy".[12] The Foreign Ministry had requested that the US not "punish us more just to get your message out",[13] and the US complied. Cope Tiger would take place at the end of January 2007 with over 800 US service members. An advisor to Surayud concluded that, "official US policy is mandatory, but we sense the Defense Department is trying to work its way around the measures. Washington understands full well that the military is in the driver's seat and China is waiting in the wings".[14] If only temporarily, Washington did finally seem to understand what Boyce had been saying since the coup—only to see him lose resolve.

Thaksin called Boyce twice in 2006 and again in the wake of New Year's Eve bomb attacks in Bangkok. After merely thanking the embassy for assisting with a US visa during the first call, in December he asked whether former President Bush would be meeting Surayud during his upcoming visit. He also sent a letter "in friendship and solidarity" to the current President Bush: "Together we have made huge strides ... I personally continue to believe that democracy is the best system of government ... I deeply believe that sustaining and enhancing the cooperation between Thailand and the United States of America continues to serve the greater good of all of our peoples and the world at large".[15] During the third call, Thaksin asked whether the US knew who carried out the New Year bombings and complained that Surayud had publicly accused him within hours of the blasts. Specifying no offense, Thai authorities told Boyce that the courts might sentence Thaksin, "but would be inclined to let him off ... the real reason for the coup had been to ensure Thaksin would remain out of power forever".[16] Thailand placed no onus on the US for the work of several Washington public relations firms on Thaksin's behalf, although protesters asked for embassy support in a Thaksin-related dispute with Singapore. The ex-premier visited the US in April 2007.

Bomb attacks in Bangkok on New Year's Eve triggered US technical assistance, but no let-up in its desire to see martial law fully lifted. Boyce "would have great difficulty recommending" that Washington welcome Foreign Minister Nitya,[17] who "appeared taken aback" by embassy maps showing where martial law remained in effect.[18] One coup-planner and long-time CIA associate said that the law was completely unnecessary. Surayud partly agreed—lifting it in Bangkok the day Cope Tiger began—but struck the embassy as "increasingly disengaged".[19] The US informed Thailand that no decision had yet been taken on Cobra Gold. In February, Sonthi and Anand were highly critical of Surayud in meetings with Boyce—"no national agenda, no strategy, no management skills, and no guts"—but asked whether he might nonetheless be invited to

Washington.[20] Boyce poured cold water on the idea, and warned "that any move to elevate a military man to the premiership would be unacceptable to the United States".[21] At the same time, he told Washington that "We have much to gain from proceeding with Cobra Gold and little to lose."[22] In May, amid fears "even to cosmopolitan interlocutors" that Thaksin was influencing US policy,[23] Sonthi "acknowledged that there had been talk of staging a follow on coup to replace Surayud".[24] Boyce informed Washington that its criticism was being seen as "'betrayal' of an old friend",[25] especially in view of "the more ingratiating approach of the Chinese".[26] But he did not recommend either scaling back or scaling up the US response; Cobra Gold was underway.

* * *

In mid-2007, the embassy endorsed the supreme commander's bid to visit the US military academy he had once attended, as he had not planned the coup and had proven a moderate since. His trip would "serve as a poignant reminder of the benefits that the Thai will lose should they further delay their return to a democratically elected government".[27] The embassy also endorsed his attending a defense conference in Hawaii. In contrast, it argued against permitting the assistant commander-in-chief to study explosives in the US, as he "professes a strong supporting role in the coup-related activities and likely gained his fourth star because of it".[28] As with other IMET matters, Boyce made the right calls.

Not subject to automatic sanctions (which surprised the Chinese), sales of US equipment were among the "beyond Section 508" measures kept as leverage against democratic slippage. A month after the coup, due to "short suspension dates" before they would be canceled or shifted elsewhere, the embassy recommended that six pending requests proceed. It should have done so conclusively for only two cases, both for the Thai navy: a $60 million purchase of two MH-60S Naval Knight Hawk helicopters and maintenance for P-3 patrol aircraft. Even without US appreciation for China's maritime strategy, the approvals were well-advised. Two requests for the air force should have been denied. The decision on two final maintenance requests for F-16s, both related to the contentious replacement of the aging fighters, was debatable. Regardless, a year later Thailand would finally put an end to the three-year saga by choosing Sweden's Gripens over new F-16s (and Russian jets). Despite the six recent approvals, the Thais publicly claimed that sanctions had forced their hand. They also noted that the Gripens left few funds remaining for mid-life upgrades to existing F-16s, meaning that a lost anchor-level deal would have ripple effects for years to come. Two years after no less than the US president had cited their "allied status" in addressing the issue, Thailand was swayed not by Moscow but by Stockholm.

Days before a July 2007 visit by Vietnam War veteran and influential US Senator Jim Webb, the embassy supported the sale of M-16 rifles to Thailand to maintain interoperability with American forces. The Thais changed their minds, however, purchasing Israeli machine-guns, and later passed on approved M-113 armored vehicles for a Ukrainian model. In his meeting with Webb, Surayud "acknowledged somewhat ruefully that it was difficult to convince the U.S. Congress that his predecessor (former PM Thaksin Shinawatra) had not set a 'good example'".[29] Yet it was not the US that was saying no. After a visiting US diplomat was asked without irony how the US managed a fully elected senate, Foreign Minister Nitya met with Congress in September 2007.

* * *

Three weeks after the coup, a US diplomat of Chinese descent visited an "American corner" at a northeastern Thai university, where Thais asked if they could practice Mandarin with her; "students stated that their interest in Chinese was fueled by the prospect of employment".[30] The university was negotiating with another in China to set up a Confucius center. Noting the irony, Boyce cabled Washington that, "Although Chinese is by no means 'replacing' the importance of English—and by analogy China 'replacing' America—it is quickly catching up in its level of importance in the eyes of the Thai people."[31] By April 2007, he conceded that "telling America's story to over 62 million Thais is a colossal task", as the embassy launched a speaker series aimed at reaching young and provincial Thais.[32] At least twenty schools and civic groups, alongside the country's five American corners, would host embassy staff that year to hear about "women's leadership, the civil rights movement, Thai films in the United States, the American high school experience, and environmental issues".[33] Five breaking-of-the-fast events during Ramadan, including one at the ambassador's residence, included presentations and yielded difficult questions ("Why does George Bush hate Muslims and think they are all terrorists?").[34]

Indeed, the US war in Iraq continued to complicate relations; Boyce and Nitya discussed it in January 2007, Senator Webb and Surayud did the same six months later. In between, the Thais again raised their Islamic insurgency and ASEAN's Muslim-majority countries as reasons for continued hesitation on the Proliferation Security Initiative. Wide knowledge by then that the US had lied about their presence in Iraq also made the PSI's focus on weapons of mass destruction problematic. The US's fast-track approach continued to slow down the process: "PSI is not a legal instrument", complained a senior Foreign Ministry official. "You cannot submit it to the cabinet for approval."[35]

The Americans' worst diplomatic own-goal was scored with foreseeable yet unforeseen consequences. On account of growing danger in Iraq, the State Department guaranteed foreign service officers one of their top five choices for their next assignment in exchange for one year in Baghdad. When a disproportionate number listed Thailand, however—as they had for decades—the department was forced to shorten the duration of their tenures from a typical four or five years to two, without the possibility of extension. This was necessary even with four other choices listed by each officer. Thus 2007 became the final year during which US diplomats in Thailand (save at the most senior levels) had the time to invest in relationships, culture, language, and knowledge. As the two-year rotations would last through the 2014 coup, the State Department ensured that Boyce was the last of his kind.

In contrast, the US was also the victim of plain bad luck, whose ill effects would likewise multiply in the coming years. Just after the coup, erstwhile private conversations between the US embassy and various Thai and foreign contacts were made public via the WikiLeaks website. Notes of closed-door meetings and accounts of other events—replete with summaries and anecdotes, quotations and commentary—became available. Exposing information and opinions clearly understood by both parties as more complete, sensitive, strategic, and candid than that intended for the public domain, the site uniquely damaged US–Thai relations. Since WikiLeaks' sources were anonymous, it was impossible to know whether the documents were indeed "leaked" by US officials or the handiwork of a hacker. But as they were recorded and sent as diplomatic "cables" by US diplomats in Thailand to Washington (and other US embassies worldwide), the Americans were seen as at least unwittingly complicit. That the conversations included Thailand's most senior people and most delicate subjects made the breach all the more serious; personal relationships were also compromised. A fellow privy councilor later recalled, "General Prem didn't take it too well. I don't think my old boss took it all that well either. But he has never talked about it to me, and the Americans have never mentioned it."[36] While a senior embassy official did in fact apologize to several Thai contacts in 2007, WikiLeaks would leave the generational shift in bilateral relations with a bitter aftertaste—and the Chinese with a diplomatic windfall.

Royal implications

The monarchy in Thailand is considered sacrosanct outside the most private and protected discussions. In 2007, authorities explored reasons to charge Thaksin with *lese majeste*, introducing an element into the kingdom's political crisis that would just as quickly occupy its center. Over the last half of the 20th century, yearly averages of *lese majeste* cases during any of the five decades ranged between one and eleven. Fewer than two cases per year were brought between 2000 and 2004, before seventeen in 2005, thirty in the year of the coup, and a staggering 127 in 2007. Thailand also blocked the YouTube website for four months in 2007 due to a clip it deemed offensive to the monarchy. In view of the king's express and public words in 2005 that he was not above reproach, the witch-hunt would say more about Thailand's royalists than its royals. In 2007, Anand told Boyce—privately—that "half the people who work at the Palace did so only to acquire status and peddle influence; only around one-third of those at the court were there solely out of devotion to the King".[37] Nitya told him, also in confidence, that it was the palace itself that had signaled for an end to the *lese majeste* effort against Thaksin. The timing of WikiLeaks could not have been worse for the US, coinciding with and ultimately contributing to growing politicization of Thailand's highest institution.

In contrast, China's exposure was limited to what it shared with the Americans, the most indelicate being merely that it saw Prem as having backed the coup. Otherwise, the main purpose of a February 2007 visit by a state councilor was to have an audience with the king. He was also the guest of honor at a dinner hosted by two privy councilors, announcing a $1 million donation to a royal foundation. In December, the Chinese defense minister and a delegation of generals attended the king's birthday celebration. Although canceled, China planned the crown prince's first-ever visit to China in 2007, as well as several more trips by Princess Sirindhorn. It also commenced a "serious effort" lasting two years to arrange a visit by the king himself; he had never traveled to China and had not been abroad since 1995. While health concerns would result in the cancelation of that trip as well, the Chinese were engaged with the royal family on a level not matched by the Americans for decades. In the words of a cabinet minister, China saw any conflict between Thaksin and the palace as between a couple: "Why bother choosing sides? One day everyone will come back."[38]

However public it would become, US contact with the layers of concentric circles around the monarchy would continue. This included the king himself, whom the elder President Bush visited in honor of his sixty years on the throne in 2006, and the crown prince, with whom Boyce spoke at length a year later. Some saw the former as "symbolic endorsement of the royalist coup";[39] the embassy as generating "considerable good will for the United States".[40] Sanctions wisely notwithstanding, the US allowed the Thai air force chief to attend a ceremony in Seattle to mark the purchase of an aircraft for the queen. In 2007, Princess Sirindhorn attended the 45th anniversary celebration of the US Peace Corps in Thailand. The Privy Council remained the main two-way conduit, although Prem's exclusion from the initial guest list for a dinner with Bush (he was later added) cast doubt on its access and accuracy. Boyce met with Prem at least twice in 2007, to say nothing of council member Prime Minister Surayud, and attended a dinner in honor of another. Prem asked for news of Thaksin's April visit to the US and denied knowledge of his claim to have written to the king.

Trading places

When Surayud spoke in 2006 of practicing "ethical diplomacy", he was referring to his predecessor's conflation of personal and national interests.[41] He also joined the PAD in promoting the king's "sufficiency economy", although that was likewise done to cast shade on Thaksin as a poster child for globalization; Thailand's old elite had not become elite by aspiring to mere sustainability. Yet Surayud could not avoid maintaining Thaksin's focus: in 2007, China overtook the US as Thailand's second largest trading partner. Bilateral trade with China rose 23 percent in 2007 over the previous year. Thailand did maintain a trade deficit, however, as imports ($6 billion to $17 billion) rose by only a slightly higher percentage than exports ($6 billion to $15 billion) from 2003 through 2007. It also complained of an undervalued yuan. While a PRC state councilor welcomed advice on improving Chinese companies' competitiveness, it was telling that his chief interlocutor was Sarasin Viraphol of the China-centric CP Group. Overall the Thais saw "no option other than riding the wave as skillfully as possible"; Surayud authorized a military C-130 to fly fruit to China for a halal festival in mid-2007.[42]

* * *

The sixteen months in US–Thai economic relations under Surayud were summarized by the fact that in 2007, a year after forfeiting its place to Japan as Thailand's leading trading partner, the US fell behind China—from first to third in two years. The trade diversion it had feared in 2006 was suddenly a reality twice over. Described as "iffy" by the US six months before the coup, prospects in 2007 of a free trade agreement that might reverse the damage were even worse.[43] With Thaksin in mind, Surayud was not keen to pursue FTAs and Parliament wanted to ensure its inclusion. Conferred by Congress, Bush's "fast track" trade authority to negotiate was set to expire in July. Even as the US trade representative claimed that "We have not given up" on an FTA,[44] the Thais said negotiations were "indefinitely delayed"[45] or would "resume when a democratic government is in place".[46] Only the Democrat Party's Abhisit was in favor of immediate resumption. According to Thaksin's former minister, after the coup "The Americans put it on ice. Frankly, it was kind of just left on the side. There was no discussion by anyone deciding not do it, it was just left on the side."[47] Boyce suggested talks might resume in 2008.

Unlike the FTA it had derailed, compulsory licensing of anti-HIV drugs transcended domestic political disputes and continued to cloud the atmosphere. Thailand announced one such license in December 2006, pledging to import generic versions of a drug and produce it domestically. That it did not negotiate with the firm beforehand irritated the Americans and offered a potential avenue for compromise. Otherwise, however, Thailand's stated goal of treating all but 11,000 of its 133,000 eligible HIV patients by the end of the year pre-empted the US response. After a second license was issued, the Americans applauded another US firm's decision to halt new drug registrations in Thailand. Fearing the US might raise Thailand a level on its watchlist for intellectual property rights (IPR) violators and revoke GSP trade privileges, the minister of public health planned to visit Washington. Personal issues forced him to cancel the trip and Thailand was duly raised the following month. Although Boyce told Parliament that compulsory licensing was only a contributing factor, no one believed him, even as penalizing a nation for entirely legal action in one area of international law only harmed credibility in advocating compliance in others.

> In a bizarre twist to the story, the RTG discovered that a pro-pharma NGO in the U.S. ... advocating Priority Watch List for Thailand was linked to former PM Thaksin. The NGO's executive director ... is

a senior adviser to Edelman Public Relations, a firm also contracted by Thaksin. Accusations flew that Thaksin had somehow used the connection to influence USTR's decision to further discredit the current government.[48]

The public health minister finally took his trip in May 2007, during which he signed an anti-HIV deal with the Clinton Foundation first mooted two years before; at least one high-profile American was working on the right side. The minister's other fear was realized, however, when the US revoked GSP privileges for certain Thai exports.

In late 2006, Thailand planned to indict US investment firm Lehman Brothers for malfeasance during the 1997 financial crisis, identifying practices that would soon lead to another crisis. It also summarily announced a one-year reserve requirement of 30 percent on foreign capital brought into the country. Designed to stabilize currency markets, it caused the Thai stock market to drop 14 percent in a single day instead. Roundly and loudly condemned by embassies across Bangkok, it was slowly relaxed over the next several months. Proposed amendments to the Foreign Business Act were widely seen as motivated by Thaksin's dealings with Singapore. After briefing a discouraged American Chamber of Commerce, the embassy sought guidance from Washington as to whether the amendments violated international trade rules. At the same time, Surayud provided assurances that the special investment privileges under the Treaty of Amity and Economic Relations would remain in effect.

One size fits all

Just as Surayud's "ethical diplomacy" emphasized China, so it did the larger region by extension. While he ignored Thaksin's ACD and Ayeyerwady–Chao Phraya–Mekong Economic Strategy as formal mechanisms, Surayud kept his "gateway" in northern Thailand wide open, 100 short kilometers from a Yunnan province claiming a 65,000-member chamber of commerce. Yet with the Mekong River's depth remaining under China's control, plans for a second port on the Thai side were temporarily shelved. The Yunnan-to-Bangkok road, via Laos, saw progress, although a critical bridge linking Thailand and Laos was scrapped for a shorter one to be financed by Thailand and China. In the meantime, a Mekong ferry slowly moved goods across the border. Partly offsetting the estimated three-year setback in speed was the slightly shorter road from

Yunnan to Thailand via Myanmar. In March 2007, officials and media from Thailand, China, and four other countries traveled the whole of it over five days. While beset by unofficial tolls in Myanmar, it accessed a potentially larger market. Progress on rail projects and the industrial estate slated for northern Thailand was limited.

For China, the strategic objective remained protecting and projecting its energy and trade interests, via diversification of regional arteries and access points. In late 2006, it began importing oil via the Mekong when two ships carried 300 tons from a northern Thai port to Yunnan. According to China's state-supported *Xinhua*, "Experts say the waterway will serve as an alternative to the Strait of Malacca" and allow 70,000 tons of refined oil to reach China each year.[49] This was technically true, but China still needed an alternative on the *western* side of Thailand's Isthmus of Kra. While a Thai petrochemical leader "oddly broached resurrecting the Kra Canal project", Surayud had more urgent matters to deal with.[50] On the other hand, the Mekong served for China's largest import from the region, one only somewhat less central to its military and industrial development: rubber. Ninety percent globally was produced in Southeast Asia, with Thailand, Indonesia, and Malaysia—all on the Straits' eastern side—leading the way.

In 2007, China achieved regionally what it had achieved bilaterally with Thailand, moving ahead of the US on ASEAN's list of trading partners (remaining behind Japan and the EU). Its trade with the region since just 2004 had nearly doubled. Although Thailand worked quietly with its neighbors in advocating the yuan's faster appreciation, the overall economic situation held far more benefits than costs. Beijing also signed an agreement with ASEAN on military cooperation, and acknowledged continued Thai interest (begun under Thaksin) in engaging North Korea via the ARF. In July 2007, the first China–ASEAN joint military exercises took place, focusing on peacekeeping and regional disasters.

Finally, in early 2007 China vetoed a UN Security Council resolution on Myanmar and told the Thais "there was evidence the US is behind" major demonstrations there in September.[51] Thailand interpreted the latter as Chinese concern for its "soft underbelly"—which geopolitically would include itself as much as Myanmar.[52] Where a visiting state councilor from Beijing said he had pressed Myanmar to retain ASEAN support, Thailand saw its guest as representing far more leverage than the regional body. Following a crackdown on the demonstrations, China's ambassador to Bangkok joined Boyce on a major talk show to discuss the issue.

Disassociation

Myanmar remained one of the few regional issues with which the US was engaged, if primarily to advocate non-engagement, and Surayud did tell Boyce that he aimed to take a stronger line than Thaksin had. But while the premier pledged not to oppose the Security Council resolution, the Foreign Ministry came out against it. Nitya also claimed that Thaksin's "Bangkok Process" was "in consonance with what President George W. Bush suggested" in November 2006 regarding ASEAN leadership.[53] Boyce told Surayud "point blank to keep an eye on" his foreign minister.[54] Further, when ASEAN adopted a slightly tougher position later in the year during Myanmar's protests, Thailand instead favored the UN's predictably impotent "Friends of Burma" initiative. Surayud himself told President Bush at a September 2007 APEC meeting that regional influence had waned as China's had waxed. Nitya said Thailand would only change its position if the army were to "start shooting monks", but when that duly happened days later, he discouraged Surayud from speaking out at the UN General Assembly in New York.[55] General Sonthi, avowed opponent of Thaksin's Myanmar policies, actually expressed public "sympathy and support" for the junta.[56] Although Surayud would override Nitya and Sonthi and admit that he had spoken too soon, tension with the Americans was mounting.

* * *

In 2007 Thailand suggested that Myanmar be a matter for the ARF. Yet for the second time in three years, and despite the US position on Myanmar, Secretary Rice "was disappointed that events in the Middle East had prevented her from joining the ARF".[57] Thailand responded by reminding a State Department official—and future US ambassador to ASEAN—that "in this region, symbols are important".[58] That the US still struggled with symbolism was evident throughout Surayud's term. At an ASEAN meeting just weeks after the coup, the White House "scrambled" to keep a US delegate from standing beside Thailand's in an alphabetized photograph, only for diplomatic karma to prevail: "I was still standing next to Vietnam!"[59] The Thais continually reiterated their call on the US to sign the ASEAN Treaty of Amity and Cooperation, noting that it "would have a very high symbolic value" in the region.[60] Although the

Americans conceded that a mere signing (a step short of Senate ratification) was a purely executive decision, the White House took no action. Where it did, inviting ASEAN leaders to Bush's Texas ranch during an APEC meeting in September 2007, the result was a "hostile atmosphere".[61] Bush conditioned the invitation on Myanmar's exclusion, and issued it only after postponing indefinitely a 30th anniversary US–ASEAN summit—itself teeming with self-evident symbolism. The visit would not occur; the summit would occur two years late.

Prem was "very interested in the APEC angle" after the coup, knowing that Bush and Surayud would both be at a November 2006 function and wanting to avoid another (mutually) embarrassing episode.[62] In contrast, General Sonthi failed to appreciate "the difficulty the President might have" in meeting Surayud.[63] Days later, a Chinese diplomat confirmed that Beijing's premier would be meeting his Thai counterpart soon, and "wondered aloud what effects it may have on the ASEAN–US relationship if the President refused to meet with Surayud".[64] Fortunately, the US National Security Council failed to prevent Bush from shaking his hand at the event, although the attempt alone belied the prevailing shallowness of the US response. The following APEC summit in late 2007 saw Bush leave a day early.

None of this lent credibility to US statements—many made in classified cables no less—concerning its "strategic interests" in the region. In stressing the importance of the U-Tapao and Sattahip (modernized by the US in the 1960s) naval bases, the US noted only that the former serviced more than seventy aircraft per month engaged in the Middle East. Despite Singapore being the only other partner in Cope Tiger, sitting at precisely the point where ships exit/enter the southern Straits of Malacca, China was not mentioned as a reason to allow the air exercises to take place less than five months after the coup. Clearly aware in 2007 that Thailand was "[l]ocated near strategic maritime choke points and … has the potential to play a greater role in U.S. Naval planning", the US did not respond even privately to Thailand's express (if brief) interest in a Kra canal.[65] And if Cobra Gold was staged as "pundits in China and elsewhere claim that the United States is not focused on Southeast Asia", it was focused on all but the most important geopolitical issue.[66] Partial exceptions existed in Senator Webb and Surayud himself. Although the former spoke only of stability, he "wanted to be sure that the U.S. was always part of Thailand's considerations" in the region.[67] Surayud, not forgetting his anti-communist past, replied that "We have China on the other side of us. We don't want to be on our own."[68]

Military justice

It was symbolic of Thailand's ideological vacuum that one of the soldiers who overthrew Thaksin had been detained after the 1991 coup that triggered the "Thai Spring". Like burglars pledging to restore goods stolen by *others*, the military government pledged to restore the democracy and human rights taken by Thaksin. Surayud did make a rare apology to southern Muslims for previous rights violations by the state, commenced an investigation into his "War on Drugs", and established centers to counter trafficking in persons. Thailand welcomed the US resettlement of some 13,000 refugees from Myanmar in 2007, though it repeated its "Mexico defense" in denying new arrivals. A US brigadier general visited camps in the far north to assess conditions (and counter-narcotics efforts). Following a police raid on a shelter for North Korean refugees, Surayud pledged to assist smaller and more discreet US resettlement efforts. Once post-coup restrictions were lifted, the authorities were less antagonistic toward the media than Thaksin had been. Regionally, Thailand took a leading role in introducing a human rights mechanism into the draft ASEAN charter; if ultimately a cosmetic body, few other nations raised the matter at all.

In mid-2007, the former commander of the Hmong militia was arrested in California for plotting to overthrow the communist Laos government. That he had been trained by the CIA decades before to prevent a communist takeover was not lost on many. To Boyce's surprise, Surayud referred to the commander as an "old friend".[69] In Thailand itself, following a false alarm concerning the forcible return of 158 Hmong in the north, the embassy asked the Thai NSC to ensure top-down instructions. Some had been recognized by UNHCR as refugees; others were denied access. Thailand then did attempt to return them, halting the operation only after Surayud himself responded to US (and other) entreaties. Claiming to be "between a rock and a hard place", the Foreign Ministry assured Laos that no Hmong would be resettled to the US, and assured the US that none would be returned to Laos.[70] Further, some of the 158 were linked to a group of 8,000 others who had been in Thailand far longer, sixty-one of whom were sent back after being denied access to UNHCR.

* * *

"Extraordinary legislation" in Thailand, conferring sweeping powers on the authorities, fast became ordinary under Surayud. A new Computer Crimes Act served as a conduit for "protecting the monarchy", and a new Internal Security

Act (ISA) gave ISOC powers during peacetime similar to those martial law gave the army at war. In most cases, provisions of the laws or their abuse resulted in rights violations. Surayud told Boyce that the ISA, "littered with Cold War language and concepts", would be similar to the US Homeland Security Act.[71] Even before the coup, martial law had been in effect in select districts of nineteen border provinces since 1991; the "Thai Spring" had its limits. Thaksin's Emergency Decree, another piece of "extraordinary" legislation, had replaced it briefly in the three southernmost provinces, before it was reinstated there *atop* of the decree. But beginning with the 2006 coup and extending through its successor eight years later, at no point were fewer than thirty-one of Thailand's seventy-seven provinces at least partially under martial law. Seldom were the Emergency Decree and/or the ISA not in effect somewhere as well. Excepting the deep south throughout and parts of Bangkok for brief periods, conditions on the ground seldom warranted the laws' application, but the politics and power at stake were irrepressible.

In late 2007, a Chinese diplomat told Ambassador Boyce that, "in accordance with the recent Chinese Communist Party's decision to take on more responsibilities in foreign affairs, the PRC government would spend the next year evaluating its ability to influence international events … the extent of China's capacity to influence other nations".[72] While no reference was made to Thailand, there was little question that the kingdom's foreign affairs would continue to be greatly affected by China. As per the authoritarianism inherent in extraordinary legislation, Thailand's domestic affairs were even more influenced by Beijing under Surayud than under Thaksin. To be sure, Thailand's military government did not resemble China's oligarchy any more than did Thaksin's elected premiership. But as in China itself, under Surayud the China Model was established by force and sweeping legal powers, not by a popular mandate as with Thaksin. The military appointed a legislature, which turned around and granted the military enormous new powers. In contrast, despite two consecutive mandates from well over 10 million voters and a bastion of illiberal tendencies, Thaksin's power had been less sweeping and slower to accumulate. Claiming to reject Thaksin's domestic governance, the coup government adopted, adapted, and deepened it.

Thaksin told Boyce on the telephone that he welcomed US efforts to return democracy to Thailand, "not for his own sake, but because it was 'good for the country'".[73] That he was being disingenuous was unremarkable; that he represented so many other Thais—supporters and opponents alike—showed how much had changed during his years in office. This was true not only within the corridors of power but on the streets outside, where the (Yellow) PAD and a new (Red) UDD faced off against each other but featured similar winner-takes-all agendas. They would oppose and favor elections, respectively, but their different means shared the same end.

SAMAK AND SOMCHAI/GREATER CHINA (2008)

Thailand held elections in December 2007, fifteen months after the coup. Thaksin's Thai Rak Thai party was reconstituted under a new name and handily won yet again at the polls. China's Foreign Ministry stated, "As a good neighbor of Thailand, we respect the choice of the Thai people. It is our sincere hope that Thailand could maintain political stability and social harmony, with the people there living a happy life, and that the strategic relations of cooperation between China and Thailand could continue to develop."[74] A month later, Samak Sundaravej, a principal of the 1976 crackdown and publicly clear about being "Thaksin's nominee", was made prime minister.[75] Chinese Premier Wen Jiabao sent a congratulatory letter, to which he responded, "Thai-Sino relations are deeply rooted and are as inseparable as relatives or brothers … 'I am an old friend of China'".[76] He was also Sino-Thai himself, his ancestors hailing from the Guangxi autonomous region. He would allocate $100,000 in aid after an earthquake in Sichuan province in May 2008, and pay the country an official visit in July. When asked about its growing influence, Samak referenced his boss in exile:

> If he had a conflict over buying F-16 fighters, he would join with China, join with India. So when you do things like this, it makes things more balanced. And the United States can't say anything. I think it is good … The US is a little bit far away, but a good old friend. But China is more than a good old friend.[77]

In February 2008, Thaksin Shinawatra returned to Thailand, facing a warrant for abuse of power but politically vindicated by the voters. Network Monarchy was suddenly on the defensive. A half-century after an international tribunal had ruled the Preah Vihear temple within Cambodian territory, the PAD accused Samak's foreign minister of treason for supporting Cambodia's World Heritage bid on the temple's behalf. A constitutional technicality forced his resignation. He was replaced by Tej Bunnag, former ambassador to both China and the US, although he would step down after just forty days. August saw Thaksin leave Thailand for the final time. "Then he ran away", recalled the CP Group's Sarasin. "He sought the help of the former chair of the Thai Olympic Committee ... to get the court's permission to attend the opening of the Beijing Olympics in 2008. That was before the judgment was passed. Did he know anything about it? I would not be surprised if he did".[78] From there he would direct UDD counter-protests against the PAD, which began a five-month occupation of Government House and protested against China's hospitality. Thaksin denied reports he was building a house on land owned by a Chinese business associate. In September, Samak himself was ordered to resign on a constitutional technicality after hosting a televised cooking show. When Thaksin then filled the premiership with his own brother-in-law, Somchai Wongsawat, the PAD clashed with the UDD, resulting in one person killed when a China-made teargas canister exploded. In November, the PAD occupied Bangkok's two international airports for several weeks, causing China to undertake its largest ever airlift of citizens abroad, and Somchai to resign, the second prime minister in three months.

Going through the motions

In symbolism likely apparent to both, Surayud's last month in office was Boyce's last in Thailand: "Ambassador noted that he had paid farewell calls on Surayud at the end of each of his three assignments to Thailand."[79] Replacing Boyce was Eric G. John, whose ambassadorship was contentious among Americans and Thais alike. In one ledger, most agreed that he carried out US "policy" adequately under challenging circumstances. An otherwise highly critical embassy official was clear that John quickly "got to where he needed to be, and so was able to be a credible conveyor of our messages".[80] This was attributable to his having been deputy assistant secretary (DAS) for East Asia and the Pacific for three years prior to landing the embassy; he was privy to Thailand's crisis on either side of the coup. Samak's first foreign minister recalled a positive relationship with him and Thaksin did not question his credentials.

In the other ledger was agreement that John's personality, gossip-wooing personal life, and management style were problematic and sometimes had professional ramifications. "Style points really", in Boyce's words, but style counts in diplomacy more than in most fields.[81] When in 2010 he was rumored to be a candidate for the special representative post in Myanmar, nearly 100 respected US citizens in Bangkok—and a dozen members of the Thai Foreign Ministry—petitioned Clinton to reconsider. John had never been a deputy chief of mission, an embassy's "number two", passing on the role in Manila for that of DAS. As it is the only other position responsible for *all* embassy programs, projects, and personnel, he lacked critical job-specific experience. That the Bangkok embassy remained among the largest in the world and was traditionally assigned to diplomats toward the end of their careers (John was forty-seven) only exacerbated the issue. One result was a negative internal review of John's management in May 2010. Yet contrary to rumors that he was recalled early to Washington, his departure four months later followed an untimely death in the family.

Without absolving John of responsibility—as indeed neither did he—his ambassadorship said more about the State Department than about its officer. He had served under Ambassador Christopher Hill in South Korea and as his deputy (as DAS), and it was widely known that Hill was behind his Thailand appointment. Although hardly unusual given their relationship and standard institutional culture, it was a miscue more than a decade in the making. True, "No one was ever going to replace Skip—you could only succeed him."[82] But John's lack of fluency in Thai alone contrasted not only with Boyce but with his Chinese counterpart. During the peak of the war in Vietnam, the State Department was putting at least a dozen officers through Thai language study each year, as well as in Southeast Asia "area studies" at major US universities. In 1968, an advisory council of over twenty Thailand specialists was established by a USAID grant. Reagan cut the budget for area studies during the 1980s, and as USAID transitioned from infrastructure to governance, it did so in Thailand with the same personnel—specialists in a different field. As late as 1986, the State Department had three desk officers for Thailand, later dropping to two, then one. Congress slashed by two-thirds the $15 million remaining for area studies in the mid-1990s, and directed the remainder to the Asia Foundation. In 2001 the foundation reported that many regional leaders were concerned that "the first generation of American specialists in Southeast Asia are beginning to retire and are not being replaced at the same rate … American policymakers and the public alike will over time be much less well-informed about the region, with negative consequences for US–Southeast Asian relations in the future".[83]

On the ground, the US maintained only three "American corners" in Thailand's south, north and northeast. USAID and Asia Foundation programs carried on and the Voice of America continued to broadcast out of the old Ramasun facility. American Studies programs at Thai universities had begun to decline after the 1997 financial crisis, consistent with the closure of the United States Information Service in 1998. While the Foreign Ministry had continued to help fund Thai Studies programs in the US and would organize conferences in Thailand in 2008 and 2009 on bilateral relations, US participation was limited. Meanwhile, by 2009 Thailand hosted twelve of China's twenty-one Confucius institutes in Southeast Asia. In a head-shaking piece of irony, a northeastern university's courses on US history and foreign policy were both being taught by Chinese teachers with salaries paid by the Chinese government. US diplomats in northern Thailand received community leaders, visited a hospital founded by American missionaries a century earlier, promoted US higher education, and donated books to ethnic minority children. They were surprised by an overwhelming misperception that student visas for the US were hard to obtain, when the acceptance rate was over 80 percent. In November 2008, the US held three simultaneous and media-friendly events for over 2,000 Thais (and Americans) to watch live coverage of the US election, "engage with the Ambassador and ... learn more about the U.S. democratic system".[84] John also traveled to the northeast and "conveyed the USG's ongoing commitment to building and sustaining cultural and economic ties that extend beyond Bangkok to all regions of Thailand".[85]

* * *

President Bush called to congratulate Samak on the elections, and John visited his residence. "Anything you want, we'll help", the new premier told him.[86] "Samak spoke warmly of the United States ... the U.S. provided an excellent example for others, and many Thais who had been exposed to the U.S. adopted American ways of thinking. He praised the American promotion of equality and harmonious relationships between diverse ethnic groups".[87] The speaker of Parliament thanked the US for his visa after the coup, and welcomed a Congressional delegation focused on peer-to-peer exchanges. He asked them to correct "wrong information" in Washington regarding Thaksin.[88] Chuan told John that many younger Thais "were not as positive about the U.S. as older figures were".[89]

In March 2008, the State Department promised to seek a meeting between Samak and Bush before the US elections, and Samak's (first) foreign minister met

Rice, the attorney-general, and the NSC director in Washington. The foreign minister asked for US assistance in improving relations with Saudi Arabia, while the interior minister asked for more counter-narcotics assistance, promising to respect human rights. Having received US training himself as a former police officer, he said "the U.S. should not forget its old friend".[90] Assisting all this was the arrest in Thailand of Russian Viktor Bout, charged with terrorism for conspiring to sell weapons to Colombian revolutionaries. His "co-conspirators" were undercover US agents in cooperation with Thai counterparts. Citing their recent extradition of a US citizen for trial in Thailand, the Americans wanted Bout sent to the US. The attorney-general would visit later in the year on Bout business and call Thai authorities three additional times from Washington. That Bush himself raised it with Samak showed both the priority and problems that would attend Bout's case.

Ambassador John hosted Thaksin and his wife for dinner in April, joined by soon-to-be prime minister Somchai Wongsawat. His guests were "expansive in their discussion", including a recent offer of sale to Thaksin of the Houston Rockets basketball team.[91] In June, police seized hundreds of stolen or fake US passports, prompting the visiting attorney-general to praise them for "sending a message that we will work together, across borders and regardless of borders".[92] The embassy spoke to Islamic scholars in Bangkok to assess the government's approach to the deep south, which saw another delegation from the US Senate. Thailand attended the Proliferation Security Initiative's fifth anniversary event, but said again that it was unable to immediately endorse it. Thailand's third foreign minister in nine months would meet with US officials in September during the UN General Assembly. In a final meeting with John, Thaksin said he would be pardoned for an upcoming conviction and regain his frozen assets in exchange for quitting politics and residing "primarily abroad".[93] Neither side would abide by the deal.

The main political event under Samak and Somchai was an August 2008 visit by Bush. Noting 175 years of diplomatic relations, Bush put on a brave face: "America looks to Thailand as a leader in the region and a partner around the world. I was proud to designate Thailand a major non-NATO ally of the United States. And I salute the Thai people on the restoration of democracy, which has proved that liberty and law reign here."[94] Yet America had not engaged Thailand as an ally for at least a decade. It would take more than one election to restore democracy, and liberty and law had been under attack since 2001. Moreover,

Bush "conspicuously refrained from commenting on the country's 16-month period of military rule ... several key Thaksin allies were not invited to the high-profile event and Thaksin himself was conspicuously absent ... Bush's handlers declined, even after heavy Thai government lobbying, to allow for a question-and-answer session".[95] Thaksin had flown to Beijing and self-imposed exile the day before.

After resigning, Samak left for Disney World. On the day the PAD protester was killed (and an American injured), the Foreign Ministry asked John to confirm that a coup would harm relations. Anand told him that there would "not be a coup in the traditional sense of the word".[96] Speaking prophetically on the phone after his conviction, Thaksin told John that his opponents "would only face larger problems"[97] and "his political allies would continue winning elections".[98] The supreme commander asked the embassy to use its "private meetings with Thai politicians to influence them in a positive way".[99] When the PAD occupied Bangkok's airports in November, the US stated that it was "not in a position to comment on the political agenda of the demonstrators ... This is an issue for the Thais to resolve. We would like to see events in Thailand proceed peacefully and in accordance with the constitution and the rule of law".[100] Members of Congress expressed misplaced concern that Thailand could become a failed state. To his credit, John traveled to the northeast to discuss the situation with provincial governors, who "expressed admiration for the 'maturity' of U.S. politics".[101] Prime Minister Somchai presented a congratulatory letter for Obama at the US election events; coup leaders were not invited. Yet John would refer to one of them as the "steadiest figure on the political stage the past four months ... who has steadfastly rejected pressure from both sides for the army to intervene".[102] In fact, the commander publicly suggested that Somchai resign, and abjectly failed to protect critical infrastructure and the safety of foreign travelers.

Boots on the ground

When Samak visited China in July 2008, he did so as Thailand's defense minister as well, agreeing with his counterpart to further strengthen military ties. "Strike 2008", successor to the inaugural joint exercises the year before, took place in northern Thailand the same month—the first time Chinese forces trained anywhere abroad. Two teams of twenty-four special forces engaged in counterterrorism drills. Nor did procurement slow, as Thailand's military budget increased by 28 percent in 2008, Surayud's parting gift to his constituents the year before.

On 6 February 2008, the US rescinded its coup-related sanctions against Thailand. Samak had this to say:

It's OK, they didn't sell them weapons ... But the US is still a guarantor of this kind of military movement across the world. They make strong statements when the world is looking, like with General Musharraf in Pakistan now, they tell him you must stop with emergency rule. But the US doesn't say much when the world's not watching.[103]

A new PACOM commander visited twice in 2008, but Thailand's army chief "declined to engage" a third time.[104] Secretary of Defense Robert Gates visited in June between trips to the US by the deputy supreme commander and his boss. Cobra Gold was much larger than the year before, with China and six other nations continuing to make up the Combined Observer Liaison Team. As some troops were diverted to respond to Cyclone Nargis in Myanmar, "local reporting stressed the benefits of the exercise".[105]

In addition to Cope Tiger and CARAT, Thailand also hosted the "Ellipse Charlie" counterterrorism exercises for the first time in five years. In the embassy's words, "That Malaysia and Cambodia were considered as hosts for the 2008 exercise but rejected ... underscores the ongoing value of the U.S. access in Thailand".[106] It involved the FBI, State Department, and special operations personnel in a range of intelligence and hostage rescue activities. The Thais were encouraged to continue the US Defense Resource Management Study, and beginning to reconcile its loss on fighter jets, the US noted the Swedish model's use of US technology. In a nascent concession to Chinese competition, the Americans focused procurement on the Thai navy, offering S-3 aircraft and "working with them to consider U.S. military articles and services over that of other countries like China".[107] With suspension lifted on Foreign Military Financing, they also encouraged purchase of SeaVue radar, P-3 aircraft, more MH-60 helicopters, and materiel in support of the Harpoon missile system.

Stagnation

China's economic prowess was cast in even brighter light in 2008 by the start of the US-turned-global financial crisis. Sino-Thai trade crested $36 billion, quadruple the figure of just six years before on the eve of their FTA. Thailand's CP Group was "playing it low but paying everyone in both countries to protect its interests. One would hardly know it was owned by Thais".[108] Looking back was Samak's foreign minister: "With strong foreign reserves, China could easily expand using economic influence to gain more friends and win the trust of Thailand. It was also easy for China to establish closer ties because most rich Thai people are Chinese. It was natural, they invested in Thailand and we invested in China."[109]

In contrast, on the 175th anniversary of the Treaty of Amity and Commerce, US commercial relations with Thailand were falling years behind China's. While bilateral trade in 2008 was only $6 billion less than the Sino-Thai figure, it had increased just 60 percent since 2002 compared to their quadruple rise. Thailand's largest export market but third largest supplier of imports (after Japan and China), the US remained its third largest partner overall. In their most advisable economic move since buying back the F-18s ten years before, the Americans proposed a regular dialogue. Beginning to appreciate the trends, however, the Thais "suggested it could be done on the margins of other international meetings".[110] In March, the US assistant trade representative tried but failed to restart FTA talks, as "the Thai government has not approached us to schedule additional rounds, although officials occasionally make public statements affirming that the FTA is a long-term goal".[111] Bush encouraged a resumption of negotiations during his Bangkok speech in August, but his fast-track authority to conduct them expired two months later.

With serial trademark infringement, lax law enforcement, and the second highest rate of movie piracy in the world, Thailand was kept on the US priority watchlist of IPR violators. Few Thais believed it went much deeper than compulsory licensing of pharmaceuticals. Samak asked for a review and dismissed the public health minister, but "it was clear that the previous government's arguments in favor of CLs continued to resonate".[112] After the US publicly denied that it planned to file a (groundless) complaint with the WTO over compulsory licensing, a joint dialogue committee was agreed. The WTO informed the US that the duties it had been placing on Thai shrimp exports since 2005, as well as its "continuous bond" requirement, were non-compliant. Yet even after the WTO's appellate body confirmed the rulings, the US refused to comply. Thailand assigned a February 2009 deadline, after which it "would have no choice but to return to the WTO to seek arbitration".[113] Thailand also asked that GSP benefits it had lost the previous year be restored, and expressed concern that a recent US ban on gems from Myanmar could harm its own industry. Bush was uncommonly on-point in stating that "America sometimes sends mixed signals about the openness of our economy."[114]

Political disruption and the previous government's decisions resulted in fewer US companies being interested in investing. Thailand responded to a request for relevant negotiations by saying it "had already provided its offer on services".[115] Visits by Samak's finance minister to the US and the undersecretary of commerce to Thailand focused on communications, transportation, financial services, and agribusiness. Ambassador John also advocated on behalf of a US company seeking to produce engines for Thailand's national carrier, and expressed concern over police refusal to protect a US automotive plant during an industrial action. Concerned about their health amidst the global crisis—and with comically poor timing—Thai banks tightened the lines of credit to US firms while the Thai finance minister was visiting Washington.

Presidential regrets

When Thaksin arrived in China to attend the Olympics and avoid a day in court, Princess Sirindhorn was there as the guest of honor at a reception organized by the Thai embassy and Chinese authorities. Uninvited, Thaksin simply walked in and entered the receiving line alongside guests from both Surayud's administration and the current one he had appointed. Not since he was prime minister were such diverse centers of power represented in the same room—only not in Bangkok but Beijing, capital of Thailand's 21st century ally. According to a Thai diplomat, "We were not informed as an embassy and we were not very happy", while the rest of the room stood in awkward silence.[116] Equally surprised, the princess allowed the former premier to greet her. The diplomat recalled that Thaksin "looked like someone who had just lost a battle".[117]

In contrast, the US–Thai royal dynamic in 2008 was characterized not by convergence but by separation. In August, "Bush failed after heavy foreign ministry lobbying to arrange a meeting with King Bhumibol Adulyadej, who was in residence at his seaside palace in Hua Hin, about 200 kilometers south of Bangkok. Government sources say that's because Hua Hin's airport lacks the runway facilities to accommodate Bush's jet."[118] A half-century past in Thailand, Herculean logistical efforts had been made to accommodate not only jets but geopolitical priorities. Recognizing further that the monarch who had enabled those efforts was the one still residing in a seaside palace, the failure of a US president to meet him was truly profound. It rendered his already vacuous speech conclusively void of meaning, and conveyed an alternative message. For a king in the twilight of his reign, US President Bush could not—would not—bridge a distance equal to that between Washington and Philadelphia. What should have been a non-negotiable meeting between the most powerful man in the world and his most steadfast regional ally since World War II "had proven logistically impossible to arrange".[119]

Two months later, Princess Sirindhorn visited the US, where she said that the PAD was not acting on behalf of the palace. In Bangkok she met with Ambassador John. Contrary to many of his counterparts who chose to skip the event, in December John attended the annual military parade in honor of the king's birthday. Prem showed interest in US efforts in Myanmar after Cyclone Nargis and Cobra Gold. Twice denying there would be another coup, he told John that Samak "ultimately would need to leave".[120] In contrast, he said he was pleased with Somchai's public acceptance of the verdict against Thaksin. "Stressing that Ambassador was the only foreigner he would share the information with", Prem's foreign minister and fellow councilor laid out a scenario for Samak's departure and replacement by Anand.[121] John "repeatedly emphasized it would amount to a coup by another name ... Anand replied that he had disagreed with the U.S. reaction to the 2006 coup".[122] Two other privy councilors told John that they would protect the king from the ongoing crisis. The king's principal private secretary "spoke fondly of his close associates in Washington such as Senator Lisa Murkowski, former Senator Sam Nunn, and former Secretary of State George Shultz".[123] His deputy had been recalled as ambassador to Washington in 2008 to serve under him. The secretary agreed with John that the crown prince might consider hosting more functions for US dignitaries, but offered that "any USG public statements on Thailand's turmoil would be 'extremely unhelpful'".[124] One foreign liaison officer for the queen told John that a coup "like what happened September 19, 2006" would not happen;[125] another "guessed Somchai would be forced from office by the end of the year".[126] Last and least, Thaksin also discussed the monarchy with John, recounting later that "Eric John was very close to General Prem, he always went to see him, and Prem was the one who really was very revengeful with me. And so Eric John got one-sided information and gave a wrong report again, a one-sided report."[127]

Chinatown

Having challenged Ambassador Boyce to a televised debate on Thailand's human rights record in 2005, Samak's (and Somchai's) record on the same did not impress. A progressive new trafficking law was balanced by talk of another war on drugs. Violations in the deep south (by both sides) continued unabated, seventy-seven new *lese majeste* cases were lodged, and the Emergency Decree was in effect in Bangkok for most of 2008's latter half. One hundred and fifty-eight Lao Hmong refugees (half of whom were children) remained in detention in Thailand, as those in the north dropped to 6,000 via returns the Thais unconvincingly claimed were voluntary. Some were refugees "because they helped you in Vietnam".[128] In August, twenty-nine years after Roslyn Carter had visited Cambodians inside Thailand's eastern border, First Lady Laura Bush visited refugees from Myanmar in the west. President Bush met dissidents from Myanmar at Ambassador John's residence—in a legal sense, US territory—after Thailand prohibited a meeting on its soil. To ensure that the Thais had plausible deniability, the embassy simply didn't tell them.

As he informed a visiting Congressional delegation, Samak "was sensitive to reasonable Chinese concerns about national unity and secessionist movements".[129] After a crackdown in Tibet caused the intended Thai torch-bearer to drop out, Samak ensured that protesters did not disrupt the running of the Olympic torch through Bangkok. Several Chinese citizens were removed from the scene. Not unlike US–Thai collaboration earlier in the decade—causing China to say "we want that too"—Thai authorities began detaining Chinese (and Islamic) Uighur "terrorists".[130] Samak also had no regard for the plight and rights of Muslim minority Rohingyas, planning for their detention on southern islands as they fled Myanmar on boats.

Samak's foreign minister recounted suppressing the Falungong religious group in Bangkok, because "we didn't want to antagonize the Chinese".[131] In fact, "the Chinese Ambassador warned officials at Government House about a possible FLG bomb during the torch relay in Bangkok", despite an unblemished history of peaceful practice.[132] Both of the group's local founders were warned by Thai police that the country must "not lose face" during the event.[133] Attempts to publicly explain their position were refused, reflecting the media's "not wanting to be seen as anti-China".[134] Otherwise, the Falungong practiced in Bangkok's largest park and in front of the Chinese embassy. Chinese diplomats "routinely called Sino-Thais ... who had investments connected to

China, warning them not to associate with FLG".[135] Thai police arrested nineteen Chinese Falungong outside their embassy; others of the 161 registered with UNHCR were detained or pushed across the borders to Myanmar or Laos. The Falungong were generally not sought by China for repatriation, but as a Thai diplomat explained, "China understands us—that Thailand will not do anything to break down relations."[136]

* * *

Samak told a Congressional delegation that "it was not necessary to push the Chinese to adopt democratic reforms", as they were "communist in name only".[137] So long as they did not act like communists, it was fine to be undemocratic. Referring to the Falungong, a Thai official told the US that "we accepted international principles not to allow other groups to use Thailand as a place to protest and worsen our relations with a third party".[138] Such principles did not exist, however, save in China and the nations within its growing sphere of influence: the international community's alternative camp. "Historically, culturally, and geographically, China is more powerful and closer to Thailand", explained the foreign minister. "Like the US government will pay more attention to Mexico than Thailand—proximity, common interests—China, *rightly speaking*, will expand influence and would like to be the leader in Asia ... the number one superpower".[139]

There were mixed signals that the US recognized the shift in Thai attitudes and admiration. In a post-mortem on the coup, Ambassador John wrote that he found "it difficult to imagine any set of foreign sanctions that could have had a decisive impact while also being compatible with the longstanding friendship between Thailand and the West". Denying that the sanctions failed to accomplish either goal, he correctly implied an Eastern alternative. Yet his complaint that Thailand's "interim authorities at times demonstrated a willingness to treat foreign attitudes as peripheral" told only half the story: they regarded American attitudes as peripheral, not those of the Chinese.

The US also encouraged Thailand to be a founding member of an Asia-Pacific Democracy Partnership (APDP), "based on Thailand's own experiences with democratic institution building".[140] It did join as an observer but preferred that the initiative not require "inclusion of civil society components from member states".[141] The US actually saw Thailand as having fully returned to democracy solely on account of its 2007 elections. That the APDP's main activity was election observation only added to the circular reasoning—to say nothing of Thailand's express desire to exclude certain "components". Moreover, as the embassy itself observed, "the most visible and active NGOs were newly-formed partisan organizations clearly linked to Thaksin".[142] On the other side lay the patronizing and contemptuous "Yellows", led but not limited by the PAD. The PAD began advocating "New Politics" of a 70 percent selected Senate (with only 30 percent elected) and a monarchy in control of both Parliament and the military. In the meantime, it called for an interim premiership filled by a privy councilor, and a "Supreme Council" which it likened to China's State Council. Indeed, three days after the US election in November, Sondhi said that "the US had long ago lost its legitimacy to preach to Thailand about democracy".[143]

ASEAN and its discontents

The Chinese told Thailand that "they will never let Burma be like Iraq", and asked for assistance in persuading the US to meet with Myanmar's leadership.[144] Yet Thailand believed that Chinese support for Myanmar would prevent it from changing. Samak favored multilateral talks, emphasizing that "the key to such a negotiation would be China".[145] The Thais also complained that its original share in an energy project had been knocked down after China arranged a majority share for itself. "China is taking 'practically everything' and had even taken over projects that the Thai had pioneered."[146] Recalling their own experience the previous year, the Thais "warned that the US sanctions policy was pushing Burma to be a satellite of China, first economically and eventually in the area of security".[147] Samak visited in March, raising not Mexico but Cuba: "The U.S. had tolerated a communist dictatorship in its backyard for many decades."[148] Thailand also maintained its practice of not voting in favor of a UN General Assembly resolution on Myanmar, despite several US requests. As John informed Washington, Samak "clearly has his own ideas about how to encourage positive change in Burma ... he would continue to bear in mind the President's concern, however, and he reiterated his interest in remaining 'a messenger' between the West and Burma".[149] Thailand admonished the Americans for making Myanmar a condition to smooth relations with ASEAN, as its new secretary-general—Chuan's foreign minister—asked for both Chinese and US support. Four days before Cyclone Nargis in May, with Thailand also set to take over as ASEAN chair, it said that the "next level" of US–ASEAN military cooperation should be on humanitarian efforts.[150] The US and Thailand then facilitated 185 humanitarian flights during the disaster, most from U-Tapao and using assets in the region for Cobra Gold.

On another border, the US embassy encouraged Thailand and Cambodia to utilize a new bilateral committee to resolve its temple dispute. When Cambodia sought a meeting of the UN Security Council, both major powers were placed on notice. The Thais then "expressed deep thanks for what they perceived as strong U.S. support July 23 in the UNSC for Thai efforts to keep attempts to resolve the Preah Vihear dispute with Cambodia in a bilateral track".[151] Following Thailand's hyperbolic suggestion that it could invoke the bilateral Thanat–Rusk memo signed the same year as the court decision, Prime Minister Somchai assured John that no further armed conflict would occur. Beijing hosted both nations' premiers for talks late in the year.

* * *

A US-friendly Thai became ASEAN's secretary-general for five years beginning in 2008, and Thailand would hold the regional chair for an exceptional eighteen months through 2009, but the US would not stem the eastward tide. In April, the Foreign Ministry told the US that "Every year, China had rolled out a new initiative, such as acceding to the Treaty of Amity and Cooperation, or setting up a periodic consultation with the ASEAN Defense Ministers."[152] The Americans merely agreed during visits by PACOM and Secretary Gates that a regular US–ASEAN defense meeting "merited consideration".[153] A new US ambassadorship to ASEAN was welcomed as a first among its dialogue partners, but the ambassador's duties were on top of those as a deputy assistant secretary of state—he remained based in Washington. Although Australia, France, India, Japan, New Zealand, Russia, South Korea, and the UK had all joined China in signing ASEAN's treaty, he passed on the most obvious introductory move. Secretary Rice urged a review of the ARF before actually attending its gathering in July, replete with a US work-plan focused on counterterrorism and the PSI. The ASEAN summit was postponed in December due to the PAD's airport occupations, although Bush joined its leaders in attending the APEC summit the same month. As ASEAN chair, Thailand was also in charge of choosing the theme of the EAS, noting for the second straight year that, "if the US decided it would like to join the East Asia Summit, then Thailand would be ready to discuss ways to help".[154] It too was postponed, but the US would not join.

Economically, China's "mask came off" during the 2008 financial crisis, exposing a hubristic view of its neighbors further enabled by US vulnerability.[155] According to former US Ambassador Boyce, its approach essentially became, "Before we start let's get one thing straight: you need us, we don't need you."[156] Certain damage was done to its image, if considerably less than that of the US in 1997, and nothing money couldn't fix. Chinese trade with ASEAN reached $193 billion in 2008, up from $45 billion in 2001 and having grown at least 20 percent annually since 2003. A China–ASEAN Center for Trade, Investment and Tourism was established, and the fifth China–ASEAN Expo and Business and Investment Summit took place. Financially, China made possible the multi-lateralization of the Chiang Mai Initiative's original bilateral swaps, resulting in an $80 billion currency pool from which member countries could borrow. Lessons from one financial crisis were being applied to the next. Finally, by 2008 China's economic aid to Southeast Asia was higher than that of the Americans.

In contrast, the US assistant trade representative "compared Thailand's economic performance unfavorably to regional competitors … who were making strides in reforming business regulations and building institutions".[157] The Thais' response would have failed to reference Chinese "strides" at US expense only with great restraint. True that more stable Southeast Asian nations were better able to boost trade and court FDI, but in the seven years since Thaksin took office the US had barely registered Thailand's northern economic gateway. The ex-premier may have had China in mind in devising the policy, but he was at his most democratic when choosing economic partners. While Bush was busy claiming that "we have supported the vision of a Free Trade Area of the Asia Pacific", the US share of ASEAN's trade was falling to 12 percent in 2008 from 17 percent the year before.[158] This knocked the US down yet another place on the region's list of trading partners, to fifth. The US did remain ASEAN's top source of FDI, but neither the Initiative for ASEAN Enterprise (2002) nor the ASEAN–US Trade and Investment Framework Agreement (2006) had changed the economic game.

Ambassador John told Thailand's minister of commerce that "U.S. business was *beginning* to view ASEAN as a single economic entity" (emphasis added).[159] The US consulate in Chiang Mai joined other US diplomats from Laos, Cambodia, and China's Sichuan province in hosting a conference on logistics, supply, and transportation in the northern Thai region. In denial of how large the Chinese presence already was, John opened by repeating that, "more China doesn't mean less of the U.S."[160] The consulate cited a US garment company, profitable since 1990 "despite competing with Chinese textile giants", as an example to other investors.[161] It said that the "success of two large corporations in northern Thailand is a testament to the potential for American investment in the region's arable and affordable land".[162] And it noted the "potential for the northern region as a high-tech manufacturing hub".[163] This was 2008, but still just "potential". That the US was expressly told that it enjoyed a reputational advantage over China in corporate social responsibility made its lack of initiative even more dispiriting.

On a multilateralized CMI, the US wished to ensure that its operations were "truly complementary to those already in place within the international financial institutions ... not redundant or counterproductive".[164] Yet the initiative's nature and purpose—backed by China—had never been to complement but to counter. The Thai official most responsible for its expansion reminded John plainly that, "during the 1997 Asian financial crisis, the IMF's policies did more harm than good and that friends like the United States could not be counted on for assistance".[165]

The dragon's tail

Thailand, China, and the four other nations comprising the Greater Mekong Subregion (GMS) signed a five-year development plan. As China's oil-laden barges continued moving up the river, the plan emphasized energy. China's Guangxi autonomous area began "advocating the combination of maritime economic cooperation, mainland economic cooperation, and Mekong sub-region cooperation".[166] In August, however, the river flooded and inundated seven northern Thai provinces, causing local and regional frustration at China. Most Thais said it had released water from three upstream dams, and that its recent blasting and dredging of the river had contributed to the problem. While Samak agreed with China's claim that heavy rains were at fault, Chinese gains in goodwill from the previous year were set back. Prime Minister Somchai backed a third meeting of the Ayeyerwady–Chao Phraya–Mekong Economic Strategy, a Thaksin initiative designed to facilitate and manage Chinese interest in the region.

Recalling that Chinese cities had inspired him as a former Bangkok governor, Samak praised the highest railway in the world linking China and Tibet. He also promoted the completion of the road connecting northern Thailand with China's Yunnan province, via Laos; "I wish to drive to China. It must be fun."[167] By March the portion between Laos and China was fully paved, but the Thai portion of the road remained incomplete and work had not begun on the bridge across the Mekong. Bangkok was "using the bridge as a bargaining chip for trade negotiations with Beijing, since the Chinese appear considerably more eager to complete the route".[168] While the alternative route through Myanmar was equally delayed, the grand plan was to have them meet at an "Indochina Junction" (continuing east to Cambodia and Vietnam) in Thailand's north. With shipments taking up to two weeks to travel that distance on the Mekong, Chinese interest and funding increased.

* * *

Samak's foreign minister concluded that the US "was playing a lesser role in this part of the world, let alone in Thailand or ASEAN, because it didn't have many interests. But when it felt China was expanding influence, it felt it had to do something ... Its interest was to control the influence of China rather than to promote bi-lateral relations".[169] He was correct on US inactivity in Asia; incorrect that it made efforts to "control" China. Far from having a proactive strategy for protecting its geopolitical interests—itself predicated on their recognition—the US was not so much as reacting to moves affecting them. And the lack of urgency, based on wishful assumptions over hard analysis, went all the way to the top: in his Bangkok speech, President Bush trumpeted "a sharp departure from the zero-sum mentality of the past".[170] On what grounds? According to Bush, a "peaceful and successful future for this region requires the strong involvement of both China and the United States".[171] This was highly debatable, considering the effects on democracy, human rights, and the rule of law where China's involvement—including in Thailand—was "strong". It also said nothing of the *United States'* geopolitical interests, both as traditionally defined and including the same democracy, human rights, and rule of law. Even after the march stolen by China after the coup—duly described by its diplomats in zero-sum terms—the US commander-in-chief insisted on believing that this was "past".

Thailand continued to participate in the "Eyes in the Sky" program in the Straits of Malacca. The US assisted in planning a joint maritime security seminar between Thailand's Laem Chabang port, 20th globally in volume of container exports to the US, and Singapore. Focused on "emergency response, terrorist attack response, hazmat (including chemical and radiological) incident response, EOD (explosive ordnance disposal), and mass casualty incident response", there was no mention of China.[172] The continued importance of the U-Tapao naval airbase was emphasized after the PAD occupied Bangkok's airports and it was opened for commercial flights. The US agreed to a second bilateral Strategic Dialogue in June 2008, but the two topics it specifically mooted for inclusion were IPR and the PSI. While not denigrating the economic aspect to strategic relations, intellectual property (read: compulsory licensing) was a far cry from the China Model. In the run-up to the event, Anand "commended the Chinese government for effective use of 'soft power' ... saying a U.S. presence in Southeast Asia was essential and in America's interest".[173] He also urged closer US–Japan relations to "*offset* what would otherwise prove to be overwhelming influence on the part of China" (emphasis added).[174] After the dialogue, a "U.S.-educated Thai Army Colonel at the National Defense College shocked a group of U.S. one-star officers ... by stating bluntly: 'The Thai perceive regional power dynamics as follows: China is rising; the U.S. is distracted/declining; and Thailand will adjust its policies accordingly'".[175]

ABHISIT/FALSE HOPE AND TRUE COLORS (2008-2011)

When in late 2008 Thailand's political dust settled for the fourth time in twenty-six months, each time seeing one prime minister depart and another take office, there was hope for the relationship among American leadership. Abhisit Vejjajiva was a Western-educated (Oxford) premier, who as opposition leader since early 2006 had cultivated relations with the US embassy. Ambassador John was the first diplomat to call on Foreign Minister Kasit Piromya (Georgetown University), saying that his "understanding of the complexities of the U.S.–Thai relationship will make working with him and the MFA on difficult issues easier".[176] He called Finance Minister Korn Chatikavanij (Oxford) "an impressive figure—sharp on the range of economic issues and well-disposed toward the U.S."[177] All three represented the Democrat Party, judged "pro-American" as early as the late 1940s, and in which Chuan remained active. Most of all, save for his defense minister and a deputy premier, thirty-four of Abhisit's thirty-six cabinet members were civilians. On the US side, newly elected President Barack Obama had pledged to shift US attention away from the Middle East, and would soon refer to himself as the "first Pacific president".[178] Less than a month in her position, Secretary of State Hillary Clinton would make Asia the destination of her first trip abroad, something that had not been done since Secretary Rusk visited Thailand in 1961. Any doubts in Bangkok that Obama's opponent and Vietnam War veteran John McCain might have shown more promise, would not linger.

Instead, they came back in force on both sides of the ocean, amidst a slew of ignored warning signs. Abhisit's party had not won an election since 1992; he took office via another "judicial coup" and a sizable defection from Thaksin's camp. The army chief claimed no role in the machinations, but added that "politicians were not disposed to listen to him" after his recent attempt to divide Samak's government.[179] He was of Queen's Guard pedigree and not an IMET graduate, while Abhisit and Korn were just forty-four years old and of prominent Sino-Thai families. The former told John that his cabinet would include "the 'old friends' the U.S. knew well", but the American era's generational shift was complete both within and outside the military.[180] Although Kasit was cut from the old cloth, he had retired early as ambassador to the US in 2005 to assist the PAD, Thailand's most anti-democratic movement since the vigilantes of the 1970s. Indeed, despite saying he wanted to avoid "Thailand passively waiting and merely reacting to whatever the US raised", his foreign policy would be mostly reacting to Thaksin Shinawatra.[181] On the American side, the embassy's post-election message that it did "not anticipate significant changes in our bilateral relationship", was cause more for concern than comfort.[182] Clinton's inaugural trip was to China, Indonesia, Japan, and South Korea; treaty and major non-NATO ally Thailand was skipped.

Finally, the color-coded pendulum would swing back yet again under Abhisit, with the Red Shirts taking to the streets and Thailand's security forces proving politicized, incompetent, and deadly. At almost no point during his thirty-one-month administration were Bangkok and its surrounding provinces not under either the Emergency Decree or Internal Security Act. ASEAN's "Plus Three" meetings in April 2009 were violently disrupted and ultimately postponed; Chinese Premier Wen Jiabao failed to reach the venue at all. Over a forty-day period in 2010, at least ninety persons were killed and over 2,000 injured.

Chinese fire drill

Abhisit complained of the difficulty in moving Sino-Thai relations forward in these circumstances, but the CP's Sarasin was less forgiving:

> The Democrats never did anything with China, they did nothing. They
> did not promote anything through the official channel, neither did they do

anything through the unofficial channel. They were just basically not paying attention to China. So by default, the Chinese were very frustrated with Abhisit. Being bogged down in domestic politics was a very weak excuse. As the head of government, you are supposed to be omnidirectional.[183]

Beijing never broke stride. Signaling early support for the new government, China canceled a talk by Thaksin at Hong Kong's press club in early 2009. That Thailand had to request similar action again, however, showed that China would continue to hedge its bets. A year later, its diplomats would tell the US "that there are so many visits to Thailand, involving not only central government officials but provincial trade delegations, that they do not assign control officers for anyone lower than a Vice-Minister".[184] Premier Wen Jiabao visited twice in 2009 alone. Abhisit reciprocated in June 2009 and in September and November 2010, when the "two sides reached broad consensus on promoting comprehensive growth of China–Thailand relations".[185] Foreign Minister Kasit took three trips to China in *each* of the two years. In 2010 he celebrated thirty-five years of bilateral relations in Beijing (June), toured Shanghai and Zhejiang province (August), and opened a new Thai consulate in Guangdong province (December). The speaker of the House visited in 2010, as did two of Abhisit's deputy prime ministers, while the chair and vice-chair of China's National People's Congress visited Thailand separately. In the words of China's Foreign Ministry, these exchanges "enhanced political mutual trust and deepened mutually beneficial practical cooperation between the two countries".[186]

For the second time in six years, the US embassy registered an uptick in the quality of Chinese diplomats. The ambassador "has spent 17 years of his career posted here and routinely makes local TV appearances. Those that do not have previous Thai experience, like the DCM, are smart, articulate, and increasingly confident in speaking up at English-language international relations seminars once the preserve of 'Western' diplomats".[187] Even Boyce had only spent eleven years in the kingdom, and he was the (retired) exception proving a new US rule. A Chinese diplomat said that, "30 of the 36 ministers in Abhisit's cabinet could be considered Sino-Thai".[188] A Thai counterpart explained: "Generations of overseas Chinese migrating to our country and their role during difficult times, they are all important ties. Do we have the same ties with the US? Not similar, not at the same level ... that the Chinese government sees the importance of this issue we appreciate, because it's a strength".[189]

Nor was this reality limited to the corridors of power and policy. By the end of 2010, in addition to the twelve Confucius institutes in Thailand, eleven Confucius "classrooms" had also been established. Approximately 2,700 Chinese instructors were teaching at all levels throughout Thailand, mostly Mandarin. Even more notably, Thailand and China had become for the other its largest source of foreign students, with roughly 10,000 from each country. According to a 2010 US embassy cable, the "number of Thai students in China and of Chinese students in Thailand now outstrips the flow between Thailand and the United States".[190] As English language study remained obligatory to the option of Mandarin, the embassy claimed it was "not clear, however, that growing Chinese soft power in education has come at the expense of the soft power of the United States".[191] Yet did not the reversal in educational exchanges itself constitute a zero-sum loss—with the Chinese *option* being the whole point? The Chinese embassy claimed that over 18 percent of Thailand's 65 million people were ethnically Chinese, while an opinion poll indicated that 70 percent of *all* Thais ranked China as the kingdom's closest friend.

* * *

A month after the 2006 coup, Chinese diplomats in Bangkok told the US that they would alter their opportunistic response only if the junta fired on civilians. When not a military but a military-backed government did so in 2010, however, China was expectedly unmoved. Abhisit recalled: "They were always very clear: 'Hey, your affairs are your affairs, we hope you just deal with it and make things stable'. That's what mattered to them. Its stance of saying 'we're not interfering' was a much easier approach to Thailand, it didn't upset anyone as such."[192] A UDD leader argued that the Chinese "didn't blame anything on Abhisit because they supported Abhisit already, you understand?"[193] Despite having arms among them, the protesters called upon the Chinese embassy for assistance in preventing bloodshed. "We did not want foreigners to interfere with our sovereignty", said the leader, "but to at least announce a statement to not shoot people. But no, it never came out."[194] Instead, after initial bloodshed its Foreign Ministry stated that, "China is deeply concerned over the situation in Thailand. We sincerely hope to see restoration of social order, political stability, economic development and people enjoying a happy and prosperous life in Thailand at an early date."[195]

The Chinese sent a representative to the UDD stage in late April for a briefing. "Immediately after the trouble took place" in May, recalled Abhisit's spokesperson, they "were called to Government House, where an explanation was very swift" of the final crackdown. Otherwise, China was less in touch with Thai political leadership "compared to the US", but was "well-connected with top military leaders".[196] Just two months after the crackdown, it welcomed General Chavalit on a "personal visit".[197] Ambassador John assessed that, lacking credibility on handling protests peacefully, China had too much to risk in getting involved in the crisis and too little to risk in not. Conversely, a Chinese official said that the US had "blundered" in its involvement.[198] Comparing them, Abhisit's spokesperson and longtime security advisor Panitan claimed that, "China is less active and uses an indirect approach and its handling of this situation was no different … China is very pragmatic, but very keen in getting information and reacting".[199] In 2015, he concluded that, "Afterward when things had moved on, the political positions the US and the Chinese took clearly showed how sophisticated the policies of the two countries were. Instead of insisting on principles alone, the Chinese adopted a more practical, pragmatic approach."[200]

Undiplomatic recollections

In 2009, Abhisit and Kasit visited the US, and Secretary Clinton traveled to Thailand. Yet only Kasit's trip was bilateral, as Clinton visited for the ARF and Abhisit traveled for the UN General Assembly, after which he met only with US legislators and business leaders. Kasit would make another visit to Washington in 2010, not long after the US embassy had "not been able to respond positively to Abhisit's repeatedly expressed desire, since he took office in December 2008, to visit Washington".[201] The Thais also failed in getting Obama to stop in Bangkok en route to Indonesia in 2010.

Abhisit's deputy prime minister said that Clinton "has a lot of fans here",[202] and Kasit would praise the undersecretary for political affairs. "But those responsible for the Asia-Pacific I was not impressed with. I thought the quality of your ambassadors all over the Asia-Pacific was hopeless, not up to the job. And even those who are up to the job do not have the attention of the State Department."[203] If more diplomatic, Abhisit himself recalled that "Other embassies—the UK embassy, the Chinese—would have people who worked here before. They would come back and speak Thai, they would know a lot about Thailand. The recent ambassadors and top people at the US embassy are not made in that mold. I am not sure whether it is unique to Thailand."[204]

Visiting in 2009, Kurt Campbell came in for singular criticism by both sides. "You did not have a first-class assistant secretary of state for East Asian and Pacific Affairs", noted Kasit.[205] He was known for having wall-to-wall daily meetings, but "seeing and treating Thailand more as a stop-over to Burma, which was more of the moment for his bosses, than as a destination itself".[206] Noting that Campbell went on to run a profitable think-tank, a senior US diplomat offered that "there was no way to monetize Thailand".[207] In turn, Campbell disliked Kasit so much that he told his control officer he would not return to Thailand until there was a new foreign minister, "and he didn't go back until that happened".[208]

While later making the mistake themselves and to far greater effect, the Americans repeatedly pointed out the absence since mid-2008 of a Thai ambassador in Washington. A senior State Department official reflected that Thailand was "not serious about external engagement" at a time it was most needed, referencing a recent Singaporean ambassador in Washington whose term had lasted twelve years.[209] At the same time, Thailand complained that the 121-member Thai–American Parliamentarian Friendship Group reached out to Congress but received no response. It also "warned that China was working actively to cultivate ties with the Thai Parliament ... while the number of Thai MPs traveling to the U.S. had declined".[210]

While a 2009 survey indicated that 86 percent of urban Thais had a favorable view of the US, Bangkok was Thailand's largest city by orders of magnitude and had long been a base of the pro-US Democrat Party. The same year, a town hall-style meeting with students "received overwhelmingly positive media coverage ... due to the witty banter between Secretary Clinton and the co-hosts that created a comfortable, at-ease atmosphere".[211] Clinton's claim that "educational and student exchanges are among the most important U.S.–Thai initiatives" belied the figures however.[212] There were 8,700 Thai students enrolled in US schools, "more or less stagnant over the last five years ... down from a peak of more than 15,000 before the financial crash of 1997" (and fewer than the 10,000 in China).[213] About 7,500 young Thais participated in a US Summer Work Travel program. Only 1,500 American students were studying in Thailand, a mere 15 percent of China's tally. And contrasting US teachers in Thailand with China's, the embassy said "the number is significantly lower".[214] There were also roughly 145 Peace Corps volunteers in the kingdom, but their influence had much declined since the "mentoring as a child by PC volunteers" recalled by Chuan's foreign minister.[215]

* * *

By 2009, the ILEA had trained some 9,000 Thai officers and pursued more than 500 cases. A new group of eighteen law enforcement agencies focused on "extradition and mutual legal assistance … counter-narcotics, counter-terrorism, trafficking in persons (TIP), intellectual property (IP) protection, money-laundering, cyber- and other white-collar crime".[216] Training for a whopping 170,000 Thai police was planned, while the nation's leading forensic scientist requested US training for her work in the deep south. The US and Thailand also announced ground-breaking results of the largest ever HIV vaccine trial, jointly conducted over six years. After a massive earthquake in Haiti in January 2010, the US assisted in the evacuation of Thai citizens and appreciated the deployment of Thai medical teams.

Otherwise, the case of Russian arms trafficker Viktor Bout continued to consume enormous diplomatic time and capital. John raised concern with Abhisit and his defense minister that money was behind a Thai navy captain's testimony that Bout had been in Thailand to discuss a submarine deal. The Americans were justified in stating that failure to ensure an honest *process* "would constitute a major setback to the bilateral relations".[217] But if rightly rejecting Thai pleas for understanding strong Russian pressure, the US would exert enormous extrajudicial persuasion of its own. Following a call by the US attorney-general in March 2009, the Foreign Ministry was ordered to testify on extradition's impact on US and Russian relations. The US itself had to testify in a criminal complaint filed by Bout against three US Drug Enforcement Agency officers in relation to his arrest. The embassy recommended that Thaksin's foreign minister Surakiart, by then in private legal practice, be retained as counsel.

In August 2009, the court denied the extradition request, shocking and disappointing the US, which immediately appealed. John recommended that Obama call Abhisit. He urged senior US and UN officials to meet with Thai ambassadors in Washington and New York. He suggested that Washington ask other nations affected by Bout's trade to contact Thailand. He argued that, based on the ruling, Thailand's southern insurgents could be considered political actors whose foreign suppliers could not be extradited to Thailand. And going for the political jugular, John stated: "At a time when the Thai government was pursuing extradition of fugitive former Prime Minister Thaksin Shinawatra, the judge's ruling subverted the RTG position."[218] He concluded that, "Without being counter-productively heavy-handed, we will make clear that we see Thai executive branch reaction to the ruling as a test of the relationship."[219]

In early 2010, the US issued a second extradition request based on new money-related allegations. This actually negated a successful appeal of the initial decision, as Bout could not be extradited until the new charges were likewise ruled upon. A US plane was left waiting on a Bangkok tarmac. With the second decision still pending in November, however, "the Thai government plucked Bout from a Bangkok prison and discreetly handed him over to waiting US officials, who bundled him onto a plane … Thai security forces armed with assault rifles surrounded Bout while hurriedly escorting him to the airport without informing the Russian Embassy in Bangkok that their citizen was being extradited".[220]

* * *

Several conclusions can be drawn from American involvement in Thailand's political crisis in 2009 and 2010. First, the US was alternately thanked and criticized by both sides as it served their interests. In contrast to China, as a senior US diplomat retrospectively pointed out, the US was "expected to weigh in, and the fact we got hit for it was just part of the game. We didn't have the option of sitting it out, and the fact that neither side was happy I took to mean we did something right".[221] Second, and to their credit, the Americans would meet with both sides at appropriate and comparable levels throughout, restating for the fourth year running their opposition to unconstitutional changes in power. Kasit agreed on "the need to pursue justice for all sides", but gave outspoken views in defense of the PAD.[222] The UDD's increasingly diverse leadership likewise expressed democratic contradictions. And assertions by both sides that communication with the other equaled endorsement of its cause belied their shared pleas for a "complete understanding". Third, it was in the Americans' interest to react to a crisis from which democracy might still have reemerged in Thailand, if in a critically weakened condition. The China Model had already won the day within the PAD's Yellow camp, but it remained in play among the UDD's Red Shirts. If a place for democracy, human rights, and the rule of law truly existed within US policy on Thailand—admittedly against the evidence under Bush—the crisis presented a late-game opportunity for Obama to prove it. In contrast to Sino-Thai relations, which had never included a common interest in upholding international law, the US still had a chance to inject priorities beyond Beijing's "order" and "stability". In the eye of the storm in mid-2009, John was thus correct in claiming that the "U.S. was not a referee, but a responsible friend of Thailand".[223] Finally, the US rendered a series of misjudgments, ranging from the avoidably careless to the consequential.

Over the five ensuing years, Deputy Prime Minister Suthep Thaung-suban would prove the most committed civilian opponent of democracy in Thai history. He told a State Department official that he had reached out to Thaksin in late 2008, but had been rebuffed; Thaksin claimed he had never been contacted. Suthep thanked John for his own outreach to the former prime minister, asked to no avail whether he knew of Red Shirt "training camps" in Cambodia, and shared his concern that Abhisit's life might be in danger. Presaging his own future exploits, he also said "that Thaksin had extensive wealth and was engaging in a public relations effort that misrepresented the nature of the anti-government movement, portraying it as focused on democracy".[224] On the Red side, a visiting US official asked Thaksin's party leaders "what the international community could do to assist Thailand to peacefully and democratically resolve the political conflict".[225] Their comments likewise anticipated later events. Former (and future) cabinet member Chaturon Chaisang advised that "Elections were not the final word in democracy."[226] Thaksin's lawyer asked that the US "consistently apply the principles followed in the Honduran" coup earlier in the year.[227] John also met again with Thaksin's sister: "While it was obvious that politics does not come as naturally to Yingluck as it does to her brother, one suspects she may well have a bright future with the party."[228]

John erred in meeting Thaksin's ex-wife two days in a row in early 2009, not on account of her political or precarious legal status, but because they dined in five-star hotels where they were bound to be seen. The second lunch, designed to clarify the first after rumors and reports quickly circulated, only compounded the error. In February, he told the press that rumors of Thaksin's US visa being revoked were untrue. Thaksin informed John on the phone that he "might travel to the U.S. in the coming months but intended not to denounce the RTG publicly".[229] He replied that his visa "did not guarantee admission into the U.S. The Ambassador reminded Thaksin of the U.S.–Thai extradition treaty and suggested Thaksin exercise his own judgment".[230] After the derailment of the ASEAN event in April, however, John recommended that the US "prudentially revoke" the visa[231] as two arrest warrants had been issued for the ex-premier and a US visit "would ensure that issues surrounding Thaksin's status would dominate the U.S.–Thai relationship".[232] Instead the decision only hindered relations with the opposition and did more to realize John's concern than prevent it. Indeed, when John rejected Kasit's requests to track Thaksin's movements abroad, the minister conceded that his return to Thailand "would probably be politically too hot to handle, and added that there were a number of people who might try to shoot him".[233]

The State Department also blundered in condemning the "unacceptable violence by the protesters"at the ASEAN event, without also acknowledging government-backed agents provocateurs.[234] Thaksin's sister would tell John "that the Red Shirts learned their lesson last April and had disavowed the use of violence", but public relations were proving a weak point across the board.[235] Two months later, John's recommendation that charges brought against Kasit be viewed as an "internal Thai matter" backfired.[236] Likely trying not to state the fact that the PAD's airport occupations fell short of "terrorism", the US appeared to the UDD suddenly selective in its lack of interest. The same month, thirty Red Shirts outside the US consulate in Chiang Mai protested at Secretary Clinton's plans to attend the ARF hosted by Abhisit. Over sixty more used former president Jimmy Carter's November visit with Habitat for Humanity to ask Obama to "boycott and not support" the government.[237]

* * *

In early March 2010, the embassy issued a statement that the UDD "forswear the use of violence" and the government "exercise appropriate restraint".[238] At the same time, Deputy Prime Minister Suthep cited "intelligence it apparently received from the United States that the protests could turn violent, as justification for pre-emptively invoking the Internal Security Act (ISA)" in Bangkok.[239] This assertion—entirely consistent with being a "responsible friend" to Thailand—would dog the US throughout the crisis and beyond. He also claimed that the US had "wiretapped telephone conversations involving Thaksin".[240] The UDD rallied briefly in front of the US embassy asking for clarification and asserting that the "black ops taught by the US is an old hat".[241]

After the first deadly clashes on 10 April, Secretary Clinton called for peaceful dialogue in a video message: "While you continue on the path to resolve your political differences, we remain confident in the strong, enduring bonds between the United States and Thailand."[242] Despite the army's amateur attempt to clear a protest area, the US rightly pointed at the Red Shirts for triggering the violence. Among them was a renegade Thai general with an anti-communist past: "Earlier, I took General Vang Pao, from the Hmong resistance, to America … I have a history of working with the CIA".[243] His message for Obama was to "Bring the United Nations in, because it is going to be like Pol Pot, Mussolini and Hitler."[244] Nine days later, the State Department reiterated its call for an end to the violence, as the embassy joined China in sending a representative to the central protest area. "In an apparent bid to counter US criticism and divide international opinion", Red Shirts briefly marched on the UN building in Bangkok and requested peacekeepers.[245]

As the US also praised Abhisit's "roadmap to reconciliation" and urged the protest leaders to condemn the violence from their stage, private meetings with them caused additional tension.[246] One recalled that they "invited us to have a discussion upstairs but nothing happened".[247] In early May the UDD warned of eventual violence by the authorities: "if the US interpreted events more carefully, they would see the true evidence".[248] Its spokesperson complained that

> a US official had "incredible details" of recent violence that he believed was gathered by the "CIA and other on-the-ground informants". He said that US officials claimed that the UDD had rigged compressed gas tanks to be used as bombs and stockpiled automatic weapons in nearby buildings … "The ambassador has apparently made up his mind that we have become an army and not a peaceful movement … the US Embassy is not as neutral as they say they are".[249]

To his colleague's mind, however, "I had a chance to talk with the US embassy but I think they still had some wrong belief" about Thaksin's interest in violence.[250] The government itself took issue with an early May meeting between a visiting assistant secretary of state and several UDD leaders; Kasit and the PAD declined his invitations, and John was called to the ministry for an official reprimand. Despite the meeting's purpose of urging the UDD to de-escalate, what had been welcome outreach six months ago had become interference.

Between 13 and 19 May, having permitted the situation to intensify for over two months, Thailand's security forces took action. In a US diplomat's accurate recollection, the Red Shirts had constructed "Mad Max-like" fortifications in a dozen locations, with sharpened bamboo, barbed wire, and rings of tires.[251] Armed clashes occurred throughout central Bangkok as soldiers retook ground and made arrests. Mere meters from a *New York Times* reporter who had just interviewed him, the renegade general was killed by a sniper's bullet to the head. Indeed, the army would unlawfully resort to lethal force inside "live-fire zones", as small but deadly groups of protesters lobbed grenades. At least sixty people were killed, most of whom were civilians, and over 1,000 others were injured. In the last hours, Red Shirts set fire to several major buildings, causing smoke to rise above the city.

During an online "Virtual Town Hall" for US citizens in Thailand, the embassy's security officer said, "Right now, I'm working with the prime minister. The army is now trying to get the city back open and it has involved responding to violence instigated by the Red Shirts."[252] Hours after the operation ended, an embassy spokesperson addressed the press: "We are deeply concerned that Red Shirt supporters have engaged in arson targeting the electricity infrastructure and media outlets and have attacked individual journalists ... We condemn such behavior and call on UDD leaders and affiliated opposition politicians to urge their supporters to stop such acts".[253] Abhisit and his yellow-clad backers would hold the Americans on-side for his remaining fourteen months in office. That the US view of the violence was far more lop-sided than the violence itself was driven by its incomplete assessment of the previous year's clashes and its persistent confusion of army reluctance for "restraint". Further, as its security officer revealed and Abhisit's spokesperson explained,

> The intelligence officers we cooperated with knew very well what was at stake on the ground, and that was reflected in the top US diplomats. The fundamental thinking about peaceful solutions and democratic principles was the same, but it was not only that anymore. There was less discussion of principles at that time, which was not bad in a time of crisis. We had a direct channel to talk to the top embassy people all the time. They voiced their concerns on the ground—real concerns on real issues—and were trying to make good comments, positive suggestions. We also reassured them on how the government would operate, how the security forces would operate.[254]

If the Americans had real concerns over the army's unlawful "live-fire" zones, they were ignored. Their statements after the fact made no mention of them.

The US was almost certainly influenced too by Thaksin's rejection of a compromise on the eve of the crackdown, heavily in his favor but excluding return of his assets. That he had told John the year before—correctly—that the Red Shirts were "driven by much more than money" suggested how much more was lost in 2010 than the lives of ninety people.[255] Like the PAD two years before, the UDD put any lingering doubts about its democratic credentials to rest in the violence. Minuscule pockets of genuine pro-democracy sentiment would remain under its nominal umbrella, but it otherwise revealed its true colors.

June saw both sides send envoys to Washington in the hopes of influencing a resolution on Thailand in the House of Representatives. Abhisit reflected that

> Thaksin did have a strong lobbying team in the US, and so his ability
> to get articles published favorable to him obviously gave a favorable
> impression of his side to a casual observer of Thailand. I didn't for a
> moment blame, say, a Congressman or a Senator who believed the Thaksin
> propaganda because that's what they would read. But when we made an
> effort to explain things, it did help.[256]

Thaksin's Thai lawyer wished to offer "friendly advice to a friend", and see a provision encouraging negotiation with Thaksin in the resolution.[257] Instead, passed near-unanimously, it stated that the House "supports the goals of the 5-point roadmap of the Government of Thailand for national reconciliation".[258] A month later, a senior State Department official would visit Abhisit and pledge executive support for the plan. After UDD protesters violated pre-agreed conditions, the embassy refused to accept its letter asking that the resolution be rescinded. Maladroit speeches by Thaksin's new foreign lawyer only discredited his client and bounced off their American target.

Finally invited to Washington in December to address the US Helsinki Commission on Thailand, Thaksin did not go. Thailand had sent warrants for him worldwide in recent months on terrorism charges, in addition to previous ones on more credible charges. It also said that it was tracking his visa applications and preparing an extradition request. Whether the US advised Thaksin in advance or he assessed the risks independently was not clear. But that an invitation from a bipartisan Congressional body was not enough to override political and legal uncertainty spoke loudly. Eric John would depart Thailand as ambassador the same month, noting four and a half years later that Thaksin no longer spoke to him.

Synchronized swimming

From 2001 through 2008, Thailand had seen only Thaksin- or military-led governments, all of which had deepened military ties with China. As further evidence that Thaksin's changes ran deep, there was no sign of the trend changing under Abhisit, beginning with a visit to Beijing by Thailand's army chief less than two months after the new government was formed. High-level visits in both directions would continue unabated over the next two and a half years, with China's defense minister reciprocating as early as December 2009. The number of Thai officers attending Beijing's National Defense University also increased. Kasit told a US diplomat that the "Chinese military was pushing hard for closer relations with Thai counterparts."[259] With no explanation necessary, the Defense Ministry told the US that this was simply "natural".[260] After Sudan denied a Thai request in 2009 relating to a humanitarian mission, the US embassy informed Washington that "the Thai do not plan to ask for significant deployment assistance from the U.S. Conversely, the Thai have told us they are looking to the Chinese for assistance—material and political—in making the deployment successful".[261] An opinion poll the same year found that only *2 percent* of Thais viewed China's growing military power as a threat.

The first drop in the military budget post-coup (the global financial crisis disguised as civilian leadership) also pointed procurement to cheaper Chinese weapons and materiel. Persistent complaints on quality and concerns on interoperability kept large-scale purchases at bay, but Chinese kit was beginning to include maintenance and training. China continued to improve Thailand's air defense equipment and offered to sell weapons systems and second-hand submarines. And as Kasit explained, "The Chinese had money in abundance, and knew what toys needed to be given to the military. And the terms and conditions of financial or economic cooperation were devoid of democratic considerations. So they bought Thai politicians, they bought the Thai military establishment."[262] In view of shared interest in submarines, most important were developments in joint exercises. "Strike 2009" was held in China, "Strike 2010" in Thailand and focused on counterterrorism. In 2009, Beijing strongly suggested large-scale bilateral exercises, which the Thais confined to special forces for the time being. A new development in

November 2010 was "Blue Strike", a maritime exercise involving both nations' navies and marine corps.

Retreat

An aide to Thailand's army chief told the Americans that his boss "favorably compared the treatment he receives in China to the 'big brother' approach of his U.S. counterparts, whom he viewed as at times more interested in pursuing potential concerns over human rights and democracy than in building relationships".[263] A year later the chief himself described a "growing sense among the Thai military and other government agencies that the benefits to the relationship accrued more greatly to the U.S."[264] Thailand's point of comparison and priorities were not surprising, as Sino-Thai mil-to-mil advances under Abhisit signaled a corresponding retreat for the US and Thailand.

The commander-in-chief did meet the US army chief of staff in mid-2009 in Bangkok and attend the Pacific Army Chiefs Conference in Hawaii. He visited Washington itself in early 2010. A senior general attended a Chiefs of Defense conference, also in Washington, while the assistant secretary of state for political-military affairs and the PACOM commander visited Bangkok in 2010. Consistent with areas for enhancement identified by the embassy, Kasit "knew that in Norfolk, Virginia there was an intense discussion on restructuring the US armed forces—rapid deployment forces, joint command, more electronic and modern armaments, computerized and knowledgeable soldiers".[265] In his 2009 meeting with Clinton, he told her that "Thailand could be good at peacekeeping operations under the UN, could do anti-piracy, and could be part of more civilian–military undertakings on disaster relief and humanitarian assistance. These were the types of things that you should do to help upgrade the Thai military establishment."[266] Despite standing "to lose the most from the additional transparency", the army continued implementation of the US-funded Defense Resource Management System, and JUSMAG helped it establish a non-commissioned officer program.[267] The US also helped Thailand transport medical supplies to Haiti in 2010, upgrade a peacekeeping training facility, and provide armor and vehicles for its troops in Sudan. Inviting ridicule for its price and impracticality, the Thais spent over $7 million on an unmanned dirigible for surveillance in the deep south.

Procurement otherwise took another hit. In 2009, with more than $2 billion worth of weapons and materiel in the pipeline, the US began "a comprehensive program that will meet Thai military needs through Foreign Military Sales, Foreign Military Financing, Direct Commercial Sales, and other programs".[268] Further to his meeting with Clinton, Kasit

> wanted her to change the terms of military procurement. We are allies so we should have better things than the Burmese or the Malaysians. You cannot say that we should get the same things as the underlings. We should get something quite good, near what they have given Taiwan, South Korea, Israel, or even the Egyptian military. I said the same thing to the US Seventh Fleet commander in Honolulu. There was some sort of a distrust, or some sort of fear that Thailand would have the overall priority over neighboring countries—and why not? We are the bloody allies.[269]

The Thais formed a committee solely devoted to increasing US acquisitions. At the top of its list were three UH-60 Blackhawk helicopters and the possibility of six more within several years. Noting that Sweden's jets had come with technology packages that outweighed the F-16's greater overall proficiency, Abhisit's spokesperson (and security specialist) Panitan requested technology transfers. He also took a page from meetings with the Chinese in seeking submarines, claiming they would afford "important strike capabilities".[270] Nonetheless, an air force general complained that it was "increasingly difficult" to make US purchases. In response to a Foreign Ministry request for more foreign military finance, a visiting Defense Department official pledged to increase it "as early as 2012".[271] The Thais bought Israeli Tavor rifles over American M4s the same month.

In April 2009, Kasit requested more excess defense articles (EDA) in accordance with Thailand's major non-NATO status, as the US drew down in Iraq and Afghanistan. Along with Abhisit, he raised it with Clinton again in July, requesting that Ambassador John pass on a specific list to JUSMAG. He pointedly informed a senior State Department official that "Thailand could not continue to say no to China's requests for more military engagement, and that the U.S. military needed to re-engage more seriously, and to respond 'at least symbolically' to Thai requests for Excess Defense Articles."[272] The army chief added that such "would go far in working against the perception that Thailand was giving more than it was receiving in the relationship".[273] Nonetheless, the US responded that EDA would not be available until *at least 2014*.

Training and joint exercises fared little better. As late as 2010, funding for IMET had not regained pre-coup levels, and "few junior officers" were studying in the US.[274] Although the former was partly due to worldwide cuts and the latter to Thaksin's anti-IMET policy, it was clearly of concern to the Thais. According to the Defense Ministry, the decrease from $2.4 million to $1.5 million "could diminish the historically close ties between the U.S. and Thai militaries".[275] Kasit was even clearer on the geopolitical and demographic realities, stating that IMET was needed to "positively facilitate the development of the next generation of Thai military leaders".[276] He looked back in frustration: "They had so much influence on the Thai military establishment. Push them to behave in a more civilized manner."[277] Defense and State Department officials said they would try. The US and Thailand continued to participate together in roughly forty bilateral or multilateral military exercises each year, with Cobra Gold remaining the anchor. The Thais requested training in the event plans for a coastguard came to fruition. In mid-2011, US marines conducted a ten-day non-lethal weapons training exercise on Thailand's eastern seaboard, including much-needed crowd-control techniques after the previous year's debacle in Bangkok.

What crisis?

In Abhisit's recollection, "Relations with China were very focused on economic ties, so most of the trips that we made were about setting targets for trade, investment, tourism, getting our agricultural goods there, the high-speed rail."[278] By the end of 2009, Thai exports to China were 115 percent higher than in December 2008 when Abhisit took office, and exceeded those to the US (and Japan) for the first time; while China had surpassed the US in overall trade with Thailand two years before, it had remained behind as an export market. Moreover, the share of Thai exports bound for China had doubled since 2002, from 5 to 10 percent. Interestingly, among the strongest was computer hard drives made by US manufacturers in rural Thailand; having outsourced their labor to Southeast Asia, the companies' products were credited as a Thai export. Another was rubber, both cause and effect of northern Thai farmers continuing since Thaksin's tenure to switch from rice. Responding to a request from Thailand and Indonesia, Beijing agreed to a six-fold increase in price. According to Finance Minister Korn, the most they had hoped for was half that. Overall bilateral trade rose 39 percent in 2010 amid discussions of a currency swap. During his June visit to China, Abhisit signed no fewer than eighteen economic agreements in what the US embassy called "an example of the Chinese paying attention to the Thai top priorities".[279]

In 2009, as Thailand opened its second and third investment offices in Shanghai, the value of Chinese investment proposals in the country increased by more than $1 billion. While China remained behind Japan, the US and the EU, it was climbing fast; "Beijing signaled its commitment more economically by serving as the largest foreign investor to Thailand in the first quarter" of 2010.[280] Moreover, while Chinese investors continued to enjoy financial-*cum*-political backing from Beijing, they did not receive the national treatment afforded the Americans under their bilateral Treaty of Amity and Economic Relations. In what would remain its single largest investment in Thailand through at least 2015, China purchased the Asia Credit Bank. Done via a competitive bid, negotiations with China proceeded "virtually at the government-to-government level".[281] Korn was clear that this was a "conscious decision by us to have one of China's main banks have a major presence in Thailand and allow trade and other investments in the future to be financed through this bank".[282] At the same time, renaming it the Industrial and Commercial Bank of China, Beijing just as clearly "wanted a foothold in a strategic country in Asia".[283] Conversely, "some analysts estimate that Thai investments in China are well over ten times the value of Chinese investments in Thailand".[284] Pride of place continued to belong to the CP Group, which not only had $6 billion worth of investments in China, but had "managed to place at least one of its top managers in a key ministerial position in every Thai government in the past decade".[285] Whatever real and feigned differences existed among such governments, access to the world's largest market was not one of them.

Yielding market share

"While all this was going on", according to Korn, "there was absolutely nothing going on between Thailand and the US, no new developments. America was in no position to do very much because of the financial crisis. At best it was really just maintenance of a very good relationship that we had all taken for granted."[286] His advice at the time, given publicly via CNN, was that they "continue to work with each other rather than to be concerned about the potential impact of China's economic rise".[287] Yet the impact was real: the US was rapidly falling further behind in trade and slowly losing its lead in FDI. While the Americans would continue to insist that the "Thai economic leadership understands

that in the long run, respect for intellectual property rights, fair labor practices, and good governance ... are necessary for sound economic growth", they
could also be honest with themselves.[288] In reference to the reversal in export
fortunes, John conceded that "The data for December were a surprise to some,
but when looking at the last three decades of Thai–Chinese economic relations,
it is obvious that this day was inevitable."[289] Indeed, Thai exports to the US in
December 2009 were only 13 percent higher compared to the same month in
2008, while the share of Thai exports bound for the US had almost halved since
2002. Overall, bilateral trade grew just 15 percent in 2010.

On the abortive FTA, Kasit said that "discussions would not be going
anywhere",[290] Abhisit that "the US has yet to send a signal to resume the
talks".[291] While Abhisit also resurrected Thaksin's trade representative position, the State Department had to wait for a new one of its own in 2009.
Ambassador John did commence a "Meet the Minister" series in which he and
US businesses engaged cabinet-level officials, and traveled to northern Thailand in 2009 to promote economic links with local government and private
industry. Although not enough to get Thailand removed from the US watchlist, Abhisit became personally engaged in IPR protection and the US initiated
an out-of-cycle review "needed to give the new government the backing" to
make progress. Kasit agreed to "talk to pharma in a friendly manner",[292] as
the deputy trade minister traveled to Washington pledging that "compulsory
licensing was not going to be a difficult issue".[293] Late 2009 saw Thailand
accede to the Patent Cooperation Treaty, amend its copyright laws, and receive
US IPR experts.

The main trade issue for Thailand was US protectionism. Although the US
finally began complying with the WTO ruling on continuous shrimp bonds,
the commerce minister "questioned how a 'Buy American' policy would be
implemented and whether it would be consistent with WTO commitments".[294]
A Thai diplomat in Washington reported in early 2009 that "new legislation is
intended to serve as a non-tariff barrier to imports to the U.S."[295] What neither
side questioned or reported was how a US effort at "protecting" its economy
was accounting for much of Thailand's export discrepancy between China and
the US. The main concern for the US, implicating both trade and investment,
were Thailand's customs laws, resulting in unfair and non-transparent treatment
of US exporters and investors. Despite a new Thai ban on US beef exports,
the US was seeking to double its exports to Thailand pursuant to a National

Export Initiative in 2010. Abhisit formed a committee to resolve the issue, while deputy premier Suthep pledged to "assist informally" via a friend at the Finance Ministry.[296] The director-general of the customs office was duly transferred to an inactive post; the US invited his replacement to address its chamber of commerce. When the largest American exporter to Thailand (Amway) was assessed a $200 million fine on the valuation of certain goods, the finance minister himself agreed to investigate.

For the second and third consecutive years, US investment in Thailand fell in 2009 and 2010. The global financial crisis, Thailand's domestic scene, and continued uncertainty on preferential treatment under the AER discouraged the 650-member American Chamber of Commerce. Abhisit's government also contained members "who, by nature of their position, have personal financial interests that brush up against those of U.S. firms".[297] In late 2008, Ambassador John toured Coca-Cola's factory in the northeast to promote investment. Korn recalled that with "the automobile industry—Ford, Chrysler, GM—which has a significant presence here, there were issues that needed to be dealt with. AIG and AIA, specific issues that needed to be dealt with".[298] In September 2009, Abhisit put on a "business roadshow" in New York to drum up investment, and rang the closing bell of the city's fabled stock exchange.[299] A Thai court then suspended on environmental grounds all activity in a huge industrial estate on the Gulf of Thailand, including those of Dow Chemical and Chevron. Most did not resume until late 2010.

Palace politics

During the six decades between World War II and WikiLeaks, American diplomats in Thailand spoke readily and honestly with and about Thailand's royal family. It would thus be unfair to assign private conversations and memos a significance beyond their having been made public. Thailand's *lese majeste* law, non-applicable to foreigners with diplomatic immunity, might have been relevant in several cases at most. Rather, it was the timing of the cables' entrance in the public domain that brought them notoriety. Thailand's crisis had long been as much about the palace as mere politics, but few factors both exposed and exacerbated that reality more than WikiLeaks. The cables were simultaneously messenger and message, and both bore the seal of the United States.

In the wake of President Bush's debacle in August 2008, even the fading generation of Thailand's monarchy no longer belonged in the US camp. A

December 2009 visit to Thailand by China's defense minister was timed to coincide with King Bhumibol's birthday celebrations, and John was not the only ambassador meeting regularly with the aging Privy Council. The next generation was looking East. A Chinese poll conducted in 2009 resulted in Princess Sirindhorn being named "the second most important of 'China's top ten international friends'".[300] By the end of 2010, she had made a reported thirty trips to China since 1981, including five during the past two years. A Thai Foreign Ministry official "stressed that the work Princess Sirindhorn had undertaken to enhance Thai–China bilateral relations is more than symbolic".[301] An institute in China was named after her, hosting students from both nations and focusing on biotechnology, alternative energy, and traditional Chinese medicine. China also built a residence for her outside Beijing. Long an active and admired proponent of Mandarin, Sirindhorn welcomed China's donation of several northern Thai university buildings, named after her and designed for Chinese studies. Moreover, Princess Chulabhorn, having been named a cultural ambassador to China as well, traveled there three times in 2009 alone. Kasit attended a performance by the princess on a Chinese musical instrument during his third trip that year.

In contrast, while the Thais were "deeply appreciative" of Obama's interest in the king's health during a 2009 APEC event, all interaction with the monarchy was done by the embassy in Bangkok.[302] John met with the crown prince at the start of 2009. In addition to discussing US investment, Cobra Gold, and the Viktor Bout case, he complimented John on his visibility and activity in the media and rural areas, and among students. In a statement suggesting resignation more than hope, he also remarked that, "Our generation grew up in the Vietnam War, and easily understood the strategic importance of having a strong alliance with the U.S."[303] In late 2009, Princess Sirindhorn joined Abhisit and John in affirming the US Peace Corps as "an anchor of the enduring Thai–U.S. bilateral partnership".[304] She spoke of how the program complemented her own work for disadvantaged children. In mid-2010, the Thai Fulbright Commission awarded her for promoting Thai–US education exchanges.

Otherwise, John hosted two lunches in 2009 for Privy Council chair Prem, and attended by up to five other councilors and the king's principal private secretaries. In the wake of the violence, they thanked the State Department for its statement and "indicated most members of the Thai political class viewed the USG as credible and balanced".[305] They also informed John that all channels of communication with Thaksin over a possible deal had been shut down. Once each in early 2009 and early 2010, John spoke with Prem individually to convey concern about the *lese majeste* law. Prem asked what the US would do if a former president became a paid advisor of another nation (as Thaksin had done in Cambodia). He spoke well of Abhisit, but "did not feel sympathetic toward either the Red Shirts or the PAD".[306] Three other meetings included his foreign minister and fellow councilor, who criticized Abhisit's "lack of resolve",[307] but "had higher hopes for" the general destined to take over Thailand in 2014.[308] John met twice each in 2009 with a political advisor to the crown prince, discussing Thaksin, Bout and the Thai police, and with the king's deputy principal private secretary.[309] To US Senator Webb, who joined one of the meetings, the deputy "apologized for 'having to play the China card' and opined that as U.S. focus on Southeast Asia has diminished over the last decade, China has increasingly become a more important partner for Thailand".[310]

Finally, the embassy informed Washington that "the future role of the monarchy ... will remain the ultimate internal Thai discourse, with Thais largely deaf or indifferent to outside voices".[311] Two months later, it mistakenly played Thailand's national—rather than royal—anthem at a large Independence Day reception. A senior US diplomat said he was "110 percent sure it was not a deliberate signal", and it dissipated quickly as an honest and awkward mistake after the embassy reached out.[312] But to politically sensitive ears at an American function, the anthem struck some as an "outside voice" best kept quiet.

Democratic rights

"Democracy" had not been so rhetorically seized upon in Thailand since the experimental 1970s—nor so abjectly trampled. Even the "Thai Spring" had not featured such constant, strident, and diverse claims to "D" as did the PAD's "New Politics" and the UDD's tyranny of the majority, both utterly bankrupt. The defense minister—a key leader of the 2014 coup—told John that Thailand "was attempting to use the U.S. as a model for the development of Thai democracy".[313]

Further, democracy's death throes in Thailand came against American naivety and dogmatism. In mid-2009, Kasit told Clinton that "the aspiration of the Thai people was to become a fully-fledged democratic society. The United States went through the democratization process ... So what I needed from the United States was to learn and share its experiences and best practices on good governance".[314] Similarly, in 2010 the UDD invited the embassy to one of its many "Democracy Schools" in the north and northeast, and asked whether US funding for more might be available. Ignoring that Kasit's democratic credibility was gone by then and that the UDD's was at its peak, the US was not given to shades of gray amidst the primary colors. Consistent with their approach in the rest of the world—if inconsistently applied—the Americans began defining democracy exclusively as the absence of a textbook coup and the occurrence of an election. In Thailand this fast became dogma, which, true to form, would blind the US to nuance, manipulation, and "understanding". It would mistake two absolutely integral elements of democracy for its sum total. Indeed, John claimed that the army chief—another key player in 2014—"has resisted pressures from all sides for military intervention … to come down on the side of democracy".[315] This also accounted for why some Thais wrongly accused the US of favoring the UDD, as both shared a "silver bullet" approach to elections.

* * *

In 1984, American scholar William Klausner warned of "the possibility that the *lese majeste* concept could come under more scrutiny and criticism if it is manipulated and misused by power brokers such as government officials, politicians, and business-men to settle political scores".[316] Exactly a quarter-century later, Prime Minister Abhisit presided over the steepest decline in freedom of expression in modern Thai history. Although it had begun in 2007 and would worsen under his successors, the drop itself under Abhisit was near-vertical. His coalition government, consisting less of seven political parties than of the Democrats, military, Privy Council, and PAD—i.e. Network Monarchy—was more sensitive than the famously touchy Thaksin. In 2010, 478 cases of *lese majeste* were filed, a three-fold increase over the previous year's figure. A year later, a joint Thai–US citizen was arrested for having administered a blog *while in the United States* that included *The King Never Smiles*. During Abhisit's thirty-one months in power, an estimated 113,000 websites were blocked. At the same time, he would tell a US diplomat that Beijing's "recent controversy with Google had exposed a more worrisome aspect of China's rise".[317]

Otherwise it was a familiar story. The deep south had become a full-blown internal armed conflict, and included the systematic use of torture by Thai security forces. Abhisit prioritized the case of a Muslim lawyer forcibly disappeared under Thaksin, but by the time he left office nothing had changed. The nation's leading forensic scientist identified a "killing field" in the north that "no one wants to investigate".[318] Having passed an improved anti-trafficking law in 2009, the Thais complained about the annual US anti-trafficking report in 2010: "This is not the way to work with friends."[319] Five years on, Abhisit was nonplussed: "The US and also Europe need to make their stance known about human rights and democracy, and when they make statements whenever there is a controversial event here, they often upset people. It's not new, we've had this for quite some time."[320] By 2010, the embassy had vetted Thai security personnel for US training or assistance nearly 500 times since late 2004.

Beginning just before Abhisit took office but continuing throughout, Thai authorities took fuel, food, and water away from Rohingya "boat people" on the Andaman Sea and set them adrift. Those who made it ashore were beaten and detained. Many were moved by people smugglers, others were or would become victims of human trafficking; all were desperate to leave Myanmar. Abhisit pledged to investigate and take legal action, but border policy was still in the hands of ISOC. The official position that the Rohingya were economic migrants was partially true, but even Kasit admitted that some could be refugees, while no status justified their inhumane and illegal treatment. Asking how the US responded to Haitians and Cubans, Abhisit was both well-advised and conveniently pragmatic in proposing a regional solution. In March 2009, Ambassador John penned an article for the regional *Irrawaddy*, voicing opposition to past and future push-backs. In June—after the US prevented the forced return of other refugees on the Myanmar border—Suthep "acknowledged that the RTG had at times" engaged in the practice.[321]

The Lao Hmong population in Thailand remained divided between 158 refugees in one northern location and some 6,000 people in another, an unknown number of whom were refugees. In violation of the most basic tenet of international refugee law, all would be sent back to Laos at the end of 2009. The Foreign Ministry asked the US in April to think "outside of the box", which for Thailand included resettlement of the 158 only *after* their return to Laos.[322] The Thais also pledged to protect the "CIA fighters" among the 6,000, while preparing to repatriate them all regardless.[323] Their population would drop throughout the year by nearly a third, via "voluntary" returns the US was not permitted to observe. In June, a military officer told the US that they "would not use physical force or compulsion but would use inducements and psychological pressure to encourage returns to Laos".[324] The following month, Abhisit himself told Secretary Clinton that there would be no forced repatriation, while a US legislative delegation visited the camps. They warned that any forcible return would result in a "major uproar" in Congress.[325] The US then joined talks with Thai and Lao authorities concerning "the eight percent" who might be refugees: humanitarian puppet theatre.[326] In November, the Americans actually "acceded to the idea of moving the Hmong back to Laos for a short period before being repatriated to a third country".[327] When Abhisit himself visited Laos nineteen days before the push-back, they wrongly assumed that at least the 158 would be protected. Instead, on 28 December Thailand forcibly returned the remaining 4,369 Hmong. In the recollection of an embassy official, "it was a measure of diminished US influence that we could not pull that off" against the People's Democratic Republic of Laos.[328]

John doubled down on his byline with an opinion editorial in the *Bangkok Post* condemning the *refoulement*. Abhisit's and Kasit's offices "called first thing in the morning" to protest, while John's deputy was summoned for personal reprimand.[329] The embassy rightly stood its ground, and warned that "Congress would soon be back in session and that there might be further repercussions".[330] Yet three months later and for the second time that decade, the US voted for Thai membership on the UN Human Rights Council, making John's 987-word op-ed the sum total of its response. In exchange for support for the US's own Council bid, the vote also came one day before Thailand's security forces began their crackdown in May 2010.

Border calls

In one of its first foreign policy moves, the Obama administration reviewed the country's outdated "Burma policy". The US "found Kasit more active on Burma than any Thai Foreign Minister since 2000", welcoming his trip there in early 2009.[331] It appreciated his facilitation of talks between its government and an ethnic minority group, and his support for US assistance to activists and dissidents. However misguided, his "understanding for the need for continued sanctions" was also applauded.[332] His ministry spoke out on Myanmar at a March session of the UN Human Rights Council, and "quietly hosted" the Council of Asian Liberals and Democrats, which did the same.[333] Clinton praised Thailand's overall Myanmar policy in May. The Americans were concerned, however, that "the Thai military for the first time since 2002 may be once again conducting its own separate approach to Burma".[334] The embassy noted that it was meeting the government at "a level Thai civilian leaders cannot match".[335] As chair, Thailand facilitated a statement on Aung San Suu Kyi at an ASEAN meeting in July, attended by Clinton. Having visited Bangkok earlier in the year, US Senator Webb met with Abhisit again in August, winning support for pressure on China to speak out on Myanmar's upcoming elections. In a move the US deemed "unprecedented", Thailand's Foreign Ministry summoned the Chinese ambassador in late 2009, to dispute that an armed conflict in Myanmar was "solely a domestic matter".[336] The US discussed its policy review with the Foreign Ministry the same month, including a conditional desire to lift the sanctions. Thailand's former ambassador to Myanmar told the Americans that, "regardless of what policy the U.S. adopted, the Burmese regime would always have the upper hand. The U.S. should work collectively with ASEAN".[337] In November 2010, days before its first elections in two decades, Abhisit visited Myanmar.

* * *

In 1965, three years after the international court decision on the Preah Vihear temple, Donald Nuechterlein wrote: "In dealing with the popular outburst of emotion against the Cambodians, the Sarit government had to use all the power and persuasiveness at its command to keep the situation under control and to prevent dissident and subversive elements from using it to try to discredit and perhaps to upset the regime."[338] Forty-four years later, the indignation was less felt than fabricated, and the currency less of "peasants" than the upper class PAD. It also posed no real threat to Abhisit despite more casualties, serving simply as a proxy war between Sondhi and Thaksin, who was spending considerable time in Cambodia. That China and the US had to at least take account of the dispute was testament to the PAD's adeptness at hatching an "international incident" for purely domestic consumption.

In fact China was more interested in an unrelated dispute between its two neighbors over claims in the Gulf of Thailand. With reserves of oil and natural gas beneath waters not separated from China by the Straits of Malacca, the Chinese could not take a chance on a temple standing in their way of accessing them; the sooner Preah Vihear was resolved, the sooner the maritime issues could be as well. The Thais asked Beijing to encourage compromise on the temple, but also made it clear that conventional weapons sales to Cambodia were not appreciated. By mid-2010 China had helped to reduce tensions.

Kasit requested and received the same from the US, which aspired to middle ground but agreed that Cambodia's retention of Thaksin as an economic advisor in 2009 was an escalation; it advised Thailand to "take the high road in moving forward".[339] Thailand also obtained US support for membership on the UN World Heritage Committee. Analogous to Chinese arms sales were the first US–Cambodia military exercises in mid-2010, which greatly aggravated the Thais. A US undersecretary of state said that "We don't see that as in any way contradicting or in conflict with our commitment to working with the Thai military."[340] In February 2011, two and a half years after the notion was first mooted, the UN Security Council heard statements from both sides on the temple, although the US and China agreed that ASEAN was better placed to address the issue.

Finally and further afield, the US welcomed a Thai statement on North Korea in May 2009; ASEAN and ARF meetings resulted in two more. As chair, Thailand allowed China to submit alternative language for the ARF statement drafted by the US. When the Americans learned that the new text had come from North Korea itself, the Thais relayed that the Koreans would otherwise abandon both the ARF and the Six-Party talks. "China now had to deliver on their end of the bargain", according to Kasit.[341] Annoyed that Thailand had acted "without consulting with us or seeking judicious editing", the US was angry that Chinese pressure proved more powerful than its own.[342] Clinton conveyed her personal disappointment to a Foreign Ministry official who had assured her otherwise. In December, however, the US welcomed the seizure of a cargo plane yielding 35 tons of weapons from North Korea; the US had provided critical intelligence before being allowed to join the Thais onboard. John recommended a call of appreciation from Obama to Abhisit, and Clinton praised Thailand in Washington two days later. As the flight and most of its five-man crew had come from former Soviet states, Thai authorities questioned Viktor Bout. It was never learned where the weapons were headed, but the assumption by both nations was Myanmar.

Too big to fail

In 2009, China became ASEAN's largest trading partner, overtaking the EU and Japan just two years after moving ahead of the US. At the start of the following year, the China–ASEAN free trade agreement came into full effect, having been signed in 2002 and come into partial effect in 2005. Trade between the regional giant and regional body had already grown six-fold since 2000. Finance Minister Korn told CNN, "The Chinese attitude diplomatically, politically, and economically with the rest of Asia has been wholly positive."[343]

Pending the completion of the bridge over the Mekong River linking northern Thailand and Laos, riverine transport remained the main China–ASEAN trade route and rubber the main export. In addition to two ports also used to ferry trucks across in lieu of the bridge, construction on a new port commenced in 2009. Construction on the bridge finally began in early 2010. Furthermore, as announced at the ASEAN summit in October 2009 in Thailand, China agreed to jointly finance at least two more Thai–Laos bridges, with plans for completion in 2012. The announcement was presided over by the premiers of all three nations. Construction on the Thai side of the road also picked up under Abhisit. On the "Indochina Junction's" other road, connecting Thailand and China via Myanmar, a new $10 million customs house was completed. The Asian Development Bank (ADB) projected that in 2015, the cost of shipping goods on the Mekong would still be no more than half that of using either road, but that the roads/bridges would take less than half the transit time.

Against the tide of optimism were two sets of complaints and controversy, the first concerning "Unofficial customs fees, poor adherence to rules of origin, and general lawlessness along the Mekong River."[344] The ADB's projections were based on rational, efficiency-driven decisions relative to the regional FTA. Yet when provincial and local players imposed their own rules and "local value-added taxes", curious distortions in the ways and means of transportation, the volume of goods, and consumer costs resulted. These were often but not always to China's economic benefit, and sometimes led to violence. A 2009 firefight on the Mekong between ethnic minority rebels and the Myanmar army resulted in the death of a Chinese sailor. Following an attack the previous year on a Chinese patrol boat, Thailand and Laos were quick to join the two nations in investigating.

The other issue was China's continued manipulation of four dams, causing additional "dry seasons" and both ecological and economic damage downstream. "Locals claim that water levels are adequate when Chinese vessels are scheduled to travel down the river, but are lower when Thai vessels attempt to make the trip upstream. Chinese officials counter that only 18% of the Mekong's flow originates in China."[345] In 2009 there was related opposition to the clearing of rock formations in twenty-one locations along the river; larger Chinese vessels trumped local fish stocks. However, China surprisingly attended the Mekong River Commission's Flood Forum in northern Thailand, engaging fellow governments and civil society. Presenting studies showing minimal impact of two future dams, it also postponed a third, conceding that "problems would come back to haunt China and they would lose face and influence in the lower Mekong".[346] China also participated in the Commission's hydropower environmental assessment in late 2009, and welcomed its team to its own flood control offices.

The following year, drought replaced deluge, as the Mekong's water levels hit a seventeen-year low and neither of Thailand's two ports was usable. For the first time, the MRC—on which China had only observer status—sent a letter to Beijing with strong backing from Abhisit. While the Chinese said it was "baseless and incorrect" to blame them, an assistant foreign minister traveled to Bangkok to provide assurances, and their embassy held a rare press conference.[347] China then sent its vice-foreign minister to an MRC meeting in Thailand, and welcomed it on a visit to several of its dams. Tension remained, however, as a Thai representative said that, "China's four dams on the upper part of the Mekong River have already destroyed the river's ecosystem. Now this giant nation plans to build 12 more dams on the lower part."[348]

Finally, meeting with his US counterpart in 2009, China's new ambassador to ASEAN said that his country wanted to expand regional investment. The next month, China announced a $10 billion investment fund and loan package, focused on infrastructure, natural resource development, and communications. Needed and appreciated in equal measure during a global crisis rooted in the US, it also recalled Beijing's $1 billion pledge in 1997 as the US looked the other way. There was more: China extended a $15 billion line of credit to ASEAN countries, $5 million to a China–ASEAN cooperation fund, and $900,000 to an ASEAN Plus Three fund. It donated 300,000 tons of rice to an emergency East Asia reserve, proposed a China–ASEAN scheme for high-yield regional crop farms, and pledged places for a thousand farmers in Chinese training courses. In the words of a Thai Foreign Ministry official, Beijing was the "main actor" in crisis response.[349] In early 2010, the $80 billion Chiang Mai Initiative was increased to $120 billion, with China contributing the second largest share. "China's support was something that we sought and received", recalled Korn. "The most significant event related to China was the upgrading of the CMI."[350]

* * *

If economics was China's stock-in-trade, it was not the only tool in its box. By early 2009 it had forty-eight separate mechanisms through which it was otherwise engaging ASEAN. China's regional ambassador told the US that separate meetings of ASEAN's Plus Three countries caused its core member states anxiety; it was thus important to "show respect for ASEAN's centrality in East Asia's architecture".[351] In view of China's success in influencing and infiltrating the body, the first statement was congratulatory, the second self-serving. A Thai Foreign Ministry official said that Beijing was "less accommodating" to ASEAN than in the past, and that the region had recently declined a Chinese proposal to conduct joint military training.[352] A Thai general was more objective toward the new 21st century reality: "With Laos and Cambodia heavily influenced by China, it was important for Thailand to develop good relations with Beijing as well in order to insure against being sidelined in the region."[353] Abhisit commented, "Within the context of ASEAN, China was very careful not to give the impression that, because of her emergence as an economic power, she was going to somehow pose a threat. But the militaries of our two countries were quite close anyway, so we were comfortable with the way things were done."[354]

False start

Following the US polls in November 2008, Prime Minister Somchai had sent the president-elect a note: "With your past experience in Southeast Asia, I look forward to seeing the United States under your leadership enhance its meaningful role in the region ... Thailand is firmly determined to work with the United States and ASEAN colleagues towards a more vigorous and fruitful US–ASEAN partnership".[355] Eight months later, during her visit to Thailand for the ARF, Secretary Clinton told a large gathering of students, media, and officials that "the United States is back ... President Obama and I are giving great importance to this region".[356] In between, an anti-Thaksin Abhisit would emphasize ASEAN in large part because the ex-premier had not, and inherit both the regional chair and a secretary-general of Democrat Party tutelage. From 2009 through mid-2011 thus spelled the last best chance for the US to make up ground on China in ASEAN. It would begin with several sure-footed political steps but also with an inherited and ill-conceived economic initiative; the former would not be sustained, the latter never fixed.

Initiated during the later Bush years, the Trans-Pacific Partnership (TPP) was seized upon by Obama and made a cornerstone of his foreign policy. Yet in a region where economic supremacy increasingly belonged to Beijing, the US asked ASEAN states to join a trade agreement that did not and would not include China. Since free trade's effectiveness and efficiency are premised on the greatest degree of inclusion—making bilateral and regional agreements mere place-holders for larger accords—this was self-defeating. Given US concern for China's trade practices, it was also illogical in excluding it from a formal process and binding deal. Making most plain the politics of the decision was that the main criteria for TPP inclusion was membership in APEC—which China had enjoyed since 1991. China was excluded because it was China. Unable to beat them, the Americans could not bear to join them. As Abhisit explained in 2015:

> The US came with the agenda of the TPP and that left out China.
> Thailand found it difficult to join the process. A proper invitation for us
> to join would only come when President Obama later visited Thailand,
> and that was rather late and made it technically difficult for us to join. So
> I see whatever shift was taking place here more as a reflection of what was
> happening in the US and her approach to China.[357]

Further, while preaching partnership abroad, Obama was encouraging protectionism at home. His ambassador to ASEAN conceded in early 2009 that, "In the region, there are some people who have put the blame on us."[358]

Against this backdrop, Korn chaired the first ASEAN finance ministers meeting in late 2009 and had a good relationship with the US secretary of the treasury, "to the extent it existed at all".[359] Abhisit and ten other Thai ministers met a US–ASEAN Business Council delegation, announcing a "one-start shop" to answer concerns and coordinate. Ambassador John and Abhisit each visited the US in 2009 for the council, and an ASEAN–US senior economic officials meeting was held in Bangkok. The "shop" came online late in the year. In a meeting with the US ambassador to ASEAN in early 2010, Thai business leaders urged "renewed dedication" to investing before the creation of a single ASEAN market in 2015.[360] Advocating a vision simply beyond their American visitors, they asked the US to "dedicate itself to economic development in the region in the same way that the U.S. once built military capacity".[361] Sarasin of the CP Group recommended packaging trade issues with investment, adding "that this was the strategy that China had adopted".[362]

Clinton's inaugural trip to Asia bypassed Thailand, but included a visit to ASEAN's Secretariat in Jakarta. She committed to attending the ARF and to signing its Treaty of Amity and Cooperation, making good on both in July

2009. The former made her "the star" of the ARF and different from her predecessor, who shunned the event.[363] But the latter came seventeen years after ASEAN's initial request and six years after China's signature. In the midst of the meetings, Clinton published a piece in the *Bangkok Post* stating, "The United States and the nations of Southeast Asia are old friends facing new challenges."[364] In another corrective move, she pledged to relocate the US ambassador to ASEAN to Jakarta; that is, to ASEAN. In Bangkok, John was open to a Thai request—expressly made to balance China's presence—that the US attend an ASEAN Inter-Parliamentary Assembly meeting in mid-2009. And two years after it was postponed, a 30th anniversary US–ASEAN summit was finally held in November. Obama thus became "the first American president to share a room with all 10 leaders of the Association of Southeast Asian Nations".[365] In the finance minister's recollection, "That was something that would have been noticed by China because there wasn't a similar formal event between the Chinese leader and ASEAN."[366]

A new Lower Mekong Initiative (LMI) was proposed by the US in 2009. Its first meeting was held to the side of the ARF, focusing on the environment, health, education, and infrastructure around the Mekong River. Critically, it included not only Thailand and its eastern neighbors, but Myanmar and China as observers. "China's presence was a catalyst", noted the US embassy, "forcing member countries to be more focused and productive in their discussions."[367] Thailand requested a Mekong–Mississippi rivers partnership, and the Chinese a bilateral dialogue. Noting "with evident satisfaction" that the US had gotten China's attention[368], Kasit went further in advocating a trilateral "Mekong Summit".[369] The second and third LMI gatherings took place in 2010, along with a host of sideline and spin-off meetings. The US pledged $7 million for environmental programs on the lower Mekong, while the MRC and Mississippi River Commission agreed to share experience and expertise. In two major missed opportunities, however, Thai suggestions that the LMI be linked to the TPP and/or "facilitate U.S. military assistance to the region" went unheeded.[370] In both cases, potential geopolitical gains at Chinese expense fell victim to a lack of vision and follow-through. Economically and militarily, China had been taking full advantage of the Mekong for years; the US was content with environmental cooperation.

Indeed, the ASEAN treaty provided the US with only its eighth (compared to China's forty-eight) mechanism with which to engage the regional body. In a 2009 meeting with John, the Foreign Ministry's director of Chinese affairs "was pleasant but direct in describing the growing role for China in Southeast Asia and a decline in the United States' stature and influence in the region".[371] And despite the 30th anniversary's pomp and publicity, Korn concluded that, "in the end it really came to nothing".[372] In December 2009, the ministry held an internal seminar on the future of China and the US in Southeast Asia. As duly relayed to Washington, Thai experts "contrasted the Chinese charm offensive to what they termed the 'lost' years of the Bush administration".[373] China continually "pursued a clear, patient, well-planned strategy of engagement in the region through repeated reciprocal visits at all levels", while renewed effort under Obama was just that: new.[374] Five years later, Foreign Minister Kasit looked back with justified dissatisfaction:

> The US could have done more with ASEAN. What would have been more generous than to support the democratization process in ASEAN? If you had a visionary assistant secretary of state for Asia-Pacific affairs, the presence and activity of the United States in Southeast Asia would have been much more beneficial to the relationship. It is not yet there.[375]

In early 2010, John himself would lament that "even government officials and academics sympathetic to the U.S. see the dynamic of China rising and the U.S. receding likely to continue, unless the U.S takes more vigorous action to follow-up with sustained efforts to engage on issues that matter to the Thai and the region".[376] At the same time, he only helped further assure such a future by once again concluding that, "the uptick in Chinese influence and activity does not automatically mean a corresponding decline in U.S. influence".[377]

South of China and the sea

An early 2009 ASEAN Defense Ministers Meeting (ADMM) decided that the ARF would conduct joint exercises on disaster response later in the year. The US pushed for the exercises but was not a member of the ADMM. Fearing that it "could otherwise likely be dominated by China", Abhisit asked the US to join.[378] Indeed, aware that the Chinese were requesting participation, the US embassy reported that they "hoped to be able to shape the goals and membership before the U.S. and others could become involved".[379] Nonetheless, the Americans were ambivalent. By early 2010, ASEAN (by then led by Vietnam) had still not decided whether membership would be offered to six nations also part of the EAS, or to the US and Russia as well. China was secure in either case; the US remained non-committal. After Clinton took in her second ARF meeting in mid-2010, the US ultimately joined the ADMM in October and took part in the second ARF joint exercises in 2011.

Compounding the Americans' willful hesitation was their strategic negligence, as the 2009 joint exercises focused on maritime security. Rather than immediately see the ADMM as an opportunity to influence the exercises and so reclaim ground lost to China, the US could not be moved to send its defense secretary to a meeting. Not even Beijing's proposal the same year of joint military exercises with ASEAN (excluding the US and over twenty other ARF members) was enough to spur US interest. Although ASEAN had declined China's offer, both parties doubtless saw the ARF as an alternative.

And those were only two of three, as 2009 also saw China propose large-scale *maritime* exercises with Thailand alone, a treaty ally of the United States. What it wanted from "Blue Strike" was "Cobra Gold-like amphibious" exercises in the Gulf of Thailand, utilizing the Vietnam War-era Sattahip naval base.[380] Thailand postponed them a year and, citing Cobra Gold, limited them to marine special forces. Despite little risk of such, one Thai official recommended that they focus on humanitarian response "to avoid causing alarm with the U.S."[381] The Thais also showed equivocation in declining China's offer to cover all costs, despite confiding to the US that budget constraints were another factor. Yet as Kasit told the embassy, "they would find it difficult to continue to say no".[382] Most on-point was a senior Thai general: "Thailand could not escape its geographic reality."[383] The exercises lasted a week and featured approximately 100 marines from each side at the platoon/company level, alongside a series of amphibious ships. That they coincided with Sino-Thai talks on submarines—already a difference-maker in the South China Sea—only emphasized Chinese planning and US passivity.

Consistent with at least fifteen years of policy, China's military outreach to the ARF, ASEAN, and Thailand was about securing and protecting its littoral geopolitical interests, primarily the South China Sea. Not only did several ASEAN states have competing territorial claims there against China, but in 2009 three filed cases under the UN Convention on the Law of the Sea. Known and calculated reserves of oil and natural gas were partly driving Chinese policy, second to what marked the sea's northernmost point: Taiwan. For Beijing, despite clear independent value in disaster relief coordination, the exercises' humanitarian purpose also served a far more strategic one. This was acceptable to the large and diffuse ARF—whose exercises were held in the Philippines and Indonesia—but not to the smaller ASEAN and its individual claimants. The Thais conceded to the US that, as chair, they felt compelled to honor an overarching "ASEAN solidarity" in declining China's suggestion of joint exercises with the regional body.[384]

China's secondary geopolitical interest in the exercises was the Straits of Malacca. In view of Malacca's sister straits Lombok, Makassar, and Sunda, all squarely within Indonesia, the ARF's 2011 exercises were particularly important. Likewise the drills with ASEAN, four of whose member states were connected to the Straits of Malacca and its sisters. Two of them, Indonesia and Malaysia, had claims in the South China Sea, but Thailand and Singapore did not. Two of them, Indonesia and Malaysia, had claims in the South China Sea, but Thailand and Singapore did not—the two nations with the most to gain and lose, respectively, if the Straits was ever made redundant by a canal though the Isthmus of Kra.

That the ASEAN exercises were deferred only made China's bilateral exercises with Thailand all the more critical. Blue Strike's sole geopolitical aim for China concerned the US-controlled Straits of Malacca. Held in 2010, it had been planned the year before when Thailand still held the ASEAN chair. Hence, while "the RTG was not suspicious" of China, it limited the exercises' scale so as not "to be seen as out in front of other ASEAN nations in expanding relations with China".[385] This too would change. Indeed, a Thai diplomat told the US as early as May 2009, that Beijing would request compensation—"possibly concerning the question of Taiwan"—for its assistance during the global financial crisis: "What can Thailand do?"[386] China's Foreign Ministry summed up bilateral relations in 2010 in characteristically understated fashion: "Strategic cooperation between the two countries made steady progress."[387]

Finally, not a maritime move as such, a railway network first mooted decades before was becoming a related element in China's geopolitical equation. In 2009, a memorandum of understanding was signed for a 51–49 percent Thailand–China joint venture for a high-speed rail connecting the two countries via Laos. Thailand established a new state enterprise to manage the project for up to fifty years. Beginning in China's Yunnan province, the rail would extend southward to Thailand's northeast, further south to Bangkok, then southeast along the Gulf of Thailand's seaboard. Another connector would go due south from Bangkok to the Thai-Malaysian border—intersecting the Highway 44 "land bridge" linking the gulf with the Andaman Sea. In Finance Minister Korn's words, it was a "clear signal to China that we wanted to do something big together" and was of "great importance strategically from China's perspective".[388] Spokesperson Panitan confirmed: "Security relationships are very complicated. This was why the link with China was critical. The Chinese wanted to come and invest more in our infrastructure, in many modern rails."[389] Why? Because if the unfinished highway were completed, China would have access to both bodies of water without using the Straits of Malacca. Oil, gas, and goods could land on either of Thailand's coasts, before going either east–west across the isthmus ("road-to-water"), or north–south through Thailand and Laos ("road-to-rail").

China proposed a three-year timetable, Thailand was more cautious, and with over 60,000 Chinese workers building the railway's Lao section, questions arose as to whose nationals would get the work. Beijing's request for a kilometer on either side of the rail in Thailand was refused, as a law put in place decades before to prevent Chinese immigrants from owning land was still in effect for all foreign nationals. Not unlike the road network, in early 2011 another railway connecting Thailand and China via Myanmar was agreed in principle, but deferred until after Thai elections. And in a related but less noticed move, in 2009 Thailand and China joined twenty-six other nations in agreeing to a Trans-Asian railway. Links between their Southeast Asian rails with those of the larger region would form a 114,000-kilometer web. Most significant for China was that Thailand was joining only three other nations—Myanmar, Bangladesh, and India—with coastlines along the elusive Andaman Sea (or its Bay of Bengal extension).

Watered down

At the ARF in 2010, Clinton offered to mediate territorial disputes in the South China Sea, and began raising the volume on freedom of navigation. Belated and necessary, the position was not welcomed in equal measure by regional states. Looking back, Abhisit said that the US

> appeared to come with the agenda that ASEAN should become more proactive on the issue of the South China Sea. And that didn't help. When we were chair, we thought that ASEAN's approach was appropriate, that any dispute had to be settled by the claimants peacefully according to international law. ASEAN's role was simply to make sure that it didn't blow up and that there was safe passage. But the US tried to push.[390]

Presaging its response to the US "pivot" the following year, Beijing characterized Clinton's offer as "an attack on China" and reminded its neighbors that it was a "big country".[391] Mentioned by neither global power was the Straits of Malacca. China had no interest in focusing US attention on a chess piece it was preparing to neutralize; the US still seemed not to realize the piece was in play. As early as December 2008, Kasit had told John that part of a $3 billion allocation was slated for "a project involving a land bridge to connect sea ports on the Gulf of Siam to the Andaman Sea (as an alternative to using the Straits of Malacca)".[392] John had informed Washington without comment. In early 2010, Kasit told PACOM that Thailand sought "to do more, as its geographic location between the Pacific and Indian Oceans was important".[393] During the same meeting, the CP's Sarasin drew attention to "the port of Ranong on the Andaman Sea. If this port were developed to handle high-volume traffic, Thailand could provide China with a safe and secure alternative to developing transportation links to the Indian Ocean through Burma. This would divert Chinese influence in Burma and provide Thailand with significant growth possibilities".[394] Sarasin was by then an ex-senior diplomat and executive vice-president of the largest foreign investor in China, whose economic links to Beijing rivaled those of Chavalit in the military. He was speaking to the US naval leader responsible for over half the world's surface and population. He outlined a geopolitical reality, offered a signal slice of Sino-Thai strategic thinking, and intimated promise and peril for the US. He proposed an alternative to both a canal across the Isthmus of Kra and the Straits of Malacca. Crucially, he proposed that the United States, having first mooted a canal in 1972 and in control of the Straits for a half-century, be its chief source of investment-*cum*-influence. He concluded by requesting "PACOM support of this endeavor".[395] PACOM declined.

Long central to US interests in Asia and beyond were Thailand's naval bases. US jets continued to use U-Tapao for over 1,000 flights each year, US ships Laem Chabang and Sattahip for over sixty visits and exercises. The former included intelligence flights, for which permission was granted "as a matter of routine, without having to answer questions to the purpose".[396] While John commented that, "Preserving such unfettered, unquestioned access requires engagement",[397] Kasit would recall that he "offered U-Tapao as an international center for disaster relief. Naval officers from Honolulu came to inspect it two or three times, but after we left office there was no continuity from the US side".[398] Little noticed at the time, in 2010 the Abhisit government also approved a US request for its National Aeronautics and Space Administration (NASA) to use U-Tapao for strictly civilian flights to study climate change.

New to the US were Thai aspirations of developing a coastguard and equipping it with submarines. For the former, Kasit suggested additional IMET funds, while PACOM proposed linking the navy with the US Coast Guard Academy. That Panitan mentioned Rohingya "boat people" in requesting assistance also spoke to submarines. While their combat utility in territorial waters averaging only 50 meters in depth was questionable, their use in countering non-traditional threats (trafficking, smuggling, environmental degradation, etc.) was clear. Most intriguing was Panitan's claim that "Thailand considered submarines critical due to the nation's trade routes, as well as its reliance on gas and oil platforms in the Gulf of Thailand."[399] Few trade routes were more valuable to every nation than the Straits of Malacca, while the gulf's gas and oil platforms were as important to Beijing as to Bangkok.

* * *

Prior to his only bilateral visit to the US, Kasit told John he would review the two Bush–Thaksin statements of 2003 and 2005, "to see what made sense to retain as part of the framework ... and what could be added to carry the relationship forward".[400] In 2015, he recounted his experience:

> I told Hillary, first, it has been a case-by-case relationship, issue by issue. There is no partnership, no joint consultation and joint strategy on what we are going to do as treaty allies. And second it has been reactive, with the Thai side reacting to series of requests from the United States: "Would you kindly send a medical team to Serbia?" "Can you allow us to use U-Tapao airbase for refueling on the way to Afghanistan and Iraq to bomb the hell out of them?" "Can you catch this terrorist passing through Thailand?" "Can you open the center for interrogation?" "Can you vote or not vote on the Israel-Palestine question?" I told Hillary that whatever you want to do with us, let's sit down to understand each other's position. Some appreciation of each side's limitations would be highly appreciated.[401]

Kasit returned to Bangkok to work with John on a third bilateral Strategic Dialogue, suggesting the Seventh Fleet and "respective views of China and its role in the region/world" as agenda items.[402] When Kurt Campbell, the senior US diplomat with whom Kasit shared a rocky relationship, accompanied Clinton to Thailand several months later, he asked the embassy to develop "a strategic map forward for a big picture".[403] John and his political counselor drafted a five-page document organized by thematic area. However, despite following up several times, the response from Campbell was "Silence. Silence."[404] In the meantime, Kasit and John added human rights, military procurement, disaster relief, civilian–military cooperation, peacekeeping, capacity-building in Indochina, educational exchanges, "and eventually Burma" to the Strategic Dialogue's agenda.[405] China remained on the list, but as in the previous dialogues it was facing increasing competition for attention. Kasit stated that Thailand would be content with a "junior" partner role "if the U.S. were to explain its overall approach to the Asia-Pacific region for the future".[406]

At the start of 2010, 69 percent of Thais thought that a US military presence in Asia was important for regional stability. A visiting deputy assistant secretary of defense suggested a military dialogue in addition to the wider strategic talks. Matched by Thai interest in ministerial participation, it would also include China's regional role and rise, as well as US access to Thai training facilities, prepositioning of humanitarian relief supplies, regional security concerns, and combating transnational crime. With both forums in mind, the new PACOM commander queried "his interlocutors for their view of Thailand's strategy over the next five to ten years".[407] The hold-up remained Campbell. His deputy privately complained that "he couldn't get ten minutes on Campbell's schedule to talk about Thailand".[408] In the words of a US diplomat involved, he "wasn't sitting down with his policy DAS for Southeast Asia to talk about a strategic framework toward a treaty ally that was going through troubled times".[409] Like most others in Washington, he lacked "an appreciation for everything that had been part of this rich fabric, which could have been grounds for an occasionally painful, occasionally passionate path together, as opposed to this gradual drift apart".[410]

The Strategic Dialogue finally took place in July 2010, chaired by Kasit and the US undersecretary for political affairs. His domestic politics notwithstanding, the foreign minister seemed genuinely concerned with China, while the undersecretary was more senior than the previous two dialogues' representatives. Yet, despite nearly five years since the suggestion was agreed by both sides, "a full day devoted to discussion of Thailand's special position with regard to China" was not forthcoming. The senior defense talks followed, likewise with China as just another item on a long list.

YINGLUCK/THE NEW NORMAL (2011–2014)

History had a habit of repeating itself in Thailand. By mid-2011, it had experienced eighteen attempted coups and was on its nineteenth constitution since 1932. It had seen twelve premier changes since 1991. And in July 2011, it saw Yingluck Shinawatra sworn in as prime minister, sister and stand-in for a Thaksin first elected a decade previously and who had repeatedly taken back the spotlight. She received 48 percent of the vote (via Thaksin's party) in another clear mandate, and would likewise leave office at the point of a gun. But repetition is not the same as *déjà vu*. Thanks to her brother's sea change in foreign policy and China's pivot, Yingluck's predecessors had continued moving Thailand further inside Beijing's sphere of geopolitical influence. The Americans had bungled Southeast Asia as badly as they had a Middle East they actually cared about. Thailand under Yingluck was different; no longer changing, it was *changed*. And unlike the coup that had ended Thaksin's tenure, the one of 2014 did not counter that fact but confirmed it.

It would not matter that the US sent to Bangkok a rising star, one of only five "career ambassadors" in the Foreign Service and the first to the kingdom in thirty years. No matter that the secretary of state would announce the "pivot" to Asia. And no matter that President Obama would make Thailand his first foreign visit just eleven days after being reelected. Just as Ambassador Boyce had described $1.7 billion in aid nine months after the 1997 crisis, it was all "Too late, too late. We did that. And we can't undo it."[411] Yingluck was less a throw-back to her brother's pro-China policies than a template for Thailand in a new Chinese century. By the time Xi Jinping took over in Beijing in March 2013, two-thirds into Yingluck's term, Thailand was already primed for his latter-day irredentism of ideology and influence. And if 2006 had seen the last American coup, 2014 was in the spirit and style of the Chinese. Even more authoritarian than Abhisit, Yingluck would herself be replaced by another junta, one whose pedigree and perspective had long been more consistent with the China Model than US democracy.

First class

Not surprisingly, Yingluck's "China" rolodex was substantially deeper and more developed than its American analogue, including Politburo members initially cultivated by Thaksin. Her ministers "claimed Chinese ancestry whether true or not" and saw their Chinese names used by imported newspapers.[412] Her foreign minister would recall that "we understood the Chinese, the way they think of us as friends or cousins", while more than 500 of his diplomats were former students of Thailand's leading China scholar.[413] Yingluck's deputy party leader traveled to China "almost every month", as often to border areas as to major cities, including the Guangxi autonomous region whose governor succeeded in luring Yingluck there as well.[414] The premier would travel to the country so often that another minister could only pledge to check the records for an actual figure. As for Yingluck's patron and puppet-master, "Thaksin was very active. In Beijing he said, 'Let's collaborate.' He didn't sing the song of democracy in Beijing, far from it. It was about how to do business. So there were two different songs he sang—very good. It was someone like that who was capable of leading a country like Thailand."[415]

Yingluck met Premier Wen Jiabao at a meeting of East Asian leaders in November 2011, where he told her that, "China cherishes its traditional friendship with Thailand."[416] Alongside a raft of areas in which he advocated further cooperation, he also pledged assistance in the wake of the worst floods in Thai history (unrelated to China's dams).[417] The following month, Yingluck welcomed in Thailand Vice-Premier Xi Jinping, who said that "Thailand and China are as intimate as relatives."[418] He mooted several areas in which their Strategic Partnership, originally agreed in 2005 and covering cooperation in fifteen areas through 2011, could be extended and enhanced. During a trip to Beijing the following April, she signed its expansion through 2016.

In November 2012, Yingluck hosted Premier Wen at the opening of a new Chinese Culture Center in Bangkok. He told attendees, "As friendly neighbors from ancient times, China and Thailand had maintained close contact and nurtured a firm friendship, giving body to the notion that 'China and Thailand are one family.'"[419] In their formal meeting, Yingluck congratulated Wen on the Communist Party's eighteenth national congress, "voicing belief China would continue to move forward steadily and play a more active role in the world … Thailand unswervingly pursued friendly policies with China and would like to enhance contact between the two countries at all levels".[420] Wen said that Beijing was "ready to help improve Chinese language teaching in Thailand and promote cooperation in tourism and youth exchanges between the two nations".[421] They concluded by signing documents formalizing future cooperation.

While Wen's visit was notable for its timing, a mere two days after President Obama left the kingdom, it was a mere prelude to three others in 2013. First, in

August the first bilateral Strategic Dialogue took place in Bangkok. Surprising only in recalling so many other similar initiatives, it was comprehensive in scope and the first substantial opportunity to discuss progress on the expanded partnership. Second, Xi met Yingluck again at an APEC meeting in October, this time as China's new president. Having reached the top of the leadership ladder since their last meeting, he said that "China–Thailand relations enjoy a solid foundation of political, economic and public opinion support."[422] Yingluck requested support for Thailand's bid to become a non-permanent member of the UN Security Council for the first time in twenty-six years.

Finally, a pinnacle was reached a week later when Wen's successor, Premier Li Keqiang, became the first foreign national to address Thailand's Parliament in its eighty-one-year history. None of the six US presidents who had visited Thailand—several more than once—had received such an honor, not even after King Bhumibol had addressed Congress in 1960. Times and tributes had changed. Attendees included the chairs of the CP Group and Bangkok Bank and regional ambassadors; the American ambassador was not present. Li received a standing ovation upon entering, before stating that their peoples were "members of the same family" and that "The China and Thailand friendship will certainly blossom and be deep-rooted."[423] He also said that China would consider reciprocating Yingluck's move to grant visa/fee exemptions for Chinese visitors (a treaty obligation the US had still not fulfilled since 1966). Thailand would soon be the nation with the most consulates in China. Claiming that "Thailand and China are meant to offer opportunities for each other", Yingluck joined Li in signing six agreements on energy and natural resources, science, and culture.[424] Echoing his boss a week earlier, Li stated that "China under my administration is glad to work with Thailand under the Yingluck government in pushing forward the Comprehensive Strategic Partnership cooperation framework."[425] He received another standing ovation upon exiting.

Tough times, worse timing

Boyce's large ambassadorial footprints, John's colorful tenure, and the historically deadly violence had combined to make 2008–2010 very transitional years in the minds of many Thais. Hopeful but not optimistic on Obama's early years, their perception of the United States—seen first and foremost in its embassy—was of a nation whose era in Southeast Asia had passed. That Clinton had declared the US as "back" conceded that it had been away.

Certainly in Thailand itself, the US was seen as having fallen far behind China, its diplomatic presence serving simply as that demotion's local and public face. As noted by one of Yingluck's advisors, "Washington had a lot of things on its mind, Thailand had not been on its radar screen for a long, long while. But the Chinese were here."[426] In the words of ex-diplomat Sarasin,

> Don't put the blame or praise on the ambassador, it was really about Washington. I used to go all the time and have sessions, at least at my level, with the deputy assistant secretary of Asia-Pacific. I would be invited by Congressional aides, various Senators, even the CIA and the Pentagon. Not anymore. Why do they have the Bureau of East Asian Affairs? It's not a small bureau.[427]

A former Thai ambassador to both the US and China was even more reflective:

> My relationship with the US embassy and the Americans went back a long time. My grandfather was in Washington, and my grandparents were very close friends of the first proper ambassador, Edwin F. Stanton. Both of my parents were educated in the States. I was the fifth member of my family to be in Washington, so I grew up in an American atmosphere, played in the garden of the ambassador's residence when I was a child. But relations have become more and more distant. I think it is partly because of the American angst after the terrorist attacks of September 2001, when they built an embassy that is a fortress. The members of the embassy no longer come out to meet people, they no longer know Thais. They just sit in their fortress. Their rotations are very fast, they don't stay here very long. They have lost touch and lost their touch with the Thai scene. Before, if I went to see my boss, the CIA station chief would always be there chatting with him as well. That is gone. I don't think the CIA station chief would be so warmly welcomed anymore, because the Thai leadership is afraid of speaking frankly to the Americans in case there are more leaks. So you would be right to say that the Chinese influence in Thailand is greater than that of the Americans these days, because the embassy is out of it.[428]

Two officials similarly noted that when they joined the Foreign Ministry two decades ago, many former and active US diplomats were married to Thais or otherwise connected to the country. "Thailand doesn't have those friends anymore", they concluded. "The US needs to forge a new generation of people who spend formative years in Thailand, who know the country, and then work. Because in just a couple of years they have no way of understanding Thailand. Why would they lose it? They had this niche before China."[429] Finally, Abhisit's spokesperson, whose term straddled those of both Ambassador John and his successor, attributed "ground losses" in the kingdom to a "lack of sophistication on the part of US diplomacy".[430]

Kristie Kenney was supposed to change all that. Described by one State Department official as a "ruthless operator", she "wanted the job, lobbied hard internally, and got it because she was seen within the system by the decision-makers as being one of the rising, shining stars".[431] Not only of career ambassador rank, Kenney had broken glass ceilings within the Foreign Service, becoming the first woman to hold the role of executive secretary (effectively chief of staff for the secretary of state). Also the first female US ambassador to Ecuador and the Philippines, she boasted relevant experience alongside a top-notch network. Given that her husband was an assistant secretary of state (and fellow career ambassador) posted in Washington, "her whole life revolved around work, office and home, networking and messaging".[432] Although not fluent in Thai, she would become more proficient than her predecessor. In short, Kenney was qualified to lead a major US embassy in ways that most were not, and "She wanted Thailand. Why? It was a big important country, an allied relationship the way the Philippines had been, and one that was very deep and broad on all sorts of operational levels."[433]

She would prove, however, the right ambassador at the wrong time. To her credit, evident to even the casual observer and confirmed by internal sources, she "wanted to be ambassador to all Thais and not just those within five miles of the embassy".[434] Thai human rights analyst Sunai Pasuk explained:

Skip Boyce was about direct personal diplomacy, and that was consistent with his time and with how Thai–US relations had evolved. But it was not sufficient anymore to have closed-door talks with the elites from both sides—Skip had access to all sides and he talked to everyone. But the weakness of that diplomacy was that it was out of touch with feelings on the ground. With Kristie Kenney you saw attempts to reach out further from the usual contacts, to real people on the ground. It was the first time in the history of the relationship that "people diplomacy" emerged.[435]

Kenney thus traveled widely in Thailand, and was "certainly the first person to try to make use of social media as a foreign policy tool".[436] Finance Minister Korn recalled that she "was at pains to visit Red Shirt villages", complaining that "nobody else had villages like the Red Shirt villages".[437] Yet it was hardly Kenney's fault that Thaksin and the UDD were more innovative than the Democrats and PAD; nor did she limit her travels to Red areas. Kenney's liberal use of Facebook and Twitter ("Twiplomacy") was consistent with a workshop held in Bangkok in 2009, in which State Department officials "challenged attendees to reach all the people we can through all the methods we can, but warned that 'new media' is a tool, and not a strategy".[438] Whether in attendance or not, Kenney's use of such tools in the Philippines was setting standards that others would be encouraged to emulate.

The problem was that, in the midst of turmoil experienced once in a generation—once a century when considering monarchical dynamics—Thailand was not the Philippines. Korn went on to claim that Kenney's visits "meant that the Red Shirts were able to portray the US as supporting and accepting their movement".[439] While the ambassador was not to blame for this either, the "challenge came when things got out of her control, when the internal Thai dynamic went sideways".[440] Yet rather than adapt and adjust, she just doubled down, increasing the visibility of her rural visits, posting even more "charismatic" photographs on Facebook, and "tweeting" voluminously—including in direct reply to other users. Instead of taking stock and exercising discretion, she attempted to be even more accessible and "democratic", only to see it backfire. No longer an appropriately engaged representative of the United States, Kenney was increasingly seen as a participant in a Thai crisis. It was here that the former finance minister was on-point:

I said to Kenney that surely she must be aware that the US was being used as a poster boy, as it were, for the Red Shirts. And did the US wonder why that was the case? And how dangerous that was? Forget right and wrong, but just how dangerous it was that they were playing to that and allowing the Red Shirts to basically take ownership of the relationship. It was very obvious to anybody who was looking. The US Independence Day

273

celebration was fully attended by Thaksin's party, taking photographs and posting them on Facebook, but not by representatives of anybody else. And so the stored up sentiment and feeling of those in the anti-Thaksin camp sort of exploded at the first perceived misstep of the US, and Ambassador Kenney's lifestyle and approach played into that narrative.[441]

That her term was extended by a year only extended the damage.

The irony was that, according to embassy officials, Kenney came in with "strong views" largely in favor of the conservative side—"until the very end, when she gave up on the Yellows".[442] She was also "scrupulous" about wanting to be seen as neutral; a coffee-only meeting with a Yellow leader had to be "consciously balanced" with a coffee-only meeting with a Red leader of the same level.[443] Moreover, while one advisor noted that Kenney "could get through to Yingluck" better than could her predecessor, the foreign minister said that she "did not take a side. Whatever was in her mind, she didn't show it".[444] Thaksin himself agreed: "Ambassador Kenney balanced the information from both sides and understood better. She understood when my sister was being bullied politically. She was also a lady, so she may have understood her better because they had a chance to talk. I think the US started to understand better with more balance during the Obama administration."[445]

A backdrop to all of this was a Washington that provided Kenney with even less support than it had John or Boyce. One US diplomat described the State Department as having had a "Fuck it approach" to Thailand, watching it fall to "last place" among the five US treaty allies in Asia.[446] Another mused that it was placed at the top of a veritable list of "Asia lite".[447] Kurt Campbell remained in place as assistant secretary for the region through early 2013. "He didn't understand Thailand and didn't want to understand it", according to yet another official, "as there were enough other issues and shiny objects for him to pursue."[448] He would be replaced by Obama's national security director for Asian affairs—the main liaison with Clinton in formulating the "pivot" in 2011. His dynamism, however, was evident in the policy's failure to launch and in its two passing references to Thailand. Indeed, perhaps the most surprising aspect of Kenney's solo act was that it came amid bold claims by her bosses that "America" was onboard. If she was guilty of confusing her social media "tool" for a "strategy", then the mistake only exposed how truly little by way of strategy Kenney was receiving.

* * *

Kenney called Yingluck upon her becoming premier, and paid a call on outgoing Abhisit, pledging to work with him as well. As Chinese media reported, "Asked if the United States is confident that there will be no more coups d'etat in Thailand, Kenney expressed her appreciation that the election went peacefully."[449] According to a member of Yingluck's government, "Washington was initially reluctant" with her, while she in turn felt that the US had not acted strongly enough against the coup five years before.[450] Her strong relationship with Kenney and a good rapport with Secretary Clinton, however, alongside Thaksin's network in Washington, helped build trust.

In November 2011, Clinton visited Thailand on a regional trip, stating that the US "was committed to the people of Thailand and to the government. We are proud and grateful for this alliance. It has delivered results, and now we have to ensure that it continues to deliver results for both of our people for decades to come".[451] Decades was per se dismissible. A $10 million donation for flood recovery and a visit to an evacuation facility were more commensurate with the relationship. The US also provided water pumps, boats, generators, and survival kits, worked on infrastructure and public health, and facilitated contributions from Coca-Cola and Chevron. "And we are identifying sites that hold historical significance to the Thai people to help protect and restore monuments of Thailand's proud and ancient culture."[452] Yingluck met Obama days later at an East Asian leaders meeting in Indonesia, and discussed "how we could deepen and broaden the partnership between our countries".[453] She also attended the UN General Assembly in September 2012, missing it the years before and after on account of floods and political rallies. However, as one observer complained, "By agreeing to meet Thai leaders for only five minutes on the sidelines of the UN … Obama made it clear the place Thailand occupies on the White House's priority list".[454]

Two months later and less than two weeks after his reelection, Obama visited Thailand. Yingluck called it "the perfect occasion to launch a celebration of the 180th anniversary of Thai–U.S. diplomatic relations next year. I thank both President Obama and Secretary Clinton for actively promoting Thai–U.S. relations … we had productive and wide-ranging discussions, mostly of friendly partnership".[455] They discussed climate change, disaster relief, terrorism, and human trafficking. Yingluck also announced that Thailand would at last join the Proliferation Security Initiative after eight years of negotiation. "Finally, we recognized the importance of continued high-level exchanges and consultations between our two countries. As part of our growing partnership, the President and I agree to stay in close touch and to have our ministries and agencies do the same on the rich agenda we discussed today."[456] Obama replied that "Thailand is America's oldest friend in Asia … I'm pleased that we've agreed to a series of efforts that revitalize our alliance to meet the challenges and opportunities of our time".[457] He noted the 50th anniversary of the Peace Corps in Thailand, and promoted initiatives in public health, food security, and wildlife protection. His conclusion, inspired if unfounded, was that "because of the progress that we've made today … we've put the U.S.–Thai alliance on an even firmer footing for many years to come".[458]

In 2012, the US issued a travel advisory on "foreign terrorists" in Bangkok, after which a joint search yielded a Hezbollah member and a room packed with bomb-making ingredients. Given Thailand's economic dependency on tourism, however, the foreign minister issued a strong rebuke, "As for what the US has done, I have already expressed my disappointment through the media and this was a diplomatic way of telling the US off for not consulting with Thailand first."[459] The defense minister was no less piqued, calling in the defense attaché and urging "the US to be more careful when a situation like this happens in the future".[460] While neither said as much, the fact that the warning was issued via Twitter could not have helped. On the other side of the ocean, Thaksin was reportedly barred from visiting Washington as a condition for receiving a new US visa in mid-2012. The ex-premier himself was ambiguous: "I had no problem entering the US, but there was no official relations, I had very little relations with officers on the political level."[461] Late in 2013 eyebrows were also raised when disclosures by US whistleblower Edward Snowden revealed the likelihood of espionage by the US embassy. Whether this focused on Thai authorities or citizens was unclear, but recalled both WikiLeaks and the wire-tapping claims of 2010. Thailand's NSC declared that it would never cooperate on any illegal activity. The same month, protests that would eventually trigger the coup prevented Yingluck from making a bilateral visit to the US.

* * *

Twice in the same week in November 2012, Thailand's King Bhumibol granted an audience to the world's two most powerful leaders, Obama and Wen. Due to the king's age and health, the meetings were more ceremony than substance, but there was no question as to which was more relevant to the kingdom's foreign policy. Obama praised "a leader of wisdom and dignity who embodies the identity and unity of this nation", but made no reference to the relationship, much less to an "alliance" for which the king had been the most central and constant protagonist.[462] The past was past. In the words of a Yingluck advisor,

> The Americans were worried when I talked to them, but I don't think they had a strategy like the Chinese. Because having a strategy for Thailand means also having to deal with the monarchy. Not only the political superstructure but because the Crown Property controls a lot of business. So if they really cared they would talk to the palace.[463]

Wen represented a nation and people who "felt the allure of the Thai princess and admired her for doing a lot of things that they do".[464] A Thai general said that China welcomed Princess Sirindhorn "with open arms" because she had "invested" herself in the country.[465] A Chinese leader admitted that she had been to more places there than he had. Bonds with Princess Chulabhorn were also continuing to grow, as were relations with the crown prince, whom Wen and Xi had met the year before.

Sarasin lamented: "Before Thaksin, all the news Chinese people would get about Thailand was about the king and the monarchy. But unfortunately the limelight is now on Thaksin, particularly in the political field. You can see how much influence he has had for years, and for part of that you have to credit Thaksin's personal efforts."[466] Displeasure notwithstanding, this only benefited Sino-Thai relations. Not only was Thaksin staunchly pro-China, but he maintained an electoral hold over Thailand, such that both nations were fully covered. Further, army leadership under Yingluck was a perfect amalgam for China. Representing the Queen's Guard faction of Network Monarchy—having regained its ascendency over the King's Guard—the army shared Thaksin's authoritarianism. By 2011, its points of reference were equally "palace and Peking", both of which would serve when taking over the kingdom again in 2014.

Force multipliers

The strategically significant "Blue Strike" maritime exercises were held again in 2012 and 2013 among both nations' navies and marines. A combined 320 special forces also conducted "Strike 2013" after two years off, focusing on counterterrorism, reconnaissance, parachuting, and sniper training over two weeks in Thailand. Yingluck's defense minister negotiated joint air force exercises with China that would occur under the junta that followed. After the navy and army—whose chief of staff spoke fluent Mandarin—this added a third area of bilateral Sino-Thai exercises. And in another huge geostrategic advance for China, it was promoted to "observer plus" status for Cobra Gold 2014.

Back in his position as a security advisor, Panitan pointed to "the relationship after ten years of close cooperation between the two defense ministries. The Chinese were well-connected to the top generals, to the top officers, fully engaged in many ways".[467] General Chavalit was never far from the scene, although as the person most responsible for Panitan's conclusion, he had mainly become redundant. While high-quality equipment was available, inexpensive kit still characterized the bulk of procurement from Beijing, with commissions of 20 percent or more providing the main incentive. The political benefits both at home and abroad were also considerable; Yingluck made herself defense minister toward the end of her term and loosened the purse strings in an attempt to forestall a coup. It was during her visit with high-level military officials in Beijing in April 2012 that the bilateral Strategic Partnership was officially extended and expanded. In a related move, the two nations continued reviewing second-hand submarine options, as Thailand would complete a dock and training facility at Sattahip naval base the same month as Cobra Gold 2014.

* * *

In his November 2012 remarks in Bangkok, President Obama said that the two nations have "been treaty allies, committed to our common defense, for nearly 60 years. Our men and women in uniform have stood together and they've bled together".[468] A year after deploying the *USS Lassen* and 2,500 troops to assist with Thailand's floods, Obama continued that "Our military has already trained and exercised together, and we're already close partners in preventing terrorism and combatting narco-traffic."[469] Cobra Gold remained the biggest and, according to military and civilian sources alike, the best regional exercises for technical training. China's new "observer plus" status in 2014 allowed its participation in an engineering project.

In a reminder that mil-to-mil cooperation remained the strongest element of the overall relationship, in 2012 and 2013 a new bilateral army exercise took place in Thailand. "Hunaman Guardian" saw several hundred soldiers from each side engage in humanitarian assistance, disaster relief, and rescue drills over ten days. According to a US commander in 2013, "They will also train on improving aviation maintenance procedures, small unit mounted and dismounted infantry tactics, counter-improvised explosive devices techniques, as well as expand on lifesaving medical skills."[470] Interestingly, the exercises began that year with a wreath-laying ceremony at a statue of Field Marshall Sarit, both militaries' patron saint of royal intercession. The commander continued: "I think it's important to keep the Hanuman Guardian exercise going. It's not as large as the Cobra Gold exercise, but it also creates a more intimate experience between us and the Thai Army."[471] An embassy official concluded that, "at least to the extent they are a professional military and not a uniformed bureaucracy", the Thais still valued US military training.[472]

Against this gain was regression in relationships away from the training grounds. JUSMAG's primary purpose for years had been to facilitate military education and exchanges, requiring at least working relationships if not a strong professional rapport with Thai counterparts. Yet a retired US colonel with extensive history, knowledge, and networks in Thailand was told that Ambassador Kenney initially discouraged contact. "Please tell me I am not hearing this", replied the colonel. "I've had hearing trouble since Afghanistan."[473] In mid-2012, the new JUSMAG chief complained to him that his staff was unable to arrange introductory meetings with senior Thai officers, admitting they had neither liaisons nor even telephone numbers. A week later, he reported that Yingluck's government was refusing to assist. The colonel finally offered three mobile phone numbers and an office line for a four-star Thai general, which led to appointments with the three armed services, the armed forces headquarters, and the Ministry of Defense. The general was set to become the ministry's permanent secretary. In early 2014, PACOM requested that the colonel send along biographies for senior Thai officers of the kind he had written for years on active duty. "They hadn't seen one since I left for Afghanistan in 2007", he said. "What are we doing? What are we doing?"[474]

One-two punch

With Thaksin back at the helm via Yingluck, no longer was Thailand's government incompetent (Surayud) or coy (Abhisit) in its furtherance of an economic agenda he had set a decade earlier. It was not a coincidence that Yingluck's foreign minister did not know the first thing about international relations, but was from an IBM background and owned his own company. An advisor noted that Yingluck was committed to China from the start: rice, rubber, and railways. The American Chamber of Commerce in Thailand boasted approximately 800 members, Japan's roughly 1,500, Taiwan's a remarkable 5,000. The Chinese would not disclose their membership, but it was believed to exceed that of their competitors. Meanwhile, Thaksin was spending increasing amounts of time at his Beijing home. Sarasin explained:

> He didn't just play golf. No, he got Yan Bin, who owns the golf course, to invite leaders or people associated with the leaders to play golf. And on the golf course he did business. He had his own lobbyist in Yan Bin, serving him full-time and very effective. And that is why, even if you go to China today—I just came back from Shanghai last night—people ask if Thaksin is Chinese.[475]

During Xi's December 2011 visit, the Bank of Thailand and the People's Bank of China agreed to a three-year currency swap worth 70 billion renminbi. It permitted exporters from both countries to settle deals in their own currencies—thus decreasing the influence of the US dollar. The visits of China's premiers Wen and Li in 2012 and 2013 both yielded economic agreements, while the Strategic Dialogue in between facilitated progress and projections. During the former, "China was willing to make concerted efforts with Thailand to actively implement the five-year program for economic and trade cooperation … advance cooperation in infrastructure construction in areas such as transportation and water conservancy".[476] The latter visit, a year into the trade program, featured similar priorities as well as private sector deals in rice, engineering, and rubber. Yingluck's foreign minister reflected that "China thought it could use Thailand for whatever it could get;"[477] Li concluded that "Thailand's greater prosperity is more than welcomed by China."[478]

The currency swap was valuable because China had passed the US as Thailand's largest export market in 2009 and was not slowing down; bilateral trade grew 21 percent in 2011. Two years later, with trade up another 13 percent over 2012, Thailand and China set a trade goal of $100 billion by 2015—twice that previously set for 2010. China reportedly agreed in 2013 to import a million tons of rice, in what would prove a source of alleged corruption and controversy for Yingluck. Claiming to have made numerous government-to-government (G-to-G) sales to China, Yingluck was unable to produce a bona fide contract. At the same time, however, she rightly claimed that G-to-G included Chinese provincial and local governments, as well as, more debatably, state-supported Chinese companies. Many of the latter had in fact been established for the purpose in China by Sino-Thai politicians and entrepreneurs, and so were "Chinese" only in a technical sense. Ultimately, "The Chinese were the ones who informed us here that they had no deal with Yingluck at all", recalled Senator Kraisak, "so there you are."[479] A public if politic statement to that effect by China was far more detrimental to the prime minister.

In 2014, having surpassed the US in 2007 for second place, China moved ahead of Japan to become Thailand's leading trading partner.

Investment-wise, even after Thaksin's early efforts, China had still accounted for only 1 percent of Thailand's net foreign investment in 2006. Perhaps nothing illustrated more powerfully China's economic reach in Thailand than that by early 2014 it had become Thailand's *second largest* source of FDI. From also-ran to runner-up in eight years, it had invested in the "gateway" of its near abroad more deftly than any of its competitors.

* * *

An advisor to Yingluck recalled that "The Chinese were willing to put their money and their firm commitment in, to push, which didn't leave Thailand much of a choice, although we wanted a choice."[480] It was not to be found in the US. During Obama's 2012 visit, Yingluck stated, "On the economic front, to generate growth and create jobs for both Thai and Americans, the President and I agree to redouble our effort to promote trade and investment."[481] Obama explained that a "trade and investment council that we've set up will further explore ways in which we can synchronize our economies so that entrepreneurs and business-people who want to trade and want to produce products, want to take advantage of opportunities in both countries, will have an easier time doing so".[482] Yet the bilateral FTA remained stuck in a 2006 time-capsule; a Thai diplomat recalled that "The US was not interested anymore, and that was too bad."[483] Each year of Yingluck's term—which made it seven consecutive years—Thailand remained on the US priority watchlist for IPR violators, with compulsory licensing still understood as the key reason. In 2011, bilateral trade grew just 9 percent, keeping the US well behind China and Japan on the kingdom's list of trading partners.

On US investment, Yingluck's advisor noted that existing investors were excellent and found it easy to do business, but that new FDI "didn't come".[484] US companies continued to receive national treatment pursuant to the Treaty of Amity and Economic Relations, but a US diplomat agreed that new investors were deterred by the "CNN effect" of the constant turmoil. As far back as 2005, Thaksin advisor Pansak Vinyaratn had admired the US Kimberly-Clark company in the deep south; a decade on he talked colorfully of the north and northeast:

> Seagate, the American hard disk maker, has been fucking around in the Red Shirt areas for the past 30 years using Red Shirt laborers. Even now they are still producing that shit there. Meaning, certain American corporations have fantastic, deep knowledge of the psyche of the Red Shirts. And they keep producing this crap, they pack it up, put it into the belly of Thai International cargo and send it to Sichuan to be assembled there as computers.[485]

Indeed, the embassy agreed that Thailand's role in the integrated chain of US technology was discounted until the floods of 2011. Yet throughout Yingluck's term, new FDI in the south was a victim of the internal armed conflict, while in the north and northeast Seagate remained an exception.

Ten more years

During his 2012 visit to Thailand, Premier Wen remarked, "Against the backdrop of complicated and profound changes in international and regional situations, China stood ready to work with Thailand."[486] A long-time member of the Thai Foreign Ministry confirmed his sincerity: "They felt they had to engage Southeast Asia and East Asia in particular, so they put focus on regional interests, especially the economy. Whereas when the US looked at the world, where was the region? Thailand was off the radar. But for China we were somewhere, we were somewhere on the radar screen."[487]

Recalling the deadly incidents of 2008 and 2009, in October 2011 two Chinese barges on a Thai section of the Mekong River were attacked, resulting in the deaths of thirteen crew. All but one was found on shore or afloat; most had been blind-folded, gagged, and shot. Alongside the barges' lawful cargo of oil and produce were found over 900,000 methamphetamine pills worth $1.5 million.

The Chinese immediately suspended all traffic, and sent a Foreign Ministry delegation from Beijing to northern Thailand. Within a week, a joint investigation concluded that nine Thai soldiers had acted "on an individual basis" in a drug-smuggling operation. The Thai army chief called the case "highly complicated"; Beijing summarily announced joint patrols of the Mekong.[488] The Thais would maintain sole patrol of the river within their territory, but sent staff to a new headquarters in Yunnan province and agreed to share intelligence. When the Thai soldiers denied the charges, the hunt was on for a Myanmar drug lord widely believed to have been behind the previous attacks as well. He was captured in late 2012 and executed by China. Attributed to a rogue outlaw from neither country, the crime caused only initial and minimal tension between China and Thailand. The joint patrols, however, were another Chinese inroad into Southeast Asia.

For two years beginning in mid-2012, Thailand became the formal coordinator for China's relations with ASEAN. Although conferred on a rotating basis, the role was especially welcomed by Beijing in view of Thailand's decade-long "gateway" policy and practices. A China specialist in Yingluck's Foreign Ministry agreed that "Thailand is trusted by China like no other ASEAN nation."[489] The same month saw ASEAN foreign ministers fail for the first time to produce a communiqué at their annual meeting, after China flexed its muscles over language on the South China Sea. The Thais thus saw an opportunity to avoid having to take a side in the sea's territorial disputes by offering to mediate as part of their coordination role. Cleverly, they would retain the mediation role even after their two-year term as coordinator expired. In 2015, a Foreign Ministry official confided and confirmed that "Thailand prides itself in this role and we think we've done well so far, partly because we are not involved in the conflict. We also see an opportunity in it. Thailand has a special relationship with China."[490] As China was a major part of the conflict, Thailand's neutrality effectively spelled support.

At the end of the year, President Xi officially launched negotiations for a Regional Comprehensive Economic Partnership (RCEP) to include ASEAN and five other nations (Australia, India, Japan, New Zealand, and South Korea). It would comprise the world's largest free trade area, and cover goods, services, investment, economic cooperation, intellectual property, competition, and dispute settlement. The RCEP excluded the US and was likely designed to compete with its Trans-Pacific Partnership; unlike the TPP, it protected sensitive industries from enhanced competition and made fewer demands for policy changes. A fourth round of negotiation took place in April 2014; Xi hoped it might come into effect by 2015.

In mid-2013, Bangkok hosted a "successful convening of a High-Level Forum on the 10th Anniversary of the China–ASEAN Strategic Partnership".[491] Prime Minister Li outlined two points for agreement and seven areas for cooperation over the next ten years—"2+7" through 2022. The points were strategic trust/"good-neighborly friendship", and economic development/"win–win outcomes".[492] In Li's words, the seven areas were "business, connectivity, finance, maritime cooperation, security, people-to-people relations, and the scientific and environmental field".[493] Specifically, he advocated improvement of the China–ASEAN free trade agreement.

* * *

The recollection of virtual Prime Minister Thaksin was measured: "Obama went to Thailand and Secretary Clinton went to Thailand, so they understood better, they had a good rapport. But still the priority of the US was not ASEAN as a lot of things happened in the world."[494] A Foreign Ministry official assigned to ASEAN was more candid: "Too bad there is not much I can tell about the US. I did not hear any concrete proposals from that side, just the political rhetoric repeated at meetings with ASEAN."[495] In 2011, the members of Clinton's Lower Mekong Initiative agreed to a five-year plan of action and a "virtual secretariat" online. Priority areas were education, the environment, health, and infrastructure—still nothing overtly economic or security related. Moreover, US engagement tapered as Obama focused on reelection and new challenges in the Middle East. It did finally join the East Asia Summit in 2011, six years after China had joined fifteen other nations at its first convening, and hosted APEC the same year. In 2012, however, after a visit to Myanmar that Yingluck rightly described as "historic", Obama skipped both the EAS and APEC—and would skip the latter again in 2013.[496]

"So in terms of my priorities", Obama said during his speech in Bangkok, "number one: expanding trade and investment ... we'll work together as Thailand begins to lay the groundwork for joining high-standard trade agreements, such as the Trans-Pacific Partnership".[497] Yingluck did not disagree: "Thailand sees the TPP as very important for the future. But we have concern for the readiness of the country, which is something that must be addressed in parallel by way of capacity-building. After that, we can work and assess. It might be better to invite all other countries, as it would mean more markets and new markets."[498] Whether by "other countries" she meant China was not known, but the TPP continued to exclude what would become not only Thailand's largest trading partner in 2014, but the *world's largest economy* the following year. Thus was Obama wrong in claiming that it would "advance our vision of a region where trade is free and fair, and all nations play by the rules".[499] In contrast, the RCEP was not envisaged with such interests, making its exclusion of the US as economically expedient as it was politically. By mid-2013, the TPP had undergone eighteen rounds of negotiation with eleven nations, with a tentative launch set for the APEC summit in October. Like Obama himself, the TPP would miss that date. Recalling the bilateral FTA, discussions with Thailand made little progress before the 2014 coup.

While you were away

In late 2011, the American who had been arrested earlier in the year on *lese majeste* charges was sentenced to two and a half years in prison. When the US criticized the law, Thailand's former palace police chief stated, "If the US or the UN are of this opinion or support this, they should know that the Thai people who worship and want to protect the King are ready to be their enemy and will fight both the US and the UN."[500] Victims of the law wrote an open letter to Obama before his visit the next year. During his speech, he acknowledged steps Thailand was taking to address human trafficking, but it retained a second-tier ranking through Yingluck's term. The Foreign Ministry complained that the Americans "weren't able to get across what the problem was. It was something else each year. Should that not have been mentioned before?"[501] The US continued to advocate protection and resettlement of North Korean refugees, as Thailand saw an exponential rise in their number. And although it would hold the line until after the coup, Thailand was facing greater Chinese pressure to capture and repatriate hundreds of Muslim Uighur "terrorists". A US diplomat confirmed that the Uighurs were "towards the top of their list and towards the top of our list".[502] A Thai counterpart complained that the Chinese "came in very heavy-handed, saying they need to be sent back without any question. They were very unforgiving in terms of how we dealt with it. We said we wanted to make sure that their rights were there. 'What rights? They are criminals'".[503]

* * *

On account of coming to power via Thailand's first legitimate election since 2005, as well as representing a party that had never lost, Yingluck was seen by the US as signaling a "return to democracy" even more than Samak in 2007. In late 2011, Clinton told her that the "United States stands firmly behind the civilian government of Thailand and the work it is doing to consolidate strong democratic institutions, ensure good governance, guarantee the rule of law, and protect human rights and fundamental freedoms".[504] Yingluck replied that Thailand was "a full-fledged democracy once again, after the July general election and with the mandate of the people".[505] The whole exchange was based on the simplistic US view that an election equaled democracy, by which logic Afghanistan and Iraq had been democratic since 2004 and 2005, respectively. For Yingluck, "full-fledged" democracy meant only that her side—rather than any other—was firmly in power.

During Obama's visit a year later, Yingluck again spoke of "our shared commitment to democracy, human rights, and free markets".[506] Obama replied that she was "committed to rule of law, committed to freedom of speech ... will strengthen democracy even further in Thailand and will serve as a good example for the region as a whole".[507] This had last been true under Prime Minister Chuan through 2000. Obama stated that "democracy is not something that is static; it's something that we constantly have to work on ... all citizens have to remain vigilant".[508] Thailand's citizens had been vigilant by joining anti-democratic movements, supporting a coup, refusing to accept electoral defeat, and committing violence. And most notably, in a desperate if stiff-lipped exhortation, Obama implicitly acknowledged that the game was lost, going so far as to name the winner:

> Madam Prime Minister, What can emerging democracies in Asia
> take away from how difficult it has been for the President to get
> Congress to agree ... with him? And why shouldn't China's system of
> government look more appealing in this region when you confront a
> situation like this in the U.S.? And I think it's important to recognize
> that, yes, democracy is a little messier than alternative systems of
> government, but that's because democracy allows everybody to have
> a voice. And that system of government lasts, and it's legitimate, and
> when agreements are finally struck, you know that nobody is being left
> out of the conversation. And that's the reason for our stability and our

prosperity. And the notion somehow that you can take shortcuts and avoid democracy, and that that somehow is going to be the mechanism whereby you deliver economic growth, I think is absolutely false …

And it's worked for us for over 200 years now, and I think it's going to work for Thailand and it's going to work for this entire region. And the alternative, I think, is a false hope.[509]

Team Thaksin redux did not share the president's position and nor did its opponents. The PAD would slowly fade, although not before Sondhi claimed that the US was trying to impose "three Western ideas" of elected government, human rights, and transparency on Thailand. Among the organizations he called out in evidence were Amnesty International and the Council on Foreign Relations. In the PAD's place and founded by Abhisit's ex-deputy premier Suthep, was the People's Democratic Reform Committee (PDRC). Boasting yet another misplaced "D", the PDRC distinguished itself from both the PAD and UDD in being as deeply opposed to democracy as the military with which it would align itself. Like the others, however, it attracted most of what little remained of Thai civil society. The PDRC called for a "People's Council" of 300 conservative professionals and 100 scholars and royalists. All would be chosen or approved by the PDRC itself, thus being not only less representative than the PAD's "New Politics", but representing only itself. It would pass laws and carry out "reform" indefinitely, toward three graduated purposes. One, overthrow Yingluck. Two, ensure that the entire Red demographic—from Thaksin to his party to the UDD to the millions of Thais living in the north and northeast—was permanently disenfranchised and disempowered. Three, transform itself into a permanent governing system via elections aping Iran and Zimbabwe. Reactionary in the extreme, the PDRC was simultaneously a pre- and post-democratic movement, led by the most committed civilian opponent of democracy in Thai history. And it looked a lot more like China's Politburo than Obama's Congress.

Nothing to fear

There was no manner in which Beijing did not continue outpacing Washington in geopolitical moves under Yingluck. While this signified no change for a decade and a half, it was surprising given how badly behind the Americans had already fallen, with their "pivot" to Asia admitting as much. Announced just three months after Yingluck took office, among the pivot's stated aims was to place 60 percent of the US navy in the region by 2020. By the time she was over-thrown thirty-one months later, it had barely advanced beyond the movement of 200 marines to Australia in April 2012. "The US was so distracted with its own domestic issues and with whatever was going on elsewhere", recalled Korn. "The Arab Spring overtook in terms of immediacy and urgency the Asia pivot. So really very little came out of it, which was very disappointing."[510] Also in April 2012, and in furtherance of a pivot long underway, China signed another Comprehensive Strategic Partnership with Thailand, never losing focus. In Bangkok later in the year, Obama said that

> when I announced our desire to pivot and focus on the Asia Pacific region,
> in part it was a response to a decade in which we understandably, as a
> country, had been focused on issues of terrorism; the situation in Iraq and
> Afghanistan. And as a consequence, I think we had not had the same kind
> of presence in a region that is growing faster, developing faster than any
> place else in the world … we see this as a central region for our growth and
> our prosperity, and it's not one that we can neglect.[511]

Yet the pivot was already becoming to the region—and to China in particular—what the response to the 2006 coup had been to Thailand: too much rhetoric for too few results. It was not, according to a former Thai diplomat, that it "smacked of a return to the containment policies and military alliances of the Cold War, threatened to set off a spiraling regional arms race, and to become self-fulfilling in terms of creating an enemy state". It was that it risked those potential effects without achieving anything in return. That it also raised "unrealistic expectations among some allies" was because the Americans were not prepared to prove such expectations realistic.[512] The pivot's foreseeable political costs were worth far less than its geopolitical gain had the US actually *pivoted*, instead of boldly pledging motion before standing still.

* * *

With the ink barely dry on Clinton's *Foreign Policy* article on the pivot, the Chinese responded and the Americans flinched. Recalled one of Yingluck's advisors, China's request for a higher level of participation in Cobra Gold "got the Americans quite nervous and got a lot of ASEAN countries to be more careful, even us".[513] Yet a US lieutenant was sadly transparent that "This is just another opportunity for us to come together and work on our tactic techniques and procedures."[514] China duly received "observer plus" status. Aggravating this was its statement that Cobra Gold "complicates the security situation in the region, especially territorial disputes over the South China Sea".[515] A year and a half since it had protested at the US offer to mediate the disputes, Beijing was forewarning that the region's largest exercises should not hinder its maritime expansion. What better way to ensure this than by "observing" more keenly?

In February 2012, the PAD said the US was trying "to create instability so that it can install its military bases to block China's influence".[516] Sondhi claimed that US capitalists were planning to overthrow Thailand's monarchy, "in a bid to rule Thailand to control natural resources in the region to contain China".[517] The US then renewed a request—previously approved by Abhisit— for NASA to use the U-Tapao airbase for climate change research flights. U-Tapao continued to host over 100 US military flights per month, including for humanitarian missions in line with a separate agreement with the US months before. When Yingluck gave the go-ahead to NASA, Abhisit suggested she had obtained a US visa for Thaksin in return, and that the flights "could jeopardize Thailand's vibrant trade ties with China".[518] The Thai press went further, claiming that they were "actually cover for secret new US intelligence operations targeting China. Three commercial Chinese airlines, namely China Airlines, China Eastern Airlines and China Southern Airlines, make regular use of U-Tapao's facilities".[519] Thaksin would get his visa in any event; "trade ties" remained vibrant. Thailand's press was more plausible, but unfortunately assumed greater US attention and resources on China than was likely the case. The PAD then won the day:

> The US has developed a project which can emit electromagnetic waves into the atmosphere to be reflected back to the earth to cause "natural disasters" at targeted areas, as a new kind of weapon to destroy enemies ... the whole world has been worried about this, and it is no surprise that the Chinese Army had to hold talks with its Thai counterparts.[520]

The military approved the request but Yingluck referred it to Parliament, causing NASA to withdraw after a final reply deadline passed. In November, Obama stated that US–Thai cooperation should include new challenges, "And Thailand I think, having experienced its own floods, understands the importance of this."[521] A role for China in Yingluck's NASA deliberation was not known, but two of its airlines using U-Tapao were based in Guangdong province and Taiwan respectively, on the mid-coast and northernmost point of the South China Sea.

Just four days after Thailand let NASA's deadline pass, it began its role as coordinator-*cum*-mediator for ASEAN–China relations. In mid-2013, Yingluck's foreign minister asked (US treaty ally) the Philippines to separate its South China Sea disputes from the wider ASEAN–China dynamic. Beijing promptly agreed to talks with ASEAN on a code of conduct in the sea, remarking that, "China and ASEAN countries are close neighbours and we are like members of one big family."[522] After the South China Sea was discussed at the first Sino-Thai Strategic Dialogue in August, the two nations signed agreements on maritime cooperation during Premier Li Keqiang's historic visit two months later. Bilateral submarine talks were also characterized as "related" to the disputes.[523] Abhisit's Democrats then drew attention to a US website claiming that Thailand had hired a firm to lobby "Congress of the strategic importance of the South China Sea".[524] Reportedly, in exchange for offering the US a naval base on its east coast, Thailand wanted more trade representation in the US. The Democrats alternately criticized Yingluck for the move and challenged her to lodge a protest with the Americans; her foreign minister denied the story.

Three months later and just three months before Thailand's coup, Cobra Gold 2014 took place with China as an "observer plus" for the first time.

* * *

A week apart in October 2013, Chinese President Xi Jinping and Premier Li Keqiang discussed a high-speed passenger rail link with Prime Minister Yingluck. Designed to run in twenty-four hours from Yunnan province to Singapore—further than the Thai–Malaysian border under Abhisit—the first stage would conclude in Bangkok (via Laos). Xi mooted financing by China's new Asian Infrastructure Investment Bank, for "As Thailand is regarded as China's major regional partner for development, plans for a new stage of cooperation between the two nations will be sought."[525] Li suggested that the railway could be partly funded by barter for Thai agricultural products. Thaksin's reply was, "You want to build the high-speed train, we will give you the high-speed train."[526] Sarasin explained:

What we needed most was rail for hauling goods, rather than hauling people, because we had adopted the American way—the road. So we had neglected the passenger railway but in the process also the cargo rail. What we needed most was the cargo rail, whereas the Chinese priority was the passenger. But here it would not pay off because you cannot make a stop every hundred kilometers, you have to have a concentration of people. In China no problem, they have over 100 cities with over a million people. But in Thailand, how many cities have a million people? One. So the high-speed passenger rail wouldn't work here, but for political reasons Yingluck agreed with the Chinese. It was all political. And who was behind Yingluck?[527]

The politics as ever pertained to geography and the Straits of Malacca, at the bottom of which sat the high-speed train's destination, Singapore. China would have another and faster land route for transporting oil, gas, and goods between Yunnan and the Straits. A US diplomat pointed out that the rail would be standard gauge rather than the narrow gauge used by Thailand's rail system: "It is just a conduit for stuff to move up and down from China."[528] Technically a passenger rail, it would also serve to transport men in uniform in the event of a crisis. Most importantly, it would be yet another north–south option intersecting the "land bridge" or a future canal across Thailand's Isthmus of Kra, making dispensable its continuance all the way to Singapore.

Out of the barrel of a gun

In late 2013, a strange thing happened on the way to a coup. After Yingluck mooted a bill conferring legal amnesty on "political offenders" dating back to 2004, Red and Yellow alike came out to oppose it. Hardly united in principle—each simply wanted to see its opposite numbers pay a legal price—they succeeded in getting the bill withdrawn. Thus did proverbial preparation meet opportunity, as the PDRC's Suthep kept his well-heeled followers on the street and began calling for military intervention. After it occupied several government buildings, Yingluck invoked the Internal Security Act. The military stood and watched. Twice the Chinese Foreign Ministry stated: "We believe the Thai government and people have the capability to handle the problem."[529] The State Department encouraged "all involved to resolve political differences peacefully and democratically in a way that reflects the will of the Thai people and strengthens the rule of law".[530] When

Yingluck called for a snap election, the PDRC called for a boycott, not able to countenance yet another in which Suthep's Democrat Party would get buried. In mid-December, 500 PDRC members marched on the US embassy, protesting its support for the election, demanding to see Kenney, and raising the Thai flag on top of a makeshift pole. An open letter said, "If you continue to 'express concern' time and again, directly or indirectly, then we presume that your growing concern is mainly based on your self-serving interests."[531]

Two weeks before the polls in February 2014, Yingluck invoked the Emergency Decree following the first death in related violence. Overall, twenty-eight would die over five months, in what the PDRC hyperbolically called the seeds of "civil war"—2011 had seen *3,307* murders in Thailand, to say nothing of the southern armed conflict. China reportedly offered to mediate, calling "on all parties concerned to resolve issues through dialogue and consultation … to restore national stability and order at an early date".[532] While Kenney told the press, "I have no intention to intervene in Thai politics", both Suthep and Thaksin's lawyer wrote letters to Obama.[533] The elections were disrupted by more violence when security forces ignored obvious security concerns. Kenney met Yingluck in April to deliver a letter from Secretary of State John Kerry. "The US particularly does not want to see a power grab or military coup", reported the foreign minister. "If this should occur, they would not be happy about it."[534] In early May, Yingluck finally stepped down after the third court order against a Thaksin-backed premier in nearly six years. The State Department responded that "a resolution should include elections and an elected government".[535] Of the security forces, a deputy secretary of defense remarked that "It really demonstrates the evolution of Thai civil–military relations in a positive direction",[536] concluding that "We don't have reason to expect that the Thai military will change their current stance."[537]

A week later, on the same day that the joint CARAT naval exercises kicked off, the army added martial law to the ISA and Emergency Decree already in effect. From the State Department: "The Royal Thai Army announced that this martial law declaration is not a coup. We expect the Army to honor its commitment to make this a temporary action to prevent violence, and to not undermine democratic institutions."[538] And temporary it was: after ordering Thailand's principal politicians to a barracks for two days of fake negotiations, army chief Prayuth Chan-ocha declared on 22 May 2014 that he was taking over the kingdom. It was the coup to end all coups in Thailand, and its twelfth since 1932. Within days, the National Council for Peace and Order (NCPO)—largely of Queen's Guard pedigree—had detained over 250 people, begun referring *lese majeste* cases to military courts, and vowed to remain in power "indefinitely".[539] There would be no "D" in its title this time.

* * *

Secretary Kerry's statement was released less than eleven hours after the coup. Its effects were equally immediate but innocuous. CARAT stopped in mid-stream and $3.5 million of a total $10.5 million in military aid to Thailand was cut. With the exception of thirty-three Thai soldiers already in training, IMET was suspended. PACOM canceled a visit to Thailand and rescinded its invitation to a general. The State Department canceled firearms training and a visit to the FBI for the police. The $3.5 million was worth 10 percent the cost of a single F-16; the State Department's spokesperson was priceless: "We don't want anything to end in chaos but we think setting a timeline for early elections is something that is not just possible but is what the appropriate step is. There is no reason they can't be held in a short time."[540]

This would remain the US mantra over the next several months and beyond, the result of having reduced a playbook once full of history, language, and culture—and experience—to a series of formulaic steps. According to a diplomat who was serving in Bangkok when the previous coup had taken place,

> Looking at how the messaging was managed in 2006 versus 2014—the language and tonality—is instructive of how a senior experienced diplomat with very deep linguistic and cultural connections handles that kind of situation, versus someone who had global experience in messaging but not a lot of depth in tough environments. The Thais knew we were going to do what was right and criticize the coup, but the backside—context and nuance—had always been there and then it wasn't anymore. That took a lot of our closest friends, people who had been admirers of the US role in Thailand for the last 30 or 40 years, aback.[541]

Kerry's original statement was only 150 words long, described by an ex-diplomat as "the path of least resistance" through the State Department's vetting process.[542] By that point, the Americans had little choice but to "reflexively fall back on and trot out phrase X that we used in country Y when something Z happened".[543]

On 2 June, a day after Prayuth promised elections within fifteen months, Secretary of Defense Chuck Hagel urged him to "release those who have been detained, end restrictions on free expression, and move *immediately* to restore power to the people of Thailand, through free and fair elections" (emphasis added).[544] It was not that fifteen months was acceptable or that Hagel was wrong per se, but that he should have known by then that Thailand had seen its last free and fair election, and that US credibility for demanding otherwise was gone. That a State Department spokesperson declared that "every political lever, economic lever where applicable" would be pulled wrongly implied that such levers still existed.[545] To wit, in a move it would have been advisable not to publicize, at the end of the month the US suspended $1.2 million more in military aid, for a total of *$24 million less* than in 2006. Fittingly, Kenny became the target of a social media campaign calling for her removal. In calculated contrast, on 4 June China's ambassador met with the junta "and assured us that they still have a good relationship with Thailand and that they hope the situation will return to normal quickly".[546] Two days later, Prayuth asked Chinese business representatives to promote tourism in Thailand, stating that he was as "committed as ever to its strategic partnership 'at all levels' with China".[547]

To its credit, the US canceled the bilateral Hunaman Guardian joint army drills, and rescinded its invitation to Thai observers for its Rim of the Pacific exercise. Kenney stated that Cobra Gold itself was "under review" and "will be a tough call at very senior levels in Washington".[548] The NCPO responded that "regional security should be considered a lasting, significant issue";[549] the Foreign Ministry that any cancelations should "not be a major cause for concern".[550] Thailand's supreme commander met with the Chinese ambassador the same day to discuss closer ties. While China's "observer plus" status made canceling Cobra Gold 2015 even more advisable than in 2007, in the end it was simply scaled back. Again in contrast, Thai generals visited Beijing in mid-June, claiming that "China regarded Thailand's political problems as an internal issue."[551] According to a poll that month, 56 percent of Thais were "not worried at all" by US sanctions, compared to 9 percent who were "very worried". China was identified by 33 percent as the friendliest and most trusted foreign entity, second only to ASEAN.

On 29 June, a Thai repeatedly shouted anti-American statements outside the US embassy and was not arrested. "This man's actions do not count as a violation of the legal ban on political protests", explained a senior police officer, "because it was merely an expression of anger."[552] On 4 July, a woman stood outside the same embassy holding a placard that said, "Long Live USA Day". She was detained for five days before being released without an explanation. In between, Kenney denied a press report that General Prayuth had not been invited to her embassy's Independence Day reception, adding meekly, "We want to work on issues like education, environment, health and other social issues."[553] During the same period, China's ambassador said that "The junta has strengthened China's confidence in Thailand, notably in terms of economic cooperation."[554] Both symbolizing the foreign policy shift underway and giving it substance, the Chinese hosted the Privy Council's General Prem and the second China–Thailand Strategic Dialogue. China "expressed that it would like to see a stable, united and thriving Thailand to play a greater role in the regional and international arena".[555] In turn, Thailand's chief delegate "expressed appreciation for the positive stance taken by the Chinese government, saying it helped consolidate long-term ties".[556] Speaking to a wider audience, he added: "Thailand is ready to work with any country that wants to cooperate, but a true friend is a friend in tough times."[557]

Chapter Ten:
Continental Drift

[T]iny Siam was now in the grip of something from which the most wily diplomacy could not free her ... It looked as though the Kingdom, by historical and geographic accident, once again was in the middle of something big, from which she might emerge badly mangled.[1]

Alexander MacDonald, 1949

The coup statement was very strong, but when things happen will you follow the statement or not? That's another problem. You make a statement, you believe in human rights, you believe in democracy. But suppose Thailand doesn't follow that. Can the US do anything with that strong statement? Can you make sanctions against Thailand? Because if you believe it, but the government does not return democracy to the people, can you do anything? That is what we have to wait and see.[2]

Surapong Tovichakchaikul, 2015

We are talking about a future of pipelines, in this case gas from offshore fields in the Bay of Bengal, that will extend China's reach beyond its legal borders to its natural geographical and historical limits. This will occur in a Southeast Asia in which the formerly strong state of Thailand can less and less play the role of a regional anchor and inherent balancer against China, owing to deep structural problems in Thai politics.[3]

Robert D. Kaplan, 2010

Ambassador Kenney left Thailand in November 2014 and her replacement would not take up his post until October 2015, leaving the embassy's top job in Bangkok vacant for eleven months. In the midst of the 21st century's Great Game in Asia, the United States left itself unrepresented in a nation being run by its own military. Illustrative of Obama's "shuffle" to the region, the US could not manage this signal step in protecting—never mind projecting—its national interests. Across town, the Chinese ambassador was busy.

TECTONIC ACTIVITY

Beyond its borders, Thailand's growing embrace of the China Model—an authoritarian government backed by a controlled market economy—is attributable to China and the United States. Since the turn of the century, the push and pull of their policies have interacted with indigenous forces and factors—an absence of ideology, a culture of impunity—in a spirited process of natural selection. Colluding with Thai history and culture in the case of China, colliding in the case of the US, the global powers have offered not only different systems of governance, but the visions and values that inform them. The result in Thailand—on the campaign trail, in the streets, in the barracks—has been a clear preference to rule and be ruled rather than to represent and be represented. Thus did Ambassador Kenney speak past her hosts in the wake of the coup: "Like most Thais, we want Thailand to live up to its democratic ideals."[4] Resistance to the junta has been virtually non-existent. In 2015, a Thai general offered that,

> From the Thai point of view, emergence of Western-style democracy in China would be disastrous, as the country would degenerate into a land of warlords fighting each other. For a small country on the land periphery of China, a strong central government in effective control of that great country is far more conducive to the pursuit of our needs. We at the same time now realize that simply mimicking the Western political system would inevitably lead us back into another political dead-end. We need to go back to the drawing board.[5]

Appreciating the difference between warlords and politicians, and without naming the China Model or US democracy, the general's comparison and verdict were clear. Perhaps because the Chinese do not share Thailand's praetorian tradition, former finance minister Korn imagined a nation in which the military stops governing but bequeaths its approach to governance:

> If our politics continue to be authoritarian in the way they are today, then the more likely it is that your scenario plays out. I wish to tell my own country that we mustn't lose context. At the end of the day, given the

choice, you would much prefer the American way of life to any other way of life, I'm not even going to say the Chinese way of life.[6]

Abhisit's foreign minister Kasit was less circumspect:

> Over the past few months there has been an undercurrent movement of one-party rule to provide stability as an alternative to a more robust and conflicting defense of opinions in street politics. "Let's go for the Chinese model." One-party rule in Thailand would see the military still in control of the political regime directly or indirectly to provide stability so that we can develop. Can the US allow this to happen?[7]

Like the general's "strong central government", Kasit's reference to (political) stability toward achieving (economic) development, speaks to the China Model's definition and its growing appeal. Thailand appreciates, however, that the reverse is also true: economic turmoil destabilizes the body politic. Although Thailand is distinct from China in condoning rather than condemning corruption, many Thais are increasingly upset by economic inequality that is among the worst in Southeast Asia. The UDD's rank-and-file made this a focus of their 2010 protests, even as the PAD and PDRC depended upon it for their power.

Thai authorities of any color face two imperatives, both far less challenging in a kingdom of 67 million people than in a China of 1.4 billion. The first is to ensure that the economy grows steadily, ideally with net gains among the poor keeping pace with inequality. Even should the rich advance at a faster rate, the poor's standard of living must not be allowed to stagnate for too long. This would result in fewer demonstrations by the grassroots and serve the China Model's focus on development. Xi Jinping's 2012 anti-corruption campaign was partly designed to placate the Chinese masses. Fifty days after the coup, Beijing reminded Bangkok that China "had focused on reforms that led to rapid development over the past 30 years, and hoped that the reforms in China could act as a role model for other developing countries in the region including Thailand".[8] In 2015, Thaksin's ideologue Pansak concluded squarely, "The 20th century major powers do not define the world's future anymore. The world's future is about solutions. And a practical intellectual solution is more valuable than the Seventh Fleet at this moment."[9]

The second lesson is political: strictly limit freedom of assembly, expression, and association, such that the few demonstrations that do arise are small and short-lived. This is preventative where possible, reactive where necessary, and serves the China Model's focus on (surface-level) stability. That China has not experienced a repeat of Tiananmen Square is largely because—as with the 2008 uprising in Tibet—it has cracked down early and hard. Xi Jinping's 2014 rule of law campaign provided retroactive rationale for this approach, while Thailand's three pieces of extraordinary legislation have allowed it to do the same since the turn of the century. One Thailand scholar recounted how, after the violence of 2010, he began hearing Thai bankers talk openly about China's "authoritarian capitalism", before going on to bankroll the PDRC before the coup: "They were prepared in a way they hadn't been before to put their money behind the defeat of democracy because of the fear of the masses."[10]

* * *

How important is Thailand's adoption of the China Model to China itself? According to Thaksin, "They just don't care. Whoever becomes the government, they do business with them. They are like entrepreneurs, they do business, they don't do politics."[11] With one eye on his constituents, Korn agreed:

> China is perfectly comfortable with whatever system Thailand operates under. And I can say this with confidence. The Democrat Party has a very warm relationship with the Communist Party of China. They continue to invest in us, they continue to invest in democratic institutions in Thailand. Arguably I think they would prefer that we went back to a democratic system, although obviously they have no problem with a military government either.[12]

Both erred, however, in the same way the Americans have been erring since the late 1990s, ignoring the other global power. If the US had no presence and interests in Southeast Asia, China would indeed not "care" and might even "prefer" a democratic system in Thailand. But in the competition for geopolitical influence, China has long seen the need to cultivate the purely political; its international aspirations require due regard to Thailand's national situation. In principle, this is no different from the Americans' promotion of democracy in the Middle East and elsewhere, save that it has been done not with gunboat diplomacy but diplomacy, with investment rather than invasion. An advisor to Yingluck noted that China does "not yet" pressure Thailand on UN votes, although its hands-off approach may be the point.[13] "The Chinese have been more sophisticated in approaching Thailand", said security analyst Panitan. "It is beyond a charm offensive, it has achieved another level in a very progressive approach to the relationship in terms of politics. The Chinese have been very quick in seeing the opportunities that have opened up since the coup of 22 May 2014. They had been preparing for that opening up of opportunities."[14]

In providing "intellectual cover" for an authoritarian Thailand since the turn of the century, China has not only conferred upon it a kind of false legitimacy, but has given itself far greater cover than the US to pursue geopolitical interests in the kingdom. Thanks to Thaksin's "gateway" policy, this has had regional implications as well. Such cover was particularly strong during the sixteen months after the 2006 coup and has been near-exclusive since the 2014 reprise. When asking the US in 2006, "If the (Thai) people accepted it, why shouldn't the international community?", the Chinese were speaking past the coup and declaring their place in that same community.[15] By defining alternative terms of good standing and deciding which nations are meeting them, Beijing has been able—as has Washington for seventy years—to further its own agenda in the process.

With rare exception, China has no independent motive in promoting or perpetrating rights violations in Thailand. Rather its interest in authoritarianism anywhere abroad exists primarily to counter an expressly contrary approach by the US. Democracy, human rights, and the rule of law are for China just factors to negotiate in pursuit of its interests, while for the US they are claimed as ends in themselves—even ones upon which others depend. Thus, for China, they are subject to the same zero-sum analysis that attends its strategic thinking in other areas. For where democracy is in greater evidence, the US is more likely to be engaged and influential; where authoritarianism has taken hold, the Americans are more likely to cede ground. Three weeks after the 2014 coup, the official newspaper of China's Communist Party weighed in: "from Kiev to Bangkok, the politics of the street and public clashes have caused deep sorrow … whether openly or behind the scenes, American and Western forces have been involved. From West Asia and North Africa to Ukraine and Thailand, each one without exception was led astray on to the path of 'Western-style democracy'".[16]

Yet, if under the guise of "non-interference" China subtly interferes, it must be judicious. In 2011, Myanmar's unease at the breadth and depth of Chinese interests and influence in its affairs intensified. While far from having become a client state of Beijing, Myanmar had been under military rule for decades and was also highly dependent on China's "intellectual cover" abroad. At the same time, two decades after it first imposed economic sanctions on Myanmar, the US reconsidered its position. The result has been a qualified weakening of China's advantage. Fortunately for China in Thailand, dissenting voices are faint and few, and the US shows no sign of repeating its success.

* * *

In 1970, David A. Wilson observed that "The Thai Government and, substantially, the Thai people do not share the view that Thailand is part of China's 'natural sphere of influence' ... opposition to the expansion of the Chinese influence into Thailand, among other places, has been the foundation of American influence in Thailand".[17] What changed of course was that the foundation buckled, before collapsing altogether. More than any other domestic or foreign factor—including China itself—the United States has accounted for Thailand's adoption of the China Model, and its foreign policy shift into China's geopolitical sphere of influence. That is, both within and outside the kingdom, the US has "lost" Thailand more than China has gained it, and more than Bangkok has itself proactively altered its approach to governance and geopolitics. "Besides giving the prestige of being equal", said Thaksin in 2015, "when the Chinese build a relationship, they give heart. They give heart. The US seems to be at haste with everything, rush in, rush out. They don't give heart."[18] Another former premier recalled telling a senior US diplomat after the recent coup, "You are just pushing us closer to China."[19] The junta's ambassador to Washington complained that he was "doing the US embassy's job" in managing the sentiments of Thais, joking that Thailand should "go nuclear" to get US attention.[20]

Yet if US policy in Thailand since the late 20th century has been the most proximate cause of the kingdom's shift, American decisions elsewhere in the world have played a supporting role. Anand noted Myanmar and Iraq—sanctions and war—with great pressure on Thailand to back both. "Particularly as they went around the Security Council with a blatant lie about WMD", he explained. "That was the time when I stopped reading Western newspapers. To sum up our resentment of the Americans would be that they were hypocrites."[21] Nor did he forget unlawful transfers of power:

> I would be the first one to admit that our coup d'etat was wrong, but we
> did not get the same treatment from the Americans. What happened in

Egypt in 2013? They helped the army dismantle a democratically elected government. If you go back, the US did that in Guatemala, in Panama, in Nicaragua, in the Dominican Republic, in Cuba. Yet, they keep on carping about this timetable, about a roadmap for when we will have democracy. It's absurd.[22]

Abhisit also cited the coup in Egypt: "The Americans said it was an 'intervention to restore democracy', and that if it took one year before they returned to elections, that was fine but in Thailand it would be too late. What would happen if General Prayuth became prime minister after elections? Would the Americans see that in the same way Egypt has evolved?"[23] Panitan noted that "more and more are aware of it thanks to modern communication, the internet, information networks. And it has played into the public's sense that something has really gone wrong between the two countries: 'Why haven't we received the kind of treatment that Egypt has?'"[24] US diplomats in both Bangkok and Washington acknowledged that the junta itself continued to raise Egypt, although one dismissed it contemptuously as a "debate point".[25] Tellingly, his remit was almost exclusively Thailand.

Trust has been the most evident casualty. Korn claimed that "America has begun to lose credibility in the thinking Thai's mind, and that's a shame."[26] Long-time "Thailand hand" Karl Jackson bemoaned that "The most disturbing thing for any American diplomat trying to operate there is the level of trust. I've never seen it so low among the Thai elite."[27] Anand looked further, lamenting that a stronger "point in history is still remembered by Thais of my generation, but I'm not so sure the new generation knows anything about it".[28] Finally a Thai general: "The sad part is, in the 53 years since I began, I have never seen such a bitter and widespread show of rejection and antagonism toward the US. In the past, whenever there was some disagreement or dislike of something, negative comments would be of cynicism or sarcasm, relatively mild or half in jest, now they are in anger and bitterness."[29]

Yet the United States should not simply attempt to make a right of two wrongs by refusing to condemn Thailand's coup, much less by calling it an "intervention to restore democracy". The former would be to join China in silence, the latter to repeat the equally discredited language of the junta itself. The US, like every member of the international community, has both a right and duty to protect civil and political rights. This is enshrined in long-settled and binding international law, as well as in many national constitutions. In the 21st century this means opposing the proliferation of authoritarianism, the China Model's political half. For when a nation's domestic affairs implicate international law—let alone violate human rights, humanitarian, or refugee law—they cease being its "domestic affairs". As a permanent member of the UN Security Council, charged with upholding "international peace and security", China knows this very well. As do other nations. Indeed, Thaksin's claim that the US "expressed more concern and took more action" than any other nation after Thailand's 2014 coup rightly condemns the others' failure.[30] To express concern, censure, sanction, even deploy troops in exceptional cases, is not to "interfere" but to exercise responsibility.

The solution then is veiled by the problem, which is not that the Americans' message is invalid or impolitic—much less reminiscent of the colonial era, as suggested in 2014 by the daughter of ex-dictator Thanom. It is that the messenger has been sufficiently discredited since the late 1990s that the Thais are no longer willing to listen. However unlikely, the first step the US should take in attempting to rebuild relations with Thailand is to retrospectively announce that Egypt's 2013 coup was a coup. For in the words of a US diplomat, "The conclusion the Thais have seemed to draw is that we are unprincipled. In Egypt, where we are perceived to have greater strategic advantages, we'll look the other way."[31] Korn concurred: "Why was our military government acceptable to the United States in the 1970s? The answer is obvious: America needed Thailand strategically and needed it to be strong to stand up to the communist threat. So at that time democracy really didn't matter. Now that needs have changed, suddenly democracy matters."[32] Appropriate to a security advisor to the junta, Panitan similarly channeled that era's realpolitik: "This is exactly what the US has been telling us all along. It is not about friendship, it is about national interests. So you can see the tide moving to get our national interests connected more with China, as told by the US, more with Russia, as told by the US: 'You should serve your national interests'."[33]

And the US is right: a solution will come, in Thailand as elsewhere, only when the US decides to consistently treat democracy, human rights, and the rule of law as *national interests*—not merely perceive or proclaim them as such, but invest strategic resources toward their protection and advancement. The problem with Ambassador Kenney's claim that "We take very seriously the whole human-rights aspect to this coup in Thailand", is that the US has not taken human rights very seriously in the relationship for two decades.[34] It has not treated them as national interests.

Nor is that all. "You have invested so much in trying to tell the Chinese to respect human rights, to implement some form of democratic process", noted Pansak in 2015. "But you allow your closest ally Thailand to have coup after coup. The Chinese would have a laugh, wouldn't they?"[35] For in Southeast Asia, the Chinese have been treating their national interests as simultaneously *geopolitical* for decades, including the China Model. In contrast, the Americans have been failing to appreciate—much less aggressively engage—the zero-sum game in which democracy and human rights are losing. Bush's "democracy by war and decree" was defined by its contradictions, with a regional agenda on which human rights barely registered. Obama's "pivot" to Asia did claim that "our most potent asset as a nation is the power of our values—in particular, our steadfast support for democracy and human rights".[36] Yet it listed their advancement last among six "key lines of action", and addressed them as distinct from US "interests".[37] Obtaining UN votes, increasing military advantage, and expanding economic markets were interests to be secured via negotiation, horse-trading, arm-twisting, even air strikes. Democracy and human rights were mere values, supposedly advanced by "encouraging", "calling upon", "urging", or levying the occasional sanctions. In a strategically located Thailand, the US has not been *competing* with China for influence in how Thai leadership perceives power, treats its people, and applies its laws.

* * *

Undergirding a strategic overhaul in Thailand and beyond, what structural changes must the Americans make to transform their aspirational and ancillary values into core geopolitical interests? Put simply, they must reverse the decisions taken since the late 1990s that have demonstrably diminished their ability to compete for influence. Most pertain to human, financial, and intellectual resources, each having a cascading effect on the others. "Tell me who the strong players are at State or the NSC, who are friends of Thailand", asked Karl Jackson. "That's a problem, a real problem."[38] A retired Thai diplomat asked to brief members of Congress just before the coup recalled his hosts "openly lamenting the lack of old Thai hands".[39] A senior State Department official complained that "No one wants to address structural problems with democracy and governance", resulting in a policy of "special interests and not strategic interests".[40]

Within the US, Congress should reinstate funding for the Thai and South-east Asia studies programs that still exist at a number of US universities. The US Foreign Service should both actively recruit candidates from these programs and support diplomats in obtaining area-specific knowledge between assignments. It should provide Thai (or other regional) language study sufficient to achieving near-fluency prior to deployment, and attach such to career advancement. While diplomats possessing skills and expertise transcending regional ring-fencing should be assigned accordingly, provision should be made for officers aspiring to spend the duration of their foreign service in Asia. Multiple "tours" to the same nation over a long career should be encouraged and facilitated. Where possible and appropriate, the Department of Defense should adopt this approach through its staff colleges, allowing officers to become regional special-ists (with JUSMAG or PACOM, for example). Congress should substantially increase funding and regional earmarking of IMET, and amend the Foreign Operations Appropriations Act to completely exempt IMET from suspension in the case of coups. Finally, as Pansak commented, "The Americans will have to argue among themselves and agree among themselves: What do they want out of this relationship? The United States, I am fully aware, does not have much time. Northern Africa is still there as a top priority, the power relationship with Russia, East and West Africa."[41] Across the globe, former senior US diplomat Stephen Bosworth agreed that time counts and must be accounted for: "The president and his top two-dozen aides, what are they focused on? All would agree that the next eighty-five years of this century will be far more dominated by China than Syria, but very few of them would say, 'OK, I'm going to clear Wednesday afternoon every week to think about China'—much less Thailand. It's depressing."[42]

In Thailand, a campaign such as that post-1997 should be developed to repair and rebuild personal relationships at the leadership level. This should entail visits by the few "old Thailand hands" still in government or military service, such as Senator John McCain and (Thai-born) Representative Ladda Tammy Duckworth. Representatives of important Congressional committees, executive agencies, and PACOM should also be included, such as the State Department's Bureau of Population, Refugees, and Migration and the military's Judge Advocate General's Corps. A senior US diplomat's comment that this book constitutes one of the few examples of "Track II" outreach needs contra-dicting, as the Clintons (foundations), Karl Jackson (universities), and Skip

Boyce (businesses) are among many natural liaisons. And barring *force majeure* on par with the Vietnam War, a new generation of Thai hands will not evolve without targeting younger talent: junior professionals in and out of uniform should be introduced to the kingdom with a full box of business cards. The US should likewise invite Thai counterparts to visit, but travel to the region should take priority. The contacts and concerns of Thailand-based American "friends" should be utilized and considered throughout, especially those residing outside of Bangkok.

Toward more effective "people's diplomacy", the US should greatly expand its "American corners" in number, size, and scope, and provide substantial funding for American studies programs at Thai and regional universities. ASEAN studies should receive attention and resources as well, in addition to a redoubling of education exchange efforts. All of these should emphasize rights-based programs and opportunities. Given the compromised state of Thai civil society, the US should "retrofit" its assistance and condition financial support on extraordinarily strict compliance.

Considering the challenges was an American diplomat who served several years in the Bangkok embassy (and a rare mid-career Thai hand): "We are able to have a nuanced policy on China, where we understand strategic interests at a level that allows us to manage all the problems ... to think and operate on two planes, sometimes public versus private. It was once there in our Thai policy as well but no longer is".[43] Thaksin agreed: "The US has to restructure its foreign policy and foreign service. Otherwise it will lose importance. Just last month I went to Washington and told policy people, both Republican and Democrat, that the US has to be a multi-tasking computer and not a single-tasking computer in foreign policy."[44]

SEA CHANGE

"Liberalism ultimately rests on power: a benign power, perhaps, but power nonetheless", writes American geopolitical analyst Robert D. Kaplan.[45] Leverage on rights comes largely from the furtherance of more traditional geopolitical interests. Following Thailand's coup, a senior US diplomat stated that "The challenge facing the United States is to make clear our support for a rapid return to democracy and fundamental freedoms, *while also working* to ensure we are able to maintain and strengthen ... our security alliance over the long term".[46] The reverse is also true, that more traditional interests often depend on circumstances in which rights are respected and protected. Another diplomat acknowledged that "taking a stand for democracy has frankly harmed our traditional, straightforward interests" in Thailand.[47]

In conjunction with the South China Sea, no single factor is more pivotal toward the defense of traditional US geopolitical interests in Southeast Asia than the Straits of Malacca. Discussing the wider region, Kaplan warns that

> The separation of geopolitics from human rights issues … plus the degree of abstraction that surrounds the naval domain in any case, will help make the South China Sea the realm of policy and defense analysts, rather than of intellectuals and the media elite. Realism, which is consciously amoral, focused as it is on interests rather than on values in a debased world, will therefore triumph.[48]

Kaplan assumes, safely thus far but not inevitable, the continued separation of US interests from values. And should the separation hold, his conclusion that realism will win over rights is accurate as far as it goes, but does not go far enough. For Kaplan ranks US foreign policy priorities relative to one another, but fails to consider the international implications of that ranking. As seen in Thailand already, the subjugation of human rights to more traditional "interests" has resulted in those interests' loss to China. That is, when rights lose to realism on the agendas of US diplomats and defense officials, the US itself loses to its global rival in realist terms. It loses geopolitically. Nor is the suspension of assistance after a coup an exception, but merely a reversal with the same result. For as also seen in Thailand, thanks to a lack of strategic deliberation and deft diplomacy, the sudden and conditional privileging of "values" over "interests" has made no difference. Rather than act as a hold on those interests, it has held them hostage. Everything simply grinds to a halt. The pursuit of democracy and human rights is a moral and legal responsibility in its own right, but the geopolitical consequences must be equally accounted for.

* * *

A 16th century Portuguese envoy was quoted as saying, "Whoever is lord of Malacca has his hands on the throat of Venice."[49] Four centuries later, referencing the equivalent powers of the Cold War, Thai Foreign Minister Thanat said that the US was paying somewhat greater attention to … the Indian Ocean and the importance of protecting the supply line from that ocean to the China Sea and the Pacific Ocean. Thus, Southeast Asia, including Thailand, is gaining a renewed strategic significance and is becoming a factor not to be neglected in the global contest between the major powers.[50]

Although that conflict ended shortly thereafter, Kaplan notes that "The fall of the Berlin Wall did not—could not—end geopolitics, but merely brought it into a new phase. You cannot simply wish away the struggle of states and empires across the map."[51] Yet that is precisely what the US has been doing in Southeast Asia for over two decades, wishing away the zero-sum dynamic that defined that Cold War in favor of a Pollyannaish pivot in which "everyone wins". Secretary Clinton noted in her 2011 article that "The stretch of sea from the Indian Ocean through the Strait of Malacca to the Pacific contains the world's most vibrant trade and energy routes", but failed to acknowledge that it is being contested. More than half of the world's merchant fleet tonnage passes through the Straits—over 60,000 vessels each year—carrying over a third of global trade. Oil and liquefied natural gas pass in even greater volume: two-thirds of the world's commercial supplies. Each day, 15 million barrels of oil transit the Straits, three times more than the Suez Canal and fifteen times more than the Panama Canal. The figures rise when Malacca's southern sisters Lombok, Makassar, and Sunda are included. The four straits together witness a third of all global maritime traffic.

To be sure, basic patrols by Thailand and other regional states notwithstanding, the United States' Seventh Fleet is the primary guardian of the Straits of Malacca. Rather than approve and monitor each vessel as it would if within its sovereign territory, in enforcing "freedom of navigation" it retains the power to take such freedom away. In a direct conflict with China, or more likely one involving China and US allies and interests, the Seventh Fleet would have a larger deterrent effect on unwelcome vessels than any other force or factor. Readily able to do the same in Lombok, Makassar, and Sunda—which already add a week to the journey—it could force ships all the way around the southern tip of Tasmania to eventually reach a Chinese port.

In 2005, the Pentagon adopted a "String of Pearls" analysis, which holds that China is developing economic projects and military outposts along coasts and within waterways. The string begins on its own Hainan Island and continues west across Southeast Asia's maritime underbelly, winding up eventually at Port Sudan in the Red Sea. No coasts are more important than those of Bangladesh and Sri Lanka (skipping US ally India), touching the Bay of Bengal. No waterways are more critical than the Straits of Malacca and Lombok. Thailand's Andaman coast links the Bay of Bengal and the Straits of Malacca. Conceptions have varied since the original "String of Pearls" analysis, but given China's road and rail projects reaching that coast—to say nothing of a potential canal—Thailand should unquestionably be included.

Thailand's U-Tapao airbase is perhaps Southeast Asia's clearest example of the US "lily pad" strategy—"dual-use civilian–military facilities where basing arrangements will be implicit rather than explicit, and completely dependent on the health of the bilateral relationship in question".[52] Hence Pansak's rhetorical challenge: "Has the Thai military modified any semi-secret relationship or contract with the United States? No. You have the right to use Thai airbases and airspace randomly, quietly all the time for your strategic operations. So what's the problem?"[53] On the one hand, "Our investment in military technology going back thirty years will continue to pay off in a major way for up to three decades to come", said former diplomat Bosworth in 2015. "It will take the Chinese a long time to match that. Having been somewhat successful in a twenty-year effort to deny us unimpeded access to the Taiwan Straits, they could conceivably do the same in other parts of the region, but it will take time and investment."[54] And the same year Clinton announced the pivot, the Pentagon pledged that looming budget cuts would not come at the expense of US force projection in Asia.

On the other hand, as Thailand's coup got underway three years later, the number of US naval ships dropped below 300, down from 600 at the end of the Cold War. A ranking defense official said that the pivot was "being looked at again because candidly it can't happen",[55] while a PACOM officer told Bosworth, "Our problem is that we're used to treating the Pacific as an American lake, and that era is over and not coming back."[56] US maritime supremacy in the Straits of Malacca may have a long future, but it is not indefinite. And in Thailand, the "lily pads" can compromise American interests as much as further them. To news that the US might cancel Cobra Gold 2015, the junta responded, "We are a strategic location for them to gain access to other countries. The US has tried to set up a base in U-Tapao and American troops are scheduled to train with Thai armed forces all year. We are the key that [the US] can't afford to lose."[57]

Such is the price for strategy not keeping pace with political developments. In a nineteen-page chapter focusing on maritime Southeast Asian "game theory" in 2014, even leading US analyst Kaplan leap-frogged from Vietnam to Myanmar. He mentioned Thailand, key to unlocking what China's Hu Jintao called the "Malacca dilemma", not a single time.

In 2015, civilian and military officials representing opposing sides of Thailand's political conflict agreed that the US was off-course. Thaksin offered that "The US interest is oil strategy, a strategy of power, but they have to look at what they are going to do with the politics in this area. In the future if something happens, the US needs to have friends here."[58] His foreign minister Surakiart agreed:

> The unity of ASEAN is in the interests of the US, the disunity of ASEAN is not. If they want ASEAN, home to 600 million people, to be the buffer of the United States against China, this approach will not achieve their objective. They know full well they will not fight with China and the Chinese know full well they will not fight the United States. Why create tension to destabilize China? Engaging and containing China has to be looked at from different perspectives, and if that were the case the US role would be welcome in Thailand as a treaty ally.[59]

To Abhisit, "The Americans are squandering opportunities, and it would be a mistake if they put us too low in priority. Geographically speaking we are in a location where our partnership with them could mean so much for their presence and influence in the whole region."[60] His finance minister Korn went further, stating that "Thailand's great advantage in its location is that, unlike other countries in Asia and ASEAN, it does not have to choose between the US and China, and yet America is almost forcing us to choose anyway."[61] Kasit narrowed the focus and alluded to the Straits:

> With these Chinese inroads, how can the United States lay low and do nothing? There is no vision out of the State Department, the White House, the US embassy, or even the American Chamber of Commerce. You cannot complain about the Chinese because the Chinese need to come down to the warm water. They need to undermine the Indians and the United States in the Indian Ocean. So what is the United States doing? Nothing.[62]

The last word, fittingly, went to a general: "Thailand can only be considered measly and insignificant to the future of American world strategy. Do you know the Aesop tale about the lion and the mouse?"[63] In the fable, a lion needlessly spares a mouse, which promises implausibly to reciprocate one day—only to make good on the promise by helping the lion escape a hunter's net.

* * *

The Chinese have long known both maritime and mainland Southeast Asia, of which Thailand is both, as the "South Sea". Its total land area, comprising ten countries, is smaller than the Indian subcontinent and is almost entirely peninsula, archipelago, or islands. According to Sarasin of the CP Group, "The Chinese see the importance of Southeast Asia definitely, the geographic and strategic importance, and they put a lot of emphasis on ASEAN. But they are more focused on the US and Russia. They see Southeast Asia through the lens of how it affects their relations with those countries."[64] Central to this is US control of the Straits of Malacca, upon which China's development and defense continue—for now—to depend.

China is the world's largest economy and its largest market by nearly every measure. It is also the world's largest net importer of oil, having doubled its demand for crude between 1995 and 2005, and is in the process of doubling it again. It consumes over 10 percent of global oil and over 20 percent of global energy overall. While Indonesia, on the eastern (China side) of the Straits, is expected to remain the largest supplier of natural gas for decades to come, the vast majority of China's oil comes from outside the region via the Straits. China is projected to import over 7 million barrels of crude oil each day by 2020, 85 percent of it through that narrow passage. As the world's energy needs double by 2030, nearly half of all new consumption will come from China and India (which, being on the Straits' western side, doesn't need it).

In 2005, China began producing and acquiring submarines at a rate of eight to one compared to the US. Five years later, China and Thailand began discussing such vessels while jointly holding the first "Blue Strike" maritime exercise. By 2014, as Beijing announced plans to increase military spending "with a special focus on enhancing the country's maritime power", it had more submarines than the US.[65] After the coup, a Thai official told former US ambassador Boyce, "Do whatever you want with Cobra Gold, we've got Dragon Gold if we need it."[66] China is expected to have more warships than PACOM in the western Pacific by the late 2020s, in Bosworth's words a "blue water navy capable of projecting power".[67]

China reportedly has never acknowledged the Pentagon's "String of Pearls", but in 2013 Xi Jinping announced a largely economic "One Belt, One Road" vision. It consists of a land-based "belt" north of China, from Russia to Europe through Central Asia, and a maritime "road" south of China, from Papua New Guinea to northeast Africa. The latter hugs the western Pacific and Indian Oceans through Southeast and South Asia, as well as the maritime Middle East to the Red Sea. Thailand is squarely incorporated. Purposely charged with historical as well as future significance, the dual-track idea has been alternately referred to by China as a 21st century "Silk Road". "I think Xi Jinping has something larger in his mind", said a Yingluck advisor in 2015, "and I don't want to see Thailand become a Chinese province. We must be partners instead of being treated as a province to the south, which we could be in ten or fifteen years. Yes it's economics, but it's always strategic positioning in this country."[68]

* * *

Consistent with Sun Tzu's 2,500-year-old *The Art of War*, China intends to prevail over the US in the Straits of Malacca without firing a shot. Despite fifteen years of comparatively more advanced mil-to-mil relations with Thailand, Beijing has spent far more political and economic capital on bypassing the Straits than on challenging the Seventh Fleet. A member of Yingluck's China team stated in 2015 that the Chinese are looking for Thailand's help in their "ultimate goal" of getting to the Indian Ocean.[69] A colleague claimed that, because Beijing sees Thailand as the center of a strategically important ASEAN, it "has no choice" but to work with Bangkok in getting to the sea.[70] Thus far into the 21st century, river, road, and rail projects joining Chuan's unfinished "land bridge" have allowed China to effectively expand its territory without having to secure and administer it. But this will change, and soon.

No later than the year 2025, construction will begin on a canal across the Isthmus of Kra with Chinese financing, engineering, and workers. Connecting the Gulf of Thailand with the Andaman Sea, it will render all other means of bypassing the Straits of Malacca ancillary and auxiliary. For China—and indeed the US—a canal is imperative, for according to the Malaysia Maritime Institute in 2015, the Straits' passage limit of 122,600 vessels per year will be reached by 2030 at the latest. That a canal will take an estimated ten years to build means that construction may commence even sooner; that it will cost at least $20 billion (at current calculations) will not be cause for delay as the Straits begins to narrow. More than twenty-five feasibility studies have reportedly been commissioned, the latest in 2005 under Thaksin.

A year after Thailand's coup, reports appeared that General Chavalit had signed a memorandum of cooperation for yet another study with Chinese authorities in Guangzhou. Both sides issued denials. The junta said that "The surrounding environment is not conducive to the project … the constitution does not allow the dismemberment of the country".[71] Yet in 2015, Chavalit's Thai–Chinese Cultural and Economic Association called a canal "inevitable".[72] Commenting on its consistency with Xi's "One Belt, One Road",[73] the association was invited by China's Communist Party to a meeting in Beijing. Security advisor Panitan was non-committal: "We don't have adequate factual information on which to base a decision on whether we should go ahead with this project."[74] Recounting his experience with the issue, Thaksin thought a canal "possible" with the generational shift in Thai leadership. "Geopolitics?", he added. "I don't know."[75] Former foreign minister Surakiart strongly disagreed:

> China is interested because it is part of what the US calls their "String of Pearls" strategy. They would not have to rely on the political pulse in the Malacca Straits, which is too much for the Chinese. But I say to the Chinese even now that they should forgo the issue, give up. It is a non-issue, it is impossible. It is an economic issue, and it is a political issue—a national issue. The digging of a canal would make people feel that Thailand is separated into two countries, and that is the factor that prevents any debate. It comes down to the territorial integrity of Thailand, and even if more perception than reality, in politics perception is reality.[76]

In the end, Thai excuses and denials are a political luxury that China's geopolitics will soon deny them. With the China Model in both countries dependent on unrelenting economic growth, neither will concern itself with territorial integrity, much less environmental concerns and local livelihoods. Billed as a commercial enterprise, a canal will double as a stanchion of China's national security, and of Thailand's by extension and alliance. Beijing will stake its claim as the primary financier, engineer, and political force, so as to exert as much control over a canal as the Seventh Fleet does over the Straits.

As for China's unsuspecting rival, a US diplomat boasted in 2015 that the Thais "are going to keep us around, they are going to play this game".[77] Yet time has all but run out and the Americans are losing badly. Having conducted the first study on a canal across the isthmus in 1972, they have not revisited the issue for over four decades. Obama's pivot had no place for one of Asia's most pivotal stretches of land, just fifty kilometers across. Symbolizing the relationship writ large, Kra is the fulcrum of a shift by Thailand long underway. In announcing the pivot, Secretary Clinton was clear: "In Asia, they ask whether we are really there to stay, whether we are likely to be distracted again by events elsewhere, whether we can make—and keep—credible economic and strategic commitments, and whether we can back those commitments with action. The answer is: We can, and we will."[78]

For the sake of America's geopolitical interests—*all of them*—there is no choice. We must.

Notes

Preface

1   See Randolph 189.

2   Interview, Chalermsuk, 19 January 2015.

Introduction

1   US Department of State, "Coup in Thailand", Press Statement, John Kerry, Secretary of State, Washington, DC, 22 May 2014.

2   Foreign Ministry of the People's Republic of China, "Foreign Ministry Spokesperson Hong Lei's Regular Press Conference on May 23, 2014", 23 May 2014.

3   Foreign Ministry of the People's Republic of China, "Foreign Ministry Spokesperson Qin Gang's Regular Press Conference on May 26, 2014", 26 May 2014.

4   The White House, 18 November 2012.

5   Foreign Ministry of the People's Republic of China, "Premier Wen Jiabao Holds Talks with Thai Counterpart Yingluck", 21 November 2012, http://www.fmprc.gov.cn/mfa_eng/topics_665678/pwjamoealapovcat_665698/t992130.shtml.

6   See Pasuk and Baker, *Thailand's Crisis* 40.

7   See "Clinton: Chinese Human Rights can't Interfere with Other Crises", *CNN*, 22 February 2009.

8   Interview, Korn, 8 May 2015.

9   Interview, State Department official with responsibility for Thailand, 9 April 2015.

Chapter 1

1   MacDonald 10.

2   See Surachart 29.

3   See Van Praagh 32.

4   See Kasian 267.

5   See Saner 23.

6   Darling 52.

7   See Fineman 35.

8   Kurlantzick, *The Ideal Man* 80.

9   See Nuechterlein 97.

10   Thak, *Thai Politics* 552.

Chapter 2

1   See Lederer and Burdick 71.

2 Stanton, October 1954.

3 Thak, *Thai Politics* 547.

4 Ibid. 597.

5 See Van Praagh 81.

6 See Fineman 72.

7 See ibid. 116.

8 See Wilson, "China, Thailand, and the Spirit of Bandung (Part I)" 154.

9 See Anuson 56.

10 Interview, Anand, 21 January 2015.

11 See Fineman 176.

12 See Van Praagh 122.

13 Fineman 145.

14 See Wilson, "China, Thailand, and the Spirit of Bandung (Part I)" 168.

15 Stanton, October 1954.

16 See Wilson, "China, Thailand, and the Spirit of Bandung (Part II)" 105.

17 Faulder.

18 Interview, Kraisak, 12 January 2015.

19 See Anuson 88.

20 Stanton, October 1954.

Chapter 3

1 See Vimol et al. 106.2.

2 See Nuechterlein 241.

3 Fineman 254.

4 See Wilson, "China, Thailand, and the Spirit of Bandung (Part II)" 126.

5 See Henderson 82.

6 Interview, Chalermsuk, 19 January 2015.

7 See Vimol et al. 106.2.

8 See Darling 187.

9 See Wilson, "China, Thailand, and the Spirit of Bandung (Part II)" 126.

10 See Connors, *Democracy and National Identity in Thailand* 70.

11 See Darling 179.

12 Interview, Kraisak, 12 January 2015.

13 See Vimol et al. 110.

14 See Randolph 49.

15 Ibid. 72.

16 Stanton, October 1954.

17 See Kien, *China and the Social World* 197.

18 See Handley 189.

19 Lane 189.

20 Randolph 16.

21 See Jackson, in Ramsay and Wiwat 107.

22 See Handley 188.

23 ASEAN, http://www.asean.org/news/item/the-asean-declaration-bangkok-declaration.

24 See Phuangkasem 16.

25 ASEAN, http://www.asean.org/news/item/the-asean-declaration-bangkok-declaration.

26 See Vimol et al. 124.

27 Ruth 25.

28 See Saner 64.

29 See Ruth 40.

30 See ibid. 79.

31 See Saner 68.

32 See Ruth 10.

33 See Saner 64.

34 See "Thailand, Laos, Cambodia, and Vietnam April 1973", A Staff Report Prepared for the Use of the Subcommittee on US Security Agreements and Commitments Abroad of the Committee on Foreign Relations, United States Senate, 1973, 8.

35 See Wiwat, in Wiwat and Warren 107.

Chapter 4

1 Interview, Kraisak, 12 January 2015.

2 Interview, Anand, 21 January 2015.

3 Ibid.

4 See Handley 220.

5 McBeth 156.

6 See Shinn, in Bunge 187.

7 Sarasin, in Wiwat and Warren 134.

8 Kasian 272.

9 See M.L. Bhansoon 274.

10 Interview, Kobsak, 14 January 2014.

11 Interview, Kraisak, 12 January 2015.

12 See Chambers, "'The Chinese and the Thais are Brothers'" 608.

13 Interview, Sarasin, 6 February 2015.

14 M.L. Bhansoon 286.

15 See Van Praagh 149.

16 See Liang 13.

17 See Saner 131.

18 See Randolph 164.

19 See ibid. 179.

20 Ibid. 169.

21 See M.L. Bhansoon 215.

22 Wiwat, in Wiwat and Warren 110.

23 See Randolph 181.

24 See M.L. Bhansoon 162.

25 Interview, Kraisak, 12 January 2015.

26 See Jackson, in Jackson and Wiwat 165.

27 See M.L. Bhansoon 224.

28 See Surachart 182.

29 Interview, Warren, 5 January 2015.

30 See Van Praagh 181.

31 Interview, Former high-ranking Thai Ministry official, 2 February 2015.

32 Interview, Kraisak, 12 January 2015.

33 Interview, Former Thai foreign minister, 2 February 2015.

34 See Pavin, *A Plastic Nation* 48.

35 See Chulacheeb 96.

36 Interview, Thai general, 22 January 2015.

37 Sarasin, in Wiwat and Warren 141.

38 See Chambers, "'The Chinese and the Thais are Brothers'" 615.

39 Interview, Former member of Communist Party of Thailand, 5 January 2015.

40 Interview, Thai general, 22 January 2015.

41 See Liang 18.

42 Interview, Rosenblatt, 7 April 2015.

43 Interview, Thai general, 22 January 2015.

44 Interview, Lane, 8 April 2015.

45 See Randolph 218.

Chapter 5

1 See Vimol et al. unnumbered.

2 Sarasin, in Wiwat and Warren 116.

3 See Van Praagh 118.

4 Jackson, in Jackson and Wiwat 172.

5 M.R. Kasem, in Ramsay and Wiwat 8.

6 Surin, in Ramsay and Wiwat 84.

7 Anonymous "Thai discussant" to Levin, in Ramsay and Wiwat 99.

8 Anand, "The United States in Asia".

9 McCargo, "Network Monarchy and Legitimacy Crises" 501.

10 See Overholt, in Ramsay and Wiwat 166.

11 Interview, Kraisak, 12 January 2015.

12 See Interview, Sulak, 11 January 2015.

13 See US Department of State, *Review of State Department Country Reports on Human Rights Practices for 1981*, Hearing before the Subcommittee on Human Rights and International Relations of the Committee on Foreign Affairs, House of Representatives, Ninety-Seventh Congress, Second Session, 28 April 1982.

14 See US Department of State, *Country Reports on Human Rights Practices for 1986*.

15 Thanat, in Jackson and Wiwat 311.

16 See Randolph 228.

17   Interview, Boyce, 4 June 2015.

18   Interview, Chalermsuk, 19 January 2015.

19   Ibid.

20   Crispin, "Thaksin's Loss".

Chapter 6

1   Interview, Jackson, 9 April 2015.

2   Interview, Korn, 8 May 2015.

3   See Rolls 96.

4   Rolls 105.

5   Pavin, *A Plastic Nation* 4.

6   Interview, Boyce, 4 June 2015.

7   Embassy Bangkok, 06BANGKOK1767, 22 March 2006.

8   Chang Noi 227.

9   Interview, Steinberg, 9 April 2015.

10   Anand, "Address of Prime Minister Anand Panyarachun to the Foreign Correspondents Club of Thailand, 25 April 1991".

11   US Department of State, Bureau of Democracy, Human Rights, and Labor, "Thailand", *Country Reports on Human Rights Practices for 1992*, 1993.

12   See Pavin, *A Plastic Nation* 83.

13   See Kasian 277.

14   Interview, Chuan, 3 August 2015.

15   See Hinton, in Evan et al. 13.

16   Crispin, "US Slips".

17   Anonymous "Thai discussant" to Sarasin, in Neher and Wiwat 52.

18   Interview, Kraisak, 12 January 2015.

19   Ibid.

20   Ibid.

21   Ibid.

22   Ibid.

23   See Interview, Surakiart, 4 August 2015.

24   Interview, Kraisak, 12 January 2015.

25   Ibid.

26   Interview, Senior Foreign Ministry official posted to Beijing, 2 February 2015.

27   Interview, Kraisak, 12 January 2015.

28   Ibid.

29   Interview, Senior Foreign Ministry official posted to Beijing, 2 February 2015.

30   Interview, Kraisak, 12 January 2015.

31   Ibid.

32   Ibid.

33   Rolls 103.

34   Interview, Kraisak, 12 January 2015.

35 Interview, Lane, 8 April 2015.

36 Interview, Fitts, 30 January 2015.

37 Interview, Anand, 21 January 2015.

38 Ibid.

39 Anand, "Address of Prime Minister Anand Panyarachun to the Foreign Correspondents Club of Thailand, 25 April 1991".

40 See Buszynski 727.

41 Interview, Jackson, 9 April 2015.

42 Interview, Boyce, 4 June 2015.

43 Interview, Karuna, 29 January 2015.

44 Interview, Anand, 21 January 2015.

45 See Handley 374.

46 Interview, Panitan, 31 January 2015.

47 Rolls 103.

48 See ibid. 103.

49 Interview, Chuan, 3 August 2015.

50 Ibid.

51 Email, Panitan, 9 June 2015.

52 Interview, Chuan, 3 August 2015.

53 See Pavin, *Reinventing Thailand* 201.

54 Interview, Chuan, 3 August 2015.

55 Chambers, "'The Chinese and the Thais are Brothers'" 626.

56 Murphy, "Beyond Balancing and Bandwagoning" 11.

57 Wurfel, in Thayer and Amer 148.

58 See Chambers, "'The Chinese and the Thais are Brothers'" 627.

59 See Pasuk and Baker, *Thailand's Crisis* 171.

60 Ibid. 3.

61 Interview, Sarasin, 6 February 2015.

62 Interview, Boyce, 4 June 2015.

63 Ibid.

64 See Interview, Bhokin, 4 February 2015.

65 See Pasuk and Baker, *Thailand's Crisis* 40.

66 See Interview, Boyce, 4 June 2015.

67 Interview, Sarasin, 6 February 2015.

68 See Pasuk and Baker, *Thailand's Crisis* 6.

69 Pasuk and Baker, *Thaksin* 17.

70 Interview, Pisan, 7 April 2015.

71 Interview, Sarasin, 6 February 2015.

72 Interview, Chuan, 3 August 2015.

73 Interview, Senior Thai politician, 6 February 2015.

74 Murphy, "Beyond Balancing and Bandwagoning" 12.

75 Interview, Chuan, 3 August 2015.

76 See Interview, Boyce, 4 June 2015.

77 http://www.academyordiplomacy.org/member/charles-e-cobb/.

78 Interview, Boyce, 4 June 2015.

79 Interview, Chuan, 3 August 2015.

80 Interview, Panitan, 31 January 2015.

81 "Address by His Excellency Chuan Leekpai, Prime Minister of Thailand", Council on Foreign Relations and the Asia Society, 11 March 1998, http://www.cfr.org/thailand/address-his-excellency-mr-chuan-leekpai-prime-minister-thailand/p57.

82 See Kusuma 191.

83 See Pavin, *A Plastic Nation* 79.

84 See Kusuma 205.

85 Interview, Chuan, 3 August 2015.

86 Chambers, "'The Chinese and the Thais are Brothers'" 621.

87 Murphy, "Beyond Balancing and Bandwagoning" 12.

88 See Chambers, "'The Chinese and the Thais are Brothers'" 625.

89 See ibid. 624.

90 Interview, Chuan, 3 August 2015.

91 See Kusuma 196.

Interface

1 Interview, Chuan, 3 August 2015.

2 Email, Boyce, 6 July 2015.

Chapter 7

1 Embassy Bangkok, 06BANGKOK4254, 18 July 2006.

2 Interview, Pansak, 21 January 2015.

3 Ferrara 87.

4 Interview, Senior State Department official, 16 July 2015.

5 Interview, Jakrapob, 26 January 2015.

6 See Lynch 339.

7 See Pavin, *Reinventing Thailand* 93.

8 Interview, Surakiart, 4 August 2015.

9 Interview, Sarasin, 6 February 2015.

10 Embassy Bangkok, 05BANGKOK3704, 6 June 2005.

11 Interview, Abhisit, 6 February 2015.

12 Interview, Sarasin, 6 February 2015.

13 Interview, Surakiart, 4 August 2015.

14 Ibid.

15 Interview, Thaksin, 21 August 2015.

16 Ibid.

17 Interview, Sarasin, 6 February 2015.

18 Email, Jakrapob, 12 August 2015.

19 Interview, Jakrapob, 26 January 2015.

20 Interview, Surakiart, 4 August 2015.

21 "Asia Cooperation Dialogue", in Surakiart 192.

22 Interview, Surakiart, 4 August 2015.

23 McCargo and Ukrist 58.

24 Ibid. 53.

25 Interview, Foreign Ministry official with responsibility for China during the Thaksin administration, 12 March 2015.

26 Ibid.

27 Interview, Ammar, 15 January 2015.

28 Embassy Bangkok, 06BANGKOK4254, 18 July 2006.

29 Embassy Bangkok, 04BANGKOK7313, 20 October 2004.

30 See ibid.

31 See Pavin, *Reinventing Thailand* 17.

32 Interview, Sulak, 12 January 2015.

33 Interview, Sarasin, 6 February 2015.

34 See Chambers, "'The Chinese and the Thais are Brothers'" 599.

35 "Where Does Thailand Stand Now?", in Surakiart 87.

36 Embassy Bangkok, 04BANGKOK7313, 20 October 2004.

37 Ibid.

38 Embassy Bangkok, 05BANGKOK7460, 2 December 2005.

39 Interview, Two Thai Foreign Ministry officials, 5 February 2015.

40 Interview, Senior Foreign Ministry official posted to Washington, 2 February 2015.

41 See Kurtantzick, *Charm Offensive* 67.

42 Embassy Bangkok, 06BANGKOK2826, 11 May 2006.

43 Embassy Bangkok, 06BANGKOK4480, 25 July 2006.

44 Embassy Bangkok, 04BANGKOK7313, 20 October 2004.

45 Ibid.

46 See Embassy Bangkok, 06BANGKOK5705, 15 September 2006.

47 Interview, Surakiart, 4 August 2015.

48 Interview, Jakrapob, 26 January 2015.

49 Interview, Pansak, 21 January 2015.

50 Interview, Thaksin, 21 August 2015.

51 Interview, Kantathi, 20 September 2015.

52 Interview, Thaksin, 21 August 2015.

53 Ibid.

54 Interview, Foreign Ministry official with responsibility for China during the Thaksin administration, 12 March 2015.

55 Interview, Kraisak, 2 February 2015.

56 Embassy Bangkok, 06BANGKOK1372, 6 March 2006.

57 Embassy Bangkok, 05BANGKOK5791, 9 September 2005.

58 See Embassy Bangkok, 05BANGKOK7116, 16 November 2005.

59 Interview, Sarasin, 6 February 2015.

60 "Asia: A Common Agenda", in Surakiart 44.

61 Embassy Bangkok, 06BANGKOK1372, 6 March 2006.

62 See Embassy Bangkok, 04BANGKOK7313, 20 October 2004.

63 Interview, Kraisak, 2 February 2015.

64 See Embassy Bangkok, 04BANGKOK7313, 20 October 2004.

65 Ibid.

66 Ibid.

67 See Embassy Bangkok, 05BANGKOK3725, 7 June 2005.

68 See Embassy Bangkok, 04BANGKOK7313, 20 October 2004.

69 See ibid.

70 Interview, Thaksin, 21 August 2015.

71 Embassy Bangkok, 04BANGKOK7313, 20 October 2004.

72 Interview, Sunai, 30 January 2015.

73 See Embassy Bangkok, 04BANGKOK7313, 20 October 2004.

74 Embassy Bangkok, 05BANGKOK7460, 2 December 2005.

75 Embassy Bangkok, 06BANGKOK6095, 5 October 2006.

76 Interview, Panitan, 31 January 2015.

77 See Macan-Markar, "China's October Revelation".

78 Interview, Thaksin, 21 August 2015.

79 Ibid.

80 Embassy Bangkok, 04BANGKOK7313, 20 October 2004.

81 See ibid.

82 Interview, Suranand, 13 January 2015.

83 Embassy Bangkok, 04BANGKOK7313, 20 October 2004.

84 Ibid.

85 "The 57th Session of the Commission on Human Rights", in Surakiart 25–26.

86 See Pasuk and Baker, *Thaksin* 141.

87 Embassy Bangkok, 05BANGKOK5018, 4 August 2005.

88 Interview, Suranand, 13 January 2015.

89 Interview, Thaksin, 21 August 2015.

90 Ibid.

91 Wyatt 275.

92 Interview, Bhokin, 4 February 2015.

93 Interview, Thaksin, 21 August 2015.

94 See Kurtantzick, *Charm Offensive* 146.

95 Embassy Bangkok, 05BANGKOK2431, 5 April 2005.

96 Interview, Thaksin, 21 August 2015.

97 See Embassy Bangkok, 06BANGKOK2359, 24 April 2006.

98 Ibid.

99 Embassy Bangkok, 05BANGKOK2431, 5 April 2005.

100 Interview, Thaksin, 21 August 2015.

101 Embassy Bangkok, 05BANGKOK2431, 5 April 2005.

102 Embassy Bangkok, 05BANGKOK3073, 9 May 2005.

103 Interview, Thaksin, 21 August 2015.

104 See "Thaksin's Thai Recipe", *Asia Times*, 25 May 2001.

105 See Embassy Bangkok, 06BANGKOK1472, 9 March 2006.

106 See Yong Mun Cheong, in Tarling 111.

107 Interview, Sarasin, 6 February 2015.

108 See Kasit, in Montesano et al. 164.

109 Chang Noi 139.

110 Interview, Sunai, 30 January 2015.

111 See Embassy Bangkok, 06BANGKOK1472, 9 March 2006.

112 Foreign Ministry Spokesperson Qin Gang's Comment on the Current Situations of Thailand, 20 September 2006, http://www.fmprc.gov.cn/eng/xwfw/s2510/2535/t272786.shtml.

113 See Embassy Bangkok, 06BANGKOK6095, 5 October 2006.

114 Ibid.

115 Ibid.

116 Interview, Thaksin, 21 August 2015.

117 Ibid.

Chapter 8

1 Interview, Thaksin, 21 August 2015.

2 Embassy Bangkok, 05BANGKOK2219, 29 March 2005.

3 See Pasuk and Baker, *Thaksin* 277.

4 Interview, Surakiart, 4 August 2015.

5 "Where Does Thailand Stand Now?", in Surakiart 91.

6 See Montesano, "Thailand in 2001" 98.

7 Asia Foundation 2.

8 Interview, Surakiart, 4 August 2015.

9 Interview, Jackson, 9 April 2015.

10 Ibid.

11 Ibid.

12 Joint Statement between the United States of America and the Kingdom of Thailand, 14 December 2001.

13 "Asian Civil Society Forum", in Surakiart 269.

14 "Inquiry Into the Treatment of Detainees in U.S. Custody", Report of the Committee on Armed Services, United States Senate, 110th Congress, 2nd Session, 20 November 2008, xiii.

15 See ibid. 14.

16 See Rodriguez and Harlow 67–68.

17 See Office of Inspector General 20.

18 Email, Jakrapob, 12 August 2015.

19 See Open Society Justice Initiative 111.

20 Open Society Justice Initiative 36.

21 Rodriguez and Harlow 54.

22 Interview, Boyce, 4 June 2015.

23 Office of Inspector General 36.

24 Embassy Bangkok, 05BANGKOK6953, 4 November 2005.

25 Interview, Surakiart, 4 August 2015.

26 Interview, Pansak, 21 January 2015.

27 See Achara, "Confess on Torture".

28 Embassy Bangkok, 05BANGKOK6953, 4 November 2005.

29 Embassy Bangkok, 05BANGKOK7529, 74 December 2005.

30 Interview, Thaksin, 21 August 2015.

31 Interview, Surakiart, 4 August 2015.

32 Ibid.

33 See Ehrlich, "Thailand Takes 'Hospitable' Action".

34 Interview, Chalermsuk, 19 January 2015.

35 See Wheeler, in Chaiwat 184.

36 Dalpino, "American Views: Southeast Asia" 62.

37 Interview, Thaksin, 21 August 2015.

38 Interview, Kantathi, 20 September 2015.

39 See Napisa and Chambers, in Chambers 83.

40 See Ehrlich, "Thailand Takes 'Hospitable' Action".

41 Interview, Thaksin, 21 August 2015.

42 See Wheeler, in Chaiwat 184.

43 Interview, Kantathi, 20 September 2015.

44 Ibid.

45 Embassy Bangkok, 05BANGKOK2838, 26 April 2005.

46 Embassy Bangkok, 05BANGKOK3208, 13 May 2005.

47 Embassy Bangkok, 06BANGKOK1215, 28 February 2006.

48 See Wheeler, in Chaiwat 180.

49 See ibid. 180.

50 Embassy Bangkok, 05BANGKOK3182, 11 May 2005.

51 Embassy Bangkok, 05BANGKOK1233, 17 February 2005.

52 See Embassy Bangkok, 05BANGKOK4108, 23 June 2005.

53 See Embassy Bangkok, 05BANGKOK5965, 16 September 2005.

54 Embassy Bangkok, 05BANGKOK3203, 13 May 2005.

55 Embassy Bangkok, 05BANGKOK2062, 22 March 2005.

56 Embassy Bangkok, 05BANGKOK3203, 13 May 2005.

57 Ibid.

58 See Embassy Bangkok, 05BANGKOK2013, 18 March 2005.

59 Embassy Bangkok, 05BANGKOK7729, 19 December 2005.

60 See Wheeler, in Chaiwat 188.

61 Embassy Bangkok, 05BANGKOK3182, 11 May 2005.

62 Embassy Bangkok, 05BANGKOK1038, 9 February 2005.

63 Interview, Bhokin, 4 February 2015.

64 See Embassy Bangkok, 05BANGKOK2062, 22 March 2005.

65 See Wheeler, in Chaiwat 179.

66 See Embassy Bangkok, 05BANGKOK5393, 22 August 2005.

67 Embassy Bangkok, 05BANGKOK6524, 14 October 2005.

68 Interview, Klein, 16 January 2015.

69 Ibid.

70 See Embassy Bangkok, 06BANGKOK3231, 30 May 2006.

71 Embassy Bangkok, 06BANGKOK2826, 11 May 2006.

72 Embassy Bangkok, 06BANGKOK2338, 21 April 2006.

73 Embassy Bangkok, 06BANGKOK5610, 13 September 2006.

74 Embassy Bangkok, 05BANGKOK6524, 14 October 2005.

75 Embassy Bangkok, 05BANGKOK3313, 19 May 2005.

76 Embassy Bangkok, 05BANGKOK5791, 9 September 2005.

77 Embassy Bangkok, 05BANGKOK7529, 7 December 2005.

78 Embassy Bangkok, 06BANGKOK926, 16 February 2006.

79 Interview, Kraisak, 2 February 2015.

80 Interview, Sunai, 30 January 2015.

81 Embassy Bangkok, 06BANGKOK5463, 6 September 2006.

82 Embassy Bangkok, 06BANGKOK1176, 27 February 2006.

83 Embassy Bangkok, 05BANGKOK2536, 8 April 2005.

84 Embassy Bangkok, 05BANGKOK5020, 4 August 2005.

85 Emergency Decree on Government Administration in States of Emergency, B.E. 2548 (19 July 2005), Section 17.

86 Embassy Bangkok, 05BANGKOK5455, 24 August 2005.

87 Kyung-won, Koh, and Sobhan 8.

88 Klausner, "Transforming Thai Culture" 288.

89 "Campaign to Spread Word on US Aims", *The Nation*, 8 November 2001.

90 Interview, Jackson, 9 April 2015.

91 Embassy Bangkok, 05BANGKOK1169, 15 February 2005.

92 Interview, Cole, 13 April 2015.

93 Interview, Thaksin, 21 August 2015.

94 Interview, Brandon, 8 April 2015.

95 Interview, Boyce, 4 June 2015.

96 Embassy Bangkok, 05BANGKOK2219, 29 March 2005.

97 Interview, Boyce, 4 June 2015.

98 Asia Foundation 10.

99 Interview, Thaksin, 21 August 2015.

100 Interview, Kraisak, 2 February 2015.

101 Interview, Thaksin, 21 August 2015.

102 Interview, Panitan, 31 January 2015.

103 Interview, Cole, 13 April 2015.

104 Interview, Sarasin, 6 February 2015.

105 See Embassy Bangkok, 05BANGKOK5393, 22 August 2005.

106 Ibid.

107 Interview, Thaksin, 21 August 2015.

108 Email, Jakrapob, 12 August 2015.

109 See Pavin, *Reinventing Thailand* 234.

110 See Wheeler, "Mr. Thaksin Goes to Washington" 3.

111 See Wheeler, in Chaiwat 188.

112 Embassy Bangkok, 05BANGKOK1573, 3 March 2005.

113 See Embassy Bangkok, 05BANGKOK1527, 2 March 2005.

114 Ibid.

115 See Embassy Bangkok, 06BANGKOK1538, 13 March 2006.

116 Interview, Surakiart, 4 August 2015.

117 Interview, Kantathi, 20 September 2015.

118 Ibid.

119 Embassy Bangkok, 05BANGKOK6138, 26 September 2005.

120 Embassy Bangkok, 05BANGKOK1233, 17 February 2005.

121 See Embassy Bangkok, 05BANGKOK3208, 13 May 2005.

122 Embassy Bangkok, 06BANGKOK1471, 9 March 2006.

123 Interview, Two Thai Foreign Ministry officials, 5 February 2015.

124 Ibid.

125 Interview, Kantathi, 20 September 2015.

126 Ibid.

127 Ibid.

128 Ibid.

129 Ibid.

130 Embassy Bangkok, 06BANGKOK1119, 24 February 2006.

131 Interview, Kantathi, 20 September 2015.

132 See Embassy Bangkok, 05BANGKOK6978, 8 November 2005.

133 See Pavin, *Reinventing Thailand* 148.

134 Embassy Bangkok, 06BANGKOK4742, 4 August 2006.

135 See Embassy Bangkok, 06BANGKOK5032, 17 August 2006.

136 Interview, Kantathi, 20 September 2015.

137 Ibid.

138 Ibid.

139 "Thailand and the United States", in Surakiart 367.

140 Interview, Kantathi, 20 September 2015.

141 Embassy Bangkok, 04BANGKOK8485, 16 December 2004.

142 Ibid.

143 Embassy Bangkok, 06BANGKOK689, 6 February 2006.

144 See Embassy Bangkok, 05BANGKOK5271, 17 August 2005.

145 Embassy Bangkok, 05BANGKOK7033, 10 November 2005.

146 Embassy Bangkok, 04BANGKOK8485, 16 December 2004.

147 Ibid.

148 Embassy Bangkok, 06BANGKOK492, 26 January 2006.

149 Embassy Bangkok, 05BANGKOK1072, 10 February 2005.

150 Embassy Bangkok, 05BANGKOK1169, 15 February 2005.

151 Embassy Bangkok, 05BANGKOK1072, 10 February 2005.

152 Embassy Bangkok, 05BANGKOK5791, 9 September 2005.

153 See Embassy Bangkok, 04BANGKOK8485, 16 December 2004.

154 Embassy Bangkok, 05BANGKOK1072, 10 February 2005.

155 US Department of State, "Open Skies Agreements", http://www.state.gov/e/eb/tra/ata/.

156 Embassy Bangkok, 04BANGKOK8485, 16 December 2004.

157 Embassy Bangkok, 05BANGKOK7033, 10 November 2005.

158 Embassy Bangkok, 06BANGKOK3354, 5 June 2006.

159 Interview, Kantathi, 20 September 2015.

160 See Embassy Bangkok, 06BANGKOK429, 23 January 2006.

161 See Embassy Bangkok, 05BANGKOK3208, 13 May 2005.

162 Embassy Bangkok, 05BANGKOK6693, 25 October 2005.

163 Embassy Bangkok, 05BANGKOK7090, 16 November 2005.

164 Embassy Bangkok, 05BANGKOK1425, 25 February 2005.

165 Embassy Bangkok, 06BANGKOK1317, 3 March 2006.

166 Embassy Bangkok, 06BANGKOK689, 6 February 2006.

167 Embassy Bangkok, 05BANGKOK1431, 25 February 2005.

168 Macan-Markar, "US Deal Rankles".

169 See Allison.

170 See Pavin, *Reinventing Thailand* 136.

171 See Embassy Bangkok, 06BANGKOK689, 6 February 2006.

172 Ibid.

173 Embassy Bangkok, 04BANGKOK8485, 16 December 2004.

174 Embassy Bangkok, 06BANGKOK3354, 5 June 2006.

175 Ibid.

176 Embassy Bangkok, 06BANGKOK4685, 2 August 2006.

177 Email, Aldis, 19 February 2017.

178 Interview, Two Thai Foreign Ministry officials, 5 February 2015.

179 Interview, Kantathi, 20 September 2015.

180 See Embassy Bangkok, 04BANGKOK7313, 16 December 2004.

181 Interview, US diplomat, 9 April 2015.

182 Ibid.

183 Ibid.

184 Embassy Bangkok, 06BANGKOK352, 19 January 2006.

185 Embassy Bangkok, 05BANGKOK7599, 13 December 2005.
186 Interview, US diplomat, 9 April 2015.
187 Crispin, "Thaksin's Loss".
188 Interview, Cole, 13 April 2015.
189 Embassy Bangkok, 05BANGKOK7599, 13 December 2005.
190 Embassy Bangkok, 05BANGKOK1105, 11 February 2005.
191 Embassy Bangkok, 05BANGKOK1635, 7 March 2005.
192 Ehrlich, "Thailand Joins Missile Game".
193 Embassy Bangkok, 05BANGKOK5456, 24 August 2006.
194 Embassy Bangkok, 06BANGKOK821, 10 February 2006.
195 Interview, Thaksin, 21 August 2015.
196 Embassy Bangkok, 05BANGKOK1266, 18 February 2005.
197 Embassy Bangkok, 05BANGKOK2010, 18 March 2005.
198 Embassy Bangkok, 06BANGKOK524, 27 January 2006.
199 Embassy Bangkok, 06BANGKOK1176, 27 February 2006.
200 Interview, Pansak, 21 January 2015.
201 Interview, Sarasin, 6 February 2015.
202 Embassy Bangkok, 05BANGKOK3130, 11 May 2005.
203 See ibid.
204 Guerin.
205 Embassy Bangkok, 05BANGKOK1038, 9 February 2005.
206 See Embassy Bangkok, 05BANGKOK706, 27 January 2005.
207 Embassy Bangkok, 05BANGKOK1431, 25 February 2005.
208 Embassy Bangkok, 05BANGKOK1157, 15 February 2005.
209 Interview, Chalermsuk, 19 January 2015.
210 Interview, Thaksin, 21 August 2015.
211 Embassy Bangkok, 05BANGKOK1157, 15 February 2005.
212 Interview, Kantathi, 20 September 2015.
213 Interview, Surakiart, 4 August 2015.
214 Embassy Bangkok, 05BANGKOK7045, 10 November 2005.
215 Embassy Bangkok, 06BANGKOK1215, 28 February 2006.
216 Embassy Bangkok, 06BANGKOK3396, 6 June 2006.
217 Ibid.
218 Ibid.
219 Interview, Kantathi, 20 September 2015.
220 Interview, Surakiart, 4 August 2015.
221 Embassy Bangkok, 04BANGKOK7313, 20 October 2004.
222 Ibid.
223 Ibid.
224 See Jeerawat.
225 See Embassy Bangkok, 05BANGKOK3725, 7 June 2005.
226 Phar.

227 Embassy Bangkok, 06BANGKOK1372, 6 March 2006.

228 Embassy Bangkok, 05BANGKOK5791, 9 September 2005.

229 Embassy Bangkok, 05BANGKOK5456, 24 August 2005.

230 Embassy Bangkok, 05BANGKOK5366, 19 August 2005.

231 Embassy Bangkok, 05BANGKOK7030, 10 November 2005.

232 Ibid.

233 Embassy Bangkok, 06BANGKOK352, 19 January 2006.

234 Embassy Bangkok, 05BANGKOK7030, 10 November 2005.

235 Embassy Bangkok, 06BANGKOK793, 10 February 2006.

236 See Embassy Bangkok, 06BANGKOK351, 19 January 2006.

237 Embassy Bangkok, 06BANGKOK1236, 1 March 2006.

238 See Embassy Bangkok, 06BANGKOK1176, 27 February 2006.

239 Embassy Bangkok, 06BANGKOK793, 10 February 2006.

240 Interview, Thaksin, 21 August 2015.

241 Embassy Bangkok, 06BANGKOK3111, 24 May 2006.

242 Embassy Bangkok, 05BANGKOK7030, 10 November 2005.

243 Ibid.

244 Embassy Bangkok, 06BANGKOK1174, 27 February 2006.

245 Embassy Bangkok, 06BANGKOK2624, 4 May 2006.

246 Ibid.

247 Embassy Bangkok, 06BANGKOK5148, 23 August 2006.

248 Ibid.

249 Embassy Bangkok, 05BANGKOK3945, 15 June 2005.

250 Embassy Bangkok, 06BANGKOK2484, 28 April 2006.

251 Embassy Bangkok, 05BANGKOK1038, 9 February 2005.

252 Ibid.

253 Embassy Bangkok, 05BANGKOK2280, 31 March 2005.

254 Embassy Bangkok, 05BANGKOK7272, 23 November 2005.

255 See Embassy Bangkok, 05BANGKOK6088, 23 September 2005.

256 Embassy Bangkok, 05BANGKOK2280, 31 March 2005.

257 See Embassy Bangkok, 05BANGKOK1187, 16 February 2005.

258 Embassy Bangkok, 05BANGKOK7460, 2 December 2005.

259 Embassy Bangkok, 06BANGKOK4803, 8 August 2006.

260 Interview, Boyce, 4 June 2015.

261 Embassy Bangkok, 05BANGKOK7460, 2 December 2005.

262 Embassy Bangkok, 06BANGKOK5705, 15 September 2006.

263 See Embassy Bangkok, 05BANGKOK7460, 2 December 2005.

264 Embassy Bangkok, 06BANGKOK3608, 16 June 2006.

265 See Embassy Bangkok, 06BANGKOK4254, 18 July 2006.

266 Embassy Bangkok, 05BANGKOK7460, 2 December 2005.

267 Embassy Bangkok, 06BANGKOK4254, 18 July 2006.

268 See ibid.

269 Embassy Bangkok, 06BANGKOK3743, 23 June 2006.

270 See Embassy Bangkok, 06BANGKOK5705, 15 September 2006.

271 See ibid.

272 Ibid.

273 Embassy Bangkok, 05BANGKOK7529, 7 December 2005.

274 Embassy Bangkok, 06BANGKOK1214, 28 February 2006.

275 Embassy Bangkok, 06BANGKOK1411, 7 March 2006.

276 See Embassy Bangkok, 06BANGKOK1601, 15 March 2006.

277 Embassy Bangkok, 06BANGKOK1302, 2 March 2006.

278 See Embassy Bangkok, 06BANGKOK1825, 24 March 2006.

279 See Embassy Bangkok, 06BANGKOK1767, 22 March 2006.

280 Embassy Bangkok, 06BANGKOK1473, 9 March 2006.

281 See Fullbrook, "Smooth-sailing".

282 Embassy Bangkok, 06BANGKOK3180, 26 May 2006.

283 Embassy Bangkok, 06BANGKOK2990, 18 May 2006.

284 Embassy Bangkok, 06BANGKOK2988, 18 May 2006.

285 Ibid.

286 See McCargo, "Toxic Thaksin".

287 See Embassy Bangkok, 06BANGKOK4212, 14 July 2006.

288 Embassy Bangkok, 06BANGKOK4038, 7 June 2006.

289 Ibid.

290 Ibid.

291 Embassy Bangkok, 06BANGKOK3997, 6 July 2006.

292 Embassy Bangkok, 06BANGKOK4041, 7 July 2006.

293 Embassy Bangkok, 06BANGKOK3963, 5 July 2006.

294 Interview, Jackson, 9 April 2015.

295 Embassy Bangkok, 06BANGKOK5463, 6 September 2006.

296 Embassy Bangkok, 06BANGKOK5423, 5 September 2006.

297 Interview, Boyce, 4 June 2015.

298 Ibid.

299 Ibid.

300 Ibid.

301 Embassy Bangkok, 06BANGKOK5973, 28 September 2006.

302 Interview, Kantathi, 20 September 2015.

303 Interview, Thaksin, 21 August 2015.

304 Ibid.

305 "U.S. Concerned about Thai Coup but not Rushing to Judgment", *International Herald Tribune*, 19 September 2006.

306 Interview, Thaksin, 21 August 2015.

307 Embassy Bangkok, 06BANGKOK6395, 19 October 2006.

308 Interview, Boyce, 4 June 2015.

309 Embassy Bangkok, 06BANGKOK5800, 20 September 2006.

310 Embassy Bangkok, 06BANGKOK5811, 20 September 2006.

311 Interview, Boyce, 4 June 2015.

312 Interview, US diplomat, 9 April 2015.

313 Interview, Jackson, 9 April 2015.

314 Interview, Anand, 21 January 2015.

315 See Embassy Bangkok, 06BANGKOK5814, 20 September 2006.

316 See Embassy Bangkok, 06BANGKOK6121, 5 October 2006.

317 Embassy Bangkok, 06BANGKOK5811, 20 September 2006.

318 Embassy Bangkok, 06BANGKOK5928, 26 September 2006.

319 Embassy Bangkok, 06BANGKOK6004, 29 September 2006.

320 Embassy Bangkok, 07BANGKOK2790, 17 May 2007.

321 See Embassy Bangkok, 06BANGKOK5814, 20 September 2006.

322 Embassy Bangkok, 06BANGKOK5928, 26 September 2006.

323 See Chambers, *Knights* 232.

324 Embassy Bangkok, 06BANGKOK5973, 28 September 2006.

325 Interview, Boyce, 4 June 2015.

326 Interview, Senior Thaksin cabinet member, 20 September 2015.

327 Embassy Bangkok, 06BANGKOK5929, 26 September 2006.

328 Embassy Bangkok, 06BANGKOK5814, 20 September 2006.

329 Embassy Bangkok, 06BANGKOK5836, 21 September 2006.

330 Embassy Bangkok, 06BANGKOK5973, 28 September 2006.

331 Montesano, "Thailand: A Reckoning with History Begins" 323.

332 Embassy Bangkok, 06BANGKOK5799, 20 September 2006.

333 Ibid.

334 Ibid.

335 Embassy Bangkok, 06BANGKOK6004, 29 September 2006.

336 Crispin, "Thaksin's Loss".

337 Embassy Bangkok, 06BANGKOK6395, 19 October 2006.

338 Interview, Boyce, 4 June 2015.

339 Embassy Bangkok, 06BANGKOK5799, 20 September 2006.

340 Interview, Chalermsuk, 19 January 2015.

341 Embassy Bangkok, 06BANGKOK6442, 24 October 2006.

342 Embassy Bangkok, 06BANGKOK6095, 5 October 2006.

343 Ibid.

344 Interview, Suranand, 13 January 2015.

345 Ibid.

346 Embassy Bangkok, 05BANGKOK1921, 16 March 2005.

347 Ibid.

348 See Embassy Bangkok, 06BANGKOK6095, 5 October 2006.

349 See Chambers, "'The Chinese and the Thais are Brothers'" 623.

350 Interview, Foreign Ministry official with responsibility for China during the Thaksin administration, 12 March 2015.

351 Interview, Chulacheeb, 18 May 2015.

352 Interview, Senior Foreign Ministry official with experience in China during Yingluck administration, 22 January 2015.

353 Interview, Suranand, 13 January 2015.

Chapter 9

1 Bush, "Remarks by President George W. Bush in Bangkok, Thailand".

2 See "Repression no Route to Reconciliation", *Bangkok Post*, 29 June 2014.

3 Interview, Abhisit, 6 February 2015.

4 Clinton.

5 Ibid.

6 Embassy Bangkok, 07BANGKOK756, 7 February 2007.

7 See "China, Thailand Seek Stronger Ties as Sondthi Visits China", *Xinhua*, 22 January 2007.

8 Embassy Bangkok, 07BANGKOK1265, 2 March 2007.

9 Interview, Foreign Ministry official assigned to China during the Thaksin and Surayud administrations, 12 March 2015.

10 Embassy Bangkok, 06BANGKOK7603, 27 December 2006.

11 Embassy Bangkok, 06BANGKOK7397, 14 December 2006.

12 Embassy Bangkok, 06BANGKOK7386, 13 December 2006.

13 See Embassy Bangkok, 06BANGKOK6561, 30 October 2006.

14 See Crispin, "Thaksin's Loss".

15 See Embassy Bangkok, 07BANGKOK226, 11 January 2007.

16 Embassy Bangkok, 07BANGKOK231, 11 January 2007.

17 Ibid.

18 Ibid.

19 Embassy Bangkok, 07BANGKOK179, 10 January 2007.

20 See Embassy Bangkok, 07BANGKOK940, 15 February 2007.

21 Embassy Bangkok, 07BANGKOK1598, 16 March 2007.

22 Embassy Bangkok, 07BANGKOK740, 7 February 2007.

23 Embassy Bangkok, 07BANGKOK2749, 16 May 2007.

24 Embassy Bangkok, 07BANGKOK2503, 3 May 2007.

25 Embassy Bangkok, 07BANGKOK2875, 23 May 2007.

26 Embassy Bangkok, 07BANGKOK2790, 17 May 2007.

27 Embassy Bangkok, 07BANGKOK3979, 20 July 2007.

28 Ibid.

29 Embassy Bangkok, 07BANGKOK4127, 31 July 2007.

30 Embassy Bangkok, 06BANGKOK6290, 13 October 2006.

31 Ibid.

32 Embassy Bangkok, 07BANGKOK2271, 23 April 2007.

33 Ibid.

34 See Embassy Bangkok, 07BANGKOK5459, 18 October 2007.

35   See Embassy Bangkok, 07BANGKOK1419, 9 March 2007.

36   Interview, Thai dignitary, 2 February 2015.

37   Embassy Bangkok, 07BANGKOK940, 15 February 2007.

38   Interview, Jakrapob, 26 January 2015.

39   Crispin, "Thaksin's Loss".

40   Embassy Bangkok, 06BANGKOK7386, 13 December 2006.

41   See Pavin, "Diplomacy under Siege" 452.

42   Embassy Bangkok, 06CHIANGMAI217, 12 December 2006.

43   Embassy Bangkok, 06BANGKOK3202, 26 May 2006.

44   See "Officials: U.S.–Thai FTA Talks not Given Up", *Xinhua*, 24 July 2007.

45   See Chanlet-Avery 13.

46   "Officials: U.S.–Thai FTA Talks not Given Up", *Xinhua*, 24 July 2007.

47   Interview, Kantathi, 20 September 2015.

48   Embassy Bangkok, 07BANGKOK2542, 7 May 2007.

49   See Macan-Markar, "Sparks Fly".

50   Crispin, "The Urge to Splurge".

51   See Embassy Bangkok, 07BANGKOK5234, 4 October 2007.

52   See ibid.

53   Embassy Bangkok, 07BANGKOK271, 12 January 2007.

54   Embassy Bangkok, 06BANGKOK7388, 13 December 2006.

55   See Embassy Bangkok, 07BANGKOK5036, 20 September 2007.

56   Embassy Bangkok, 07BANGKOK5126, 27 September 2007.

57   Embassy Bangkok, 07BANGKOK4644, 29 August 2007.

58   Ibid.

59   Interview, Senior State Department official, 16 July 2015.

60   Embassy Bangkok, 07BANGKOK1973, 4 April 2007.

61   See Embassy Bangkok, 07BANGKOK5569, 28 October 2007.

62   Embassy Bangkok, 06BANGKOK6395, 19 October 2006.

63   Embassy Bangkok, 06BANGKOK6324, 16 October 2006.

64   Embassy Bangkok, 06BANGKOK6442, 24 October 2006.

65   Embassy Bangkok, 07BANGKOK358, 18 January 2007.

66   Embassy Bangkok, 07BANGKOK740, 7 February 2007.

67   Embassy Bangkok, 07BANGKOK4127, 31 July 2007.

68   Ibid.

69   See Embassy Bangkok, 07BANGKOK3499, 25 June 2007.

70   Embassy Bangkok, 07BANGKOK3755, 9 July 2007.

71   Chang Noi 230.

72   Embassy Bangkok, 07BANGKOK5585, 30 October 2007.

73   Embassy Bangkok, 06BANGKOK7359, 10 December 2006.

74   Foreign Ministry of the People's Republic of China, Foreign Ministry Spokesman Qin Gang's Remarks on Thailand's General Election, 26 December 2007, http://www.fmprc.gov.cn/eng/xwfw/s2510/2535/t393199.shtml.

75 See Horn.

76 "Thai New PM Stresses to Enhance Thai–Sino Relationship", *Xinhua*, 31 January 2008.

77 See Crispin, "The Thai Military's".

78 Interview, Sarasin, 6 February 2015.

79 Embassy Bangkok, 07BANGKOK6158, 14 December 2007.

80 Interview, Senior US embassy official who served under John, 10 April 2015.

81 Interview, Boyce, 4 June 2015.

82 Interview, US diplomat, 9 April 2015.

83 Yamamoto, Pranee, and Ahsan 56.

84 Embassy Bangkok, 08BANGKOK3298, 5 November 2008.

85 Embassy Bangkok, 08BANGKOK3659, 16 December 2008.

86 See Embassy Bangkok, 08BANGKOK340, 1 February 2008.

87 Ibid.

88 See Embassy Bangkok, 08BANGKOK609, 26 February 2008.

89 Embassy Bangkok, 08BANGKOK382, 6 February 2008.

90 Embassy Bangkok, 08BANGKOK1632, 28 May 2008.

91 Embassy Bangkok, 08BANGKOK1290, 28 April 2008.

92 See Ehrlich, "US Helps Thailand".

93 Embassy Bangkok, 08BANGKOK2243, 1 August 2008.

94 Bush, "Remarks by President George W. Bush in Bangkok, Thailand".

95 Crispin, "US, Thailand".

96 See Embassy Bangkok, 08BANGKOK3119, 16 October 2008.

97 Embassy Bangkok, 08BANGKOK3167, 21 October 2008.

98 Embassy Bangkok, 08BANGKOK3191, 22 October 2008.

99 Embassy Bangkok, 08BANGKOK3209, 24 October 2008.

100 Embassy Bangkok, 08BANGKOK3492, 26 November 2008.

101 Embassy Bangkok, 08BANGKOK3640, 15 December 2008.

102 Embassy Bangkok, 08BANGKOK3632, 12 December 2008.

103 See Crispin, "The Thai Military's".

104 Embassy Bangkok, 08BANGKOK3119, 16 October 2008.

105 Embassy Bangkok, 08BANGKOK1670, 2 June 2008.

106 Embassy Bangkok, 09BANGKOK213, 28 January 2009.

107 Embassy Bangkok, 08BANGKOK2591, 29 August 2008.

108 Interview, Foreign Ministry official with experience in China after the Thaksin administration, 12 March 2015.

109 Interview, Noppadon, 18 June 2015.

110 Embassy Bangkok, 08BANGKOK1006, 31 March 2008.

111 Embassy Bangkok, 08BANGKOK1218, 22 April 2008.

112 Embassy Bangkok, 08BANGKOK1006, 31 March 2008.

113 Embassy Bangkok, 08BANGKOK2999, 2 October 2008.

114 Bush, "Remarks by President George W. Bush in Bangkok, Thailand".

Thailand

115 Embassy Bangkok, 08BANGKOK606, 26 February 2008.

116 Interview, Foreign Ministry official with experience in China after the Thaksin administration, 12 March 2015.

117 Ibid.

118 Crispin, "US, Thailand".

119 Embassy Bangkok, 08BANGKOK2343, 1 August 2008.

120 Embassy Bangkok, 08BANGKOK2643, 5 September 2008.

121 Embassy Bangkok, 08BANGKOK2619, 3 September 2008.

122 Ibid.

123 Embassy Bangkok, 08BANGKOK429, 8 February 2008.

124 Embassy Bangkok, 08BANGKOK3492, 26 November 2008.

125 Embassy Bangkok, 08BANGKOK3143, 17 October 2008.

126 Embassy Bangkok, 08BANGKOK3317, 6 November 2008.

127 Interview, Thaksin, 21 August 2015.

128 See Embassy Bangkok, 08BANGKOK968, 27 March 2008.

129 Embassy Bangkok, 08BANGKOK609, 26 February 2008.

130 Interview, Sunai, 30 January 2015.

131 Interview, Noppadon, 18 June 2015.

132 Embassy Bangkok, 08BANGKOK2269, 25 July 2008.

133 See ibid.

134 Ibid.

135 Ibid.

136 See ibid.

137 Embassy Bangkok, 08BANGKOK609, 26 February 2008.

138 Embassy Bangkok, 08BANGKOK2269, 25 July 2008.

139 Interview, Noppadon, 18 June 2015.

140 Embassy Bangkok, 08BANGKOK1254, 24 April 2008.

141 Embassy Bangkok, 08BANGKOK3099, 16 October 2008.

142 Embassy Bangkok, 08BANGKOK1293, 28 April 2008.

143 Crispin, "What Obama Means".

144 Embassy Bangkok, 08BANGKOK835, 14 March 2008.

145 Embassy Bangkok, 08BANGKOK724, 7 March 2008.

146 Embassy Bangkok, 08BANGKOK835, 14 March 2008.

147 Ibid.

148 Embassy Bangkok, 08BANGKOK609, 26 February 2008.

149 Embassy Bangkok, 08BANGKOK1327, 30 April 2008.

150 Embassy Bangkok, 08BANGKOK1283, 28 April 2008.

151 Embassy Bangkok, 08BANGKOK2259, 24 July 2008.

152 Embassy Bangkok, 08BANGKOK1283, 28 April 2008.

153 Ibid.

154 Ibid.

155 Interview, Boyce, 4 June 2015.

156 Ibid.

157 Embassy Bangkok, 08BANGKOK1006, 31 March 2008.

158 Bush, "Remarks by President George W. Bush in Bangkok, Thailand".

159 Embassy Bangkok, 08BANGKOK904, 21 March 2008.

160 See Embassy Bangkok, 08CHIANGMAI52, 28 March 2008.

161 Embassy Bangkok, 08CHIANGMAI35, 5 March 2008.

162 Embassy Bangkok, 08CHIANGMAI28, 26 August 2008.

163 Embassy Bangkok, 08CHIANGMAI60, 17 October 2008.

164 Embassy Bangkok, 08BANGKOK3336, 7 November 2008.

165 Ibid.

166 Fu-kuo Liu.

167 See "Thai New PM Stresses to Enhance Thai–Sino Relationship", *Xinhua*, 31 January 2008.

168 McCarten, "Roadblocks".

169 Interview, Noppadon, 18 June 2015.

170 Bush, "Remarks by President George W. Bush in Bangkok, Thailand".

171 Ibid.

172 Embassy Bangkok, 08BANGKOK1733, 6 June 2008.

173 Embassy Bangkok, 08BANGKOK487, 14 February 2008.

174 Ibid.

175 Embassy Bangkok, 10BANGKOK269, 2 February 2010.

176 Embassy Bangkok, 08BANGKOK3757, 29 December 2008.

177 Embassy Bangkok, 08BANGKOK3747, 24 December 2008.

178 See Allen.

179 Embassy Bangkok, 08BANGKOK3778, 30 December 2008.

180 Embassy Bangkok, 08BANGKOK3700, 19 December 2008.

181 Embassy Bangkok, 08BANGKOK3707, 22 December 2008.

182 Embassy Bangkok, 08BANGKOK3341, 10 November 2008.

183 Interview, Sarasin, 6 February 2015.

184 Embassy Bangkok, 10BANGKOK269, 2 February 2010.

185 Foreign Ministry of the People's Republic of China, 22 August 2011, http://www.fmprc.gov.cn/eng/wjb/zzjg/yzs/gjlb/2787/.

186 Ibid.

187 Embassy Bangkok, 10BANGKOK269, 2 February 2010.

188 Crispin, "US Slips, China Glides".

189 See ibid.

190 Embassy Bangkok, 10BANGKOK310, 4 February 2010.

191 Ibid.

192 Interview, Abhisit, 6 February 2015.

193 Interview, Weng, 6 January 2015.

194 Ibid.

195 Foreign Ministry of the People's Republic of China, 12 April 2010, http://www.fmprc.gov.cn/eng/xwfw/s2510/2535/t678881.shtml.

196 Interview, Panitan, 31 January 2015.

197 Crispin, "US Slips, China Glides".

198 See ibid.

199 See ibid.

200 Interview, Panitan, 31 January 2015.

201 Embassy Bangkok, 10BANGKOK269, 2 February 2010.

202 See Embassy Bangkok, 09BANGKOK1305, 1 June 2009.

203 Interview, Kasit, 23 January 2015.

204 Interview, Abhisit, 6 February 2015.

205 Interview, Kasit, 23 January 2015.

206 Interview, Senior State Department official who served under Campbell, 11 April 2015.

207 Interview, US diplomat, 9 April 2015.

208 Ibid.

209 Interview, Senior State Department official posted to Bangkok during the Abhisit administration, 16 July 2015.

210 Embassy Bangkok, 09BANGKOK1196, 15 May 2009.

211 Embassy Bangkok, 09BANGKOK1763, 24 July 2009.

212 See ibid.

213 Embassy Bangkok, 10BANGKOK310, 4 February 2010.

214 Ibid.

215 Embassy Bangkok, 09BANGKOK2860, 9 November 2009.

216 Embassy Bangkok, 09BANGKOK706, 20 March 2009.

217 Embassy Bangkok, 09BANGKOK385, 13 February 2009.

218 Embassy Bangkok, 09BANGKOK2002, 13 August 2009.

219 Embassy Bangkok, 09BANGKOK1998, 13 August 2009.

220 Ehrlich, "Bout Finally Gets the Boot".

221 Interview, Senior State Department official posted to Bangkok during the Abhisit administration, 16 July 2015.

222 Embassy Bangkok, 09BANGKOK888, 7 April 2009.

223 Embassy Bangkok, 09BANGKOK1817, 24 July 2009.

224 Embassy Bangkok, 09BANGKOK1305, 1 June 2009.

225 Embassy Bangkok, 09BANGKOK1841, 30 July 2009.

226 Ibid.

227 Ibid.

228 Embassy Bangkok, 09BANGKOK3003, 25 November 2009.

229 Embassy Bangkok, 09BANGKOK865, 3 April 2009.

230 Ibid.

231 Embassy Bangkok, 09BANGKOK1132, 7 May 2009.

232 Ibid.

233 Embassy Bangkok, 09BANGKOK1223, 20 May 2009.

234 See Askew, "Confrontation and Crisis in Thailand, 2008–2010" 54.

235 Embassy Bangkok, 09BANGKOK3003, 25 November 2009.

236 Embassy Bangkok, 09BANGKOK1653, 10 July 2009.

237 See Embassy Bangkok, 09CHIANGMAI172, 16 November 2009.

238 See Crispin, "Bombs Away".

239 Crispin, "Bloody Desperation".

240 See Crispin, "Bombs Away".

241 See ibid.

242 See Pavin, in Montesano et al. 253–254.

243 See Ehrlich, "On Guard".

244 See ibid.

245 Crispin, "Why Thailand's Reds".

246 See Askew, "The Ineffable Rightness of Conspiracy" 82.

247 Interview, Weng, 6 January 2015.

248 See Crispin, "US Slips, China Glides".

249 Crispin, "Why Thailand's Reds".

250 Interview, Weng, 6 January 2015.

251 Interview, Senior State Department official posted to Bangkok during the Abhisit administration, 16 July 2015.

252 See Ehrlich, "Revelations".

253 See Pavin, in Montesano et al. 254.

254 Interview, Panitan, 31 January 2015.

255 Embassy Bangkok, 09BANGKOK865, 3 April 2009.

256 Interview, Abhisit, 6 February 2015.

257 See Murphy, in Montesano et al. 210.

258 See Pavin, in Montesano et al. 263.

259 Embassy Bangkok, 09BANGKOK2851, 6 November 2009.

260 Embassy Bangkok, 10BANGKOK186, 23 January 2010.

261 Embassy Bangkok, 09BANGKOK934, 9 April 2009.

262 Interview, Kasit, 23 January 2015.

263 Embassy Bangkok, 10BANGKOK269, 2 February 2010.

264 Embassy Bangkok, 10BANGKOK197, 25 January 2010.

265 Interview, Kasit, 23 January 2015.

266 Ibid.

267 Embassy Bangkok, 09BANGKOK1720, 16 July 2009.

268 Embassy Bangkok, 09BANGKOK213, 28 January 2009.

269 Interview, Kasit, 23 January 2015.

270 Embassy Bangkok, 10BANGKOK411, 18 February 2010.

271 Embassy Bangkok, 10BANGKOK259, 1 February 2010.

272 Embassy Bangkok, 10BANGKOK269, 2 February 2010.

273 Embassy Bangkok, 10BANGKOK197, 25 January 2010.

274 Embassy Bangkok, 10BANGKOK186, 23 January 2010.

275 Embassy Bangkok, 10BANGKOK259, 1 February 2010.

276 Embassy Bangkok, 10BANGKOK411, 18 February 2010.

277 Interview, Kasit, 23 January 2015.

278 Interview, Abhisit, 6 February 2015.

279 Embassy Bangkok, 10BANGKOK269, 2 February 2010.

280 See Crispin, "US Slips, China Glides".

281 Interview, Korn, 8 May 2015.

282 Ibid.

283 Ibid.

284 Embassy Bangkok, 10BANGKOK286, 3 February 2010.

285 Ibid.

286 Interview, Korn, 8 May 2015.

287 See Embassy Bangkok, 10BANGKOK286, 2 February 2010.

288 Ibid.

289 Ibid.

290 Embassy Bangkok, 08BANGKOK3707, 22 December 2008.

291 See "Thai PM Says Not Sure When Thai–U.S. FTA Talks to Resume", *Xinhua*, 23 September 2009.

292 Embassy Bangkok, 09BANGKOK23, 7 January 2009.

293 Embassy Bangkok, 09BANGKOK527, 3 March 2009.

294 Embassy Bangkok, 09BANGKOK370, 13 February 2009.

295 See ibid.

296 Embassy Bangkok, 09BANGKOK1305, 1 June 2009.

297 Embassy Bangkok, 09BANGKOK1574, 2 July 2009.

298 Interview, Korn, 8 May 2015.

299 See Embassy Bangkok, 09BANGKOK2401, 21 September 2009.

300 Embassy Bangkok, 10BANGKOK269, 2 February 2010.

301 Ibid.

302 Embassy Bangkok, 09BANGKOK2962, 20 November 2009.

303 See Embassy Bangkok, 09BANGKOK206, 27 January 2009.

304 Embassy Bangkok, 09BANGKOK2860, 9 November 2009.

305 Embassy Bangkok, 09BANGKOK1166, 13 May 2009.

306 Embassy Bangkok, 09BANGKOK865, 3 April 2009.

307 Embassy Bangkok, 10BANGKOK192, 25 January 2010.

308 Ibid.

309 See Embassy Bangkok, 09BANGKOK567, 5 March 2009.

310 See Embassy Bangkok, 09BANGKOK23, 7 January 2009.

311 Embassy Bangkok, 09BANGKOK1200, 15 May 2009.

312 Interview, Senior State Department official posted to Bangkok during the Abhisit administration, 16 July 2015.

313 Embassy Bangkok, 10BANGKOK411, 18 February 2010.

314 Interview, Kasit, 23 January 2015.

315 Embassy Bangkok, 10BANGKOK298, 4 February 2010.

316 Klausner, "Law and Society" 136.

317 Embassy Bangkok, 10BANGKOK413, 18 February 2010.

318 See Embassy Bangkok, 09BANGKOK291, 4 February 2009.

319 See Embassy Bangkok, 09BANGKOK2355, 16 September 2009.

320 Interview, Abhisit, 6 February 2015.

321 Embassy Bangkok, 09BANGKOK1305, 1 June 2009.

322 See Embassy Bangkok, 09BANGKOK2041, 18 August 2009.

323 See Embassy Bangkok, 09BANGKOK650, 16 March 2009.

324 Embassy Bangkok, 09BANGKOK1485, 19 June 2009.

325 Embassy Bangkok, 09BANGKOK3018, 30 November 2009.

326 See Embassy Bangkok, 09BANGKOK2041, 18 August 2009.

327 Embassy Bangkok, 09BANGKOK3018, 30 November 2009.

328 Interview, State Department official, April 2015.

329 Embassy Bangkok, 10BANGKOK114, 14 January 2010.

330 Ibid.

331 Embassy Bangkok, 09BANGKOK1653, 10 July 2009.

332 Embassy Bangkok, 09BANGKOK888, 7 April 2009.

333 See Embassy Bangkok, 09BANGKOK841, 2 April 2009.

334 Embassy Bangkok, 09BANGKOK721, 23 March 2009.

335 Ibid.

336 Embassy Bangkok, 09BANGKOK2464, 28 September 2009.

337 Embassy Bangkok, 09CHIANGMAI151, 13 October 2009.

338 Nuechterlein 250.

339 Embassy Bangkok, 09BANGKOK2962, 20 November 2009.

340 See McCoy, "US and Cambodia".

341 Embassy Bangkok, 09BANGKOK1939, 7 August 2009.

342 Embassy Bangkok, 09BANGKOK1842, 30 July 2009.

343 See Embassy Bangkok, 10BANGKOK286, 3 February 2010.

344 Embassy Bangkok, 09CHIANGMAI67, 19 May 2009.

345 McCartan, "Manhunt".

346 Embassy Bangkok, 09BANGKOK2682, 20 October 2009.

347 See Roughneen.

348 See ibid.

349 See Embassy Bangkok, 09BANGKOK1190, 14 May 2009.

350 Interview, Korn, 8 May 2015.

351 Embassy Bangkok, 09BANGKOK528, 3 March 2009.

352 See Embassy Bangkok, 10BANGKOK259, 1 February 2010.

353 Embassy Bangkok, 10BANGKOK186, 23 January 2010.

354 Interview, Abhisit, 6 February 2015.

355 See Embassy Bangkok, 08BANGKOK3298, 5 November 2008.

356 See Embassy Bangkok, 09BANGKOK1763, 24 July 2009.

357 Interview, Abhisit, 6 February 2015.

358 See McDermid.

359 Interview, Korn, 8 May 2015.

360 Embassy Bangkok, 10BANGKOK379, 12 February 2010.

361 Ibid.

362 Ibid.

363 See Embassy Bangkok, 09BANGKOK1842, 30 July 2009.

364 See Jakkapun and McDermid.

365 McCartan, "A New Courtship".

366 Interview, Korn, 8 May 2015.

367 Embassy Bangkok, 09BANGKOK2682, 20 October 2009.

368 See Embassy Bangkok, 09BANGKOK1939, 7 August 2009.

369 Embassy Bangkok, 09BANGKOK2851, 6 November 2009.

370 Embassy Bangkok, 10BANGKOK413, 18 February 2010.

371 Embassy Bangkok, 09BANGKOK1190, 14 May 2009.

372 Interview, Korn, 8 May 2015.

373 Embassy Bangkok, 10BANGKOK269, 2 February 2010.

374 Ibid.

375 Interview, Kasit, 23 January 2015.

376 Embassy Bangkok, 10BANGKOK269, 2 February 2010.

377 Ibid.

378 Embassy Bangkok, 10BANGKOK186, 23 January 2010.

379 Embassy Bangkok, 09BANGKOK2851, 6 November 2009.

380 Ibid.

381 Embassy Bangkok, 10BANGKOK269, 2 February 2010.

382 Embassy Bangkok, 09BANGKOK2851, 6 November 2009.

383 Embassy Bangkok, 10BANGKOK186, 23 January 2010.

384 See Embassy Bangkok, 09BANGKOK1190, 14 May 2009.

385 Ibid.

386 See ibid.

387 Foreign Ministry of the People's Republic of China, 22 August 2011, http://www.fmprc.gov.cn/eng/wjb/zzjg/yzs/gjlb/2787/.

388 Interview, Korn, 8 May 2015.

389 Interview, Panitan, 31 January 2015.

390 Interview, Abhisit, 6 February 2015.

391 See Roughneen.

392 Embassy Bangkok, 08BANGKOK3757, 29 December 2008.

393 Embassy Bangkok, 10BANGKOK413, 18 February 2010.

394 Ibid.

395 Ibid.

396 Embassy Bangkok, 09BANGKOK213, 28 January 2009.

397 Embassy Bangkok, 09BANGKOK1662, 13 July 2009.

398 Interview, Kasit, 23 January 2015.

399 Embassy Bangkok, 10BANGKOK411, 18 February 2010.

400 Embassy Bangkok, 08BANGKOK3707, 22 December 2008.

401 Interview, Kasit, 23 January 2015.

402 Embassy Bangkok, 09BANGKOK1223, 20 May 2009.

403 Interview, US diplomat, 9 April 2015.

404 Ibid.

405 Embassy Bangkok, 09BANGKOK1939, 7 August 2009.

406 Ibid.

407 Embassy Bangkok, 10BANGKOK413, 18 February 2010.

408 Interview, US diplomat, 9 April 2015.

409 Ibid.

410 Ibid.

411 Interview, Boyce, 4 June 2015.

412 Interview, Kobsak, 14 January 2015.

413 Interview, Surapong, 13 May 2015.

414 Interview, Bhokin, 4 February 2015.

415 Interview, Sarasin, 6 February 2015.

416 Foreign Ministry of the People's Republic of China, "Wen Jiabao Meets With His Thai Counterpart Yingluck", 19 November 2011, http://www.fmprc.gov.cn/mfa_eng/topics_665678/wjbdyldrhy_665726/t879333.shtml.

417 Ibid

418 See Singh, "China and Thailand".

419 Foreign Ministry of the People's Republic of China, "Premier Wen Jiabao Holds Talks with Thai Counterpart Yingluck", 21 November 2012, http://www.fmprc.gov.cn/mfa_eng/topics_665678/pwjamoealapovcat_665698/t992130.shtml.

420 Ibid.

421 Ibid.

422 Foreign Ministry of the People's Republic of China, "President Xi Jinping Meets with Prime Minister Yingluck Shinawatra of Thailand", 6 October 2013, http://www.fmprc.gov.cn/mfa_eng/topics_665678/xjpfwynmlxycx21apec_665682/t1085654.shtml.

423 See Achara, "Thai–Chinese Rail Link Tipped".

424 See ibid.

425 See ibid.

426 Interview, Suranand, 13 January 2015.

427 Interview, Sarasin, 6 February 2015.

428 Interview, Former Thai ambassador to the US and China, 2 February 2015.

429 Interview, Two Thai Foreign Ministry officials, 5 February 2015.

430 Interview, Panitan, 31 January 2015.

431 Interview, State Department official with responsibility for Thailand, 9 April 2015.

432 Ibid.

433 Interview, US diplomat, 9 April 2015.

434 Interview, State Department official with responsibility for Thailand, 9 April 2015.

435 Interview, Sunai, 30 January 2015.

436 Interview, US diplomat, 9 April 2015.

437 Interview, Korn, 8 May 2015.

438 Embassy Bangkok, 09BANGKOK 2554, 6 October 2009.

439 Interview, Korn, 8 May 2015.

440 Interview, US diplomat, 9 April 2015.

441 Interview, Korn, 8 May 2015.

442 Interview, State Department official with responsibility for Thailand, 9 April 2015.

443 Interview, State Department official, April 2015.

444 Interview, Surapong, 13 May 2015.

445 Interview, Thaksin, 21 August 2015.

446 Interview, State Department official with responsibility for Thailand, 9 April 2015.

447 Ibid.

448 Interview, US diplomat, 9 April 2015.

449 See "US Ready to Cooperate with New Thai Gov't: Envoy", *Xinhua*, 5 July 2011.

450 Interview, Senior member of Yingluck's government, 13 January 2015.

451 Ministry of Foreign Affairs of Thailand, "Remarks Hillary Rodham Clinton Secretary of State Government House Bangkok, Thailand", 16 November 2011.

452 Ibid.

453 The White House, 18 November 2012.

454 Kavi, "China–Thailand Ties".

455 The White House, 18 November 2012.

456 Ibid.

457 Ibid.

458 Ibid.

459 See Ehrlich, "US, Thailand Tussle".

460 See ibid.

461 Interview, Thaksin, 21 August 2015.

462 The White House, 18 November 2012.

463 Interview, Suranand, 13 January 2015.

464 Interview, Sarasin, 6 February 2015.

465 Interview, Retired Thai general, 22 January 2015.

466 Interview, Sarasin, 6 February 2015.

467 Interview, Panitan, 31 January 2015.

468 The White House, 18 November 2012.

469 Ibid.

470 Richardson, Staff Sgt. Kyle J., "Hunaman Guardian Opening Ceremony", US Army, 21 June 2013.

471 Ibid.

472 Interview, State Department official, April 2015.

473 Interview, Cole, 13 April 2015.

474 Ibid.

475 Interview, Sarasin, 6 February 2015.

476 Foreign Ministry of the People's Republic of China, "Premier Wen Jiabao Holds Talks with Thai Counterpart Yingluck".

477 Interview, Surapong, 13 May 2015.

478 See Achara, "Thai–Chinese Rail Link Tipped".

479 Interview, Kraisak, 2 February 2015.

480 Interview, Suranand, 13 January 2015.

481 The White House, 18 November 2012.

482 Ibid.

483 Interview, Two Thai Foreign Ministry officials, 5 February 2015.

484 Interview, Suranand, 13 January 2015.

485 Interview, Pansak, 21 January 2015.

486 Foreign Ministry of the People's Republic of China, "Premier Wen Jiabao Holds Talks with Thai Counterpart Yingluck".

487 Interview, Two Thai Foreign Ministry officials, 5 February 2015.

488 See Winchester.

489 Interview, Senior Foreign Ministry official with experience in China during Yingluck administration, 22 January 2015.

490 Interview, Two Thai Foreign Ministry officials, 5 February 2015.

491 "China, Thailand Convene First Strategic Dialogue", *Xinhua*, 19 August 2013.

492 ASEAN–China Centre, "ASEAN and China", http://www.asean-china-center.org/english/2010-06/23/c_13365143_2.htm.

493 The State Council, The People's Republic of China, "Take China–ASEAN Relations to a New Height", Remarks by H.E. Li Keqiang, Premier of the State Council of the People's Republic of China at the 17th ASEAN-China Summit, Nay Pyi Taw, Myanmar, 13 November 2014.

494 Interview, Thaksin, 21 August 2015.

495 Email, Thai Foreign Ministry official with responsibility for ASEAN, 25 January 2015.

496 The White House, 18 November 2012.

497 Ibid.

498 Ibid.

499 Ibid.

500 See "Visit: We have to Fight even the US and UN", *Prachatai*, 21 December 2011.

501 Interview, Two Thai Foreign Ministry officials, 5 February 2015.

502 Interview, State Department official, April 2015.

503 Interview, Two Thai Foreign Ministry officials, 5 February 2015.

504 Ministry of Foreign Affairs of Thailand, "Remarks Hillary Rodham Clinton Secretary of State Government House Bangkok, Thailand", 16 November 2011.

505 Ibid.

506 The White House, 18 November 2012.

507 Ibid.

508 Ibid.

509 Ibid.

510 Interview, Korn, 8 May 2015.

511 The White House, 18 November 2012.

512 Kobsak.

513 Interview, Suranand, 13 January 2015.

514 See Yang.

515 See ibid.

516 See "The US is Behind all Political Turmoil in Thailand", *Prachatai*, 6 February 2012.

517 See "Sondhi L: US Capitalists behind Campaign to Overthrow Monarchy", *Asian Correspondent*, 13 February 2012.

518 Trajano.

519 Cole and Scacchitano.

520 See "PAD Discloses US Plan for U-Tapao Airport", *Prachatai*, 25 June 2012.

521 The White House, 18 November 2012.

522 See Ten Kate.

523 See Heifetz.

524 Post Reporters, "Democrats Urge Protest over US Naval Base Claims", *Bangkok Post*, 15 December 2013.

525 See "Yingluck, Xi Strengthen Bilateral Project Alliance", *Bangkok Post*, 7 October 2013.

526 Interview, Sarasin, 6 February 2015.

527 Ibid.

528 Interview, State Department official, April 2015.

529 See "China Hopes for Political Stability in Thailand", *Xinhua*, 11 November 2013.

530 See "US, Germany Call for Calm", *Bangkok Post*, 11 December 2013.

531 See Paritta.

532 See Thanida, "Decree Spurs Flurry of Travel Warnings".

533 See Wassana and Achara, "Kenney Stays Out of Crisis".

534 See Wassana, "US Cautions Govt Against Coup, Chaos".

535 See "US Urges Restraint in Thailand following Premier's Ouster", *Xinhua*, 7 May 2014.

536 See Beattle.

537 See ibid.

538 US State Department, "Statement by State Department Spokesperson Jen Psaki: Thailand".

539 See Fuller.

540 See "US Unimpressed by Year-long Road Map to Elections", *The Nation*, 31 May 2014.

541 Interview, State Department official, 9 April 2015.

542 Interview, Former State Department official, 16 July 2015.

543 Interview, US diplomat, 9 April 2015.

544 See Post reporters and *Agence France-Presse*, "Uni Alumni Blast US 'Meddling' in Coup", *Bangkok Post*, 2 June 2014.

545 See Jory.

546 See LeFevre and Pracha.

547 See "NCPO Boosts China Trade Ties", *Bangkok Post*, 7 June 2014.

548 See Campbell.

549 See "Thailand Urges U.S. to Reconsider Plan to Relocate Cobra Gold Military Exercise", *Xinhua*, 25 June 2014.

550 See "China Steps Into the Breach", *The Nation*, 26 June 2014.

551 See Jory.

552 See "Police Say Anti-American Protest not Violation of Martial Law", *Khaosod English*, 29 June 2014.

553 See Wassana and Achara, "US Embassy Snubs Top Brass Over Invites".

554 See "China Steps into the Breach", *The Nation*, 26 June 2014.

555 Foreign Ministry of the People's Republic of China, "The Second Round of China–Thailand Strategic Dialogue Held in Beijing", 12 July 2014, http://www.fmprc.gov.cn/mfa_eng/wjbxw/t1175118.shtml.

556 See "Prem Gets an Invite to Visit China", *The Nation*, 12 July 2014.

557 See ibid.

Chapter 10

1   MacDonald 215.

2   Interview, Surapong, 13 May 2015.

3   Kaplan, *Monsoon* 208.

4   See "Repression No Route to Reconciliation", *Bangkok Post*, 29 June 2014.

5   Email, Thai general, 25 December 2014.

6   Interview, Korn, 8 May 2015.

7   Interview, Kasit, 23 January 2015.

8   "Prem Gets an Invite to Visit China", *The Nation*, 12 July 2014.

9   Interview, Pansak, 21 January 2015.

10 Interview, Baker, 6 January 2015.

11 Interview, Thaksin, 21 August 2015.

12 Interview, Korn, 8 May 2015.

13 Interview, Suranand, 13 January 2015.

14 Interview, Panitan, 31 January 2015.

15 See Embassy Bangkok, 06BANGKOK6442, 24 October 2006.

16 See "Beijing Blames Thai Example", *Bangkok Post*, 10 June 2014.

17 Wilson, *The United States and the Future of Thailand* 163.

18 Interview, Thaksin, 21 August 2015.

19 Interview, Former Thai prime minister, 1 February 2015.

20 Interview, Pisan, 7 April 2015.

21 Interview, Anand, 21 January 2015.

22 Ibid.

23 Interview, Abhisit, 6 February 2015.

24 Interview, Panitan, 31 January 2015.

25 Interview, State Department official with responsibility for Thailand, 9 April 2015.

26 Interview, Korn, 8 May 2015.

27 Interview, Jackson, 9 April 2015.

28 Interview, Anand, 21 January 2015.

29 Email, retired Thai general, 29 January 2015.

30 Interview, Thaksin, 21 August 2015.

31 Interview, State Department official, April 2015.

32 Interview, Korn, 8 May 2015.

33 Interview, Panitan, 31 January 2015.

34 See Campbell.

35 Interview, Pansak, 21 January 2015.

36 Clinton.

37 Ibid.

38 Interview, Jackson, 9 April 2015.

39 Interview, Kobsak, 14 January 2015.

40 Interview, Senior State Department official, 16 July 2015.

41 Interview, Pansak, 21 January 2015.

42 Interview, Bosworth, 27 May 2015.

43 Interview, US diplomat, 9 April 2015.

44 Interview, Thaksin, 21 August 2015.

45 Kaplan, *The Revenge of Geography* 11.

46 "Repression no Route to Reconciliation", *Bangkok Post*, 29 June 2014.

47 Interview, State Department official, April 2015.

48 Kaplan, *Asia's Cauldron* 16–17.

49 See Kaplan, *Monsoon* 7.

50 Thanat, in Jackson and Wiwat 310.

51 Kaplan, *The Revenge of Geography* 10.

52 Kaplan, *Monsoon* 11.

53 Interview, Pansak, 21 January 2015.

54 Interview, Bosworth, 27 May 2015.

55 See Heydarian.

56 Interview, Bosworth, 27 May 2015.

57 See Wassana, "US Threats".

58 Interview, Thaksin, 21 August 2015.

59 Interview, Surakiart, 4 August 2015.

60 Interview, Abhisit, 6 February 2015.

61 Interview, Korn, 8 May 2015.

62 Interview, Kasit, 23 January 2015.

63 Email, senior Thai general, 29 January 2015.

64 Interview, Sarasin, 6 February 2015.

65 See Heydarian.

66 Interview, Boyce, 4 June 2015.

67 Interview, Bosworth, 27 May 2015.

68 Interview, Suranand, 13 January 2015.

69 Interview, Senior Foreign Ministry official with experience in China during Yingluck administration, 22 January 2015.

70 Interview, Bhokin, 4 February 2015.

71 See Jeerawat.

72 See ibid.

73 See ibid.

74 See ibid.

75 Interview, Thaksin, 21 August 2015.

76 Interview, Surakiart, 4 August 2015.

77 Interview, State Department official with responsibility for Thailand, 9 April 2015.

78 Clinton.

Sources

Achara Ashayagachat, "Confess on Torture, Activists Urge", *Bangkok Post*, 7 February 2013.

Achara Ashayagachat, "Thai–Chinese Rail Link Tipped", *Bangkok Post*, 12 October 2013.

Alagappa, Muthiah, ed., *Asian Security Practice: Material and Ideational Influences*, Stanford, Stanford University Press, 1998.

Algie, Jim, et al., *Americans in Thailand*, Bangkok, Editions Didier Millet, 2014.

Allen, Mike, "'America's First Pacific President'", *Politico*, 13 November 2009.

Allison, Tony, "Thailand, US Inch Ahead on Trade Accord", *Asia Times*, 14 January 2006.

Anand Panyarachun, "The United States in Asia: Changing Perceptions", Keynote Address, Hilton Hotel, Bangkok, 11 July 1985.

Anand Panyarachun, "Address of Prime Minister Anand Panyarachun to the Foreign Correspondents Club of Thailand, 25 April 1991", *Management, Reform, and Vision: A Selection of Speeches by Prime Minister Anand Panyarachun, April–November 1991*, The Secretariat of the Prime Minister, Office of the Prime Minister, Government House, Thailand.

Anuson Chinvanno, *Thailand's Policies towards China, 1949–54*, London, St. Antony's College, Palgrave Macmillan, 1992.

Armacost, Michael H. and J. Stapleton Roy, "Overview", *America's Role in Asia*, San Francisco, Asia Foundation, 2004.

Askew, Marc, "Confrontation and Crisis in Thailand, 2008–2010"; Marc Askew, ed., *Legitimacy Crisis in Thailand*, Chiang Mai, Silkworm Books, 2010.

Askew, Marc, "The Ineffable Rightness of Conspiracy: Thailand's Democrat-ministered State and the Negation of Red Shirt Politics"; Montesano, Michael J., Pavin Chachavalpongpun, and Aekapol Chongvilaiwan, eds., *Bangkok May 2010: Perspectives on a Divided Thailand*, Singapore, Institute of Southeast Asian Studies, 2010.

Ball, Desmond and David Scott Mathieson, *Militia Redux: Or Sor and the Revival of Paramilitarism in Thailand*, Banglamung, White Lotus Press, 2007.

Bangkok Embassy: WikiLeaks, Thailand, Embassy Bangkok and Chiang Mai cables, 2004–2010, http://www.wikileaks.org

Beattle, Victor, "US 'Reasonably Confident' no Military Coup in Thailand", *Voice of America*, 14 May 2014.

Belanger, Julie and Richard Horsey, "Negotiating Humanitarian Access to Cyclone-affected Areas of Myanmar: A Review", *Humanitarian Practice Network*, December 2008.

Bush, George W., "Remarks by President George W. Bush in Bangkok, Thailand", Office of the Press Secretary, 7 August 2008.

Bunge, Frederica M., ed., *Thailand: A Country Study*, Foreign Area Studies, The American University, February 1980.

Buszynski, Leszek, "Thailand's Foreign Policy: Management of a Regional Vision", *Asian Survey*, Vol. XXXIV, No. 8, August 1994.

Campbell, Charlie, "The U.S. is Freezing the Thai Junta out of Military Exercises", *Time*, 26 June 2014.

Central Intelligence Agency, "Overview of CIA-Congress Interactions Concerning the Agency's Rendition-Detention-Interrogation Program", 2014.

Chambers, Michael R., "'The Chinese and the Thais are Brothers': The Evolution of the Sino-Thai Friendship", *Journal of Contemporary China*, Vol. 14, No. 45, November 2005, 599–629.

Chambers, Paul, ed., *Knights of the Realm: Thailand's Military and Police, Then and Now*, Banglamung, White Lotus Press, Bangkok, 2013.

Chang Noi, *Jungle Book: Thailand's Politics, Moral Panic, and Plunder, 1996–2008*, Selected Columns, Seattle, University of Washington Press, 2009.

Chanlett-Avery, Emma, "Thailand: Background and U.S. Relations", Congressional Research Service, 19 December 2008.

Chaturon Chaisang, *Thai Democracy in Crisis: 27 Truths*, The Institute of Democratization Studies, Bangkok, A.R. Information & Publication Co. Ltd., 2009.

Chulacheeb Chinwanno, [*35 Years of Sino-Thai Diplomatic Relations, 1975–2010: Past, Present and Future*], Bangkok, Openbook Press, 2004.

Clinton, Hillary, "America's Pacific Century", *Foreign Policy*, 11 October 2011.

Cole, John and Steve Sciacchitano, "Baseless Controversy over Thailand's U-Tapao", *Asia Times*, 22 June 2012.

Connors, Michael K., *Democracy and National Identity in Thailand*, Copenhagen, NIAS Press, 2007.

Connors, Michael K., "Thailand: Four Elections and a Coup", *Australian Journal of International Affairs*, Vol. 62, No. 4, December 2008, 478–496.

Crispin, Shawn W., "Thaksin's Loss, US's Gain", *Asia Times*, 9 February 2007.

Crispin, Shawn W., "The Urge to Splurge in Thailand", *Asia Times*, 3 November 2007.

Crispin, Shawn W., "The Thai Military's Democratic Nightmare", *Asia Times*, 16 November 2007.

Crispin, Shawn W., "US, Thailand, a Conflicted Alliance", *Asia Times*, 8 August 2008.

Crispin, Shawn W., "What Obama Means to Bangkok", *Asia Times*, 7 November 2008.

Crispin, Shawn W., "Bloody Desperation for Thailand's Reds", *Asia Times*, 17 March 2010.

Crispin, Shawn W., "Why Thailand's Reds beat a Retreat", *Asia Times*, 8 May 2010.

Crispin, Shawn W., "Bombs Away in Thailand", *Asia Times*, 2 April 2010.

Crispin, Shawn W., "US Slips, China Glides in Thai Crisis", *Asia Times*, 20 July 2010.

Dalpino, Catharin, "American Views: Southeast Asia", *America's Role in Asia*, Asia Foundation, 2004.

Dalpino, Catharin, "US-ASEAN Relations: With a New White House and Congress", Discussion paper for US-Thai Think Tank Summit, Bangkok, 13-14 October 2008.

Darling, Frank C., *Thailand and the United States*, Washington, DC, Public Affairs Press, 1965.

Ehrlich, Richard S., "Thailand Joins the Missile Game", *Asia Times*, 6 November 2003.

Ehrlich, Richard S., "Thailand Takes 'Hospitable' Action on Iraq", *Asia Times*, 1 October 2003.

Ehrlich, Richard, "US Helps Thailand Rub Out Fake Passports", *Asia Times*, 26 June 2008.

Ehrlich, Richard S., "On Guard on Bangkok's Front Lines", *Asia Times*, 11 May 2010.

Ehrlich, Richard S., "Revelations of a US Securocrat", *Asia Times*, 29 September 2010.

Ehrlich, Richard S., "Bout Extradition Stuck on the Runway", *Asia Times*, 27 August 2010.

Ehrlich, Richard S., "Bout Finally Gets the Boot from Thailand", *Asia Times*, 18 November 2010.

Ehrlich, Richard, "US, Thailand Tussle Over Terror Plot", *Asia Times*, 18 January 2012.

Emails to author from: Aldis, William, 19 February 2017; Boyce, Ralph "Skip", 6 July 2015; Jakrapob Penkair, 12 August 2015; Kent, George, 8 June 2015; Panitan, 9 June 2015; retired Thai general, 29 January 2015; senior Thai general, 29 January 2015; Thai general, 25 December 2014.

Evan, Grant, Christopher Hutton and Kuah Khun Eng, eds., *Where China Meets Southeast Asia: Social & Cultural Change in the Border Regions*, Bangkok, White Lotus Press, 2000.

Faulder, Catherine, "A Childhood Spent in the Dragons' Den", *Bangkok Post*, 19 July 2015.

Ferrara, Federico, *Thailand Unhinged: Unraveling the Myth of a Thai-style Democracy*, Jakarta, Equinox Publishing, 2010.

Fineman, Daniel, *A Special Relationship: The United States and Military Government in Thailand, 1947–1958*, Honolulu, University of Hawai'i Press, 1997.

Foreign Ministry of the People's Republic of China: Press Statements 2006-2014.

Fu-kuo Liu, "China's embrace leaves US in the cold", *Asia Times*, 16 May 2008.

Fullbrook, David, "Smooth-sailing for Thai Economy", *Asia Times*, 18 February 2005.

Fuller, Tom, "Thai General Says Coup has King's Backing", *New York Times*, 27 May 2014.

Funston, John, "Political Reform in Thailand: Real or Imagined?", *Asian Journal of Political Science*, Vol. 8, No. 2, December 2000, 89–108.

Funston, John, ed., *Divided Over Thaksin: Thailand's Coup and Problematic Transition*, Singapore, Institute of Southeast Asian Studies, 2009.

Guerin, Bill, "The Not So Ugly Americans", *Asia Times*, 11 January 2005.

Handley, Paul M., *The King Never Smiles: A Biography of Thailand's King Bhumibol Adulyadej*, New Haven, Yale University Press, 2006.

Heifetz, Justin, "Yes, We Have No Submarines", *Bangkok Post*, 9 February 2014.

Henderson, William, ed., *Southeast Asia: Problems of United States Policy*, Cambridge, MA, MIT Press, 1963.

Heydarian, Richard Javad, "New Ties, New Risks in the South China Sea", *Asia Times*, 27 March 2014.

Hewison, Kevin, R. Robinson, and G. Rodan, eds., *Southeast Asia in the 1990s: Authoritarianism, Democracy & Capitalism*, St. Leonards, Allen & Unwin, 1993.

Horgan, Denis, *The Bangkok World*, West Hartford, Bluefoot Books, 2013.

Horn, Robert, "Thailand's PM Proxy: Samak", *Time*, 19 December 2007.

Ivarsson, Soren and Lotte Isager, eds., *Saying the Unsayable: Monarchy and Democracy in Thailand*, Copenhagen, NIAS Press, 2010.

Jackson, Karl D. and Wiwat Mungkandi, eds., *United States–Thailand Relations*, Berkeley, Institute of East Asian Studies Press, 1986.

Jakkapun Kaewsangthong and Charles McDermid, "Clinton Talks Tough in Thailand", *Asia Times*, 26 July 2009.

Jeerawat Na Thalang, "Kra Canal Dream Still Far From Reality", *Bangkok Post*, 7 June 2015.

Jory, Patrick, "China: Winners from Thailand's Coup", *Asia Sentinel*, 20 June 2014.

Kaplan, Robert D., *Monsoon: The Indian Ocean and the Future of American Power*, New York, Random House, 2010.

Kaplan, Robert D., *The Revenge of Geography: What the Map Tells Us About Coming Conflicts and the Battle Against Fate*, New York, Random House, 2012.

Kaplan, Robert D., *Asia's Cauldron: The South China Sea and the End of a Stable Pacific*, New York, Random House, 2014.

Kasian Tejapira, "The Misbehaving Jeks: The Evolving Regime of Thainess in Sino-Thai Challenges", *Asian Ethnicity*, Vol. 10, No. 3, 13 November 2009.

Kavi Chongkittavorn, "China-Thailand Ties to Turn Strategic", *China Daily*, 12 October 2013.

Kavi Chongkittavorn, "Thai-US relations in multilateral dimensions"; Refreshing Thai-US Relations, Institute of Security and International Studies and the American Studies Program conference, Chulalongkorn University, Hua Hin, 9 January 2009.

Khien Theeravit, "The Indochina Issue"; Ramsay, Ansil and Wiwat Mungkandi, eds., *Thailand-US Relations: Changing Political, Strategic, and Economic Factors*, Berkeley, Institute of East Asian Studies Press, 1988.

Kien Theerawit, [*China and the Social World*], Bangkok, Duangkamol Press, 1976.

Klausner, William J., *Transforming Thai Culture: From Temple to Drums to Mobile Phones*, Bangkok, Siam Society, 2004.

Klausner, William J., "Law and Society"; *Thai Culture in Transition: Collected Writings of William J. Klausner*, The Siam Society, Bangkok, 2002.

Kobkua Suwannathat-Pian, *Thailand's Durable Premier: Phibun through Three Decades, 1932–1957*, Singapore, Oxford University Press, 1995.

Kobsak Chutikul, "New US Secretary of State Kerry Can Thwart Slide to War", *Bangkok Post*, 6 February 2013.

Koh, Tommy, "The United States and Southeast Asia", America's Role in Asia, Asian and American Views: Recommendations for U.S. policy from both sides of the Pacific, 2008, The Asia Foundation, 2008.

Kulick, Elliott and Dick Wilson, *Thailand's Turn: Profile of a Dragon*, New York, St. Martin's Press, 1992.

Kurlantzick, Joshua, *Charm Offensive: How China's Soft Power is Transforming the World*, New Haven, Yale University Press, 2007.

Kurlantzick, Joshua, *The Ideal Man: The Tragedy of Jim Thompson and the American Way of War*, Hoboken, John Wiley & Sons, 2011.

Kusuma Snitwongse, "Thai Foreign Policy in the Global Age: Principle or Profit?", *Contemporary Southeast Asia*, Vol. 2, No. 23, August 2001.

Kyung-won, Kim, Tommy Koh and Farooq Sobhan, "Asian Views: Overview", *America's Role in Asia*, Asia Foundation, 2004.

Lane, Charles Dennison, *People's War and the United States in Southeast Asia: A Study in Social Philosophy*, PhD dissertation, University of Hong Kong, April 1994.

Lederer, William J. and Eugene Burdick, *The Ugly American*, New York, W.W. Norton & Company, 1958.

LeFevre, Amy Sawitta and Pracha Hariraksapitak, "Thai Junta Claims Support from China, Vietnam Amid Western Unease", *Reuters*, 4 June 2014.

Liang Chi Shad, "Thailand's Foreign Policy: An Analysis of its Evolution since World War II", July 1977.

Lynch, Daniel C., "International 'Decentering' and Democratization: The Case of Thailand", *International Studies Quarterly*, Vol. 48, Issue 2, June 2004, 339–362.

Macan-Markar, Marwaan, "China's October Revelation", *Asia Times*, 28 October 2003.

Macan-Markar, Marwaan, "US Deal Rankles with Thais", *Asia Times*, 14 April 2005.

Macan-Markar, Marwaan, "Sparks Fly as China Moves Oil up the Mekong", *Asia Times*, 9 January 2007.

MacDonald, Alexander, *Bangkok Editor*, New York, The MacMillan Company, 1949.

McBeth, John, *Reporter: Forty Years Covering Asia*, Singapore, Talisman Publishing, 2011.

McCargo, Duncan, "Network Monarchy and Legitimacy Crises in Thailand", *The Pacific Review*, Vol. 18, No. 4, 2005, 499–519.

McCargo, Duncan, "Toxic Thaksin", *Foreign Affairs*, 27 September 2006.

McCargo, Duncan and Ukrist Pathmanand, *The Thaksinization of Thailand*, Copenhagen, Nordic Institute of Asian Studies Press, 2005.

McCartan, Brian, "Roadblocks on the Great Asian Highway", *Asia Times*, 23 January 2008.

McCartan, Brian, "Manhunt is on for Mekong Robin Hood", *Asia Times*, 7 April 2009.

McCartan, Brian, "A New Courtship for Southeast Asia", *Asia Times*, 19 November 2009.

McCoy, Clifford, "US and Cambodia in Controversial Lockstep", *Asia Times*, 31 July 2010.

McDermid, Charles, "Protectionism is a Dirty ASEAN Word", *Asia Times*, 3 March 2009.

M.L. Bhansoon Ladavalya, *Thailand's Foreign Policy Under Kukrit Pramoj: A Study in Decision-Making*, Ann Arbor, University Microfilms International, 1980.

Ministry of Foreign Affairs of Thailand, "Remarks Hillary Rodham Clinton Secretary of State Government House Bangkok, Thailand", 16 November 2011.

Montesano, Michael J., "Thailand: A Reckoning with History Begins", *Southeast Asia Affairs*, January 2007, 311–339.

Montesano, Michael J., "Thailand in 2001: Learning to Live with Thaksin?", *Asian Survey*, Vol. 42, No. 1, January/February 2002.

Montesano, Michael J., Pavin Chachavalpongpun and Aekapol Chongvilaiwan, eds., *Bangkok May 2010: Perspectives on a Divided Thailand*, Singapore, Institute of Southeast Asian Studies, 2010.

Mulder, Niels, *Thai Images: The Culture of the Public World*, Chiang Mai, Silkworm Books, 1997.

Murphy, Ann Marie, "Beyond Balancing and Bandwagoning: Thailand's Response to China's Rise", *Asian Security*, Vol. 6, No. 1, 2010, 1–27.

Murphy, Ann Marie, "Compulsory licensing in U.S.-Thai relations: A new type of intellectual property dispute"; Refreshing Thai-US Relations, Institute of Security and International Studies and the American Studies Program conference, Chulalongkorn University, Hua Hin, 9 January 2009.

Narumit Sodsuk, [*The Diplomatic Relations between Thailand and the People's Republic of China*], Bangkok, Thai Wattana Phanit Press, 1981.

Neher, Clark D. and Wiwat Mungkandi, eds., *US–Thailand Relations in the New International Era*, Berkeley, University of California Press, 1990.

News outlets: *Asia Sentinel, Asia Times, Asian Correspondent, Associated Press, Bangkok Post, Bloomberg, China Daily, CNN, Far Eastern Economic Review, Financial Times, Foreign Policy, Khaosod English, Los Angeles Times, Phuket Wan, Politica, Prachatai, New York Times, Reuters, South China Morning Post, Straits Times, The Guardian, The Nation, Time, Voice of America, Washington Post, Xinhua*.

Nostitz, Nick, *Red v. Yellow, Volume 1: Thailand's Crisis of Identity*, Bangkok, White Lotus Press, 2009.

Nuechterlein, Donald, *Thailand and the Struggle for Southeast Asia*, Ithaca, NY, Cornell University Press, 1965.

Office of Inspector General, "Special Review: Counterterrorism Detention and Interrogation Activities (September 2001-October 2003)", Central Intelligence Agency, 2003-7123-IG, 7 May 2004.

Office of the Press Secretary, The White House, "Joint Statement Between President Bush and Thai Prime Minister Thaksin Shinawatra", Washington, DC, 19 September 2005.

Open Society Justice Initiative, *Globalizing Torture: CIA Secret Detention and Extraordinary Rendition*, Open Society Foundations, 2013.

Owen, Norman G., ed., *The Emergence of Modern Southeast Asia: A New History*, Singapore, Singapore University Press, 2005.

Panitan Wattanayagorn, "Thailand"; Pal Singh, Ravinder, *Arms Procurement Decision Making Volume I: China, India, Israel, Japan, South Korea and Thailand*, Oxford, Oxford University Press, 1998.

Paritta Wangkiat, "Demonstrators March to US Embassy, City", *Bangkok Post*, 20 December 2013.

Pasuk Phongpaichit and Chris Baker, *Thailand's Crisis*, Chiang Mai, Silkworm Books, 2000.

Pasuk Phongpaichit and Chris Baker, *Thaksin*, Chiang Mai, Silkworm Books, 2009.

Pasuk Phongpaichit and Sungsit Phiriyarangsan, *Corruption & Democracy in Thailand*, Chiang Mai, Silkworm Books, 1996.

Pavin Chachavalpongpun, "Diplomacy under Siege: Thailand's Political Crisis and the Impact on Foreign Policy", *Contemporary Southeast Asia*, Vol. 31, No. 3, 1987.

Pavin Chachavalpongpun, *A Plastic Nation: The Curse of Thainess in Thai-Burmese Relations*, Lanham, MD, University Press of America, 2005.

Pavin Chachavalpongpun, *Reinventing Thailand: Thaksin and His Foreign Policy*, Singapore, Institute of Southeast Asian Studies, 2010.

Pavin Chachavalpongpun, "The Necessity of Enemies in Thailand's Troubled Times", *Asian Survey*, Vol. 51, No. 6, November–December 2011, 1019–1041.

Peleggi, Maurizio, *Thailand: The Worldly Kingdom*, London, Reaktion Books, 2007.

Phar Kim Beng, "China Mulls Oil Pipelines in Myanmar, Thailand", *Asia Times*, 23 September 2004.

Phuangkasem, Corrine, *Thailand's Foreign Relations, 1964–1980*, Singapore, Institute of Southeast Asian Studies Press, 1984.

Ramsay, Ansil and Wiwat Mungkandi, eds., *Thailand–US Relations: Changing Political, Strategic, and Economic Factors*, Berkeley, Institute of East Asian Studies Press, 1988.

Randolph, R. Sean, *The United States and Thailand: Alliance Dynamics, 1950–1985*, Institute of East Asian Studies, University of California Berkeley, 1986.

Reynolds, Craig J., ed., *National Identity and Its Defenders: Thailand Today*, Chiang Mai, Silkworm Books, 2002.

Richardson, Staff Sgt. Kyle J., "Hunaman Guardian Opening Ceremony", US Army, 21 June 2013.

Rodriguez, Jr., Jose A., and Bill Harlow, *Hard Measures: How Aggressive CIA Measures After 9/11 Saved American Lives*, New York, Threshold Editions, 2012.

Rolls, Mark G., "Thailand's Post-Cold War Defence Policy and Security Programme", *Contemporary Security Policy*, Vol. 15, No. 2, 1994.

Roughneen, Simon, "US Dips into Mekong Politics", *Asia Times*, 14 August 2010.

Ruth, Richard A., *In Buddha's Company: Thai Soldiers in the Vietnam War*, Honolulu, University of Hawai'i Press, 2011.

Saner Chantra, "A Study in Thai–China Relations, 1945–75: From Outright Hostility to Tentative Friendship", Master of Arts in Diplomacy and World Affairs Thesis, Occidental College, Los Angeles, May 1976.

Scappatura, Vince, "The US 'Pivot to Asia', the China Spectre, and the Australian–American Alliance", *The Asia-Pacific Journal*, Vol. 12, Issue 36, No. 3, 6 September 2014.

Singh, Teshu, "China and Thailand: Analyzing Xi Jinping's Visit", Institute of Peace and Conflict Studies, 24 January 2012.

Sirin Phathanothai, *The Dragon's Pearl: Growing Up Among China's Elite*, New York, Simon & Schuster, 1994.

Skinner, G. William, Charnvit Kasetsiri and Phanni Chatphonlarak, [*Chinese Society in Thailand: An Analytical History*], Bangkok, The Foundation for Promotion of Social Sciences and Humanities Textbooks Project Press, 1986.

Sng, Jeffrey and Pimpraphai Bisalputra, *A History of the Thai-Chinese*, Bangkok, Editions Didier Millet, 2015.

Sorasak Ngamcachonkulkid, *Free Thai: The New History of the Seri Thai Movement*, Chulalongkorn, Institute of Asian Studies, Chulalongkorn University, 2010.

Stanton, Edwin F., "Spotlight on Thailand", *Foreign Affairs*, October 1954.

Stanton, Edwin F., *Brief Authority: Excursions of a Common Man in an Uncommon World*, New York, Harper & Brothers Publishers, 1956.

Surachart Bamrungsuk, *United States Foreign Policy and Thai Military Rule 1947–1977*, Bangkok, Editions Duangkamol, 1988.

Surakiart Sathirathai, *Forward Engagement, Thailand's Foreign Policy*, Collection of Speeches by Dr. Surakiart Sathirathai, Minister of Foreign Affairs of Thailand, Volume 1: 2001–2002; Volume 2: 2003–2004, Bangkok, Ministry of Foreign Affairs, 2003; 2004.

Tarling, Nicholas, ed., *The Cambridge History of Southeast Asia: From World War II to the Present,* Vol. Two, Part Two, Cambridge, Cambridge University Press, 1999.

Teddy Spha Palasthira, *The Last Siamese: Journeys in War and Peace*, Bangkok, The Post Publishing Company Limited, 2013.

Ten Kate, Daniel, "China Agrees to Asean Sea Talks Amid Philippines Warning", *Bloomberg*, 1 July 2013.

Terwiel, B.J., *Thailand's Political History: From the 13th Century to Recent Times*, Bangkok, River Books, 2011.

Thak Chaloemtiarana, ed., *Thai Politics: Extracts and Documents, 1932–1957*, Social Science Association of Thailand, 1978.

Thak Chaloemtiarana, *Thailand: The Politics of Despotic Paternalism*, Ithaca, NY, Cornell University Press, 2007.

Thanet Aphornsuvan, "The United States and the Coming of the Coup of 1947 in Siam", *Journal of the Siam Society*, Vol. 75, 1987.

Thanida Tansubhapol, "Decree Spurs Flurry of Travel Warnings", *Bangkok Post*, 24 January 2014.

Thayer, Carlisle and Ramses Amer, eds., *Vietnamese Foreign Policy in Transition*, Singapore, ISEAS, 1999.

The White House, Office of the Press Secretary, "Remarks by President Obama and Prime Minister Shinawatra in a Joint Press Conference", 18 November 2012.

Thongchai Winichakul, *Siam Mapped: A History of the Geo-Body of a Nation*, Chiang Mai, Silkworm Books, 1994.

Trajano, Julius Cesar I., "Old Allies, New Dynamics in US Pivot", *Asia Times*, 31 August 2012.

Ukrist Pathmanand, "A Different Coup d'Etat?", *Journal of Contemporary Asia*, Vol. 38, No. 1, February 2008, 124–142.

US Senate Select Committee on Intelligence, "Executive Summary", *Committee Study of the Central Intelligence Agency's Detention and Interrogation Program*, 2014.

US State Department: Country Reports on Human Rights Practices 1978-1993, and Press Statements 2006-2014.

Van Praagh, David, *Alone on the Sharp Edge: The Story of M.R. Seni Pramoj and Thailand's Struggle for Democracy*, Bangkok, Editions Duang Kamol, 1989.

Vichitvong Na Pombhejara, *Pridi Banomyong and the Making of Thailand's Modern History*, Bangkok, Siriyod Printing Co., 1980.

Vimol Bhongbhibhat, Bruce Reynolds and Sukhon Polpatpicharn, eds., *The Eagle and the Elephant: 150 Years of Thai-American Relations*, Bangkok, United Production, 1982.

Warrick, Joby, and Peter Finn, "Internal Rifts on Road to Torment", *Washington Post*, 19 July 2009.

Wassana Nanuam, "US Cautions Govt Against Coup, Chaos", *Bangkok Post*, 9 April 2014.

Wassana Nanuam, "US Threats to Relocate CG 2015 Fall Short", *Bangkok Post*, 1 July 2014.

Wassana Nanuam and Achara Ashayagachat, "Kenney Stays Out of Crisis, Calls for Peaceful Solution", *Bangkok Post*, January 2014.

Wassana Nanuam and Achara Ashayagachat, "US Embassy Snubs Top Brass Over Invites", *Bangkok Post*, 5 July 2014.

Wheeler, Matthew, "The USA, the war on terror, and the violence in southernmost Thailand"; Imagined Land? The State and Southern Violence in Thailand, Chaiwat Satha-anand, ed., Tokyo University of Foreign Studies, Research Institute for Languages and Cultures of Asia and Africa, 2009.

Wheeler, Matthew Z., "Mr. Thaksin Goes to Washington", Institute of Current World Affairs Letters, 10 July 2003.

Wilson, David A., "China, Thailand, and the Spirit of Bandung (Part I)", *The China Quarterly*, No. 30, April–June 1967.

Wilson, David A., "China, Thailand, and the Spirit of Bandung (Part II)", *The China Quarterly*, No. 31, July–September 1967.

Wilson, David A., *The United States and the Future of Thailand*, New York, Praeger Publishers, 1970.

Wimon Wiriyawit, ed., *Free Thai: Personal Recollections and Official Documents*, Bangkok, White Lotus Press, 1997.

Winchester, Michael, "Deadly Fog on the Mekong", *Asia Times*, 5 November 2011.

Wiwat Mungkandi and William Warren, eds., *A Century and a Half of Thai-American Relations*, Chulalongkorn, Chulalongkorn University Press, 1982.

Wyatt, David K., *Thailand: A Short History*, Chiang Mai, Silkworm Books, Second Edition, 2004.

Yamamoto, Tadashi, Pranee Thiparat, and Abul Ahsan, "Asian Views 2001", *America's Role in Asia*, Asia Foundation, 2001.

Yang Dingdu, "US Touts Asia-Pacific Military Presence with Cobra Gold", *Xinhua*, 14 February 2012.

Yuangrat Wedel and Wedel, Paul, *Radical Thought, Thai Mind: The Development of Revolutionary Ideas in Thailand*, Bangkok, Assumption Business Administration College, 1987.

Interviews by author

Named (alphabetical): Abhisit Vejjajiva, Bangkok, 6 February 2015; Ammar Siamwalla, Bangkok, 15 January 2015; Anand Panyarachun, Bangkok, 21 January 2015; Baker, Chris, Bangkok, 6 January 2015; Bhokin Polakul, Bangkok, 4 February 2015; Bosworth, Stephen, Boston, 27 May 2015; Boyce, Ralph "Skip", Singapore, 4 June 2015; Brandon, John, Washington, 8 April 2015; Bunnag, Peter, Bangkok, 22 January 2015; Chalermsuk Yugala, Bangkok, 19 January 2015; Chaturon Chaisang, Bangkok, 20 January 2015; Chulacheeb Chinwanno, Bangkok, 18 May 2015; Chuan Leekpai, Bangkok, 3 August 2015; Cole, John, Hawaii/phone, 13 April 2015; Fitts, Robert, Bangkok, 30 January 2015; Jackson, Karl, Washington, 9 April 2015; Jakrapob Penkair, Skype/Undisclosed location, 26 January 2015; John, Eric, Seoul/Skype, 16 July 2015; Kantathi Suphamongkhon, Bangkok, 20 September 2015; Karuna Buakamsri, Bangkok, 29 January 2015; Kasit Piromya, Bangkok, 23 January 2015; Kent, George, Washington, 28 April 2015; Klein, Jim, Bangkok, 16 January 2015; Kobsak Chutikul, Bangkok, 14 January 2015; Korn Chatikavanij, Bangkok, 8 May 2015; Kraisak Choonhavan, Bangkok, 12 January 2015, 2 February 2015; Lane, Denny, Washington, 8 April 2015; Noppadon Pattama, Bangkok, 18 June 2015; Panitan Wattanayagorn, Bangkok, 31 January 2015; Pansak Vinyaratn, Bangkok, 21 January 2015; Pisan Manawapat, Washington, 7 April 2015; Pravit Rojanaphruk, Bangkok, 28 January 2015; Rosenblatt, Lionel, Washington, 7 April 2015; Sarasin Viraphol, Bangkok, 6 February 2015; Steinberg, David, Washington, 9 April 2015; Stent, Jim, Bangkok, 16 January 2015; Sulak Sivaraksa, Bangkok, 11 January 2015; Sunai Pasuk, Bangkok, 30 January 2015; Surakiart Sathirathai, Bangkok, 4 August 2015; Suranand Vejjajiva, Bangkok, 13 January 2015; Surapong Tovichakchaikul, Bangkok, 13 May 2015; Thaksin Shinawatra, London, 21 August 2015; Thanet Aphornsuvan, Bangkok, 2 February 2015; Tomseth, Victor, Skype, 15 May 2015; Warren, William, Bangkok, 5 January 2015; Whorton, William, Bangkok, 2 February 2016; Weng Tojirakarn, Bangkok, 6 January 2015; Williams, Derek, Bangkok, 8 January 2015.

Anonymous (by date): Senior Thaksin cabinet member, Bangkok, 2015; former member of Communist Party of Thailand, Bangkok, 5 January 2015; senior member of Yingluck's government, Bangkok, 13 January 2015; Thai general, Bangkok, 22 January 2015; retired Thai general, Bangkok, 22 January 2015; senior Foreign Ministry official with experience in China during Yingluck administration, Bangkok, 22 January 2015; high-ranking member of Thailand's Ministry of Foreign Affairs, Bangkok, 26 January 2015; former Thai prime minister, Bangkok, 1 February 2015; senior retired Foreign Ministry official, Bangkok, 2 February 2015; former high-ranking Thai Ministry official, Bangkok, 2 February 2015; former Thai foreign minister, Bangkok, 2 February 2015; senior Foreign Ministry official posted to Beijing during the Chatichai government, Bangkok, 2 February 2015; senior Foreign Ministry official posted to Beijing during the Prem administration, Bangkok, 2 February 2015; senior Foreign Ministry official posted to Washington during the Thaksin government, Bangkok, 2 February 2015; Thai dignitary, Bangkok, 2 February 2015; former Thai ambassador to the US and China, Bangkok, 2 February 2015; two Thai Foreign Ministry officials, Bangkok, 5 February 2015; senior Thai politician, Bangkok, 6 February

2015; Foreign Ministry official assigned to China during the Thaksin and Surayud administrations, Undisclosed/Skype, 12 March 2015; Foreign Ministry official with responsibility
for China during the Thaksin administration, Undisclosed/Skype, 12 March 2015; Foreign
Ministry official with responsibility for China after the Thaksin administration, Undis-
closed/Skype, 12 March 2015; State Department official, Undisclosed, April 2015; State
Department official, Washington, 9 April 2015; State Department official with responsibility for Thailand, Washington, 9 April 2015; US diplomat, Washington, 9 April 2015;
senior US embassy official who served under John, Washington, 10 April 2015; senior State
Department official who served under Campbell, Washington, 11 April 2015; senior State
Department official, Washington, 16 July 2015; senior State Department official posted
to Bangkok during the Abhisit administration, Washington, 16 July 2015; former State
Department official, Washington, 16 July 2015; senior State Department official, Washington, 16 July 2015.

Index